TELEVISION AND AMERICAN CULTURE

Television
and
American Culture

JASON MITTELL

MIDDLEBURY COLLEGE

New York   Oxford
OXFORD UNIVERSITY PRESS
2010

Oxford University Press, Inc., publishes works that further Oxford University's
objective of excellence in research, scholarship, and education.

Oxford   New York
Auckland   Cape Town   Dar es Salaam   Hong Kong   Karachi
Kuala Lumpur   Madrid   Melbourne   Mexico City   Nairobi
New Delhi   Shanghai   Taipei   Toronto

With offices in
Argentina   Austria   Brazil   Chile   Czech Republic   France   Greece
Guatemala   Hungary   Italy   Japan   Poland   Portugal   Singapore
South Korea   Switzerland   Thailand   Turkey   Ukraine   Vietnam

Published by Oxford University Press, Inc.
198 Madison Avenue, New York, New York 10016
http://www.oup.com

Oxford is a registered trademark of Oxford University Press

Library of Congress Cataloging-in-Publication Data
Mittell, Jason.
   Television & American culture / Jason Mittell.
       p. cm.
   Includes bibliographical references and index.
ISBN-13: 978-0-19-530667-5 (pbk.alk. paper)
   1.   Television broadcasting—Social aspects—United States.   I. Title.
II. Title: Television and American culture.
   PN1992.6M58 2009
   302.23'450973—dc22   2008033828

Printing number: 9 8 7 6 5 4 3 2

Printed in the United States of America
on acid-free paper

BRIEF CONTENTS

CONTENTS

For more information about this book, including updates, corrections, links, videos, and teaching resources, visit the companion website at http://tvamericanculture.net.

ACKNOWLEDGMENTS

Writing a book like this is a truly collaborative act, even when there is only one author's name on the cover. I have tried to synthesize a field with decades of scholarship, which in turn is built on the foundations of many other disciplines. In writing this book, I hope to have honored the work of past and current scholars in whose debt I remain, and take responsibility more for any mischaracterizations than insights.

Many peers have offered feedback on the book, pointed me in key directions, and have otherwise supported my efforts. I owe special thanks to Christine Becker, University of Notre Dame; Becca Cragin, Bowling Green State University; Chad Dell, Monmouth University; Henry Jenkins, Massachusetts Institute of Technology; Anandam Kavoori, University of Georgia; Derek Kompare, Southern Methodist University; Elana Levine, University of Wisconsin-Milwaukee; Thomas J. Loehr, Spring Hill College; Amanda Lotz, University of Michigan; Tasha Oren, University of Wisconsin-Milwaukee; Jaime Poster, University of Wisconsin-Milwaukee; Faith Rogow, founding president, NAMLE; Sharon Ross, Columbia College Chicago; Susan Ryan, The College of New Jersey; Stacy Takacs, Oklahoma State University; Ethan Thompson, Texas A&M University, Corpus Christi, and a number of anonymous readers for their willingness to review chapters to provide helpful commentary and encouragement. Jonathan Gray of Fordham University has probably offered more direct feedback than anyone, and I have enjoyed our friendship and collaborative relationship that have grown throughout this writing process. The entire diaspora of University of Wisconsin media scholars has offered advice and guidance for a number of questions that arose throughout the writing process, extending the collegial community I joined more than a decade ago. The readers of my blog, Just TV, have provided feedback on a number of the book's sections, and inspired me to write with a voice that encourages dialogue and engagement.

At Middlebury College, I am surrounded by tremendous colleagues from a wide range of disciplines. In embarking on this interdisciplinary approach, I have turned to local experts from other fields often to set me straight and reorient my thinking, and am specifically appreciative for the input offered by Holly Allen, Jason Arndt, Jonathan Isham, Rachael Joo, Sujata Moorti, Caitlin Myers, Michael Newbury, and Carlos Velez. Chris Keathley has been my sounding board since the origins of this book, and I cannot imagine that it would ever have been finished without his friendship and advice.

As a pedagogically focused book, most of its contents were tried out first in the classroom. I am grateful to the hundreds of Middlebury students who have allowed me to teach them about television, and I'm sure many can find their own feedback and conversations shaping ideas in this book. Three outstanding students had a more direct hand in the book: Grace Armstrong served as my research assistant for the early chapters; Astri von Arbin Ahlander prepared most of the illustrations; and Ioana Literat compiled the index. These exceptional young women remind me why I have dedicated my life to teaching and helping to shape the intellectual experiences of students, and I hope this book helps extend that goal beyond my classroom.

This book was a marathon that could not have been run without the constant encouragement and feedback from my editor Peter Labella. We both welcomed new sons into our families as we worked together to gestate this book, making the process longer and more sleepless than planned, but hopefully well worth the effort. The entire staff of Oxford University Press, especially Miriam Sicilia, offered what every author wants—making the publishing process as simple and stress-free as possible.

Finally, my family has provided years of support and encouragement in my unusual career choice as a television scholar and its need for persistent "research." My wife Ruth helps keep me grounded and focused on what really matters, while my children Greta, Anya, and Walter enlighten me with fresh perspectives on their own discoveries, of both television and the love of learning. I thank the four of them with deep love and gratitude.

TELEVISION AND AMERICAN CULTURE

WHY TELEVISION?

What is television? At first glance, the answer might seem obvious, especially to anyone who has grown up in a television-saturated society. But the question is trickier than it may appear, as television is far more multifaceted and complex than we tend to see it. For a useful parallel, imagine you are *on television*—as a contestant on the popular game show *Jeopardy!*. That show's gimmick is that contestants must respond to a given "answer" by posing the correct "question" for that answer. So the correct response to the answer "a domesticated bird known for laying eggs" would be "What is chicken?" But you could provide this response to a range of statements, as the question "what is chicken?" actually has many potential answers, depending on the context or your frame of reference—chicken could be "the most popular poultry meat," "a slang term for a coward," "a game where two people drive cars at one another," "a mild form of pox common to children," "a novelty dance popular at weddings," "a kind of wire commonly used in gardens," or "the mascot of the San Diego Padres." All are potentially correct ways to answer the question "What is chicken?"

But this is a book about television, not chicken. So what *Jeopardy!* statement might prompt the question "What is television?" Television could be defined as "the most powerful and prevalent mass communication medium in America

> ## JEOPARDY!
>
> *Jeopardy!* (NBC, 1964–75; syndicated 1984–present): One of the most successful game shows in television history, *Jeopardy!* features trivia framed through the gimmick of trying to find the questions for provided answers. The game show, which has been hosted by Alex Trebek in first-run syndication since 1984, is known as one of the most difficult and serious competitions, with successful contestants hailed as masters of trivia and knowledge.

(and the world)." However, other, more specific definitions show how television's commonplace role masks its multiple facets and structures:

- Television is an enormously profitable industry, grossing over $100 billion annually through advertising, cable fees, DVD sales, and other sources of revenue.
- Television is part of democracy, informing American citizens and serving the public interest through news and electoral coverage, and governed by public policy decisions and regulations.
- Television is a unique creative form, with a distinct narrative structure and set of genres that distinguish it from other media.
- Television is a mirror of our world, offering an often-distorted vision of national identity, as well as shaping our perceptions of various groups of people.
- Television is a part of our lives, as viewing and talking about it plays a central, albeit underexamined, role in our everyday routines.
- Television is a technology, serving as the central screen for a number of digital entertainment and information media in the home, from DVDs to video games.

All six of these definitions of television are central to its function in American culture. The main point of this book is to explore television in each of these crucial functions: as a **commercial industry**, a **democratic institution**, a **textual form**, a **site of cultural representation**, a **part of everyday life**, and a **technological medium**.

Few people would disagree with the claim that television functions in these six ways. The stickier point involves relative importance—which aspects of television are most vital to study, and which might be downplayed or ignored altogether? Different academic traditions emphasize various facets—economists focus on how industries generate profits, political scientists look at democratic institutions, anthropologists foreground everyday life, and film scholars analyze media texts. But even interdisciplinary approaches to television have their points of emphasis and blind spots—mass communications researchers examine institutions, politics, and the quantifiable effects media have upon audiences, while cultural scholars of media generally focus on representations, texts, and audience practices. This book tries to bridge the gaps that can arise between these disciplinary approaches, highlighting how each facet of television is vital to a broader understanding of the medium, and no single point of emphasis takes priority over others in explaining the complex functioning of television in American culture.

But how does such a multifaceted examination of television work in practice? Take for example a recent and rather notorious televised moment: Janet Jackson's so-called "wardrobe malfunction" during the 2004 Super Bowl half-time show. A brief review of the infamous event: at the end of a series of pop musical performances, Jackson and Justin Timberlake performed a duet to conclude the show. Just after Timberlake sang the lyrics "I'm gonna have you naked by the end of this song," he ripped off part of Jackson's bustier, exposing her right breast for less than a second before she covered herself and the network cut to a distant shot of the stadium. The exposure was barely visible, yet the cultural uproar was intense: blame was passed around, apologies were made, protests were filed, fines were levied, and laws were changed—all in reaction to a microsecond of television that was hardly visible to the naked eye. Why did this event happen as it did, and why was there so much furor over it? To fully

Super Bowl wardrobe malfunction: This split second image of Janet Jackson's exposed breast launched a political scandal and cultural uproar, despite being nearly impossible to see during the live broadcast.

SUPER BOWL

Super Bowl (multiple networks, 1967–present): Typically the highest-rated television event of the year, the National Football League Super Bowl is significant for launching advertising campaigns and gathering massive audiences for networks to promote their regular programming.

---

understand the reasons behind these reactions, and their cultural significance, we need consider this brief moment, and its cultural aftermath, in the context of all six facets of television outlined earlier. In doing so, we will mention some specific details of television that might be unknown to you but that should be quite familiar by the end of the book. Taking a moment to explore the multiple facets of television that matter in this brief incident will offer insight into how the rest of the book will analyze television and provide you with a broad understanding of the medium from a variety of perspectives.

Certainly the **television industry** created this moment and is thus a good place to start analyzing. The Super Bowl always ranks among the highest-rated programs of the year, so CBS relished the opportunity to rake in hundreds of millions of dollars in advertising revenue, as well as to promote its regular programming to an enormous audience. The network tapped MTV to produce its halftime show—both were owned by media conglomerate Viacom at the time—to appeal to a youthful audience by using flashy production values and hip contemporary performers. However, the sensibility of MTV's youth niche market contrasted with the mass audience of 143 million who tuned in to at least part of the game—the halftime show featured dancing, costumes, and lyrics that many viewers found offensive even before Jackson's reveal. Although CBS and MTV both fell under the same corporate umbrella, they functioned, and still function, differently within the television industry—most important, CBS uses the public airwaves to broadcast its programming, while MTV's location on cable and satellite places it outside many government regulations. Even though CBS claimed to have no advance knowledge of the pop duo's choreographed disrobing, CBS-owned stations ultimately were held responsible and fined over $500,000 for broadcast indecency by the Federal Communications Commission (FCC), the government agency that regulates television. Thus, although the goals of both CBS and MTV were the same—drawing an audience to sell to advertisers, and promoting their own Viacom-owned brands—the structure of the television industry treated, and still treats, broadcasting and cable differently, as do audiences; the latter tend to be more fragmented and select for cable channels. These differences in both attitude and regulatory scope concerning cable versus broadcast television had a direct impact upon the ensuing scandal.

The industry's conception of its audience relates to the specific **cultural representations** offered by the broadcast. Super Bowl broadcasts always assert a set of ideas to unite viewers in their national identity as Americans, with frequent use of flags, anthems, and other icons of patriotism. The halftime show was similarly suffused in nationalism, as it focused on the pro-voting message of "Choose or Lose" in a year of a hotly contested presidential election taking place during a controversial war. However, other identity differences disrupted the patriotic celebration, fragmenting the audience along lines of age, gender, race, and moral norms. MTV promoted its youthful brand with pop stars such as Timberlake, Jessica Simpson, Nelly, and Kid Rock. This was a departure from more traditional halftime shows, which previously tended toward uncontroversial, mainstream acts from country music, such as Shania Twain, and an older generation of R&B and rock performers, such as Stevie Wonder and Aerosmith. Additionally, the actual breast-baring resonated with certain historical norms of group identity in America, with the image of a white man ripping the clothes off a black woman tapping into deep-seated assumptions about female sexuality and the history of racially charged sexual content—in the ensuing scandal, Jackson was generally framed as the perpetrator of indecency and took most of the blame, even though Timberlake was the one who'd ripped her clothes off! Even if these gender and racially charged notions were not made explicit in viewers' reactions, the histories behind such images make certain ideas resonate more significantly than others in American culture and fuel the ensuing scandals. The event also triggered a moral debate over decency and censorship—even though more than three quarters of Americans polled found that the action was not worth government prosecution, a vocal minority inflamed sufficient public outrage to prompt the FCC's largest fine in history.[1] While the Super Bowl often tries to unite a nation around shared American icons such as football, advertising, and beer, this event highlighted and sustained divisions in American identity, helping to foster the uproar and justify the political reaction, especially during an election year.

Another crucial aspect of the event's presentation was a component of its **textual form**: live broadcast. Had the Super Bowl been taped for later broadcast, there would have been no issue, as CBS would have edited out the offending moment. But television features a broad mix of production modes, from live broadcast to filmed programming, in-studio to on-location production. Most of these modes of productions are linked to specific genres—sporting events are nearly always broadcast live, capturing surprises as they happen but also running the risk of airing unforeseen content. Even though live broadcasting raises the risk of airing unexpected material, in the case of the 2004 Super Bowl, television's production mechanisms both enabled the offending exposure to be seen, and then removed it from the air. The presence of dozens of cameras allow television producers to provide images to viewers that simply could not be experienced in person—no one in the crowd at the Super Bowl saw the wardrobe malfunction, except as it was presented on the Jumbotron television screen at the stadium. But just as television can provide perspectives unavailable in real life, the medium ultimately controls what viewers see. When producers realized what Timberlake had just done, they cut to a wide shot of the stadium and fireworks, disabling our close view of the action and leaving viewers to ponder what they'd just seen. Television's form encourages the replaying of live material—hence the numerous replay angles on every play of the Super Bowl. Yet this halftime highlight would never air again as it was first seen, as subsequent replays (generally on news programs) obscured the details of Jackson's exposure through digital blurring or a similar effect. One of the aftermaths of the controversy was a shift in television's production modes, as many special event programs, such as sporting events and award programs, instituted a few-second delay to monitor for potentially offensive content, changing the meaning of "live broadcast."

The industry's textual control of visual access has been offset to some degree by **media technologies**. Had this event occurred in the 1970s or before, the television industry would have maintained complete control of the offending image—most people wouldn't have realized what they'd seen, and CBS would have buried it to hide all evidence of the potentially divisive moment. But a number of technological innovations from the 1980s and onward have changed the balance of power controlling broadcast images. The popularity of the VCR in the 1980s allowed viewers to tape programs as they were being aired, and certainly this moment could have been archived and studied via videotape. But digital technologies of the twenty-first century have given viewers even more immediate power to replay and redistribute images—households with digital video recorders such as TiVo replayed this moment in record numbers, viewing it repeatedly in slow motion to discern what had really happened. Technologically savvy viewers digitized their video recordings and distributed still images and movie files on the Internet, quickly making the Janet Jackson wardrobe malfunction the most frequently searched-for image online. Due to these technological shifts, CBS was not able to control the image it had broadcast, as viewers used technologies of recording and distribution to turn a live broadcast into an archived moment that long outlived its split-second origins.

Clearly these technologies impact the role of television in **everyday life**, as viewers were able to seize the image for their own purposes. These purposes ranged from the prurient to the parodic to the prudish, as the so-called "nipplegate" overshadowed what was seen as one of the most exciting Super Bowl games ever played. Online discussions raged about the aesthetics of Jackson's nipple-adorning jewelry, and parodies surfaced online and in other media outlets. Television events often become the content of public debate and discussion, with these "water cooler" moments arising outside of the industry's planning or control. In this instance, the discussion moved well beyond water coolers—special interest organizations that regularly complain about the immoral quality of television content, such as the Parents Television Council, quickly seized upon Jackson's breast as the symbol of everything wrong with the medium. They filed complaints with CBS, Viacom, and the FCC, sending their outrage via online petitions and angry letters. One Tennessee viewer even went so far as to file a class-action lawsuit on behalf of all viewers against Viacom, CBS, MTV, Jackson, and Timberlake, claiming that the "outrageous and lewd acts" caused viewers emotional distress and unspecified "serious injury"—not surprisingly, this lawsuit was dropped mere days after it was filed. While all accused parties both apologized and attempted to pass blame on to others, the FCC took the views of this vocal minority of viewers quite seriously by acting upon the more than five hundred thousand complaints it received, most through organized online petitions and email campaigns. As this example attests, the industry's control diminishes as soon as the material is aired, as viewers can reuse images, circulate interpretations, and send feedback into the media system via technologies and practices that surpass the limits that the industry imagines for its own broadcasts.

In this case, the public outcry had a profound and serious impact on the industry and **democratic regulation** of the airwaves, serving as the "tipping point" for government intervention into cultural norms, a common occurrence during a presidential election year. The FCC pursued the complaints against CBS, levying the largest fine in broadcast history over a single incident. This event called attention to an oft-ignored and rarely enacted role of the FCC in regulating broadcasting: the agency cannot censor or judge content prior to its airing, but it can levy fines on or even revoke the licenses of broadcasters who air material deemed "indecent" by its commissioners. Congress responded to the event by further empowering the FCC, proposing bipartisan bills to drastically increase fines for indecency. Although these actions certainly follow the democratic tradition that the airwaves are a public resource used by private industries to serve the public interest, there are underlying political agendas at work, as with most things in Washington. As this took place in a presidential election year, both the Republican and Democratic parties used the incident as a way to promote their own "traditional morals" and condemn a perceived "Hollywood elite." Likewise, the FCC was coming off of a particularly rough 2003, as its proposed lifting of ownership caps had triggered an unprecedented wave of public activism in favor of media regulation, resulting in congressional action attempting to limit media consolidation—beleaguered FCC chair Michael Powell gleefully pounced upon Jackson's breast exposure to reposition himself and his agency as champions for decency and the public interest.

The immediate impact of this government clampdown on decency was an overreaction by the industry to self-regulate, resulting in broadcasters either editing out potentially questionable content, such as the partially nude body of an eighty-year-old woman on an operating table in *ER*, or avoiding airing controversial material altogether, as sixty-six ABC affiliates did when they chose not to air the network's unedited Veteran's Day broadcast of the graphic WWII drama *Saving Private Ryan* containing copious profanity, for fear of FCC rebukes. In this instance, and its aftermath, television programming stands at the crossroads of competing democratic impulses: using the airwaves to serve the public interest and community standards, while protecting the dual freedoms of speech and the press to present controversial ideas without government interference.

This brief account of how a split-second moment of live television had such wide-ranging and politically vital impacts on American culture demonstrates the complexity of television as a medium. Any one of the six facets of television explored earlier might be seen as the most important aspect of this example—you might feel that ultimately the event boils down to the public protecting itself from immoral broadcasters; or view it as a demonstration of the ability of new technologies to empower viewers. However, to understand the full story of how television impacts American culture, we need to explore how the medium functions within all six of the facets. The rest of this book seeks to do just that, exploring each aspect of television in depth—including clarifying some of the concepts briefly alluded to in this discussion of the 2004 Super Bowl broadcast—while emphasizing that none of the six facets operates in isolation from the other five. For instance, examining television's representation of national identity leads us to the industry's construction of audiences, which react to and shape viewers' own practices. Likewise, regulations of television help determine technological standards, which in turn mold production norms and textual forms. We can consider all six facets of television as individual points in a broader **circuit of culture** model, in which all parts are interconnected to comprise American television.[2] Any approach that excludes or overemphasizes one part of the circuit cannot account for the complexity of television. Thus this book promotes a multidisciplinary approach that considers all six facets of television both on their own terms and wired within a larger circuit.

The Janet Jackson case points to a second distinctive feature of this book: it does not offer a "neutral" or objective survey of key facts and historical moments in American television, but rather makes explicit arguments about the politics, meanings, and practices involving television. This book offers its own distinctive arguments about how television works and how it impacts American society, while recounting key facts and historical moments. You may notice some explicit arguments against particular "commonsense" notions about television, ideas that many people assume to be true because they've heard them so many times: *Television is bad for you. The television industry simply gives viewers what we want. Television content is predominantly liberal, or predominantly conservative. Watching television is a passive pastime. Televised violence causes violent behavior. Television is not worth taking seriously.* All of these assumptions, which

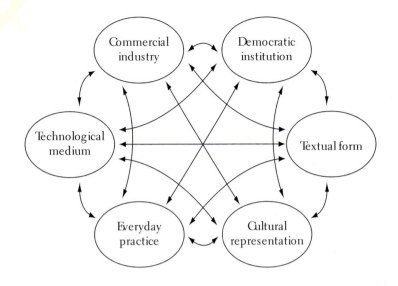

Figure 0-1 The six facets of television are all interweaved together, operating in tandem, based on the "circuit of culture" model.

should sound familiar even if you don't share them, will be debated throughout this book. You will be asked to think carefully, critically, and deeply about that screen sitting in your living room and beyond. After reading this book you will have absorbed a lot of information about television, but it is hoped you will have learned even more about *how to look at television,* and its assumed place in American society, in a new way. You may disagree with some of the book's arguments, politics, and interpretations, but a thoughtful reader will be able to rebut those arguments with more engaged and nuanced thinking about television than just common sense.

A third way in which the Janet Jackson case models the rest of this book is in that it relies on a number of academic traditions, but without getting bogged down in scholarly jargon or name-dropping. To understand the multifaceted realm of television, you have to be able to think across disciplines, dabbling in economics, political science, sociology, aesthetics, social history, psychology, and mass communication theory. This book draws upon these disciplinary traditions to explore complex ideas, but avoids language that makes those ideas comprehensible only to experts—or at least explains unusual terms when used. Some discussions are rooted in advanced theoretical concepts such as poststructuralism and subjectivity, and the theoretical writings of authors such as Louis Althusser and Michel Foucault, but these terms and names will not be mentioned explicitly again—the end of each chapter offers a guide to further reading if you wish to delve into the more specialized literature on specific topics. Likewise, the book is influenced by a number of theoretical traditions, such as feminist criticism and critical race theory, but it attempts to foreground the core ideas emerging from these traditions, rather than explain their academic origins and theoretical nuances.

By exploring each of the six facets in depth, using a range of academic traditions, this book tries to demonstrate how to think critically, and with sophistication, about television, but using ideas and language accessible to interested novices. Thus it should prepare you for more thoughtful insights into the various roles television serves within American culture and your own life—and get you ready in case you need to respond with "What is television?" on an upcoming appearance on *Jeopardy!*

A NOTE ON HISTORY

This book does not offer a survey of television's history—there are many other high-quality books providing a chronological account of American television's development and evolution—but it is not ahistorical. Underlying the book's cultural approach is the belief that we can understand media only in their historical contexts, placing them within a specific set of circumstances tied to a particular moment. Although each chapter explores a particular facet of how television works, we need to avoid the temptation of thinking of television as a timeless essence remaining unchanged and unchanging across its multi-decade history. It is useful to consider the history of television as typified by distinct eras, with each offering a general outline of how television fits into American culture within a specific period. Although the history of television is more complex than this simple periodization, this book will focus on three eras of American television, with each chapter considering specific ways television has been transformed over the following three periods.

The Classic Network Era

Starting with the emergence of television as an outgrowth of the radio industry in the mid-1940s and lasting until the mid-1980s, this era established norms that persist today for all facets of television. The defining structure of this era is the network system, in which nearly all programming was presented by three national networks (ABC, CBS, and NBC), and audiences watched shows *en masse* simultaneously across the country. The classic network era set long-lasting standards for television programming formats and advertising-supported channels, while heralding the rise of television as a central outlet for political and public affairs information. The various ways viewers engage with television, and television's role as the primary medium that defines American culture, were established during this period, setting norms that remain today. While many of these modes of engagement have diminished, the possibility of television's role as a mass medium with one shared cultural reference resonating throughout American culture still persists in rare instances, as exemplified by the Janet Jackson instance.

The Multi-Channel Era

The 1980s was a transitional decade, as television shifted from being dominated by national broadcast networks to enjoying new technologies of cable and satellite programming. In the multi-channel era that defined the 1990s, mass audiences were supplanted by demographically defined market segments, as channels emerged to reach a wide range of target audiences in a system often termed **narrowcasting**. The television industry developed new formats and strategies to reach valued audience segments, and new networks such as Fox and Univision to compete with the Big Three; yet the basic system of advertiser-supported television remained in place. Technologies such as remote controls and VCRs redefined people's viewing habits, and households became more likely to have multiple sets, changing the domestic role of television. As the mass audience gave way to smaller market segments, television's cultural function transformed, becoming structured around more diffused audience groups and programs appealing to niche groups. However, the multi-channel era still saw television as the central information and communication medium for the American public.

The Convergence Era

Television's third era is still emerging, with the medium under transition as this book is being written in 2008. As digital media have grown in importance, the role of television is evolving as it is challenged by a range of technologies such as the Internet and video games. Television still remains central in American homes, but it is no longer experienced only as dictated by national networks or cable channels; rather, the television set is emerging as the centerpiece of a range of video-based technologies. This technological convergence forces us to question the underlying economic models of both broadcast and multi-channel television, as viewers are taking control of schedules and using digital distribution technologies to offer alternatives to television programming and to resist the advertising that has traditionally been the primary source of income for the television industry. While certainly any claims of the death of television as a medium are exaggerated, there is no doubt that we are entering a new era in which the norms of the past fifty years will be challenged and redefined in unforeseen ways.

Each of these eras intersects with all six facets of television, and thus every chapter will consider how historical transformations impact the issues pertinent to a particular facet. Since each era is predicated on a technological shift—from over-the-air broadcast to cable and satellite transmission to digital convergence—many of the larger issues about how television has transformed across these eras will be considered in most depth later in the book, in chapter 11. Yet as historical changes weave themselves throughout every facet of television, it should be clear that technology alone does not cause or trigger such broad transformations—just as we need to understand how all six facets of television operate to make sense of television's cultural role today, we also need to consider how all facets respond to and often stimulate historical change.

Finally, the book's historical and analytic scope is focused tightly on American television. In some ways this is easy to justify, as television has been defined since its beginning as a national system, governed by national legislation and regulations. Additionally, American viewers have few opportunities to see television from other countries—the United States exports a great deal of media around the world, but imports very little onto its television schedule. These boundaries are starting to erode in recent decades, as the multi-channel era opened up possibilities for more imports on cable channels such as BBC America and as digital technologies became more global and unbound by national regulations. Thus while this book focuses on American television programming and its circulation within the United States, the conclusion briefly widens its scope to consider a more global context, considering how American television circulates throughout the world and the influence of imports on American culture.

FURTHER READING

Most overviews of American television take an explicitly chronological approach to television history. For important chronologies of television history, see Erik Barnouw, *Tube of Plenty: The Evolution of American Television*, 2nd ed. (New York: Oxford University Press, 1990); Michele Hilmes, *Only Connect: A Cultural History of Broadcasting in the United States* (Belmont, Calif.: Wadsworth/Thomson Learning, 2002); Michele Hilmes, ed., *The Television History Book* (London: British Film Institute); J. Fred MacDonald, *One Nation Under Television: The Rise and Decline of Network TV* (New York: Pantheon Books, 1990); and Christopher H. Sterling and John M. Kittross, *Stay Tuned: A History of American Broadcasting*, 3rd ed. (Mahwah, N.J.: Lawrence Erlbaum Associates, 2002).

Some other introductions to American television approach the subject matter topically, using a variety of critical approaches. For instance, Robert C. Allen, ed., *Channels of Discourse: Television and Contemporary Criticism* (Chapel Hill: University of North Carolina Press, 1992); and Leah R. Vande Berg, et al.,

Critical Approaches to Television, 2nd ed. (Boston: Houghton Mifflin, 2004), provide an overview of critical theories applied to television, while Jeremy G. Butler, *Television: Critical Methods and Applications*, 3rd ed. (Mahwah, N.J.: Lawrence Erlbaum Associates, 2007), focuses on television's form and representations. More detailed examinations of television's specific aspects will be recommended at the end of each chapter.

NOTES

[1]"Poll: Janet's Revelation No Crime," Associated Press, February 21, 2004.

[2]See Paul duGay et al., *Doing Cultural Studies: The Story of the Sony Walkman* (London: Sage Publications, 1997) for an influential account of the circuit of culture.

SECTION 1

Television Institutions

American television is comprised of many elements, but to understand the complex ways programming is made, circulates, and matters within American culture it is useful to start with the major institutions that manage and govern television. These institutions range from commercial networks to nonprofit community organizations, government agencies to creative production companies. Understanding the relationship among these various institutions that form the commercial and public structures of television is the goal of the next four chapters. Only by comprehending television's economic and regulatory basis can we claim to understand the medium's broader cultural values and practices.

The next two chapters outline television as a **commercial industry**. Chapter 1 explains how television programs are produced and find their way to your homes. Chapter 2 lays out the underlying economics of advertising and television ratings, explaining how programming is funded and how commercial television functions as a lucrative industry, and concluding with a case study of reality television.

Although American television is primarily a commercial enterprise, it is also bound up in governmental and public service systems—the subsequent two chapters describe how television operates as a **democratic institution**. Chapter 3 explains television's regulatory system and explores how noncommercial public television systems complement the dominant commercial industry. Chapter 4 details television's primary public service role as a journalistic enterprise, focusing on how television shapes electoral politics. These first four chapters, covering two of the most essential facets of American television, will provide the institutional basis for understanding the medium, without which any attempt to study the meanings and cultural practices of television would be incomplete.

CHAPTER 1

EXCHANGING PROGRAMMING

Throughout the classic network era, most people thought of watching television as a "free" activity—even though households needed to purchase a television set, that initial purchase provided access to an unlimited supply of free programming. In the multi-channel and convergence eras, more direct costs exist for viewers, with subscriptions to cable, satellite, and digital video recording services. But aside from the still relatively marginal system of pay-per-view or digital downloading, the assumption persists that watching an individual television program is something we do for free, paying only the cost of the time it takes to watch.

In contrast to the commonsense notion that "television is free" is another broadly held assumption: television is overly commercial. Viewers realize that the primary goal of most broadcasters is to make money, and thus programming decisions are made to maximize profit more than to serve public interest, the common good, or creative expression. Yet it doesn't take an economist to recognize that there seems to be a contradiction here: How can something that is offered for free be an overly commercial product?

This chapter and the next attempt to explain the commercial logic underlying this apparent paradox: an enormously profitable industry spends an incredible amount of money creating a product that it offers to millions of people seemingly for free. There are many ways to study the television industry, but these chapters will focus on how it functions as a commercial system and fits within the market logic of American capitalism—later chapters consider its political, aesthetic, and cultural roles more explicitly. To understand the economic logic of the commercial television industry, we need to explore three interrelated types of commerce surrounding the creation and distribution of television programming. First is the high-profile **exchange of programming**, as the television industry creates and distributes shows to be transmitted into viewers' homes—this detailed system forms the focus of chapter 1. The next chapter focuses on two less prominent but equally important economic systems: the **exchange of advertising**, as sponsors and advertising agencies create commercials and purchase airtime, funding most of American television; and the **exchange of audiences**, as the ratings system creates a currency of imagined attention to be sold to the advertisers who fund the creation of programs—and creates tremendous profits. By understanding these three exchanges, we can rethink the "free" label of television by redefining the core commercial function of the television industry: *to use freely accessed programming as a lure to sell audiences to advertisers.*

How does a show get onto television? There is no single way, as the system of program creation is as varied as the range of shows themselves. How a new sport makes its way to ESPN is vastly different from a how CBS programs a new sitcom. Depending on the program and channel, the process could involve dozens of different companies, years of development, and multiple versions of a program before anything even makes it to the air—and the vast majority of program

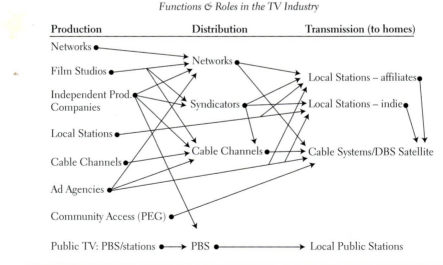

Functions & Roles in the TV Industry

Figure 1-1 The major functions of companies in the television industry are interrelated in a web of distribution and sharing, more than in direct competition.

ideas never even come close to our television screens. Despite the complexity and variability of the program creation endeavor, we can give a basic overview of the processes that bring programs to the air within most commercial television practices. Companies serve three central functions in ushering a program onto television: **production, distribution, and transmission,** roles that parallel other industries' systems of manufacturing, wholesaling, and retail sales. With each role, we can see how different types of companies fit into the television industry and how each company is able to turn a profit in the somewhat counterintuitive economics of television.

PRODUCTION

Most people think of a program as being identified by the channel it is on: for instance, both *ER* and *Law & Order* are popular NBC shows running through the 1990s and 2000s. But *ER* is not made by NBC; it is produced by a number of companies, including Warner Bros. Television, Amblin Entertainment (Steven Spielberg's production company), Constant c Productions (co-creator Michael Crichton's company), and John Wells Productions (another co-creator of the show). *Law & Order* and its spin-offs are produced by NBC Universal Television Studio, but only since 2004, when NBC merged with Universal Entertainment, which had produced the show, along with creator Dick Wolf's company, Wolf Films, since its debut in 1990. However, the NBC network that viewers identify as the home of *Law & Order* is quite different from NBC Universal Studios, which produces the program—the two companies are distinct divisions within the enormous multinational corporation General Electric. Yet few viewers think of *ER* as a Warner Bros. show or *Law & Order* as a Universal program. In the television industry, there is a crucial division of duties between the company that distributes the program (NBC) and the companies that produce it (Universal and Warner Bros.), even when they are owned by the same conglomerate.

You might recognize Warner Bros. and Universal as **film studios.** Most fictional television programs are actually produced by television production divisions of film studios, an arrangement that dates back to the late 1950s. But, like *ER*, most fictional programs have a multitude of companies involved in their production—watch the end credits of a show to see a parade of logos for each company involved. What role does each company play in creating the program? And what does a production company actually do?

The primary role of a **production company** is to manage the creative process, producing a program ready to be distributed over the airwaves or cable system. This is a misleadingly simple task, however, as television programs are unlike most other commercially manufactured commodities. One challenge is

ER

ER (NBC, 1994–2009): This series, probably television's most successful medical drama, became a ratings smash in the mid-1990s as part of NBC's "Must See TV" lineup. *ER* combines high production values, accelerated action sequences, and a blend of personal and professional conflicts among its cast of doctors and nurses to dramatize life in a Chicago emergency room.

LAW & ORDER

Law & Order (NBC, 1990–present): A crime procedural covering both police and legal departments in New York City, *Law & Order* combines a focus on real-life issues with a gritty on-location visual style. The show's long-running success has launched a franchise with three spin-offs and has made the program a reliable brand name for NBC.

that each television program must be unique—while typical industries such as automobiles and snack foods bank on the consistency that every Toyota Prius or Snickers bar will be virtually identical, no one would want to watch the exact same program over and over again. Television is similar to other **cultural industries**, as film, book, and music creators must all offer products that are distinctive enough to warrant interest from consumers, yet also familiar enough to have a clear home in the marketplace.

Television has additional challenges, however, as the series format that dominates American television schedules demands that each series be distinct from one another, but also that each episode within the series be unique as well. This leads to a remarkable amount of original content that must be produced regularly, a duty that falls upon production companies to manage and create. The number of new episodes depends on the program's genre and schedule: today, sitcoms typically air approximately twenty-two half-hour episodes per year, while soap operas produce five hours a week continuously. An extreme example, ESPN's *SportsCenter*, has aired multiple versions each day since 1979, and it showed its twenty-five thousandth episode in 2002. Compared with other storytelling media, fictional television shows generate a huge amount of original content—for example, over the course of 9 seasons, the producers of the sitcom *Everybody Loves Raymond* created 210 original half-hours, or the rough equivalent of 52 feature films!

Production companies feature logos or bumpers at the end credits of programs, highlighting their creative and corporate pedigree from both major media corporations like 20th Century Fox and producer-owned companies like J.J. Abrams's Bad Robot.

Production companies both develop new programs and produce ongoing series. Creating new programs is the most risky facet of the television industry, as the vast majority of ideas for new television programs fail to get on the air— and most that eventually do make it are cancelled before producers recoup the costs spent to develop the show. Production companies invest their own funding and resources to develop and produce programming via a system termed **deficit financing**, accruing significant debt over the first few years of a series, even if it is successful. The **license fees** that distributors such as networks and cable channels pay to producers in exchange for airing programs typically cover only a portion of production costs, placing the greatest financial risk upon production companies.

So if a production company must go into debt for years, how could this be a profitable industry? Because when a show is a hit, the long-term windfall can be enormous. The main asset that producers get for their creative and funding efforts is ownership of the rights to the program itself—typically a series will be licensed to a network or channel for an exclusive window, after which the production company can find other ways to recoup costs through additional means of distributing reruns, as discussed in the next section. Additionally, once a show is a hit, producers can demand higher license fees for new episodes, as networks want to retain flagship series on their schedules—by the end of its run, NBC was paying Warner Bros. around $7 million per episode of the sitcom *Friends*, although most of that went to pay for the six lead actors who had leveraged the show's success into record salaries of $1 million per episode each (plus revenues from future syndication sales). For a production company, the profits from one hit series can offset the losses of many failures, so producers continue to rack up debts in search of the next blockbuster series—for instance, Wolf Films has had more than a dozen pilots and series commissioned by networks, but only the *Law & Order* franchise shows have managed to last beyond two seasons.

Production companies must manage the production process from concept to continuing series; the aptly named coordinator of this process is the program's **showrunner**. Typically this person will be the program's creator (at least at first), although production companies sometimes will bring in a showrunner with a longer track record to oversee less-experienced creators. Showrunners are typically listed as executive producer in a program's credits, and their names are often the first to appear in the closing credits. On television, the role of producer means many things, from major creative force behind a show to rights-holder who negotiates an ownership stake in a show at the early stages of production. The various credits of executive producers, supervising producers, and co-producers suggest a hierarchy of authority and seniority among the production staff that varies by production company and program. The majority of television producers for scripted programming are part of a show's writing staff, leading many critics to note that fictional television is a writer's medium, especially when compared to the central creative role of directors within filmmaking. When considering the vast number of hours of programming that must be created over the course of a series, it certainly makes sense that those in charge be the most intimately involved in creating the stories and characters.

FRIENDS

Friends (NBC, 1994–2004): Part of NBC's hit "Must See TV" lineup, *Friends* is a trendy, and trend-setting, sitcom focused on a group of young singles in New York City and incorporating long-term story arcs involving the web of relationships among the six main characters.

Producer credits help sort out the various production companies involved in creating any program. As previously noted, *ER* has four production companies credited, each of which serves a different function in getting the program to the air. Warner Bros. is the primary production studio—since television production is both expensive and risky, major media corporations such as film studios are increasingly the only companies that will bear the risk of deficit financing. Warner produces more fictional television programming than any other company, maximizing the infrastructure of its Hollywood studios and spreading the risk across numerous projects. Constant c Productions is Michael Crichton's company, as Crichton wrote the original film script from which *ER* was adapted; his company credit grants him partial ownership of the lucrative series, but is less involved in the ongoing production process. Amblin Entertainment is Steven Spielberg's company, which also owns a portion of the show; Spielberg was initially an executive producer of the show, but served mostly as a consultant to shape the initial creative vision and offer deal-making clout to bring the program to the air. John Wells Productions gives partial ownership to Wells, who was the initial showrunner and frequent writer of the program, often credited as the architect of the show's innovative style and compelling narrative. All production companies share some degree of ownership and profit-sharing in a program, divided as devised in initial contracts; typically creators and showrunners will own a portion of their programs in the form of a personal production company, positioned to gain tremendous windfalls if a series proves successful.

Although Hollywood studios produce or co-produce most fictional programming, other companies can be involved. **Independent television producers** have played an important role in bringing programming to the air, especially in the classic network era. Working apart from major media companies such as networks and film studios, independent production houses were responsible for many major hits and innovations in earlier decades: for instance, Desilu Productions (*I Love Lucy, Star Trek*), Mark VII Productions (*Dragnet, Adam-12*), MTM Enterprises (*The Mary Tyler Moore Show, Hill Street Blues*), Aaron Spelling Productions (*The Love Boat, 7th Heaven*), and Carsey-Werner Company (*The Cosby Show, That '70s Show*). These independent companies offered potential alternatives to the major media corporations, often embracing controversial content or formal innovations, with successful independent producers yielding tremendous profits when their risks paid off through hit programming. The role of independent producers was nurtured by the FCC in the 1970s through regulations discussed later in this chapter, but their industrial importance has diminished since the 1990s in the wake of regulatory shifts—many of these companies were either purchased outright by media conglomerates or were forced to affiliate with studios or networks, as the costs and risks of production grew too steep without the efficiencies and shared costs that large studios can utilize. Today, most programs are produced in conjunction with studios or networks, making true independent producers a rarity.

The other major producers of television programming are networks and channels themselves, which function primarily as distributors, but have always been involved in television production. Some genres, such as news, sports, public affairs, and special events, have been primarily self-produced by the channel or network that airs the program, with the news divisions of most networks and local stations functioning as in-house production companies. In the multichannel and convergence eras, media companies were part of large conglomerates in which each major network shared ownership with a film production studio that created a portion of its programming—for instance, ABC/Disney, NBC/Universal, CBS/Paramount, and Fox/20th Century Fox. Even though these companies do share common ownership, typically the production and distribution divisions are sufficiently separate that each production company also licenses shows to competing networks, mirroring the more traditional distinction between producer and distributor. Most studios work within their conglomerates the majority of the time, licensing between 60 and 75 percent of their programming within their corporate umbrella; Warner Bros., as the most prolific production company, saw only around one third of its programming aired on its former WB network, and even fewer on The CW. Cable channels typically are more invested in self-production, as original fictional series on channels such as HBO, Comedy Central, Nickelodeon, and FX are typically co-produced by the channel, while nonfiction channels such as CNN, ESPN, and Food Network self-produce as the norm. But all types of television producers—film studios, independent producers, networks, cable channels, local stations—must work with distribution companies to circulate their programs.

DISTRIBUTION

It might seem that the production companies, which create television programming, would be the central player in determining the shape of television content and style. But undoubtedly the most crucial role, in terms of both control of the industry and securing most of the profits, is **distribution**, ultimately determining what shows make it to the air, and managing the promotion and scheduling of programming, which help create hits or try to prevent flops. Producers must get a distribution commitment before they can proceed in producing their program, as distributors provide crucial funding and are the only means to get a show seen by viewers. Producers do have a few potential avenues for distribution, with three primary types of companies serving this role within American television: networks, channels, and syndicators, each of which offer differing relationships to producers, transmitters, advertisers, and audiences. While each of these three company types serves the shared role of getting programming from producers to viewers, their functions are vastly different, and within the industry they would not be considered as functioning equally as distributors. However, networks, channels, and syndicators all function as crucial intermediaries, and together they control what appears on television schedules, even if they are not commonly called distributors in industry terminology.

Networks are the best known and still the most powerful distributors in television. The network system emerged in the 1940s, from the radio industry, as the three major radio networks all quickly established themselves as television's Big Three: ABC, CBS, and NBC. Modeled after the radio industry, these national television networks operate in a system of **affiliation** by which local stations contract with one of these national companies to carry network programming. In any local market, one station may affiliate with each national network, entering into a complex arrangement between the two parties that results in the affiliate airing the bulk of the network's programming. The affiliate station is paid a fee for **clearance**—that is, opening its airwaves to the network programs— and it gains exclusive access to the network's national schedule and promotion within the affiliate's broadcast area, which generally outstrips the caliber and popularity of programming a local station could self-produce. The network gains access to each affiliate's region of viewers, building the largest potential national audience to sell to advertisers.

For many years, the Big Three controlled the national television market, with 90 percent of viewers turning to network programming when watching prime time television through the 1970s. This control was incredibly profitable, as the networks used their guaranteed audience and lack of external competition to maximize advertising revenues and minimize risk, resulting in decades when even the last-place network turned a neat profit, such as when slumping NBC was still yielding $48 million in profits in 1981.[1] In the mid-1980s, Fox took the risky step of launching a new network—a move that was, at the time, nearly universally regarded as foolish and doomed to failure. Today Fox is virtually equal in popularity and number of affiliates to ABC, CBS, and NBC during its broadcast time—although it still airs far less programming, with no network news and little broadcasting outside of its condensed two-hour prime time lineup and weekend sports coverage. By the mid-1990s, UPN and The WB emerged as networks, following in Fox's path to compete with traditional broadcasters, although neither was able to rival Fox's success in reaching sizable audiences, gaining strong affiliates, or creating major hit programming. In 2006, The WB and UPN disbanded and were recreated in a new combination, called The CW, a network co-owned by Warner Bros. and Viacom that was aiming to compete more effectively with the more established broadcast networks. Univision emerged in the 1990s as a powerful Spanish-language broadcasting network, with ratings that rival The CW and often beat larger networks and cable channels in select markets. The rise of these newer networks has contributed to the demise of the classic network era, as the Big Three no longer are guaranteed the majority of the viewing audience given greater competition from smaller networks and cable channels.

A network's primary function is to develop a schedule of programming and attract viewers to its affiliates. Networks are heavily invested in the process of program creation: hearing pitches from producers, financing pilots for new shows, and ordering episodes for ongoing series. During the production process, every showrunner works with a network representative to provide notes on the content from the network's perspective, and each network has a **standards-and-practices** department that approves or censors content throughout the production process. Ultimately networks feel responsible for the programs they air, so they tend to take a hands-on approach with producers, which can make creators feel compromised by network executives who don't share their creative vision. Nearly all programming aired on networks is created exclusively for the network, with networks paying licensing fees to producers for new and continuing series; the one exception to this model are theatrical films, which are licensed to networks and other distributors once the film studio has maximized revenue from theatrical and home video distribution.

One key distribution role mirrors the wholesaling function of most other industries: physically distributing the producer's project to make it available to consumers. For television, this involves a complex infrastructure of both wired and satellite connections among affiliates, enabling broadcasters to air programs from around the world simultaneously and often live. In television's early years, this technical challenge was significant, especially in covering multiple time zones before satellite transmissions were feasible. However, today, as satellites, cable, Internet, and home video all offer alternative ways for viewers to access programming, the more crucial function of television networks might be thought of as the **distribution of attention**: establishing knowledge, of and desire for, a network's programs in the minds of viewers. The attention of audiences is a valuable commodity that networks look to capture via a number of key strategies.

One especially successful way in which networks attract attention to television programming is via **scheduling**. Many scheduling practices are so entrenched in American viewing habits that they seem natural, such as the designation of evening programming from seven to eleven (or earlier, depending on time zones) as **prime time**, or the tradition of series running in **seasons** from fall to spring. These practices were established back in the days of network radio, but they linger to this day as ways of understanding television programming: prime time shows are more culturally central and valued than daytime or late-night programs, and summer is primarily filled with reruns. Other scheduling practices appear to be common sense but derive from network strategies: scheduling programs in half-hour segments, running news programs in morning and dinner time slots, and airing soap operas in daytime. While many of these scheduling practices are becoming less universal in the multi-channel and digital eras, that each of these practices still seems natural today is a testament to how powerful networks have been in establishing the norms for how Americans watch television.

Networks also use specific scheduling strategies to promote specific programs and lineups, techniques that were most effective in the classic network era given the limited competition among channels. Each network attempts to create an evening's prime time schedule that will maximize **flow**, the continuous viewing across programs and (most important) advertising. Sometimes networks will use thematic evenings of programming—in the 1990s, NBC successfully scheduled its hugely popular "Must See TV" Thursday lineup (featuring *Friends, Seinfeld, Will & Grace*, and *ER*) as "destination programming" for viewers to be tapped into contemporary popular trends; while in the mid-2000s, Fox Sundays featured "Animation Domination," with *King of the Hill, The Simpsons, Family Guy*, and *American Dad*. Typically networks schedule compatible programs next to one another, especially with a popular program as a **lead-in** to a show that is new or struggling in the ratings. A network might schedule a weaker program between two hits, a strategy called **hammocking**, to boost the ratings for the middle show as audiences stay in the flow. All of these techniques were common in the classic network era—in recent decades, both the proliferation of channels and recording technologies make it more difficult for networks to use schedules to boost ratings, a set of challenges discussed more in chapter 11.

In the face of increased competition among channels and schedule-shifting technologies, networks increasingly integrated scheduling strategies within the programming itself in the multi-channel and convergence eras, working with production companies to create flow across a lineup. Networks created **stunts** over an evening's lineup—for instance, Elizabeth Taylor, in an effort to promote her new perfume, guest-starred on CBS's entire sitcom lineup of *The Nanny, Can't Hurry Love, Murphy Brown*, and *High Society* on one evening

	8:00pm	8:30	9:00pm	9:30	10:00pm	10:30
2 NECN	NewsNight with Jim Braude		Business Day	News at 9	News at 10	
3 WCAX	The Big Bang Theory (CC) HDTV	How I Met Your Mother Repeat TVPG	CSI: Crime Scene Investigation Repeat TV14 (CC) HDTV		Without a Trace Repeat TV14 (CC) HDTV	
4 WVNY (abc)	Lost Repeat TVPG (CC) HDTV		Lost (CC) HDTV			
5 WPTZ (NBC)	My Name Is Earl Repeat TV14 (CC) HDTV	Last Comic Standing TV14 (CC)			The Office Repeat TVPG (CC) HDTV	
6 WETK (PBS)	Report From Washington		Eden at the End of the World Repeat TVPG (CC) HDTV		Wild! TVG (CC) DVS	
7 WGMU (my)	Hoosiers TVG (CC)				South Park TV14 (CC)	Frasier (CC)
8 WWBI	Breakthrough (CC)	Joni Lamb	Celebration		Destined to Reign With Joseph Prince	It's Supernatural
9 WFFF	So You Think You Can Dance TVPG (CC)				FOX 44 News at 10 [NEWS]	TMZ TVPG (CC)
10 ESPN	◄ Women's Softball (CC) HDTV		Women's Softball (CC) HDTV			►
11 ESPN2	◄ MLS Soccer (CC) HDTV			Madden Nation (CC)	Baseball Tonight (CC) HDTV	

	8:00pm	9:00pm	10:00pm
12 QVC	Electronic Gifts (CC)	philosophy---beauty (CC)	
13 DSC	911: The Bronx TV14 (CC)	911: The Bronx TV14 (CC)	911: The Bronx TV14 (CC)

Today scheduling grids are more likely to be found online, but were a staple of newspapers and *TV Guide* throughout the network and multi-channel eras.

in 1996, despite the shows' being produced by differing companies. More commonly, networks featured **crossovers** between programs, such as continued storylines in the same week on NBC's *Crossing Jordan* and *Las Vegas* or CBS's *CSI: NY* and *Cold Case*, or the shared character of Lisa Kudrow's Ursula between NBC's *Mad About You* and *Friends* or Richard Belzer's John Munch, who was a regular on both NBC's *Homicide: Life on the Street* and *Law & Order: SVU*. Crossovers can allow for some playful creativity, as with *The X-Files* episode shot and constructed as a fictionalized episode of the reality show *Cops*, or animated versions of *X-Files* leads Mulder and Scully showing up on *The Simpsons* to investigate aliens, all programs airing on Fox. Occasionally, crossovers can span networks, when production companies can leverage their clout behind hit shows to allow for creative exchanges, such as between Fox's *Ally McBeal* and ABC's *The Practice* (both produced by David E. Kelley Productions and 20th Century Fox Television) or NBC's *Seinfeld* and CBS's *Murphy Brown* (both produced by subsidiaries of Warner Bros.). Yet these cross-network promotions are quite rare compared to stunts and crossovers within a network, testifying to the degree of control that distributors have over production companies.

Networks realize they are competing for ratings against other networks and channels, and thus they design their schedules in reaction to what their competition offers. In some cases, this results in direct competition: morning

SEINFELD

Seinfeld (NBC, 1989–1998): One of television's most popular and innovative shows, *Seinfeld* focuses on an unlikable foursome of New Yorkers and their comic conversations about mundane everyday life. The show combines subtle wordplay, complex narrative structure, outlandish farce, and pop culture catchphrases to become an unlikely hit that remains popular in syndication.

GREY'S ANATOMY

Grey's Anatomy (ABC, 2005–present): A hit medical drama, the show depicts life among a racially diverse group of doctors in a Seattle hospital. Especially popular with female audiences, *Grey's Anatomy* combines media storylines with romantic dramas between attractive cast members.

magazines (such as the *Today* show), soap operas, evening news, and late-night talk shows all try to beat one another in the same time slots. In these cases, networks compete with one another for a share of the largest audience block during these time slots, rather than serving viewers who might want an alternative to that time slot's normal fare. In prime time, networks more often **counter-program** against other networks, using programs that might attract a different audience than the competition, especially when facing a hit show. For instance, in 1996, *Seinfeld* was ranked the number two show on television, but did poorly among African-American audiences (ranked number sixty-eight); Fox scheduled *New York Undercover,* featuring black and Latino police, in the same Thursday night time slot, successfully reaching minority audiences (ranked number two among black audiences, number eighty-seven among all households) looking for an alternative to NBC's white-centered sitcoms.[2] Another scheduling strategy is **challenge programming**, where a network moves a hit into a time slot dominated by another network in order to try to take over the night's ratings—in 2006, ABC effectively challenged CBS by moving *Grey's Anatomy* to Thursday to directly overtake longtime hit *CSI.* Through all of these strategies, scheduling represents a primary means for networks to develop awareness, build an audience for its programming, and try to differentiate among networks.

Another key role for networks is **promotion**, advertising their own programs. While networks use nearly all media to promote programs, from newspapers to

CSI

CSI (CBS, 2000–present): This blockbuster crime procedural highlights the science behind homicide investigation, using innovative camerawork and flashy visuals to create a compelling variation on the police show. The Las Vegas original, which was a surprise hit, has spawned two successful spin-offs, giving CBS a crime franchise surpassing NBC's *Law & Order* in popularity.

billboards, their primary promotional strategy uses network airtime during their programs to broadcast ads for their other shows, typically dedicating around 25 percent of any show's advertising time to promos for network programming. In the face of heightened competition, networks are increasingly encroaching on programming itself by shrinking closing credits to show promos for future programs, and using on-screen network **logos** and **snipes**, or pop-up ads overlaying the bottom portion of the screen promoting other shows. Promotion strategies can often make or break a new program, as networks typically focus their promotional efforts on only a few new programs each season. Fans of prematurely cancelled shows often blame poor network promotion and scheduling for a show's low ratings, although sometimes hits can unexpectedly overcome weak scheduling and promotion—in 2000, CBS put its promotional muscle behind *The Fugitive* (which failed to get high enough ratings to last more than one season), only to see the under-the-radar *CSI* overcome a weak Friday time slot to become the season's biggest hit and eventually television's number one program. A hit show offers a host of benefits to a network beyond high advertising rates, as it provides scheduling anchors to raise ratings for other programming via lead-ins and hammocks, and opportunities to promote an entire lineup to a large audience.

Hits can also help define a network's **brand** identity. In the classic network era, each network strived to appeal to the broadest potential audience, yet each had certain reputations at particular moments: CBS was known both as the upscale "Tiffany network" in the 1950s, and as the "heartland network" for its rural-themed programs of the 1960s, while ABC had a more kid-friendly escapist brand in the 1970s, and NBC established itself as the urbane "quality" network of the 1980s. The role of branding became more central in the multi-channel era, as networks needed to define themselves as tied to the demographic profile of their audiences: NBC ruled the 1990s with hip sitcoms and gritty dramas that reached the young, affluent audiences desirable to advertisers, while CBS had to overcome its reputation as the elderly network of *60 Minutes* and *Murder, She Wrote*, which it did in the early 2000s, with hits such as *Survivor* and *CSI*.

NBC's hit show *Heroes* finds its image taken over by a snipe for new series *Bionic Woman* in 2007.

Branding is even more central for the second major type of television distributor: **cable and satellite channels**. The difference between cable and satellite channels and networks can be slippery, as the terms are used inconsistently throughout the industry. Although many cable channels call themselves "networks" (such as Cartoon Network or Food Network), they do not have affiliates and thus are not truly "networked"—instead, they are either single national channels that air identically across the country or regional cable channels typically airing sports or area news, such as FSN Midwest or New England Cable News. Likewise, for the everyday viewer, a channel on your cable box is the same whether it's a national cable channel such as CNN or a network such as Fox, but there is a crucial distinction for the industry: the Fox you watch is actually a local station affiliated with the network, not a national channel. Thus while the terms *network, channel,* and *station* are often used interchangeably within the industry and for everyday use, each has its own specific structure and role within the television system, and thus it is worth distinguishing what is meant by each term.

As cable television became widely adopted technology in the 1980s, channels unique to cable (and later satellite) systems established themselves as alternatives to network programming. Cable channels expanded the offerings of television programming, but as their audience shares were smaller than traditional networks, most channels established themselves using a specified brand identity. Some channel brands are based on genre (Comedy Central, Sci-Fi Channel, CNN for news, ESPN for sports), some defined by audience (Lifetime for women, BET for black viewers, Nickelodeon for kids), but nearly all channels need some marker of distinction to gain a significant place within a viewer's routine.

MTV was an important innovator concerning branding. When launched in 1981, it functioned much like commercial radio, running promotional music videos (obtained free from record companies) as hosted by "videojockeys," or VJs. As the channel became popular with teenagers, it diversified its programming to include shows with few links to the "music television" MTV ostensibly stood for, but consistent with the young countercultural identity that the channel had fostered through its ties to rock music. Soon MTV become iconic more for its attitude and style than for the distinct music video genre it had popularized, as its youthful, rebellious brand became the appeal to many viewers and the unifying factor for the channel. Notably, music videos are comparatively rare on MTV today, as the company has launched spin-off channel MTV2 to feature primarily music videos, as in MTV's early years. Most cable channels have learned from MTV's success, attempting to forge a distinct brand identity that unifies their programming, advertising, and assumed audience, and when successful, following MTV's path by leveraging that identity into spin-off channels and projects, such as Nickelodeon's TV Land or Cartoon Network's Adult Swim.

Cable channels follow most of the practices networks use to create an audience for their programming: promotion, scheduling, financing new productions, and developing channel identities. Typically cable channels lack the diversity of programming formats and sources of networks, as they strive to reach a more narrowly defined audience, and thus few channels feature the full array of news,

MTV established itself as the home for teenage audiences in the 1980s through its aggressive branding strategy, making the channel itself linked to a rebellious and playful lifestyle.

24

24 (Fox, 2001–present): An espionage show that debuted shortly after the September 11 terrorist attacks, *24* uses the innovative narrative technique of "real-time" storytelling to create an addictively exciting series. The series has generated controversy for its portrayal of torture and Middle Eastern terrorists, and praise from conservative politicians as a sympathetic fictional representation.

sports, comedy, drama, children's programming, and special events found on broadcast networks. Yet despite the comparative uniformity of any one channel's offerings, particular challenges emerge. Cable channels usually run twenty-four hours a day, whereas networks may schedule as little as two hours each day, but rarely more than twelve, leaving the remaining time to local affiliates. Thus to fill their vast amount of airtime, cable channels build frequent repetition of programming into their schedules, and often sell overnight time slots to advertisers for infomercials. Critics frequently condemn the repetitive mode of such schedules, especially for news channels, where the need to fill airtime often leads to the endless hyping of news stories and excessive pontification by pundits.

Like networks, cable channels procure programming from a range of sources: film studios, independent producers, and channel self-production. Cable channels often take advantage of their different regulatory structures to air programs that broadcast networks would refuse to air due to risqué content, such as Comedy Central's *South Park*, FX's *The Shield*, or MTV's *Jackass*; premium channels such as HBO and Showtime market themselves precisely using their ability to show mature representations of sexual material, as on *Sex and the City* and *Queer as Folk*, or explicit language and violence, as on *The Sopranos*, *The Wire*, and *Dexter*. Yet cable channels rely on network hits, too, often featuring off-network reruns. A newer strategy combines network and cable runs, as a new series debuts on a network and is shown later that week on a cable channel, typically one owned by the network—for instance, Fox aired *24* (a Fox Television production) on Tuesday nights in 2002, with its FX channel replaying the show twice during the week and contributing to licensing costs for the ongoing season.

Prior to the multi-channel era, off-network reruns were licensed to local stations solely through the third major method of distribution: **syndication**. While both networks and cable channels use programming to sell advertising and can use scheduling techniques to promote their identity, syndication does not feature a centralized schedule or channel identity. Syndicators license programming directly to individual local stations or a national cable channel, giving the stations control of scheduling and promotion duties—typically syndicated programs are **stripped**, that is, scheduled each day at the same time (for instance, Monday through Friday, at 5:30 p.m.). Why would a station pay to license from a syndicator rather than get paid to air network programming? Some stations have no network affiliations; for these independent stations, syndication provides the only access to established hit programs, even if they are years old. Even network affiliates need to program for the fringe times of their schedules that networks do not fill—few local stations have the resources to produce programming beyond news, sports, public affairs, and local event coverage, so syndication represents the easiest way to fill out a schedule with programs with proven audience appeal. And syndicated programs allow local stations to sell advertising time to local sponsors, offering a strong potential return on their license fees.

Syndicators distribute two kinds of programming: off-network reruns and first-run programs. **Off-network reruns** are a staple of syndication on local stations, filling out schedules with sitcom and dramatic repeats. Typically a network or channel purchases the license to run a new episode for a limited window (usually one year) and a set number of times (two or three); after that initial period, producers are free to re-license the program to other distributors. Broadcast networks rarely renew their licenses for old episodes beyond one season, as their reputations are built on showing the newest programming available. Within the industry, the term *reruns* typically refers to multiple presentations on the original network, as typically prime time episodes are rerun once or twice each season and the following summer. However, everyday viewers often use the term *rerun* to refer to all repeats, whether on- or off-network via syndication to local stations or a cable channel. Thus a hit show such as *CSI* has reruns air on CBS over the course of a season, in syndication across the country at a variety of local stations, and on national cable channel Spike TV—all of which yield tremendous profits for the show's producers.

Licensing fees from networks are rarely enough to finance an ongoing scripted series, and thus producers look to reruns to recoup their investments and turn a profit. If a show is successful, producers can reap tremendous financial rewards by licensing packages of reruns through syndication on local stations and cable channels. TV Land and Nickelodeon's evening lineup Nick at Nite have established their entire identity based around off-network reruns, repackaged as "Our Television Heritage." Vertical integration can bypass the syndication system in distributing reruns—for instance, Warner Bros. owns the channels Cartoon Network and Boomerang, both of which feature a large number of programs from the conglomerate's library of Warner, MGM, and Hanna-Barbera cartoons, and thus avoid paying an intermediary syndicator. In the convergence era, producers reap rewards from other ways to distribute off-network programming—home video sales and rentals on DVD, often released shortly after a network airs a season, direct downloads via iTunes or AOL during a season, and online streaming on network websites or affiliated sites such as

Hulu.com—although it is still too early to see how these practices will impact the syndication market.

Syndicators also distribute original programming, called **first-run syndication**. These shows are aired across the country at various times, although typically they fill the late-morning, late-afternoon, early-evening, or late-night fringe times that networks do not program. Most first-run syndicated shows are in genres that networks rarely distribute, such as game shows (*Wheel of Fortune*), talk shows (*The Oprah Winfrey Show*), tabloid news (*Entertainment Tonight* and *Inside Edition*), and courtroom reality shows (*Judge Judy*). But there are fictional and entertainment first-run syndicated programs more similar to network shows, some of which have proven to be significant hits, such as *The Muppet Show* and *Mary Hartman, Mary Hartman* in the 1970s, and *Star Trek: The Next Generation, Xena: Warrior Princess*, and *Baywatch* (after one failed season on NBC) in the 1990s. In each of these cases, networks passed on the program because they incorrectly doubted its audience appeal. Producers use first-run syndication as an alternative way to achieve their creative control while potentially reaching an audience share competitive with networks; it remains to be seen how much first-run syndication of fictional shows will continue, given the growth of such programming on cable channels in the 2000s.

TRANSMISSION

If the central role for distributors is to procure and promote programs from producers, there is still one more function needed to complete the programming exchange: enabling viewers to watch shows. **Transmission companies** serve this function, taking programming received from distributors and producers and making it available to viewers, much like the retail function of most consumer industries. However, in television, there is not a direct retail exchange comparable to the box office of a movie theater—audiences just turn on the television to access these cultural products. Because of television's unusual economic model, the practices of transmission companies may appear to be more complex and counterintuitive than producers and distributors, yet they are crucial to understanding the structure of the television industry.

In the classic network era, the transmission function was undertaken by one type of company: the **broadcast station**. Technically, broadcasting is a process that modulates radio waves to transmit images and sounds, following a government-mandated standard to ensure that any television was able to decode these transmissions into programming. Using the system established for radio in the 1920s, television stations each operate at a particular frequency tied to a specific channel number; as discussed in chapter 3, all stations are required to be licensed by the FCC, which assigns them exclusive access to a particular broadcast frequency in their region, at no cost. To avoid interference among broadcasts, the FCC limits the number of stations licensed within any geographical area and restricts a station's power to a local area, creating a **scarcity** of transmission companies within any particular market. Thus viewers have only a few broadcast channels to choose from in their region, and new entry into the broadcast transmission business is severely limited. Even though today the majority of viewers receive television signals through cable or satellite, stations still transmit via over-the-air broadcasting for free access to television programming in local markets.

Broadcast station assignment is further complicated by the dual system of **VHF** (very-high frequency) and **UHF** (ultra-high frequency) channels. In 1948, the FCC halted station licensing because of widespread signal interference during the early growth of television, freezing the medium's expansion until these technical problems could be resolved. The 108 already licensed stations across the country, all located in the VHF band between channels 2 and 13, continued to operate, with most affiliating with the already dominant networks. The FCC ended the freeze in 1952 by unveiling the UHF band of channels 14 through 83, allowing for greater growth of stations in any region, but creating an imbalanced mixed system. VHF transmission was more reliable and reached a broader geographical area than UHF, a distinct advantage to VHF stations. One effect of this **intermixed** system was to create two tiers among stations in any given region, with VHF broadcasters typically using their technical advantages to secure valuable affiliation arrangements with networks, a situation that effectively encouraged television to grow as a nationally networked rather than locally produced medium. Even though these distinctions mean less today, as most viewers access local stations through cable or satellite, the most prized affiliates still broadcast on VHF bands in major markets—although this system will become obsolete after the shift to digital television discussed in chapter 11.

Initially, most stations were locally owned and run, typically emerging as outgrowths of other regional businesses. Broadcast stations are consistently profitable, especially when affiliated with a network: affiliate stations receive clearance fees from networks to carry national programming and sell local advertising during both network and local programming, with minimal production costs for local news and sports coverage. Network affiliates fill the majority of their schedules with national programming, including morning news, daytime soap operas, evening news, prime time entertainment, late-night talk shows, and weekend sports. Nearly all stations rely on syndication to fill the rest of their schedules, buying the rights to established off-network hits or first-run shows. Besides syndication licenses and local news divisions, the primary cost for broadcasters is the technology needed to serve their geographical region, which became pricier as digital television emerged. Nonetheless, local broadcasting remains a profitable and lower-risk facet of the television industry.

Because of the profitability of local broadcasting, major media companies have increasingly purchased stations across the country, forming **station groups** of more thirty stations held by corporations such as Tribune Company and Sinclair Broadcast Group. These group-owned stations do not function as networks (and most groups own affiliates of different networks), but they often do share news resources, syndication packages, and editorial policies. National networks have always had an ownership stake in select stations, with these affiliates termed **owned and operated** (or **O&O**) stations; until 1985, the FCC capped the number of stations that any network could own at five. Not surprisingly, networks own the stations in the largest local markets, giving them access to the largest potential audience share—in the 1970s, all three networks owned affiliates in New York City, Chicago, and Los Angeles, with select O&Os in Philadelphia, San Francisco, St. Louis, Washington, and Cleveland. O&O stations are a key part of a network's revenue, since they do not need to pay for clearance time and can share in both local and national ad revenue. They also often represent the main revenue source for a network—in 1970, 70 percent of all network earnings came from O&O stations.[3] Since the mid-1980s, the networks have repeatedly lobbied the federal government to raise the caps on O&O ownership. In 2006, the cap stood at 39 percent of the national market share, resulting in networks each owning between ten and thirty-five stations. As discussed in chapter 3, media ownership regulations have prompted intense public debate over the role of local control and corporate responsibility in America.

In the multi-channel era, another kind of transmission company emerged: the **cable system**. Cable television was an early innovation designed to serve rural regions where broadcast reception was difficult—a local company would build a large antenna and charge each household to connect via cable to a system called **community antenna television (CATV)**. This system was transformed by the 1970s to the cable television of today, in which a company offers a range of subscription packages to households to carry both local broadcasters and national channels. Because of the physical infrastructure needed to connect a local area with cable service—as any household must literally have a cable connection to the company's headquarters—typically a municipality issues exclusive **franchise rights** to a cable system. These franchise rights guarantee each cable system a monopoly within the locality to justify the cost of cabling the area, also ensuring that cable systems need not face direct competition over customer service or price. Just as local broadcast stations have become conglomerated into larger national groups since the 1980s, local cable systems have been purchased by national companies known as **multiple-system operators (MSOs)**, such as Time-Warner Cable or Comcast, which use their economy of scale to decrease costs and increase profits, with over two thirds of cable subscribers receiving service from one of the five largest MSOs.

Cable systems provide access to television transmission for around two thirds of American households, paying a small monthly **subscription fee** per subscriber to all channels they carry; this cost ranges widely, from five cents for marginal or new channels, to more than two dollars for staples of basic cable such as ESPN. Thus ESPN, with more than ninety-six million households receiving the channel, receives almost $200 million each month in subscriber fees alone. Cable channels have a guaranteed monthly income based on how many subscribers have access to their channels regardless of ratings and advertising rates, while cable systems pass along these costs to households through ever-increasing monthly fees. Despite widespread frustrations with the customer service and price increases of the cable industry, consumers continue to subscribe to and opt for additional channels to access the wide range of programming to which a cable system offers nearly exclusive access in most areas.

Cable systems and broadcasters have long been pitted against one another in trying to reach their local audiences. Per federal **must-carry** regulations, which ensure that local broadcasters have access to the clearer reception offered by cable transmission, cable systems must transmit local broadcast stations, a law that during the early years of cable assured broadcasters that cable would not overtake their business. The spread of cable subscriptions helped UHF stations significantly, overcoming their weaker reception and putting them on more equal footing with their local VHF competition for cable subscribers. As cable became more widely adopted, broadcast stations wanted to be paid for their retransmission via cable; now broadcasters can waive their must-carry status in exchange for **retransmission consent**, in which cable systems must pay them a subscription fee for carrying their stations. Since broadcasting still provides the most watched television content, cable systems are typically willing to pay major local stations to carry their signals, as a cable system not offering local broadcast stations would generate complaints from its customers. The effect of this system is that fringe broadcast stations can be guaranteed carriage on local cable systems, while the systems must pay fees to carry the major local stations, typically network affiliates.

MSOs take advantage of this system on both ends—because they dominate the cable market, channels often negotiate lower bulk rates to access prime channel space on the major MSOs. Cable subscribers typically choose particular tiers of channel options, with increased costs tied to the number of channels packaged within each tier; the lower the channel number on a cable system, the more likely that consumers will have access to the channel, so channels negotiate for a lower position on the cable lineup. All cable channels are dependent on being adopted by cable systems, as each system that carries a channel both adds revenue in subscription fees and expands the potential audience to sell to advertisers; thus channels work to sell themselves to potential viewers, encouraging them to lobby their local cable providers to add the channel to its lineup. As detailed in Table 1-1, many MSOs have ownership stakes in cable channels—Time Warner owns CNN, Cartoon Network, TNT, and many other channels; while Comcast owns Golf Channel and part of E!—thus keeping subscription fees under the same corporate umbrella and guaranteeing placement in lineups for self-owned channels.

Cable systems typically negotiate with channels to allow a portion of the channel's advertising time to be sold by the cable transmitter, adding local advertising as another revenue stream for cable systems. Other transmission strategies offer additional revenue for cable transmitters and distributors. **Premium channels**, such as HBO and Showtime, are among the most popular options for the cable industry, as subscribers pay around ten dollars monthly, split between the channel and cable system, for access to advertising-free and uncensored channels showing movies, sports, and high-profile original programming. **Pay-per-view (PPV)** movies and events and the more recent **video-on-demand (VOD)** service both allow cable customers to pay for programming directly, a direct-sales model that is otherwise unavailable via television; thus far, these services have proven to be less popular than premium subscriptions or video rental, as most television viewers have not embraced a retail model for programming that has habitually been available without direct charges. Cable systems have also moved aggressively in providing broadband Internet and telephone services as part of their home media packages, part of the digital convergence discussed in chapter 11. In general, the varying revenue streams and lack of competition have made cable systems one of the more profitable realms of the television industry.

The main direct competitor to cable comes from **direct broadcast satellite (DBS) systems,** which emerged in the mid-1990s. DBS systems, such as DirecTV and Dish Network, require a household to purchase or rent a miniature satellite dish, uplinking to a satellite to receive packages of programming, premium channels, pay-per-view, and even broadband to compete with cable. The structure of the DBS industry is comparable to cable systems—national DBS systems pay fees for carrying channels and charge consumers monthly subscription fees. DBS has competed successfully with cable, especially in rural areas where cable service is limited by geographical obstacles and low population density—cable still reaches almost three times the number of subscribers as DBS, but satellite's customer base continues to grow as cable's portion of the market shrinks. DBS adoption was somewhat limited in the 1990s, in part because of a regulation blocking DBS providers from carrying local broadcasters if they could be received via a traditional antenna, a policy lobbied for by the cable industry. Once this regulation was lifted in 1999, DBS became a more popular option, suggesting that even in the multi-channel era, local broadcasters and network affiliates are still at the core of most people's television consumption. Like cable MSOs, DBS systems have ownership interests in cable channels to maximize their role in the industry—notably, until 2008

Table 1-1 Major media corporations have significant ownership stakes in cable channels and MSOs.

	Comcast	Disney	NBC/Universal	News Corporation	Viacom	Warner Bros.
Networks and channels owned or partly owned	E!; Comcast Sports Networks; G4; Versus; Golf Channel	ABC; ESPN; Disney Channel; Toon Disney; ABC Family; SOAPnet; Lifetime; A&E; History Channel	NBC; CNBC; MSNBC; Telemundo; Bravo; Sci Fi; USA; Universal HD; Oxygen; Weather Channel; A&E; History Channel; Sundance Channel	Fox; Fox News; Fox Movie Channel; FX; Fox Sports Net; Fox Reality; Fox Business; National Geographic	MTV; VH1; Nickelodeon; TV Land; Spike; CMT; BET; Comedy Central; Logo; Noggin (split with CBS & Showtime in 2006)	The CW; HBO; Cinemax; CNN; TBS; TNT; TCM; Cartoon Network; truTV
Cable/DBS systems	Comcast Cable Systems			DirecTV (until 2008)		Time Warner Cable

DirecTV was owned by News Corporation, which owns Fox, FX, Fox News Channel, and Fox Sports.

Partly in response to DBS competition, cable systems have rolled out **digital cable** options, which has resulted in improved picture quality, a greatly expanded number of channels, and VOD services. Cable's continued loss of subscribers persists, in part due to the industry's long-held reputation for poor service and price hikes that routinely exceed inflation. All of the transmission companies active in the television industry represent the most direct connection consumers have with the industry, as viewers make choices in subscriptions and contact their local affiliates to comment on the quality of programming and transmission. While typically transmitters have little to do with the nationally distributed programming they air through cable channels and networks, they are the key site in which television connects with viewers, and thus they are central to the industry's traditional business model—but they are threatened by the rise of downloadable and online video, which in the convergence era have allowed distributors to connect directly with viewers.

THE WEB OF OWNERSHIP

Throughout the discussion of the programming exchange, you might have noticed how some of the same corporate names, such as Warner Bros. and Fox, appear in many segments of the industry. One of the most important trends in all media industries over the past few decades has been the growing **conglomeration** of the industries, with major corporations buying out smaller companies and moving into multiple sectors of the media. Such conglomeration has been a great concern for critics and media activists, who see corporate takeover of the media as a threat to democracy. Chapter 3 discusses these critiques in more depth, but first it is important to understand how conglomeration fits into the television industry's commercial strategies, why this trend has become so prevalent, and how conglomeration works against the same free market values such businesses claim to embrace.

Television has always been an industry dominated by major corporations rather than independent small businesses, as it is the only mass medium to have been introduced with an existent industrial structure. While other media such as film, radio, recorded music, and the Internet emerged through an experimental period of hobbyists and inventors developing technologies without a shared business plan, television was a direct outgrowth of the commercial radio industry, with the same technological and programming companies that dominated radio of the 1930s and 1940s shifting their focus to this new medium. NBC, CBS, and ABC have always been the major defining companies in American television, functioning as an **oligopoly**, or a group of companies that restrict competition and control the industry; thus it would be naïve to believe that television might ever return to a pre-corporate era that never existed.

However, the landscape of media ownership has certainly changed in recent decades, as the expansion of the multi-channel era has reshuffled the players involved in the oligopolistic control of the industry. One key change is the place of television within larger corporate structures, which have become more conglomerated in recent decades. However, networks have always been enmeshed with other media interests—NBC has always been owned by a larger parent company, beginning, in the 1920s, as a government-endorsed monopolistic subsidiary of radio manufacturer and recording label RCA, which was bought out by General Electric in 1985. ABC was created in 1943 as a court-mandated divesture of one of NBC's two radio networks, merging with cinema chain United Paramount Theaters in the 1950s. CBS was an independent corporation until the 1980s, but also owned a music label, Columbia Records, and publishing interests. All three networks have always maintained their O&O stations, and have had varying interests in television production as well.

Thus networks have long practiced the two key strategies of corporate concentration: **vertical integration** and **horizontal integration**. Vertical integration refers to one company participating in all stages of its business—in the case of television, this means production, distribution, and transmission. With O&O stations and production units, television networks have always been vertically integrated, which allows companies to save costs and close out competitors through privileged relationships with their own subsidiaries. Likewise, cable MSOs that also own cable channels with production divisions are similarly vertically integrated. A horizontally integrated company has holdings across different industries, using a common ownership to share resources and promote projects—thus CBS radio, television, and Columbia records might all feature the same musical artist to create **synergy**, a situation in which one corporation's shared resources across media use cross-promotion strategies to yield a bigger overall hit than if each medium were independently controlled. For instance, Warner Bros. is horizontally integrated across most media, with vast television, film studio, music label, publishing, and Internet holdings, which allows the company to maximize the impact of any hit property. Both vertical and horizontal integration are ownership structures that promote commercial success of large diversified corporations by restricting entry of new competitors and maximizing efficiencies across different industrial functions.

Corporate concentration may mean increased profits and efficiencies for the largest conglomerates, but a concentrated market is not a free market: competition is needed to ensure the benefits from market forces. Thus the federal government regulated against market concentration in a wide range of industries throughout the twentieth century in order to promote free market economics, through **antitrust** policies and laws. However, such regulations have waxed and

Table 1-2 Most media corporations are highly conglomerated, with complex webs of horizontal and vertical integration, typified here by Time Warner.

	Television	Film	Digital	Print
Production	Warner Bros. Television; HBO Films; Cartoon Network Studios; TNT Originals; CNN Originals; Hanna Barbera	Warner Bros. Studios; Castle Rock Entertainment; Warner Bros. Animation	MapQuest; Moviefone; GameTap; Super Deluxe; Monolith Productions (games)	DC Comics; over 100 magazines including *Time, People, Entertainment Weekly, Sports Illustrated*, and *Fortune*
Distribution	The CW; HBO; Cinemax; CNN; TBS; TNT; TCM; Cartoon Network; truTV; Airport Network; Telepictures (syndication)	Warner Bros. Pictures; New Line Cinema	Weblogs, Inc.; Advertising.com; CNN.com; CartoonNetwork.com; Warner Bros. Games	
Transmission/ Retail	Time Warner Cable	Warner Home Video; numerous international movie theaters	America Online; Road Runner; Netscape; Winamp	WBshop.com

Formerly owned properties of Time Warner include Warner Music Group, The WB Network, Time-Life Books, Lorimar Productions, World Championship Wrestling, Atlanta Braves, Six Flags theme parks, Warner-Amex Satellite Entertainment, Warner Bros. Studio Stores, and numerous local broadcast stations.

waned throughout the history of television, as regulatory policies and court rulings have not been consistent across eras. Throughout the 1960s, networks grew more powerful in the television industry, increasingly demanding both co-ownership and control of future syndication rights for the programs they aired, with little intervention from a passive FCC. In the early 1970s, the FCC became more interventionist and recognized that oligopolistic control of networks reduced access for independent producers to get their programs on to the airwaves or required producers to give up ownership stakes in their productions. The FCC passed a number of anti-concentration measures to increase competition within the television industry, discussed more in chapter 3. Most notably, the **Financial Interest and Syndication Rules (Fin-Syn)** forced networks to reduce their vertical integration by limiting the number of self-owned programs aired in prime time, and requiring networks to divest the syndication wings of network corporations. Arguably the 1970s and early 1980s were a boom era for independent producers, but these regulations did not create a truly free market system for national broadcasting, as distribution was still an oligopoly controlled by the Big Three.

The 1980s saw a sea change in FCC attitudes toward concentration, as the Reagan administration appointed FCC commissioners who embraced a hands-off policy toward media ownership. New regulations and reduced enforcement of existing policies led to a major shift in the media landscape in the mid-1980s, as all three networks changed ownership multiple times and became more horizontally integrated with other media. Additionally, Fox received waivers on a number of regulations to allow it to enter the television network market. This might seem like free market economics at its finest, as Fox was able to overcome barriers of entry to pose a legitimate competitive threat to a long-entrenched network oligopoly. However, Fox was able to compete only because of its horizontal and vertical integration, as its parent company, News Corporation, owned numerous broadcast stations, a film studio with a major television production wing, and numerous newspapers and magazines used to promote the new network. Without the economies of scale and cost-sharing enabled by News Corporation's horizontal and vertical integration, it is hard to imagine a network being able to compete with the Big Three—no independent network could possibly have matched Fox's success. By not enforcing antitrust measures, the government endorsed a system of limited competition, with major corporations jockeying to expand both vertically and horizontally and close out competition from independent companies outside of conglomerates.

The 1990s saw this trend accelerate, as the Fin-Syn rules were repealed and the 1996 Telecommunications Act lifted even more antitrust regulations, encouraging expansion of O&O holdings and cross-media synergies. On its face, the multi-channel era appears to have heightened competition, as the traditional networks have seen their audience numbers dwindle in the face of cable channels and new networks, and viewer choices proliferate. But by looking at the ownership holdings of these companies, it becomes clear that networks have not lost viewers as much as shifted them to other corporate holdings. Thus ABC might have had a smaller audience in 2005 than it did in 1975—a top ten hit in 1975 might yield thirty million viewers, while in 2005 it would take only eighteen million—but many of those missing viewers were watching ESPN, Disney Channel, Lifetime, History Channel, E!, or ABC Family, all of which were at least partially owned by ABC's parent company, Disney.

Today the television industry is an oligopoly of five major media corporations, each of which is vertically and horizontally integrated, participating in nearly all spheres of the industry and across all major media. For instance, Disney owns ABC, numerous cable channels, ten broadcast affiliates, a major television production studio, a syndication distributor, a fully integrated film studio, record labels, dozens of radio stations, a retail chain, theme parks, a hockey team, a book publisher, many magazines, numerous popular websites, and a theatrical producer. Each of the parent companies for the networks has similar diversified cross-media holdings: Viacom (both CBS and UPN/CW), General Electric (NBC), Warner Bros. (WB/CW), and News Corporation (Fox). Of the major film studios, only Sony lacks significant television distribution interests, although it does produce a number of series, dominates the video game console market, and is a major manufacturer of television sets and accessories.

What is the significance of such market concentration? One particular concern involves how conglomerates treat public affairs and news stories as part of diversified media holdings, an issue addressed in chapter 4. From a business point of view, concentration reduces competition and new entry into an industry—if you have an innovative idea for a television program or channel, you must work with one of the major conglomerates to access the medium, which means operating on their corporate terms. Ted Turner, the media mogul who founded CNN, TBS, Cartoon Network, and many other cable channels, argues that there is no way he could have succeeded with his own innovations in the concentrated marketplace of the twenty-first century.[4] The expansion of cable in the 1980s enabled new entry by independent companies such as Turner Broadcasting because most broadcasters refused to consider an alternate transmission and distribution strategy; today media conglomerates seek to control all communication modes, effectively buying out and co-opting innovators through an integrated and concentrated market. Despite the rhetoric used by policymakers promoting deregulation, a concentrated system is not a free market—on the contrary, innovation and entrepreneurship are often closed out in exchange for safe formulas that will maximize synergy and cross-promotion.

Stockholders and corporate boards expect each component of a large conglomerate to turn a profit. Even though commercial television has always been motivated by profit, companies whose primary business is broadcasting tend to recognize the creative and public interest sides of the industry, as their leaders usually entered into the field driven by a commitment to journalism or creative expression. Conglomerates such as General Electric or News Corporation demand only returns on shareholder investment from each component, treating all subsidiaries as lines on a profit-and-loss statement. Thus news divisions and children's television are expected to be profitable, and innovative programs are rarely given an opportunity to prove themselves if they do not become immediate hits. As a whole, the rise of conglomeration has accelerated a tendency that has always existed in television: any new idea is judged solely by its ability to attract the large audience desired by advertisers. Thus underlying the programming exchange is a deep-seated commercial logic that typically tints the creative process involved in generating programming.

FROM PITCH TO HIT

Clearly the economic structure of the television industry is based on creating programs attractive to large enough audiences to generate advertising revenue, which pays for every step in the programming exchange. But how does television develop programs? As with all cultural industries, each individual program must be unique, but follow particular norms such as length, genre, and tone to meet viewer expectations. Every new program is inherently risky, and the television industry is notorious for its inability to predict hits and flops. Risks are unavoidable in any cultural industry, as it is impossible to guarantee what products will be popular with viewers, but the television industry has developed strategies to manage the risks of uncertainty.

One prime tactic is the use of **formulas**—producers and distributors study what other programs have recently been successful and attempt to capture a similar sensibility. Any new hit program will typically trigger a three-stage programming cycle: an **innovation** will garner audience attention, producers will attempt to mimic this success via **imitation**, resulting in **saturation** of similar programs that typically fade, leaving only the original hit on the air. The cycle of innovation–imitation–saturation can be seen throughout television history, from Westerns in the 1950s to prime time cartoons in the 1990s. Chapter 2 examines the reality TV cycle of the 2000s in these terms.

The imitative logic of television creativity takes many forms. If a producer creates a successful program, a common technique is to create a **spin-off** by relocating one character in a new situation after the original series ends, such as *Frasier* from *Cheers*, or while the original still remains on the air, as with *Angel* spinning off from *Buffy the Vampire Slayer*. Another strategy is creating a branded **franchise**, in which a production team uses new characters but similar sensibilities under a shared label, such as the multiple incarnations of *Law & Order* and *CSI* as fictional examples, or *Dateline* and *60 Minutes* as nonfiction ones.

A production company that doesn't have a hit show ready to be franchised or spun off can still employ formulaic strategies. **Clones** typically follow an innovative hit, as with the failed animated sitcoms *Fish Police* and *Family Dog*, which followed the surprise success of *The Simpsons* in the early 1990s. With a bit more subtlety than direct cloning, many producers create **recombinants**, taking elements from two or more popular programs and mixing them to create something that at least appears original—*Roswell* combined the teen drama of *Beverly Hills 90210* with the paranormal intrigue of *The X-Files*. Through all of these strategies, television producers manage the risks of creating new programs by balancing the competing demands of originality versus familiarity that both audiences and networks demand. As chapter 6 discusses, the use of genres and formulas can still result in innovative and accomplished programming.

Just as the television industry uses proven formulas to manage the risks of new ideas, production companies follow **routines of production** to minimize risks and maximize efficiencies once a program is in production. Nearly all television programs follow the production techniques established by their predecessors, resulting in a series of production norms discussed in chapter 5. **Staffing** is a key component of the process, as companies use clear divisions of duties to ensure that every production role is carried out effectively, from talent-centered roles such as actor and writer, to technical crew such as the camera operator and set builder. Since creating original programming is quite costly and risky, producers rely upon the **track record** of personnel to try to stave off failures; established stars are seen as bankable, and writers with numerous shows on their résumés are more likely to get continued work within the industry, even though hit programs often come from relatively unproven talent with innovative new ideas. The process by which an idea becomes a series highlights both how the industry operates as a closed system and its inherent logic of safe and least objectionable choices.

Imagine that you have a great idea for a new television series—how would you get it produced? The best strategy would be to become a writer for an established program, build a track record for a few years, and then pitch your idea to a network or channel. Because of the industry's belief in track record, nearly every new television program is created by experienced television writers, producers, or stars. Whereas in other media, an independently made project might emerge as a surprise hit—as with the films *The Blair Witch Project* and *Juno*, or musical acts Hawthorne Heights and Franz Ferdinand—television is much more centrally controlled by major distributors than other media, as projects are produced only with the backing of a network, cable channel, or syndicator to distribute and co-finance the project. Most new series develop from the relationships among established writers, their agents, production companies, stars, and networks. There have been some exceptions to this pattern since the 1990s, as with *South Park*, as discussed in chapter 7, or new strategies of talent development using online video as a breeding ground for potential innovations, but such examples are still quite rare and found more with niche cable channels than on mainstream network programming.

A writer who is working for a series might sign a development deal with that program's production company or network, establishing a mutual commitment to work toward creating new projects; some writers use their agents to forge connections to get the elusive **pitch meeting**, where they can try to sell their ideas. A pitch is a brief synopsis of the series idea, with an emphasis on selling the idea to the production or distribution company as a "can't-miss hit series." Pitches exemplify the formulaic logic of commercial television: a new idea must seem new enough to stand out among the hundreds of pitches that executives hear each year, but still fit into the established norms of hit programming that the industry believes represents viewers' tastes. For instance, FX's *The Shield* was pitched, by established television writer Shawn Ryan, as consistent with many aspects of the cop show genre. But the show drew upon recent police scandals to suggest an edgier and more controversial tone focused on rogue cops bending the rules, distinguishing itself from other programs and exemplifying the "similar but different" logic of television creativity.

Ideas for new programs typically come from writers and producers, but network and channel executives also devise programming concepts, farming the actual creative process to a production team. A legendary instance of this from the 1980s was NBC executive Brandon Tartikoff, who allegedly wrote down the words "MTV Cops" on a napkin over lunch and asked Universal Television to develop a series based on this two-word concept. The resulting program was *Miami Vice*, a hit police show that incorporated MTV's flashy visuals and pop music, true to Tartikoff's recombinant concept. Likewise, *Lost* emerged out of an ABC executive's idea for a drama about plane crash survivors—producers J. J. Abrams and Damon Lindelof were hired to flesh out that basic scenario, turning the initial premise into a highly complex supernatural mystery that now appears to be a wholly original product of the writers' imagination. Networks and channels spread the word to producers and agents about what types of programs they wish to air, and producers shape their creative work to fulfill distributor expectations in search of the goal of every television producer: a place on the network schedule.

FX launched into original fictional production via the innovative cop show, *The Shield*, helping to establish the channel's brand image of edgy, controversial programming through the "bad cop" Vic Mackey played by Michael Chiklis.

THE SHIELD

The Shield (FX, 2002–08): One of the first basic-cable series to achieve broad recognition, this police drama followed HBO's style of morally complex characters, heightened intensity, and serial plotting by highlighting a corrupt group of Los Angeles police who muddy the line between justice and criminality. The show's success helped spur FX and other cable channels to launch their own original dramatic programming.

MIAMI VICE

Miami Vice (NBC, 1984–89): A quintessential 1980s cop show, *Miami Vice* uses stylish clothes, flashy editing, and pop music to portray the police's pursuit of Florida drug gangs. The show's use of glossy production values and trendy fashion and music influenced many series trying to capture its "MTV style."

LOST

Lost (ABC, 2004–present): An innovative serialized program that became a global hit, *Lost* mixes genres to offer elements of mystery, science fiction, romance, and espionage through an unusual narrative style of flashbacks and time travel, as well as experiments in transmedia storytelling. The series typifies how shows that would have been restricted to a cult audience in the network era can become mainstream through digital convergence.

Once a network has approved a pitch, it provides the creator limited funding to develop the concept. If the creator is not already working with a production company, producers are brought onto the project. Throughout the development process, the creator and producers shape their ideas to fit the goals of the distributor: What audience is the network trying to reach? What other shows might the series be scheduled with as lead-ins or hammocks? What is the brand identity of the channel? While it would be nice to think that every program on television represents the pure artistic vision of the show's creators, the commercial logic of television extends to the conceptualization of programming—any creator knows that if the network or channel does not fully endorse the concept, the show will never be seen. Thus the first audience necessary to approve of any creative work is the network or channel executive hearing the pitch. This first stage of development moves the new program from broad idea into a specific conceptual document outlining the show's setting, characters, and potential episodes, and into a script for the debut episode—all of these facets must convince the network that the show has a strong chance of succeeding with audiences and will fit into the network's broader branding strategies.

Every channel and network hears hundreds of pitches a year, of which a small portion receive the funding for further development. Distribution executives review these more elaborated proposals and scripts, and select a limited number for the next development stage: **pilot production**. A pilot is the premiere episode of a series, and it is ultimately what distributors judge to fill out their programming schedules; a network or channel funding a pilot has an exclusive option on the future series. Networks partially finance pilots, although pilot production generally signals the beginning of deficit financing for production companies—pilots typically are even more expensive than ongoing episodes, due to start-up costs such as set construction and casting, not to mention the flashy visuals designed to impress both executives and viewers. Pilots pose creative difficulties, as they must fulfill a number of roles: provide exposition for the story and situation that will drive the series, establish engaging characters, set the show's tone, and make viewers want to see future episodes. Networks tend to be closely involved in pilot production, providing notes and feedback on casting, set design, visual style, and content; because the future of a series is riding on a network embracing a pilot, producers tend to work with networks and channels to make decisions that please their potential distributors.

Most people involved in television programming recognize that the pilot process is highly flawed—very often the best pilots result in poor series, and successful series may have weak pilots. Rarely are pilot episodes looked back upon as strong entries in a long-running series, as many programs take multiple episodes to really find their tone and style. For the development process, however, pilots are seen as the best representative of what the series will be. Networks use pilots to conduct market **testing**—showing the pilot (or even just reading a synopsis of it) to a sample audience and measuring reactions via surveys, interviews, and focus groups. Testing is generally regarded as highly speculative and inexact, with examples of poor testing for future hits and strong testing for eventual flops. Networks use testing to predict the ultimately unpredictable reaction that a show might have with a mass audience; long-term appeal, however, can rarely be measured by sampling just the pilot of a potential series, as low-testing pilots that became landmark hits such as *All in the Family* and *Seinfeld* demonstrate. But for network executives, testing is used primarily to confirm their instincts about a program, adding legitimacy to a show they want to air and conclusiveness to a series they have their doubts about. Clearly ongoing creative work cannot reliably be subjected to the same form of market research as most consumer goods, yet networks and channels search for every potential tool for predicting the next hit series. Testing can result in major changes in a series after the pilot, including recasting, altering settings, or even shifting a show from a comedy to a drama.

After selecting successful pilots, distributors order new series and renew existing programs to constitute a scheduled lineup for their network or channel. Most pilots are never broadcast, with the network passing on projects that seem too risky, too safe, too controversial, or too bland. The success rate of ideas for programming is quite low, as only around 10 percent of pitches move forward in development, with less than 1 percent getting a series order. Despite this winnowing process, the majority of programs that make it to the air fail to meet network expectations and are cancelled by the end of the first season. In the classic network era, this process of creating shows from pitch to pilot followed a regular annual cycle to be ready for debuting series each fall; in the multi-channel era, cable channels and increasingly networks have jettisoned the standard season schedule, so new programs debut throughout the year, making the development process less streamlined and regularized. Networks still follow a seasonal schedule for the most part, especially in presenting their annual schedules to advertisers during that May **up-fronts**, where advertising spots are first sold to sponsors via glitzy presentations of the fall season. However, following the Writers Guild of America strike of 2007–08, signs have suggested that networks are moving away from glamorous up-fronts and traditional fall launches as the primary model of scheduling.

Because of the extreme uncertainty in predicting future successes, producers and distributors focus every decision on maximizing the commercial appeal of programming, hoping to capture that unknown quality that audiences wish to see. However, many creators argue that this process of formulaic creation-by-committee is exactly what dooms most shows to failure, as audiences recognize the lack of creative voice and integrity in programs designed to appeal to focus groups. Shows that do become hits often are those whose producers are given more control to pursue an original idea. Sometimes these innovations become instant surprise hits, such as *The Simpsons*, *The West Wing*, and *Roseanne*, but often they need a few seasons to establish their tone and build a word-of-mouth following, as with *Cheers*, *Seinfeld*, and *The X-Files*. What seems clear is that programs that are primarily imitative and formulaic are more likely to make it to the airwaves, but rarely become major hits; most hits feature innovative ideas distinguishing themselves from the rest of the schedule, but the challenge is to determine which innovations will work with audiences and which will be seen as too out of line with viewer expectations.

Throughout the process of bringing programming to viewers, the television industry follows a commercial imperative, creating content to fit the perceived market. Producers shape their creative output for the goals of distributors and imagined audiences, networks devise their schedule to maximize viewership, cable channels brand themselves to earn subscriptions from cable systems, local stations affiliate with networks and purchase syndicated programming to appeal to their audiences, and cable systems structure tiers and packages to maximize subscription revenue. Despite the system's overriding commercial imperatives and the industry's reliance on safe formulas and predictable content to avoid alienating potential viewers, distributors, and transmitters, innovative and creative work does often emerge, as discussed more in chapters 5 and 6.

It is clear that millions of dollars flow through the system of program creation, but where does all this money come from? To truly understand the commercial logic of television programming, we must explore the logic of television commercials and the audience exchange, discussed in the next chapter.

FURTHER READING

Numerous media scholars have chronicled the production and distribution processes of the television industry. A groundbreaking work covering the classic network era is Todd Gitlin, *Inside Prime Time* (Berkeley: University of California Press, 2000); while Julie D'Acci, *Defining Women: Television and the Case of Cagney & Lacey* (Chapel Hill: University of North Carolina Press, 1994), provides a comprehensive case study into one controversial program from the 1980s. John Thornton Caldwell, *Production Culture: Industrial Reflexivity and Critical Practice in Film and Television* (Durham, N.C.: Duke University Press, 2008), is a more recent account of production practices; and Robert Kubey, ed., *Creating Television: Conversations with the People Behind 50 Years of American TV* (Mahwah, N.J: Lawrence Erlbaum, 2004), offers in-depth conversations with television producers and creators.

The structure of the industry is covered in a number of books, with a solid overview in Douglas Gomery and Luke Hockley, eds., *Television Industries* (London: BFI, 2006). For a good discussion of one distribution company's impact on television history, see Michele Hilmes, ed., *NBC: America's Network* (Berkeley: University of California Press, 2007). A strong account of the recent transformations in the digital convergence era is Amanda D. Lotz, *The Television Will Be Revolutionized* (New York: New York University Press, 2007). The vital history of syndication can be found in Derek Kompare, *Rerun Nation: How Repeats Invented American Television* (New York: Routledge, 2005). The cable industry is chronicled in Megan Mullen, *The Rise of Cable Programming in the United States: Revolution or Evolution?* (Austin: University of Texas Press, 2003).

NOTES

[1]Peter J. Boyer, "Triumphant NBC Faces Uncertain Future," *New York Times*, April 22, 1986.

[2]"How Blacks Differ from Whites in TV Show Choices," *Jet*, March 17, 1997.

[3]Todd Gitlin, *Inside Prime Time* (Berkeley: University of California Press, 2000).

[4]Ted Turner, "My Beef with Big Media," *Washington Monthly*, August 2004, http://www.washingtonmonthly.com/features/2004/0407.turner.html.

CHAPTER 2

EXCHANGING AUDIENCES

Certainly the common understanding of the television industry focuses on how programs are produced, channels and networks are scheduled, and local stations and cable systems bring programming to our homes. However, these systems generate little revenue on their own—the commercial television industry is not fueled by programming, but by the sales of advertising. Thus to understand how the industries economics and structure truly operates, we must take an in-depth look at advertising and the related exchange of audiences that fuels the industry.

THE ADVERTISING EXCHANGE

In the programming exchange outlined in chapter 1, distributors function as the lynchpin determining television's content, schedule, and promotion, acting as the buyers of programming from producers. But the economic logic of television distribution ranks licensing programs as a secondary concern, the bait in the mousetrap. The primary goal for networks and channels is to sell airtime for advertising—this is the main source of revenue that funds American television and sets the tone for the content featured throughout the industry.

For anyone growing up in America it might seem that television's commercial function is natural, simply the way it has always been. But advertising-supported television has generally been the exception rather than the norm in most countries, where television has typically operated through nonprofit, non-commercial, and/or state-supported systems, with commercial channels as alternatives on the margins that only recently have begun to emerge as major players in most foreign television systems. The opposite is true in America: profit-driven, advertising-supported television has always been the primary model for the television industry, with marginal public and nonprofit alternatives. The commercial logic of the television industry has an important and distinctive history that illuminates why television has functioned so differently in America from in the rest of the world; the history and social impact of television advertising illustrate how this commercial system molds American culture in quite profound ways.

The Origins of Television Advertising

As with most facets of television, the origins of advertising derive directly from other media, adopted from the industry's radio ancestors. When radio emerged as an organized industry in the 1920s, there was no consensus as to how it would be a viable commercial enterprise. Most early radio broadcasting was either was an amateur activity, practiced by hobbyists exploring the technology, or run by companies with other business interests, such as department stores, newspapers, and radio manufacturers. These early commercial stations promoted the company's primary business, often functioning only to encourage consumers to purchase radio sets—a business model with poor long-term prospects once American households became saturated with radios. Since there was no feasible way to charge for receiving a wireless radio signal, most companies saw broadcasting as a promotional gimmick with little potential revenue.

In an experiment with long-lasting consequences, New York City station WEAF offered an alternative business model termed **toll broadcasting**: acting as a "toll booth to the airwaves," WEAF sold access to use its broadcast frequency. The first company to purchase a time slot was the Queensboro Corporation, which in 1922 paid one hundred dollars for fifteen minutes of airtime to air a direct promotional pitch for its new apartment complex in Jackson Heights, thus creating what is thought to be the first **commercial**. Sales skyrocketed in response to the advertisement, and word quickly spread to a range of potential advertisers and broadcasters that toll broadcasting might be a viable business model.

This model had to overcome widespread opposition to direct broadcast advertising. Print advertising was a long-established and accepted industry, but a distinction between how broadcasting and print functioned raised concerns for many interested parties: readers controlled the way they read magazines and newspapers, with the ability to skip over unwanted advertising, but broadcasting controlled listeners' time, forcing people to either listen to a commercial or tune out a broadcast. Commentators across the political and economic spectrum resisted the notion of direct broadcast advertising, predicting that it would doom radio's public support and lead to the degradation of the medium. To some degree, these naysayers were correct, as listeners soon tired of the direct advertising offered by the earliest toll broadcasting, choosing to tune out broadcasting that offered nothing but sales pitches.

But instead of noncommercial broadcasting securing alternative funding sources to stave off commercialism, such as the license fee or taxation systems used in other countries, American broadcasting developed a model of indirect advertising or **single-sponsorship**. Potential advertisers would still pay "tolls" to broadcasters to access airtime, but instead of direct sales pitches, they would offer entertainment programming designed to appeal to listeners. These programs were sponsored by the advertiser, with the name of the program often featuring the sponsor's brand name, and short pitches for the product peppered throughout the program. These early sponsored programs were typically musical or variety shows modeled on vaudeville theater, with announcers promoting the sponsor's product throughout; as dramatic programs became more popular in the 1930s, they followed a similar model of single-sponsorship. Throughout the 1930s, this system became entrenched, with the majority of programming produced by advertising agencies, distributed by national networks, and incorporating commercial pitches into the entertainment content and brand names in the show titles.

This was the system imported to television in the late 1940s. Network television programs, many adapted from their radio counterparts, were nearly all single-sponsored shows, often produced or co-produced by advertising agencies, which would purchase airtime from networks or local stations. These shows were often named for their sponsor rather than content: television pioneer Milton Berle starred in *Texaco Star Theater,* while NBC's original news broadcast was called *Camel News Caravan* (sponsored by Camel cigarettes). An important early genre was the **anthology drama**, which featured a distinct "teleplay" each week with new casts, settings, and stories, unified under branded program titles such as *Kraft Television Theatre, The Philco Television Playhouse,* and *The United States Steel Hour.* Even shows not titled for sponsors often incorporated commercial content into their dramatic action; for instance, an episode of *The George Burns and Gracie Allen Show* features a traveling salesman entering into the fictional home of the main characters to demonstrate the wonders of the show's sponsor, Carnation Evaporated Milk. For single-sponsored programs, the line between entertainment and commercial content often blurred, but sales pitches were typically understated and took little time away from the program's primary appeals.

Clearly this system does not fit with the programming exchange detailed in chapter 1, as advertising agencies are not significantly involved in the creation and distribution of most programming today. How did this system of

TEXACO STAR THEATER

Texaco Star Theater (NBC, 1948–56): Television's first smash hit was better known as *The Milton Berle Show*, offering a range of musical acts and comedic sketches but centered on its larger-than-life host. Berle's humor used physical gags and outlandish costumes to set it apart from radio comedy, and the live format was well suited to his improvisations and direct addresses to the audience.

single-sponsorship transform into the contemporary mode of commercial spots airing within established programming? Throughout the 1950s, networks realized that they could further maximize their own assets by controlling and scheduling their conduit to the increasingly popular television airwaves. Under a single-sponsor system, a network sells time slots to advertisers; since the programming is the sponsor's responsibility, networks cannot fully capitalize on big hits or manage a schedule to promote a full lineup of programming. Additionally, advertising agencies often found single-sponsorship costly, as production expenses and network airtime exceeded what many sponsors wished to spend. Even though technically most shows were owned by sponsors, programs in the early 1950s were often produced by independent companies, with sponsor partnerships arranged by the producers and networks.

Although better known as *The Milton Berle Show*, television's earliest hit officially bore the name of its single sponsor.

TODAY

Today (NBC, 1954–present): One of the first attempts to offer network programming during "fringe" time periods, NBC's morning show established the standard for the time slot and has continued to offer its mix of news, interviews, feature stories, and entertainment for more than fifty years.

An alternative system of advertising was more attractive both to networks and to advertising agencies, and potentially more economically feasible for sponsors: **magazine sponsorship**. Modeled after the print advertising system in which each page features one or more different ads, networks sold short segments within their programming to place **commercial spots**. Innovated by NBC's morning program *Today* in the early 1950s, this system allowed advertisers to spread their budgets across different programs and reduce the risks and costs of creating new shows. Magazine sponsorship placed responsibility for program procurement and scheduling in network hands, which gave networks more control and leverage to profit from hit programs. The single-sponsor system gradually disappeared throughout the 1950s, and today exists only in rare cases, replaced by the classic network system of distribution and commercial spots.

The shift from single to magazine sponsorship directly impacted the tone of television advertising. On a program such as *Texaco Star Theater*, the sponsor used the entire hour to reach audiences, as every repetition of the sponsor's name and the catchy theme song "We're the Men from Texaco" reminded viewers which company brought their favorite "Uncle Miltie" to their home every Tuesday evening. While announcers might offer short product pitches during the program, the primary function of sponsorship was to promote the company's brand name and create positive associations with the viewing public. Under a magazine system, sponsors have a brief and costly window to promote their product, creating commercials that must stand apart from the surrounding programming; thus the style of commercial spots is more direct advertising, highlighting a product and creating a more aggressive message to promote consumer behavior—and make each spot stand out among the pack of other commercials. Thus the magazine system may be more profitable for networks and advertisers, but it has also led to a more aggressive commercialized culture, playing a significant role in making American society more consumerist in mind-set and promoting a brand-centered lifestyle that dominates in the twenty-first century, a facet of advertising discussed later in this chapter.

The Economics of Television Advertising

Just as the programming exchange involves a variety of companies that serve often overlapping functions, the advertising industry is comprised of a number of key players. At the center of the industry are advertising agencies, which come in various forms. **Full-service agencies** offer clients a broad range of services, typically divided into four departments: **market research**, to identify potential promotional strategies; **creative development**, to produce advertising campaigns; **media buying**, to place ads within media; and **account services**, to manage clients. Major advertising campaigns are typically cross-media, with television commercials coordinating with print, billboard, direct mail, radio, and any other promotional opportunity that can be imagined. Smaller **boutique agencies** specialize in particular media, creative styles, demographic groups, or facets of the advertising industry, although as with other media, advertising agencies have been concentrating into large global conglomerates since the 1980s. The top four firms—Omnicom Group, WPP Group, Interpublic Group, and Publicis Groupe, each of which contains numerous subsidiaries spanning the entire advertising and marketing business—now control over two thirds of the world's advertising industry and over half of the American market.

In addition to advertising agencies, a broad range of consulting firms, media strategists, marketing gurus, media buyers, production houses, and other support companies participate in the enormous market for creating and placing advertising. This process plays out similarly, although at different scales, at both the national level, on networks and cable channels, and regionally, via local stations and cable systems—in fact, many stations and cable systems contract with regional advertising agencies or sponsors to produce local commercial spots as an auxiliary business.

The advertising exchange typically begins with a company hiring an advertising agency to manage its account. Depending on the size of the client company and the scope of its marketing efforts, the agency might coordinate the company's entire promotional strategy for all media and products, or it might focus on a particular line of products, advertising medium, or specific ad campaign. Clients convey to agencies the brand identity that they wish to promote, their product's business strategies and goals, and their own sense of what advertising strategies would best suit their goals. Agencies strive for creative autonomy to devise and research campaigns freely, but ultimately they recognize that they must please sponsors to retain business, so they sculpt campaigns to fit their clients' assumptions. Agencies conduct research as to what strategies best fit client goals, pitch potential commercial ideas, and devise media buying plans to place ads within specific television programs, channels, and other media. An agency may subcontract some of these duties to support companies, such as video production or market research firms, but large agencies typically use their economy of scale to control all facets of an account.

Once a client has signed on with an agency and approved a campaign, the crucial economic exchange is the purchasing of slots for commercials. For a national campaign, agencies will define the size and demographics of the audience they wish to reach, looking for good matches for programming on network and cable channels. While agencies typically purchase a large package of audience segments from a network rather than specific ad spots, the industry does try to estimate comparative prices for different programs, even if actual ads are not typically sold that way. Prices for advertising on network programming vary widely—for instance, in 2004 a thirty-second spot on Fox's top-rated *American Idol* cost on average more than more than $600,000, while the same ad on NBC's *Dateline* might average only $70,000. These discrepancies are tied both to total size of the audience and its composition, with advertisers typically paying more for younger viewers in the "all-important" eighteen-to-forty-nine-year-old demographic that comprises far more of *American Idol*'s audience than *Dateline*'s. Networks try to sell the majority of ad slots before the television season begins as **up-front** ad buys; after up-front sales, typically around one quarter of potential slots remain for networks to sell throughout the season, in what is called the **scatter** market, with prices adjusted in response to ratings and schedule shifts. Agencies generally get paid on commission, adding a 10 to 15 percent surcharge on all advertising purchased for an account, so agencies have a direct incentive for their clients to advertise broadly via expensive outlets, as on prime time network hits.

When placing their commercials onto television programs, sponsors are purchasing a somewhat unknown asset, as it is hard definitively to predict the audience composition and size for a program before it airs, especially with new shows. Distributors often offer some guarantees—networks will set a minimum guaranteed rating for a sponsor's package of advertising spots, providing sponsors free **make-good** spots in their lineup if a purchase does not reach the minimum rating stipulated or if shows are preempted or cancelled. Since advertisers are a network's only paying customers, they will go out of their way to keep their business. Agencies measure the price of advertising in the unit of **cost per thousand** viewers, or **CPM** (with the *M* representing the Roman numeral for one thousand), reflecting the expense incurred to reach audiences—the average CPM for prime time network television is more than twenty-two dollars, a figure that ranges widely depending on time slot, network, and demographics. Even though ratings for network programming have dropped significantly in recent years, the CPM rate has actually risen, suggesting that the mass audience appeal of programming available only through major networks is still valued to advertisers in the multi-channel narrowcasting era.

Since the 1980s, advertisers have increasingly targeted more specific and narrowly defined audience segments. Certainly cable channels have been a key avenue for such narrowcasting, offering a more defined set of audience characteristics than most network programming. These segments are typically defined by **demographics**: age, race, gender, economic status, religion, ethnicity, and region are all valuable determinants for advertisers wishing to target a slice of the American public, although age, gender, and income are the most emphasized categories. Increasingly, market researchers have used **psychographics** as a way to group consumers across demographic categories by attitude, lifestyle, values, and interests—thus advertisers will target campaigns to consumer clusters with descriptive labels such as "mainstreamers," "good-timers," and "innovators." Advertising agencies search for the perfect match between product, ad campaign, and television program to reach the type of consumer most likely to be persuaded by the commercial. One effect of this system is that television distributors and producers shape their creative programming to meet the assumed tastes of the specific segments that advertisers most want to reach, narrowing the scope of programming that makes it to the air. For instance, few programs explicitly target senior citizens, as they are not seen as a particularly valuable audience for advertisers, even though they watch significantly more television on average than younger viewers.

Certain commercial opportunities are highly prized for advertisers, most notably the annual NFL Super Bowl broadcast. Typically the Super Bowl is the highest-rated broadcast of the year, and it is one of the few ways to guarantee access to the audience of male professionals who typically view television less than other groups. Because of the high total ratings and desirable demographics, Super Bowl ad buys are incredibly expensive, with costs for thirty-second spots exceeding $2 million in recent years. Successful Super Bowl ads can become cultural touchstones—one of the most famous and historically important was Apple's Super Bowl ad in 1984 announcing the new Macintosh computer, a Ridley Scott–directed commercial that framed IBM as George Orwell's "Big Brother" and heroic Apple smashing its market domination Apple paid to air this spot only the once, but its notoriety and success in launching a brand keeps the ad alive in specials, websites—and textbooks—for more than twenty years. Today, advertisers receive more than the thirty seconds of Super Bowl promotion they pay for, however, as the phenomenon of Super Bowl advertising itself has become a news story, with media coverage featuring critics analyzing ads, polling viewers about their preferences, offering behind-the-scenes stories on selected commercials, and even airing television specials highlighting the history of Super Bowl ads. By treating advertising as news, the press offers extended "free" coverage to its own sponsors, as long as they continue to purchase high-priced ad spots.

While purchasing commercial spots is the primary means of using television for advertising purchases, there are other models that contribute to television's promotional function. Some advertising airs independently of other programming, as sponsors purchase entire half-hour time slots for promotional

Apple's ad introducing the Macintosh in 1984 used sophisticated visuals to portray IBM as an oppressive "big brother," to be liberated by colorful and vibrant Apple.

messages. Typically, these are **infomercials** that run in off-hours on local stations and cable channels; infomercials try to wrap a long-form commercial message in an entertaining and informative package, although they are regarded as a less respectable form of promotion than traditional advertising spots, and are typically used to sell household gadgets, fringe health products, and self-improvement courses. **Home shopping channels** extend the infomercial model to a twenty-four-hour format, promoting products and enabling direct purchasing; while many critics and viewers view home shopping as somewhat crass, channels such as HSN and QVC have proven to be quite profitable in selling large quantities of merchandise for minimal production budgets.

If home shopping and infomercials explicitly prioritize commerce above content, the inverse strategy has also grown quite popular: incorporating promotional materials into entertainment. For some genres, this has always been standard practice—game shows give away prizes in exchange for promotional mention, and talk shows regularly feature guests promoting their new books, films, and music releases. Sports broadcasting, on both the national and local levels, has been a leader in commercial infiltration, as sponsors place their brand names on any program feature that broadcasters will license to them, resulting in Aflac trivia questions, Taco Bell replays, and Ameriquest halftime shows. As discussed later in this chapter, reality television has emerged as the hotbed of

ALIAS

Alias (ABC, 2001–06): An innovative spy show with a cult following, *Alias* uses stylistic visuals and complex storytelling to present the balance between a female double agent working for the CIA and her treacherous family of spies. Although never a significant hit, the show boosted the careers of star Jennifer Garner and creator J. J. Abrams.

product integration, with sponsors spending millions of dollars to have their goods incorporated into the "reality" being portrayed.

Commercial product integration techniques extend to fictional programming. In the mid-1990s, Diet Coke spent more than $30 million on a multimedia campaign featuring the stars of *Friends* and to highlight the product in the show itself, blurring the line between commercial and creative content. Sponsorship strategies have come full circle back to the 1950s, as increasingly sponsors are involved in program production and provide funding to stand out as the primary or sole sponsor of a show. For instance, ABC's 2001 pilot for *Alias* was presented "commercial-free" by Nokia, which offered extended ads at the beginning and end of the program, as well as frequent close-ups of Nokia phones in action throughout the episode—the phones were featured to such an extent that some critics commented that it felt as if Nokia were a character in the drama. More subtle product integration pervades contemporary television, as any brand name product that appears in a program has probably paid for that appearance through money or guaranteed ad buys for the series.

Companies invest billions in advertising and other promotional strategies to increase sales of their products, spending more than $71 billion in television commercials in 2006, but what return do they get on their investment? It is hard to say, as the impact of advertising is difficult to measure in direct sales—aside from outlets such as home shopping or infomercials, which invite viewers to buy products immediately via phone, advertising is a long-term investment in brand identity and awareness. Advertising agencies provide research to suggest how commercials lead to stronger sales, but clearly the agencies have an ulterior motive to promote their own services. Most sponsors realize that advertising typically offers uncertain and immeasurable results—an often-repeated quotation (attributed to many different sources) notes, "We know that half of our advertising budget is wasted, but we don't know which half." So why do companies still spend huge sums on advertising with somewhat indefinite outcomes?

Part of the answer is competition—if your competitors are actively advertising their products, can you afford to risk not advertising yours? While it

THE MICKEY MOUSE CLUB

The Mickey Mouse Club (ABC, 1955–59): A popular daytime show aimed at children, *The Mickey Mouse Club* featured teen performers called Mouseketeers singing songs, doing skits, and presenting cartoons. The show helped establish the potential for advertising directly to children and build Disney's reputation as America's main source of children's entertainment.

is hard to argue that excessive advertising is cost effective, there is no doubt that commercial blitzes promote awareness and legitimacy to both consumers and retailers, ensuring shelf space that might otherwise go to a competitor. Advertising can also help stave off competition—Coke and Pepsi battle each other through their billion-dollar global ad campaigns, but their exorbitant spending benefits both companies by ensuring that no other soft drink company can compete in their league, leaving them to operate in a highly concentrated market. For a small company to enter the realm of national television advertising requires an enormous economic risk. For instance, in the mid-1950s a new toy company named Mattel made a move that put it on the map but could have easily led to its demise, investing its entire corporate value of $500,000 to sponsor ABC's *Mickey Mouse Club* for a year—a cost of more than $3 million in twenty-first-century value, and an amount that today would buy only one thirty-second prime time spot on a hit show.[1] In the late 1990s, dozens of technology companies ran high-profile television ad campaigns as part of the dot-com boom; many were out of business within five years. Although a television commercial can be a high-profile way to break into an industry and increase competition, often the cost and scope of national television advertising reinforce limited competition and discourages new entries into an advertising-driven industry.

Advertising can also be viewed as subsidized by the government—advertising is tax-deductible as a business expense in the United States, so companies see a portion of their ad budgets returned to them via reduced tax bills. While it may be a stretch to claim that the American government has endorsed excessive advertising through tax policies, such policies certainly increase the amount of money spent on television and other media advertising. Likewise, by not investing much funding in noncommercial public media as discussed in chapter 3, the American government encourages the commercial system to expand and dominate; today's hypercommercial media culture is at least government sanctioned, if not explicitly endorsed. Television advertising is reinforced as a cultural and business norm via these governmental and corporate policies, perpetuating the commercial system even while some commentators question advertising's cost-effectiveness.

Strategies of Television Advertising

Television commercials are incredibly expensive productions, with a national thirty-second spot often costing more than $350,000 to produce. Because of the high costs to both produce and air an ad, agencies and producers control every single detail within a campaign to ensure that all elements are unified in achieving the sponsor's goals. While clearly most sponsors advertise in order to increase their sales, the goals of an ad campaign are more layered than simply a direct sales boost. Many ads strive to convey product knowledge, providing information about what people might purchase, how it compares to competitors' products, and how it might improve viewers' lives. Some ads focus less on individual products but rather on building brand awareness, linking positive attitudes with the company's name so that shoppers will trust and desire an entire product line. Additionally, almost all ads encourage consumerist behavior broadly, reinforcing attitudes that purchasing products is a useful strategy for solving problems and achieving happiness; in this way, each commercial reinforces other ads by promoting consumerism as a way of life.

Traditionally the primary goal of advertising was to convey information about a product—although as the single-sponsorship system attests to, strategies of brand awareness have a long history as well. **Product knowledge** is a broad category, including both factual information about a product's price and features, and emotional associations with the product. While most people would agree that advertising can serve consumers' interest by providing useful knowledge about products, most ads do not attempt to convey such information. Advertisers have learned that, for the most part, consuming goods is not primarily a rational process in which buyers try to make an informed decision to maximize the value of a purchase—consumption, especially in twenty-first-century America, is an emotionally charged practice, as many people see what they buy and own as defining their identity and place in society. Thus advertisers work to link positive desirable values with consumer goods, often in ways that defy rational analysis—think of Clairol's Herbal Essences campaign featuring women becoming sexually aroused by shampoo with the suggestive tagline "a totally organic experience"!

In promoting product knowledge and associations, advertisers often come close to crossing the line of deception. The Federal Trade Commission (FTC) monitors advertising for outright false and deceptive claims, but it allows for exaggerated claims of value and quality that are not outright deceptive or motivated by the intent to mislead. This type of advertising, often called **puffery**, celebrates products as "the best a man can get," "the King of Beers," or "the ultimate driving machine," all claims that cannot be proven to be deceptive, but that state dubious value judgments as fact. Puffery addresses consumers as emotional rather than rational beings, asking them to be moved by superlatives and hyperbole without providing evidence for a product's claims of superiority.

Advertising's appeals spread beyond claims of quality; the majority of ads try to create **emotional associations** between the product and personal contentment. Many ads portray a consumer-enabled **utopia**, in which beautiful people experience life to the fullest while using the sponsor's product. Such commercials link products to images of luxury, wealth, friendship, sexual fulfillment, beauty, familial harmony, nature, and humor, usually with no explanation as to how a particular bar of soap or pair of shoes might lead to such bliss. Other ads take a more **dystopian** approach, highlighting what is wrong in the viewer's world and how the product might solve those problems; such ads exaggerate the problems caused by dandruff, thirst, or stained laundry to the point of crisis, offering a magical cure to all that ails you, available at a retailer near you. Both strategies rely on the **creation of discontent** in viewers: something is wrong in your life if it doesn't match the perfect world of advertising, and products hold the solution to your troubles. Advertising rarely makes viewers feel good about the status quo, so emotional appeals in commercials tie positive feelings to consumer goods, and imply negative values about your own life that can implicitly be cured by purchasing the advertised products.

Such emotional advertising strategies operate at a conscious level—we can all perceive these strategies in ads if we stop to think about them—but in a culture in which we see hundreds of commercial messages daily, we rarely do stop to think about them. People often talk about such appeals as "hidden messages" to be uncovered, but they are not actually hidden—we consciously realize that Coors is linking its beer with scantily clad women. Likewise, this is not **subliminal advertising**, which refers to a discredited and mostly ineffective practice of hiding messages beneath the level of awareness, such as split-second flashes of persuasive words in a film or masking pictures in background images. Instead, emotionally associative advertising might be better thought of as **implicit persuasion**, forging links between products and our culturally shaped values and images at the level of implication rather than rational argument—these associations create positive feelings about products, feelings that sponsors hope consumers will recall when standing in a store aisle choosing from among many products. Think of the successful iPod campaign, in which a dancing silhouette conveys ideals of youth, energy, freedom, and rebellion, which are then linked to the iPod itself as the purchasable embodiment of those values—such campaigns are not overtly deceptive or misleading, but they encourage the troubling belief that such values and personal fulfillment can be easily bought.

If you're a careful viewer of television commercials, you might notice that many ads seem to tell you almost nothing about the product, or even what the

Apple's successful iPod campaign uses silhouettes to convey youthful energy and rebellion, all with the iconic white iPod and cord.

specific product is. These ads promote **brand awareness** more than any explicit product knowledge—the goal is for you to retain the name of the company and forge positive association with it and its associated visual images and slogans. Nike is probably the most successful sponsor in defining its brand for more than twenty years, linking itself to star athletes and an active lifestyle summed up with the phrase "Just Do It" and the company's iconic swoosh logo—with only rare mention of the specific features of its sneakers or other products. Nike's advertising campaigns have popularized an entire Nike lifestyle and attitude to the point that people identify with its image sufficiently that they purchase hats and T-shirts prominently displaying the swoosh and motto, thus turning consumers into amateur advertisers. Whether or not wearing a shirt with a swoosh truly signifies that you are an active, energetic go-getter, Nike has done an impressive job making it culturally desirable to brand yourself with its icon to evoke such positive connotations. Brand promotion relies nearly exclusively on these associative appeals, tapping into emotional currents that encourage consumers to seek personal fulfillment and self-identification via a mass-produced brand, a dubious pitch for individuality through conformity.

Advertising has faced a challenge in recent years through the rise of **clutter**. Over the years, television has seen more of its time dedicated to commercials, which today occupy more than one quarter of each prime time hour. Likewise, commercials themselves have declined in length, with more frequent fifteen- and twenty-second ads, raising the total number of ads viewers see. Advertisers must therefore cut through this clutter to make their ads stand out, using loud audio, fast elaborate visuals, and sensationalist content on one extreme, or subtle minimalism, dry humor, and understated appeals as a contrast to the hypercommercial norm. Being able to cut through the clutter to create a distinctive ad is truly a talent—many successful commercial directors have become prominent film directors due to their ability to create compelling ads—and memorable commercials definitely do offer great creativity. But ads are always driven by commerce first, with the most memorable and creative ads unsuccessful if they do not convey the sponsor's message. For example, many new technology dotcom companies created amusing and memorable advertisements in the 1990s, such as the series featuring the Pets.com sock puppet, but the businesses themselves did not see their brand awareness translate into a viable business model once the technology bubble popped.

One particularly interesting attempt to stand out from commercial clutter is the rise of what might be termed ironic **anti-ads.** These campaigns address viewers as savvy consumers who recognize the manipulative techniques of advertising and can see through them. Some campaigns parody other commercials, such as Energizer Bunny and Geico ads, while others explicitly comment on the process of advertising, such as Sprite's "Image Is Nothing" campaign, which mocks its own celebrity endorser, basketball player Grant Hill. These ads are typically clever and enjoyable, appealing to viewers by acknowledging their intelligence and critical abilities—but ultimately they, too, rely on implicit persuasion. Each of these ads tries to associate the values of intelligence, wit, and critical thinking with wholly unrelated products such as soft drinks, batteries, and car insurance. The goal is that while choosing a drink or battery, you will implicitly feel that Sprite or Energizer understands you more than its competitors, that the product reflects on your own sophisticated lifestyle, and that consuming the brands will make you even smarter and cooler by association—the same misleading and manipulative advertising strategies that such anti-ads seem to mock.

All ads share a common side effect to their primary goals of product knowledge and brand awareness: **promoting consumerism** as a general activity. Nearly all commercials rely on a basic underlying assumption: consuming goods can solve problems and foster happiness. Thus ads use implicit persuasion both for specific products and for the act of buying itself. We consume in part because advertising has reinforced the idea that buying products fosters positive feelings. This American consumerist ethos is a hallmark of contemporary society, forming the basis for the national economy and pervading all facets of social life. While television advertising is certainly not the sole cause for widespread consumerism, it is one of its main support mechanisms. Not surprisingly, this consumerist ethos pervades commercial television content as well—even when shows feature no clear product integration, the fictional and factual worlds featured on television typically revolve around consumer society, promoting a materialist worldview entirely consistent with commercial spots running on programs.

The Social Impacts of Television Advertising

There is no doubt that advertising has a direct impact on individual viewers' behavior and that of society at large—if it didn't, why would sponsors spend billions of dollars attempting to influence people? Chapter 9 discusses the questions surrounding television's broader social and psychological impacts, but advertising is a special case, given that its entire mission is to persuade and influence people. This chapter focuses on the economic logic of television, but there are by-products of economic exchanges that cannot be understood simply through the logic of the market. Economists have labeled costs or benefits felt by people outside a specific exchange as **externalities**. A classic example of a negative externality is air pollution as a by-product of manufacturing, where neighborhoods (and the entire planet) are impacted by an economic exchange that they do not directly participate in. We can consider the social impacts of advertising as externalities that might have both positive and negative outcomes. These impacts have been the frequent object of analysis by critics looking to uncover the social implications of media.

Certainly advertising's overall promotion of consumerism can be viewed as an externality, with potentially both positive and negative impacts. Business advocates suggest that advertising sustains consumerism, which drives the American economy, raises the country's standard of living, and provides a wide range of choices in an open market of goods. Critics question the sustainability of a consumerist economy, however, noting that this contemporary economic system is predicated on high levels of consumer debt, an erosion of the manufacturing base, and the creation of tremendous levels of waste—a combination of factors that seem to have come to a head in the 2008 economic crisis. While advertising is not the cause of consumerism, it certainly fuels consumerist practices and focuses social and economic priorities toward the consumption of goods.

The more vehement critiques of advertising focus on the psychological and social impact of commercial culture rather than its economic system. For many critics, advertising is part of a process of **dehumanization**, in which people are treated as goods to be bought and sold, or reduced to the sum of their purchases. Advertisers often will pursue the persuasive goals of their commercials at the expense of ethical concerns for the impact that an ad might have on viewers beyond promoting consumption. Thus the strategy of promoting discontent actually tries to make viewers less happy about their lives, with widespread unhappiness as an externality generated in the name of selling products that may not live up to the magical curative properties promised by advertising. Such critiques of advertising are powerful, but go against our commonsense experiences of viewing ads: most of us don't find ourselves dehumanized after an hour of television. But if you agree with this perspective, dehumanization and creating discontent are long-term processes, impacting viewers after years of watching ads that treat us as commodities and highlight our flaws. No single ad causes such effects on its own, but the cumulative impact of a commercialized culture arguably forges how we think about ourselves in destructive ways, a process discussed more in chapter 9.

A specific form of dehumanization involves the representation of the human body in ads—many critics foreground how advertising objectifies people's bodies, especially in representing women and sexuality, as considered more in chapter 8. Appeals to sexual arousal are one of the most common and successful means of selling products, so advertisers link a broad range of products with beautiful bodies and erotic images to stimulate audiences, forge emotional associations, and cut through the clutter. Critics argue that these strategies promote unrealistic and unhealthy beauty norms, not only promoting people's consumption of a product in the vain effort to match the images on the screen, but also damaging self-esteem in ways that can contribute to conditions such as eating disorders and depression. Many ads present fragmented images of women's bodies on display like consumer goods, which some critics claim equate body parts such as breasts and legs with products to be bought and sold; some extreme critiques argue that these images can reinforce or stimulate violent sexual behaviors in susceptible viewers. Regardless of the degree to which such critiques of dehumanization and objectification are convincing (and there is much debate around these claims), there is no doubt that for the majority of advertisers, the goal of promoting consumption trumps ethical and moral concerns about advertising's social impacts.

Advertising has its defenders as well. The economic defense is most common: advertising provides consumers with information to make rational decisions in the marketplace, fuels the economy, and supports "free" media systems. However these defenses have trouble accounting for the emotional appeals and implicit persuasive techniques that dominate advertising, strategies that actively try to convince consumers to make decisions that are neither rational nor informed: to choose expensive brand names over identical generic products or seek emotional satisfaction in disposable goods. While commercials certainly do stimulate America's consumer economy, there is so much wasteful and ineffective spending in advertising that it remains unclear to what degree the economy as a whole actually benefits from it. The most persuasive defense of television advertising is as a necessary evil to fund television—most viewers would probably rather continue to watch ads in exchange for "free TV" than pay directly for programming or contribute to a state-sponsored noncommercial system. Such choices have never been made widely available as an alternative to American television, although the success of subscription models to cable, satellite, and premium channels suggest that many viewers may be willing to pay directly to receive a broader range of programming and avoid commercials.

Social and cultural defenses of advertising are rarer. Most defenders argue that commercials support economic and media systems, but do not offer their own independent value. Many people dismiss extreme condemnations of advertising via common sense. Few people who watch ads see themselves as being manipulated, brainwashed, dehumanized, or objectified by commercials, so that would suggest that such impacts are overstated by critics imagining viewers as more vulnerable than they truly are. As chapter 9 discusses, many critics tend to overestimate the power of images to shape behaviors and attitudes, assuming that any negative message must have a negative effect. Advertisers are typically not in search of an immediate response to a commercial, not expecting you to jump in your car and go purchase the advertised product (although this behavior would certainly be welcomed by most sponsors). Rather, they see advertising as a long-term process of setting cultural norms and defining the terms by which we view consumption. The moment of truth for a commercial is when the consumer decides on the product based on the implicit associations forged over the course of months of seeing an ad campaign. These long-term persuasions are harder to detect, although most of us can think of instances in which our brand choices were influenced by a successful long-term ad campaign.

Some defenders contend that advertising functions as a medium of shared cultural values and creative expression, and thus should be prized as a window into American identity.[2] Based on this argument, it would hold that the market logic of consumerism seeks to meet the needs of people, and advertising is the direct expression of communal goals and needs. Thus any meanings featured in advertising are simply the manifestation of the broader cultural ideals the ad has tapped into. Therefore, by critiquing an ad, are we not condemning the will of the American people who hold the values the ad tries to mirror? According to this argument, if we see advertising as treating our bodies as objects and commodities as cures to what ails us, then there must be viewers who hold these ideals, and therefore such ads reflect their cultural beliefs. There is some validity to this perspective, as advertising must tap into established cultural norms to resonate with an audience. However, as chapter 7 discusses, this "reflection theory" of media is deeply flawed, as it ignores the way media help shape the society they aim to reflect, and how the industry selects, omits, and distorts aspects of the social world to fit its economic goals. Think of your own values and beliefs; some may be highlighted in advertising, while others are absent. This distorted mirror on society presents the shared values most conducive to consumerism and ignores those that cannot be effectively harnessed to sell products. Additionally, the advertising industry is not democratic in its feedback mechanism—the only way to vote on whether you like an ad is by choosing among products, a decision that has many other determinants besides advertising—and thus it is hard to argue that we simply get the advertising we most want.

Given all of these critical positions on advertising, how do you assess the arguments? Some questions need empirical research, exploring the degree to which advertising has beneficial economic impacts or does psychological harm. But at the level of common sense, imagine if our world had no advertising. Would it be a better place? Do the benefits gained from discovering new products outweigh the clutter of ads found in every medium and public space? Is it worth paying directly for noncommercial media to avoid the objectification and manipulation that advertising might encourage? Given the opportunity to avoid ads by using a recording device such as TiVo, buying digital downloads or DVDs, or subscribing to a premium channel such as HBO, would you take it, and at what cost? What is an ad-free experience ultimately worth? These issues are for each of us to consider and debate, as we make choices both as individuals and as part of a larger society. The key lesson is that advertising is not a "natural" or inevitable facet of the media. We must understand and question the system of advertising, the strategies used in its creation and circulation, and the impact it may have on our lives as citizens and media-literate consumers.

THE AUDIENCE EXCHANGE

The core economic exchange of commercial television is advertisers buying airtime from distributors and transmitters. This exchange uses television programming to build an audience for commercials to address, so what advertisers are really paying for is access to a television audience. Hence networks and channels deal in two distinct commodities: *programming* to attract an audience, and *audiences* to attract advertising buys. The economics of television revolve around audiences, and thus this third exchange may be the most crucial of all: *selling audiences to advertisers*. But what exactly are these audiences that are exchanged as a commodity? And how do these commoditized audiences relate to what we all do when we watch television? To understand the audience exchange, we need to examine the term *audience* as used by the television industry, and explore the chief mechanism for turning the act of watching television into a tradable commodity: the ratings system.

Defining the Audience

Whenever you watch a television program, you might consider yourself part of a large audience of millions of viewers watching the same program simultaneously. But if you look at press about the television industry, you read that what everyone really cares about are the viewing habits and tastes of the "eighteen-to-forty-nine-year-old audience," a category that spans two generations. Even if you fall within that age range, are you part of that audience? How does the television industry know what you want in television programming? If you're on the low end of that age range, do you really want the same thing in television programs as your parents? And if you're not within that age range, do you matter to the television industry at all?

These questions point to one of the more slippery concepts in thinking about television: defining the audience. We need to be careful with the term *audience* and contrast it with another similar term, *viewer*. **Television viewers** are the actual people who watch television—you, your friends and family, and millions of other real people watching television. **Television audiences** are the way the industry thinks about viewers: categorizes them, measures them, designs programming for them, and sells them to advertisers. But there is a crucial gap between the behaviors of real viewers and the industry's understanding of audiences, a distinction that directly impacts our understanding of how the television industry functions.

Viewing television is a more complicated practice than most people realize. While it is not necessarily a difficult activity, much more may be going on than depicted in the typical image of the "couch potato" passively watching whatever appears on the screen. Chapter 9 details the various ways viewers engage with television as part of their everyday lives. As a contrast to the industry's notion of audiences, think about how you watch television. Do you always sit mesmerized by the action, or do you watch while eating, exercising, folding laundry, talking on the phone, playing a game, or doing other activities? Do you watch a program straight through, mute the commercials, switch between channels, or time-shift via recording devices? Do you watch alone, talk with others about the program, yell back at the screen, or simply leave the television on in the background while you go about your daily life? Do you watch all programming the same way, or are the ways you view a baseball game, the Weather Channel, and *Grey's Anatomy* different? Do you watch the commercials in the same manner as you watch programming? After you watch a show, how does it affect you, and how long does the experience stay with you? And why do you watch a television program in the first place? There are many variables here, all of which suggest that viewing television is a multifaceted practice that cannot be reduced to a simple question of who is watching what.

However, the television industry does try to simplify the complexities of viewing behaviors into more streamlined and quantifiable terms. While certainly advertisers would like to know if you mute or fast-forward through commercials, and creators are interested in what reactions their programs might provoke in you, these are not aspects of viewing typically reflected in the industry's notion of the audience. The television industry poses two central questions about the audience: *Who is watching? What are they watching?* While particular segments of the industry might examine more nuanced facets of television viewing—such as a network testing a new program's appeal to a group of viewers, or an ad agency studying what commercials inspire viewers to pay attention—as a whole, the television industry is chiefly interested in knowing the *who* and *what* in defining audiences, not the *how* or *why.*

In this way, we might claim that *the television industry creates audiences,* a statement with two meanings. The first would be that television programmers work to attract an audience to their shows, and thus a successful program "creates" an audience. The second meaning is both more abstract and more significant: the television audience is a construction, a concept created by the industry to try to measure the real-world behavior of viewers. When you watch television, you are not part of an audience; you are a viewer acting as an individual or part of a small community watching a show. The audience for that program is how the industry understands the behavior of viewers, chiefly in terms of *who* and *what.* As an individual, you are never part of the television audience; *the audience is a categorical grouping defined by the television industry that does not represent actual viewers.*

The distinction between industry-created audiences and everyday viewers can be tricky. It may be useful to think about what other categorical groups you might be considered part of—Arab American, suburban, college student, Christian, hockey fan, working-class, environmentally conscious, and so on. In each of these cases, you may see yourself as part of a larger category based on who you are, what you believe in, and what you have chosen to do. However, if you think about broader cultural assumptions about that category, you may find that you diverge from the commonsense ideas about the group—you might be a college student who doesn't drink alcohol, has a full-time job, or is middle-aged, all of which point away from commonly held ideas about college students as a group. Categories and groups always rely on shared traits and typical behaviors more than acknowledging the diversity of people who may fit into the category. This doesn't mean that you don't belong within a given group, but rather that such categories can never capture the broad range of identities and practices that constitute individuals' lives, even around a seemingly simple practice such as watching television. For the television industry, the economic need for a common currency to buy and sell leads to a highly simplified and reductive categorization of viewers into audience groups.

The industry's use of audience categories pervades nearly all the practices detailed in this chapter. Clearly audiences are bought and sold by broadcasters and advertisers, targeted by creators and networks, and defined by market researchers. The industry has always used audiences as an abstraction to be used in the advertising exchange; in the classic network era, the preferred concept of the audience was the **mass audience**, as programmers typically aimed for the largest audience size with little concern for the composition of that audience. Specific time slots were more focused—daytime for the female audience, Saturday morning for the children's audience—but as a whole, networks measured success by the total size of the audience. In the multi-channel era, the question of *who* has become more prominent, as cable channels and networks have focused on reaching smaller, more concentrated **audience segments** as defined by demographic and psychographic characteristics. Thus the concept of the television audience has become more fragmented, with specific segments such as the eighteen-to-thirty-four-year-old male audience, the urban professional audience, or the working woman audience emerging as the key categories used within the industry.

Specific audience categories are often used to define programming trends and cable branding. For instance, the channel BET defines its audience in its name: Black Entertainment Television. Defined by a demographic category of racial identity, BET might seem to construct its audience as all African-American viewers, but the actual programming and promotional choices target a more specific notion of a "black audience." BET constructs a particular vision of its black audience as embracing a youthful, urban, hip-hop lifestyle, a construction that certainly does not encompass all people who are black (nor the white and Latino viewers who watch BET). Similarly, Univision constructs a Spanish-speaking audience through its language, but generally addresses its programming to a hypothetical "pan-ethnic" Hispanic audience, not specific Latino ethnicities or cultures. The television industry thus creates audience categories that put forward a vision of cultural groups that often diverges from the identity of the viewers themselves.

Identity categories also can be used by the industry to construct audiences in other ways. As discussed in chapter 8, a notable trend of 1990s television was the increase in lesbian and gay representations—shows with homosexual main characters such as *Ellen*, *Will & Grace*, and *Spin City* emerged along with the inclusion of gay themes and guest characters in a wide range of popular programs, such as *Roseanne*, *Friends*, *Frasier*, *Seinfeld*, *NYPD Blue*, and *ER*. Certainly one of the goals behind including this traditionally marginalized group within television programming was to appeal to the gay and lesbian audience, which the industry constructed as urban, financially stable, and consumerist-minded—all appealing qualities for advertisers, but certainly not universally held traits of all gay and lesbian viewers. But these representations were not targeted solely toward the comparatively small gay and lesbian audience; rather the industry saw that incorporating gay content in an accepting and affirmative style would be appealing to a larger audience of heterosexual viewers who were sympathetic to gay rights. One critic labels this audience as "slumpies," or "socially liberal, urban-minded professionals," a psychographic category that is particularly valuable for advertisers looking to reach consumers with disposable income.[3] Even though many of these programs prompted protests, complaints, and boycotts, advertisers and networks risked alienating viewers who might find gay content objectionable because they viewed such an anti-gay audience as older, more rural, less educated, and more conservative in their spending habits than the "quality audience" desirable to advertisers.

This example highlights how the industry's mode of categorizing audiences oversimplifies the complex social experience of viewers, identities, and beliefs. Many individuals might have opinions about gay representation that do not coincide with the industry's use of these categories—a young New York City law-yer might object to representations of homosexuality, while an older Nebraska farmer might be quite accepting, or even gay himself. Because audiences are groupings of individuals, the industry uses composite profiles of groups, rather than capturing the diversity inherent in any group. Many of these profiles are accurate in collective terms—as a group, industrially conceived audience cat-egories usually match typical behaviors and demographics as determined by well-funded market research—but the categories rarely capture the complexities of who we are as individuals and how we consume media. A useful exercise is to watch programming targeted to a specific audience category that you might fit into demographically, and consider how your own experiences diverges from the assumptions the industry makes about this group.

Another crucial facet of the industrial creation of audiences is that not all groups are created equal. Some categories are more broadly conceived in size—the female audience is much larger than the "do-it-yourself" audience—and thus more programming typically addresses the larger segments. But even among similarly sized audiences, some categories are much more valued and prioritized than others. Typically the industry aims at audiences that advertis-ers believe to be more valued consumers, targeting those with more money, more consumerist tendencies, and less hardened consumption habits—a group deemed the **commodity audience**. This typically translates into a young, urban or suburban, upper-middle-class audience, which advertisers see as the bedrock of American consumption even for products that may be out of reach—luxury cars are advertised to teenagers not because BMW believes a sixteen-year-old will buy their car, but to forge a long-term desire for the car as a symbol of suc-cess in adulthood. While specific sponsors might want to reach particular audi-ences outside of this main commodity audience, the vast majority of television targets the same core group of consumers, effectively neglecting viewers who fall outside this "quality demographic," such as senior citizens, working-class view-ers, and smaller racial groups such as Asian Americans and Native Americans.

The concept of the commodity audience returns us to the question that started chapter 1: How can a billion-dollar industry offer its product for free? The answer is that viewing is not actually an activity without costs, even when watching over-the-air broadcasting that does not charge direct fees. When we watch free television, we pay by allowing ourselves to be transformed from an individual viewer into part of a commodity audience to be bought by advertisers. Thus we pay the price not only by watching ads and paying higher prices for consumer goods to fund that advertising, but also by consenting to the system that defines individuals through market segments and psychographic lifestyles. Since the industry is interested in audience groups, we allow ourselves to be categorized into segments that may bear little relationship to our personal lives. Nearly all programs, commercials, channels, and genres are designed for these constructed audiences, and thus by consenting to be transformed from viewer to audience, the cost we pay is by allowing the industry to utilize the shared cultural resource of television to address individuals as predefined market segments.

This cost might be a bargain—no matter what you think of television, you can probably think of a few programs that you believe were truly meaningful, pleasurable, or had a positive impact on your life. Allowing yourself to be treated as a commodity might be a fair exchange for the amount of entertainment and information television makes available. But it is important that viewers recognize how this system works—that "free TV" has its costs, and that other alternatives are unavailable or marginalized because of the commercial drive of American television and its narrow definition of audiences. To be a media-literate viewer and citizen, you must recognize that when you watch television you are giving something up, and you should decide for yourself whether the price is worth what you pay in allowing yourself to be defined as a commodity on the industry's terms.

Measuring the Audience

In suggesting that there is a difference between television viewers and television audiences, it might appear that there is no relationship between these two concepts. But the industry works hard to ensure that its definitions of the audience are grounded in the real-life experience of viewers, as ultimately advertisers strive to impact real viewers, not just imagined audiences, through their persuasive messages—after all, real people must consume products to justify the costs of advertising. The television industry relies on a number of techniques to understand viewer behavior and translate those practices into audience categories. Of the various techniques used for **audience measurement**, by far the most influential is the system of **television ratings**. Because there are typically no direct sales of television programming to measure, such as the box office in film or retail sales of publishing and music, ratings are the system by which audiences are converted into a quantifiable currency that facilitates the exchange between advertisers and programmers, and thus the ratings system is crucial to understanding how the television industry operates.

Like many components of the television industry, ratings were adapted from the radio medium. While there have been some competing audience-measurement services, Nielsen Media Research Company has held a virtual monopoly on reporting television ratings since the 1950s. Nielsen sells a wide range of ratings reports and detailed breakdowns to nearly every company in the television industry, including networks, channels, stations, and advertising agencies. Because these numbers are uniformly viewed as defining audience sizes across the industry, Nielsen ratings function as a common currency to facilitate the exchange of audiences between distributors and advertisers. Their widespread usage results in a system that values consistency in terms of audience measurement more than proven accuracy in measuring the behaviors of actual viewers.

Ratings numbers are used outside the industry, too, with newspapers, magazines, and websites reporting ratings to the general public, as many people chart the popularity of television programs. There are two crucial numbers included in most reports: ratings and shares. **Ratings** measure the percentage of television households tuned into a program at a given moment—a 15 rating estimates that 15 percent of all television households are watching that program. As of 2008, Nielsen estimated that there were approximately 112 million television households in the country, so each rating point equals around 1.1 million households. Nielsen also estimates the number of total viewers of every program, as many households contain multiple viewers—for instance, a rating of 11.9 represents just over 13 million households and more than 18 million estimated individuals, accounting for households with multiple televisions and group viewing. Nielsen reports these numbers in fine detail, tracking changes in ratings throughout a program and subdividing ratings into many subcategories of audience groups.

The other major number reported in a Nielsen report is the **share**, the percentage of households actually watching television that are viewing a specific program. The total shares of all programs in a given time slot always equals 100, so shares compare which programs have larger portions of the television-viewing audience, ignoring televisions that are not being used. In time slots with smaller total audiences (such as late night or midmorning), ratings might be quite low but shares can be high, suggesting that a show performs well among the comparatively small audience watching television. Shares gauge competition between channels and networks, and are typically used most to measure head-to-head battles between similar programs, as with evening news, soap operas, and late-night talk shows.

So what is a good rating for a program? It completely depends on context, as changes in technology and history have altered the scale for ratings measurement. In the classic network era, there was little competition for the three networks and thus ratings for prime time programming were high—top programs would get ratings between 30 and 40 and a program with a 15 rating would likely be cancelled. In the 2000s, viewers have many more choices of channels and competition from other media such as home video, video games, and the Internet, and thus ratings for network programs have shrunk considerably. The top-rated programs today get ratings between 10 and 20, and high-profile events do not reach numbers typical of the classic network era—for instance, the 2004 finale of *Friends* received just under a 30 rating, a number that would have been considered a flop for the highly promoted finale of a hit show in earlier decades, but was the highest-rated scripted program of the 2000s. Cable programs reach even lower numbers, with ratings rarely exceeding 5 points and any program over a 1 rating generally considered a success. Thus a network show that would be considered a major hit today would have been cancelled with similar numbers in the 1960s.

Rating numbers can also be selectively presented to make different claims. For instance, both Fox News and CNN can rightly claim to have the highest viewership among cable news channels depending on how you parse the ratings. Fox typically averages higher ratings per program than CNN, and usually posts higher shares at any one moment, justifying the claim that more people are watching Fox News than CNN at any given time. But CNN has more unique total viewers each day than Fox, measured as **cumes** to count the cumulative audience of unique viewers—the total number of different individuals who watch CNN is 20 percent higher than Fox each day. Fox viewers seem to watch more hours of the channel and thus raise ratings across many programs, but CNN has more unique total viewers each day—a situation that allows each to claim that it is the most popular news channel. Advertising rates for CNN generally exceed those for Fox, seemingly because advertisers like to reach more casual viewers, who are otherwise harder to target, more than heavy viewers, who see many commercials each day. Fox News touts its status as the highest-rated cable news channel to trump CNN, but it is not the measure that matters most to its core customers of advertisers, nor is it as simple as equating high ratings with quantity of viewers.[4]

Clearly much is riding on these numbers, as programming decisions and advertising rates are all based on Nielsen ratings. So where do these numbers come from? Nielsen uses a range of techniques to measure viewer behavior and generate rating numbers, and is actively changing its techniques to adapt to the realities of the digital convergence era. As of the mid-2000s, the main source of national network and channel ratings come from **People Meters**, small boxes installed on the televisions of around ten thousand randomly selected American households that upload data automatically to Nielsen each night. These devices track what programs are watched, while viewers press a personalized button to signal which household members are viewing at any given time. Additionally, approximately twenty thousand households in major cities are wired with passive set meters, which measure only television activity, not which viewers are watching; these households are used to track local stations in major markets and provide quick "overnight" national estimates.

There are more than two hundred distinct television markets in the United States, and Nielsen's national methods cannot successfully measure the local stations in each market. To supplement the national numbers and serve smaller markets not measured with meters, Nielsen collects more than one hundred thousand diaries of viewing behavior four times each year during month-long **sweeps** periods in February, May, July, and November. These additional data allow Nielsen to report ratings for local stations and offer more comprehensive breakdowns of national numbers. Because these four months are when all affiliates can use ratings to set their local ad rates, networks tend to schedule high-profile events and movies, offer casting and cross-over stunts, and remove low-rated programs from schedules during sweeps, hoping to inflate their numbers sufficiently to keep affiliate and O&O ad rates high.

It might seem odd that the entire economic system of commercial television is based upon the viewing habits of 10,000 households—even during sweeps, data from fewer than 200,000 households is used to represent the viewing of 112 million homes, less than .2 percent of the population. The accuracy of Nielsen's ratings is a much-debated point in the media industry and among critics of the commercial system. Nielsen employs a sampling method to mirror the demographic composition of American television households, hoping that its ten thousand Nielsen families are a representative slice of the entire country. Nielsen's sampling methods have often been criticized for underrepresenting urban minority viewers, as Nielsen workers have allegedly avoided neighborhoods they viewed as potentially unsafe and have ruled out non-English-speaking families. Nielsen defends their methods, claiming that their sample mirrors the demographic profile of the United States, and have adjusted their sampling techniques in recent years to address these concerns, unveiling specific initiatives to measure African-American and Hispanic audiences. Another significant limitation has been that Nielsen traditionally only samples television as viewed in a household, not collecting viewing data for other locales, such as college dorm lounges, sports bars, and hospitals, a limitation that might skew ratings of programs with particular audiences; although in recent years Nielsen has added college dorms and hotels to its sample. Nielsen is in the process of incorporating new technologies such as the Portable People Meter to allow more comprehensive coverage of such locales and to track viewing by individual, regardless of their location or mode of viewing. As digital technologies for watching television evolve, numerous competitors are attempting to break Nielsen's monopoly by offering competing services that are arguably more accurate in measuring viewership, but for ratings to function as a common currency in the industry, there must be shared adoption of data and reports across networks, channels, and advertisers, a position that only Nielsen currently holds.

Even if Nielsen's random sample is sufficient to mirror the general population of television viewers, all sampling research has a **margin of error**, the statistically likely range within which real behaviors might fall; the potential for errors increases with smaller samples, as with cable ratings or narrowly targeted audience segments that advertisers particularly desire. In addition to standard sampling errors, other errors exist, such as those stemming from households who decline to participate (who might differ in television habits than those who do agree to be Nielsen families), who fail to follow the protocols for using diaries or meters, or who adjust their viewing habits to influence ratings. Unlike most public opinion polling conducted in politics and market research, Nielsen ratings use a comparatively static sample—Nielsen families typically are measured for two years, with little turnover among the sample over the course of a television season. This static sample means that any errors in representation persist from week to week, whereas other polling relies on complete sampling turnover to minimize errors from poll to poll. Official Nielsen reports contain disclaimers about the limits of ratings as a measure and include relevant margins of error. However, the industry typically disregards these caveats, and the press rarely reprints them, treating the numbers as proven facts rather than approximate estimates. The consequences for these errors can be significant—programs in the middle-of-the-pack in ratings could shift their position up or down many ranks if accounting for margins of error, even swapping places with direct time slot competitors. Although the industry argues that even inexact numbers are useful if used consistently, many decisions are justified based on perceived ratings that may be quite inaccurate.

Nielsen's importance in defining the television audience stems from its universal adoption by the industry—because it is a common currency without an interest in the results, participants treat its numbers as definitive. In recent years, some innovations have raised questions about Nielsen's future role in television. Ideally, nearly everyone in the industry would love more accurate data that would not rely on small samples, although any shift in measurement techniques triggers complaints from any stakeholders who find their own programming appearing less popular. The most accurate data on viewer behavior come from programs with a direct-response component, whether infomercials with a direct purchase phone number or shows such as *American Idol* that ask viewers to vote on contestants; these responses are direct evidence of people watching and responding to the program. But it is hard to imagine such techniques working for measuring other genres, such as cop shows or news. Digital technology in cable set-top boxes and digital recorders can log every click of your remote control to report to research firms, although this model raises privacy questions if viewers are unaware of what data is being collected. While these alternative models of audience measurement are being pursued by Nielsen and its competitors, no system of measurement will have much of an impact on the central construction of audiences unless it is adopted as part of a commonly agreed upon currency in the audience exchange.

Rethinking the Audience

Clearly the techniques used to measure audiences impact the way the industry thinks about, targets, and constructs audiences for programming and advertising. The vast majority of knowledge about viewing behavior is filtered through the data provided by Nielsen, boiling down the complex practices of viewers into quantifiable measures of the size and demographics of the audience. Whether Nielsen is accurate in its measurement of audience size and demographics is ultimately less relevant as a critique of the system than questioning how the measurement system obscures other aspects of viewing behavior, and how the increasing emphasis on demographics alters the practices of the television industry. As techniques and uses of audience measurement have changed over time, programming decisions have responded to new conceptions of the audience.

As a key example of these shifts, in the late-1960s CBS was the top-rated network, with hit prime time shows such as *The Beverly Hillbillies, Mayberry R.F.D.,* and *The Red Skelton Show.*[5] These long-running traditional programs were particularly popular with older and rural audiences, often called the "heartland audience," but in a system in which the total numbers of viewers was the most valuable competition in prime time ratings, the specific identity of viewers mattered less to the network. But by 1972, CBS had cancelled these programs and other hits such as *Hee Haw* and *Green Acres*, replacing them with more risky and often controversial programs *All in the Family, The Mary Tyler Moore Show, M*A*S*H, The Bob Newhart Show,* and *Maude.* Given the logic of the television industry—favoring safe formulas over risks, proven hits over innovations—how can we account for this major schedule overhaul by the top-rated network?

Two major factors contributed to CBS's programming and branding transformation. Throughout the 1960s, in response to advertisers wishing to be more targeted in their ad buying, Nielsen began to augment its basic ratings report of total viewers with more demographic information. Although these demographic reports were far less detailed than those seen today, conceiving of the prime time audience in terms of segments rather than a mass changed how networks and advertisers carried out their business. Advertisers began to focus on how they could most cost-effectively reach their ideal young, upwardly mobile consumers, and networks responded by devising programs to reach this demographic, gradually emphasizing audience composition throughout the 1960s.

This shift in constructing audiences was tied to a realization within CBS's own ratings reports. While it was consistently the top-rated network nationally in the late sixties, its "country lineup" played far worse in urban markets, often ranking behind ABC and NBC in major cities. Not only did this limited urban appeal drive away demographically minded advertisers, but it hurt CBS's owned-and-operated stations—in the 1970s, networks were limited to five

In the early 1970s, CBS shifted away from rural-themed hits like *Green Acres*...

...and embraced urban-themed sitcoms like *The Mary Tyler Moore Show* to capture a younger and more urban "quality audience."

O&Os, which were all in major cities. CBS's O&O stations in New York, Los Angeles, Philadelphia, and Chicago were losing to their competitors, despite the network's national strength. Thus CBS recognized that to maximize income across its vertically integrated holdings, it needed to reach the urban audiences in its O&O markets.

The new programs that reversed this trend offered innovative ideas to capture younger urban viewers using social controversy, younger stars, city locales, and a sophisticated tone—a risk that paid off not just among urban audiences but nationwide, as CBS remained the top network nationally despite its major overhaul, and each of these programs qualified as a major hit. Programs such as *All in the Family*, *Mary Tyler Moore*, and *M*A*S*H* were certainly successful in part because of the extraordinary caliber of the writing and performances, and they still rank among the most praised shows in television history. CBS managed to successfully transform its lineup not just by offering quality programs, but also by taking extreme measures to redefine and reconstruct its audience. This transformative moment is key in the history of the television industry, as it marks the ascendancy of the **quality audience** that is still the primary target of network programming and advertisers: young, urban-minded, upwardly mobile, educated consumers. (Chapter 7 discusses the cultural impact of these programs.) But clearly these innovations would not have been possible without an industrial system that valued particular audiences over others.

This example highlights one of the downsides of the industry's construction of audiences: not all viewers are treated equally. While a Nielsen family in Philadelphia may represent an equal statistical slice of America as their counterpart in Topeka, Kansas, within the industry's logic, the urban audience is more valuable than the rural one. The degree to which your own tastes for programming are served by television depends on how closely you fit into well-established audience categories desired by advertisers—if your demographic and psychographic profile and associated buying power do not match those of the audiences the industry wishes to attract, then it may be harder to find programming that appeals to you. Even if you do match the demographics of the commodity audiences advertisers wish to reach, the way the industry will target your group is through what it views as the group's most commonly held (and thus often least interesting and distinctive) traits, treating complex individuals as simplistic categories.

This system of measuring and exchanging audiences raises questions about a core myth of the commercial television system: Since success on television is measured by popularity, don't we just get the programming the majority of viewers want to watch? It is tempting to view commercial television as a democracy, with viewers voting for the programs they wish to see, but this parallel breaks down in three crucial ways. First, the ballot is closed—the industry offers a limited slate of shows for viewers to watch, all of which have been carefully constructed to maximize appeal to the industry's conception of audience desires (although some might say the same is true of political candidates). Selecting from a limited menu is not the same as having free choice, as the industry cannot respond to viewer interests that are not available options for viewers.

Second, as the example of CBS in the 1970s attests, television is not always interested in a majority of all viewers, as some viewers are more valued than others—the majority of rural viewers who liked *Hee Haw* and *Green Acres* were not well served by CBS's innovative shift in programming. If watching television is like voting, not all votes are given equal weight.

Third, in the exchange of television audiences, most votes are not counted. If you are among the 99.9 percent of American television households not measured by Nielsen, then your viewing practices do not affect a show's popularity. In order to register their opinion with the television industry, unmeasured viewers must actively provide feedback with letter-writing campaigns, fan websites, or protests, aspects of the viewing process that rarely trump ratings for networks in making programming decisions. Without a system of direct revenue such as box office or retail sales to measure consumption, the vast majority of television viewers have no voice in the exchange of audiences that justifies the economics of the industry. Even if the ratings system is fairly accurate in its measurement of viewing, it is mistaken to suggest that the fate of television programming is democratically decided in a system in which almost no votes count. Thus even though we who view television enter into an exchange with the industry, offering our attention for advertisers to receive programming, our participation does not register as consumer demand within the industry's market logic—only a select .1 percent of households are able to influence the industry's practices through their consumption patterns. If the commercial television industry is to be viewed as a democracy of viewers registering their opinions, then it must be seen as a representative democracy in which we have no hand in picking who our representatives are, have no idea who they are, and lack the ability to impact the system unless we happen to be selected as one of these rare representatives—in other words, it does not resemble any recognizable form of democracy.

The exchange of audiences is at the core of the television industry, but it is ultimately the least effective and efficient facet of the industry in serving its economic goals. For programmers and advertisers, the Nielsen ratings are rough approximations that function as a common currency, but ultimately offer little insight into why certain programs are popular or what viewers truly do while watching television, an understanding that could allow television to reach people more effectively. Instead, the industry uses ratings to help support its own assumptions about viewer behaviors and tastes. From the perspective of viewers, ratings and industrial systems of creating audiences oversimplify the complex practices that comprise our viewing behaviors as discussed in chapter 9, allowing a tiny minority of anonymous households to influence and shape television programming practices. While certainly much of what is popular on television has widespread appeal, it is a mistake to assume that viewers ultimately choose what programming succeeds on television.

THE INDUSTRY AT WORK:
THE CASE OF REALITY TELEVISION

One of the most striking success stories in recent American television is the rise of **reality television** over the past decade, a development that has led many commentators to assert that such programming is what viewers really want—or, more cynically, what we ultimately deserve. As the last section details, programming trends are not simple expressions of popular tastes, but rather the result of careful constructions of audience categories, combined with decisions by producers, distributors, and advertisers. Reality television can serve as a useful example for seeing how the television industry works to exchange programming, advertising, and audiences in tandem. The economics of reality television also highlights the limits of our ability to understand the medium's full importance by only focusing on the industrial facet instead of the entire circuit of television. This echoes one of the central points of this book: understanding a phenomenon such as reality television requires us to consider the many facets of the television medium.

The Economic Logic of Reality Television

On its face, reality television might seem like a form that emerged from a fluke surprise hit series, *Survivor*, which debuted to huge success during the summer of 2000, even though summer had traditionally been a dumping ground for broadcast networks to air programs seen as unsuitable for standard schedules. However, the origins of reality television stretch back throughout television history and across the globe. Predecessors of today's reality television were present in the early years of television in the 1950s, in hidden-camera programs such as *Candid Camera* and emotionally charged contests such as *Queen for a Day*, and in innovations of the 1970s, such as PBS's documentary series *An American Family* and the voyeuristic *That's Incredible!*. Television has a long history of presenting unscripted programming featuring real people, from game shows to talk shows, but it was not until the summer of 2000 that reality television began to be thought of as its own central category by the American television industry and broader public.

There were a few key predecessors in the late 1980s and 1990s that set the stage for the industry to embrace the reality trend. The Writers Guild of America labor strike of 1988 led networks to turn more to unscripted programming, opening up schedule slots for innovative shows that did not require writers. As Fox was establishing itself as a network, it used unscripted **tabloid shows** such as *Cops* and *America's Most Wanted* as low-cost material to fill out its schedule; both shows proved to be long-running hits scheduled among the more common fictional fare of prime time. These shows, as well as other 1990s predecessors of

THE REAL WORLD

The Real World (MTV, 1992–present): This long-running reality program puts a group of young strangers in a house with video surveillance, editing footage in narrative arcs of conflicts, relationships, and scandals. One of the first reality shows, *The Real World* helped build MTV's appeal outside of music videos, shifting the channel into a youth-centered lifestyle brand, rather than focused exclusively on music.

THE AMAZING RACE

The Amazing Race (CBS, 2001–present): One of the most critically acclaimed reality competitions, *The Amazing Race* pits contestant pairs in a race around the world. Combining exotic locales, unusual contests and tasks, and often volatile personalities, the show has received more praise than most reality programs for avoiding exploitation and questionable taste.

reality television such as *America's Funniest Home Videos, Unsolved Mysteries,* and *Rescue 911,* offered low production costs to avoid the deficit financing system typical of scripted programming; most of these tabloid or found-footage shows were produced or co-produced by networks themselves, so they were highly profitable ventures even with modest ratings. Thus unscripted programming became known as a low-risk option for networks, justifiable even without top ratings or key audience demographics.

Another important predecessor came from cable television, as MTV debuted *The Real World* in 1992. The innovation of this show was to couple the dramatic structure of soap operas and teen dramas with an unscripted mode of production and presentation. *The Real World* was the first successful reality program offering ongoing characters, plots, and situations in a format some label the **docusoap,** engaging a youthful audience that was, in the eyes of MTV programmers, somewhat jaded by the formulas of soap operas and prime time dramas. As with the tabloid programs, *The Real World* offered lower production costs, as writers and actors, typically the highest paid participants on a scripted program, were replaced by a team of editors and volunteer cast members. The show's success and appeal to youthful audiences, which was strong for MTV but never reached ratings comparable to those in network programming, spawned similar programs such as *Road Rules,* which joined competitive tasks with unscripted melodrama, setting clear precedents for reality competitions such as *Survivor* and *The Amazing Race.*

> ## WHO WANTS TO BE A MILLIONAIRE
>
> *Who Wants to Be a Millionaire* (ABC, 1999–2002; syndicated 2002–present): Imported from a British game show, ABC's surprise hit helped launch the reality boom and allow game shows to return to prime time. After ratings faded due to overexposure in prime time, the show was repackaged as a syndicated game show with Meredith Vieira taking over hosting duties from Regis Philbin in 2002.

The final program that helped set the stage for the reality boom might be considered more of a traditional game show than a reality show, but its blockbuster success certainly led networks to consider the potential for prime time unscripted hits. *Who Wants to Be a Millionaire?* debuted on ABC in the summer of 1999, becoming an unlikely ratings smash. The program was an import of a popular British quiz show, and in many ways it was a throwback to the hit prime time quizzes of the 1950s, such as *The $64,000 Question* and *Twenty-One*, but with higher stakes (and without the scandalous behind-the-scenes scripting discussed in chapter 6). The success of *Millionaire* made networks realize the potential for unscripted programming with low production budgets to reach huge prime time audiences, running counter to the long tradition of keeping game shows such as *Jeopardy!* and *Wheel of Fortune* as early-evening first-run syndicated programs and *The Price Is Right* as morning schedule fillers. As is typical whenever an innovation proves successful, networks followed *Millionaire* with imitative clones such as *Greed*, *Winning Lines*, and a remake of *Twenty-One*; all of these programs were short-lived, as they were unable to capture the buzz and ratings of *Millionaire*. However, *Millionaire*'s success did encourage programmers to look at European television for other potential innovative hits, which directly led to the reality boom.

Traditionally, the American television industry has been reluctant to import programming **formats** or actual shows from other countries, as the industry's common sense is that American audiences will reject foreign programs and that Hollywood television production is superior to that of other smaller industries—as discussed in the book's conclusion, aside from a few British sitcoms on PBS, Spanish-language broadcasting, and Japanese animation, almost no imported programs have aired on broadcast television throughout American television history. Adapting popular shows from other countries has a stronger tradition, however; successful 1970s shows *All in the Family*, *Sanford and Son*, and *Three's Company* were all adaptations of hit British sitcoms, while other more recent British adaptations, such as *Cracker*, *Coupling*, and *Men Behaving Badly*, fared less well on American television.[6] Adapting the format of unscripted

BIG BROTHER

Big Brother (CBS, 2000–present): One of the most popular reality franchises around the world, *Big Brother* never reached a mass audience in America, although CBS runs the program every summer to modest ratings. The show, isolating a group of contestants in a house under constant surveillance while they compete for a large cash prize, was one of the first to incorporate online footage and an expansive website.

programming such as quiz shows and reality competitions is somewhat easier than producing scripted shows, as the *Millionaire* model demonstrated—producers could import the concept and structure of an unscripted program in the form of a "brand name" and "playbook" for how to produce the show, but cast an American host (such as Regis Philbin), use American contestants, and switch the content of the questions to nationally relevant material. The ease of this format adaptation led to the original British *Millionaire* being adapted to more than one hundred different countries, creating a lucrative model for international franchising of unscripted programming.

In the summer of 2000, CBS decided to counter ABC's hit quiz show with two international unscripted adaptations of its own. The program that generated the most anticipation and advance buzz was *Big Brother*, which had been a breakout Dutch hit in 1999 and had spawned successful European versions in Germany, Britain, and Spain prior to its debut on CBS. The **gamedoc** format merges a game show competition with a documentary visual style, while drawing dramatic elements from *Real World's* docusoap model: isolating a small number of strangers in a house under constant video surveillance, and subject to viewers voting them out to determine who will be left in the house to win a final cash prize. CBS aired *Big Brother* multiple times each week in the model of *Millionaire*; the show was not a clear ratings hit, but it generated sufficient profits to be renewed for multiple seasons, due to CBS's participation as a co-producer and the show's low production costs. *Big Brother* pioneered the integration of audience participation in voting for contestants and the inclusion of additional footage online via affiliated websites, two trends that continue in reality television.

CBS's other reality offering in the summer of 2000 was a surprise smash; based upon a hit Swedish gamedoc called *Expedition Robinson*, *Survivor* isolates contestants on an undeveloped island, requiring them to compete in tasks and undertake political machinations to avoid being voted off by their fellow castaways in the quest for a million-dollar prize. The show received remarkable ratings with strong demographics, peaking with more than fifty million viewers

SURVIVOR

Survivor (CBS, 2000–present): The first massive reality hit in the United States, *Survivor* combines wilderness adventure with interpersonal drama to create a long-running series that defined the gamedoc format in America. The show is notable for its industrial innovations as well, with the production company taking the lead in selling advertising and product-integration opportunities.

watching the first-season finale, an astounding response for a series in the multichannel era. The success of *Survivor* triggered a rush to reality programming across all networks and channels, as they saw the genre offering the potential for solid overall ratings, strong performance among younger demographics, lower production costs, and opportunities for co-production arrangements to maintain ownership in hit programs.

The economics of a reality series highlight the potential windfalls that networks and producers saw in the genre. *Survivor* producer Mark Burnett worked with CBS to redefine the terms by which the show would be financed. Instead of CBS paying a standard licensing fee to help fund the show's production, Burnett negotiated to self-fund the production, but split the program's advertising revenue

The first season of *Survivor* discovered that putting real people atypical for television in a remote locale can inspire dramatic action and gameplay, generating a surprise mass hit.

with CBS, pre-selling some sponsorships before the series aired. For the first season in 2000, eight sponsors paid roughly $4 million each to run ads during the series and have their products featured in the program; this arrangement effectively financed the production costs of $1 million per episode, avoiding the deficit-financing model and turning all additional ad sales into pure profit for both CBS and Burnett. While such splits in advertising revenue are still comparatively rare, producers of reality programming almost never deficit-finance, relying instead on co-production with networks or channels to finance program creation. Production costs for reality shows are typically lower than *Survivor's*, with an average of $700,000 per hour-long episode, far less than for typical scripted programs, which typically cost more than $2 million per hour. The genre is quite profitable for producers, networks, and channels. Even though back-end revenues from reruns and DVD releases of reality television have not been typically as strong as for scripted programs, a hit show can export its format around the globe, creating a huge revenue stream for the original producers.[7]

One of the key economic strengths for reality producers is the role of product integration. While products are placed within nearly all sorts of programming, reality television seems particularly suited for such sponsorship opportunities. If product integration within fictional shows places brand names as props within dramatic action, reality programs often make products the center of the drama itself—starving *Survivor* contestants competing in a desperate effort to win a bag of Doritos; dramatizing the filming of a Ford Focus commercial starring *American Idol's* singers; teams on *The Apprentice* devising strategies to promote Crest toothpaste. Sponsors recognize that such placement is more than just creating passive brand awareness, but is actually making their products objects of desire and achievement, all in programs explicitly labeled as "real"—such product integration, in which sponsors are intimately involved with the production process, is often hailed as the ultimate promotional opportunity and potentially the future of advertising on television. Reality television thus presents a vision of the "real world," which is saturated with consumer goods, brand names, and opportunities to celebrate products, all in exchange for lucrative "promotional consideration."

Once *Survivor* emerged as such a breakout success for its producer, network, and sponsors alike, the imitative logic of the industry rushed to capitalize on the reality trend. While many programs such as *The Amazing Race* and *The Apprentice* mimicked the gamedoc structure of *Survivor*, the unscripted format proved amenable to a wide range of scenarios and genre mixtures: reality romances (*The Bachelor*), talent shows (*America's Next Top Model*), sitcoms (*The Osbornes*), how-to shows (*Trading Spaces*), lifestyle makeovers (*Queer Eye for the Straight Guy*), sports (*The Contender*), and even parodies (*The Joe Schmo Show*). Many programs were similarly imported European adaptations: *American Idol*, *Trading Spaces*, *The Weakest Link*, and *Wife Swap* were all adapted from British hits, and Dutch company Endemol produced numerous globally franchised

AMERICAN IDOL

American Idol (Fox, 2002–present): The current leader in reality ratings, *American Idol* reworked a British talent show to become the most popular show in America, launching the careers of numerous singers. The show combines a traditional talent show with audience participation via phone-in voting, as well as the ongoing drama of contestants returning for months to become well-known pop culture figures.

THE APPRENTICE

The Apprentice (NBC, 2004–present): A reality show that focuses on finding an employee for real estate magnate Donald Trump through a competition, *The Apprentice* was a hit in its first seasons before fading in the ratings. The show uses product integration as subjects for its competitions, such as designing a new Mattel toy or developing a marketing plan for Crest toothpaste.

programs such as *Chains of Love, Fear Factor,* and *The Mole,* in addition to *Big Brother*. While many specific programs and types of reality programming have come and gone quickly—for instance, *Joe Millionaire* was one of the biggest hits of 2003, but a notorious flop the next season—there is no doubt that as a broad mode of unscripted production, reality television has lingered far more than many critics initially assumed it would.

Reality television clearly offers cost-effective strategies for producers, distributors, and sponsors to achieve their commercial goals, but how does the audience exchange tie to the genre? Certainly the ratings for these programs have often been quite spectacular, with the programs performing strongly across demographic groups but particularly well with young audiences. Many reality programs enable other measures of audiences beyond ratings—*American Idol* and *Big Brother* rely on viewers voting via phone and text messaging to determine the outcome of their competitions, a practice that partner telecommunications companies use to generate substantial revenues as well. The industry can look to such evidence of direct participation as another way to construct the size and engagement of the audience, monitoring information such as the more than five hundred million telephone votes that were cast throughout the 2005 season of *American Idol*. While such data do not factor directly into the currency of the audience exchange the way ratings do, arguably evidence that viewers can be so engaged with a program to call in their opinions can serve to justify high costs for advertising and product integration, as the audience is demonstrated to be highly active and participatory.

The active participation of reality viewers can have its drawbacks to the television industry, however. Some viewers have used the feedback system of reality television to impact programs in ways that run counter to producer intentions. For instance, viewers have organized campaigns to promote *American Idol* contestants they regard as the least talented singers in an effort to sabotage the competition. *Big Brother* faced more direct interventions in its first season—a group of activist "culture jammers" attempted to sabotage the show by shattering the contestants' communication quarantine by throwing notes over the house's surrounding fences, shouting messages via megaphone outside the house, and flying banners above the house on rented planes. Such activism almost resulted in the contestants' quitting in a group walkout, but even unsuccessful moments of sabotage and activism highlight how viewers can take advantage of the unscripted format to insert their input in the dramatic action in ways that pit viewers against the show's producers.[8] While these are exceptions to the much more common participatory actions endorsed by the industry, the unscripted nature of reality television highlights how the industry can never truly capture viewers' diverse opinions and actions via the crude quantitative measures of ratings to construct convenient audience categories.

The Limits of Economic Logic

Chapters 1 and 2 outline the commercial system of television through the three exchanges of programming, advertising, and audiences. Even though there is no doubt that reality television, like all commercially produced and distributed television, would not exist in its current form were it not for this economic system, it would be a mistake to view this economic logic as overly deterministic—other key facets of television help shape what we see and how we experience the medium in ways not directly determined by the market. What aspects of reality television escape our perception if we view the phenomenon in only economic terms, and how does this case study point to the broader limits of economic logic for television as a whole?

Certainly one of the key features of reality television is that it constructs a vision of the "real world" that is highly selective and distorted. If outsiders were to try to characterize America based solely on its reality television, how would they view the country? Reality television represents an America filled with highly attractive young adults who are obsessed with competition, greed, and consumerism to the point that they will eat bugs or marry strangers to win, with few ethical hurdles standing in the way of success in business (*The Apprentice*), fashion (*America's Next Top Model*), or survival (*Survivor*). Ethnically, reality television portrays an America that is more white than the country's actual demographics, with occasional African-Americans adding diversity, but almost no other racial groups even close to representing their share of the country's population. Reality television also offers a more accepting view of homosexuality than commonly held among Americans, with straight men embracing gay culture on *Queer Eye for the Straight Guy* or a married gay couple winning *The Amazing Race* to widespread acceptance among their competitors. We need to consider such questions of representation as addressed in chapter 8 to understand what meanings reality television offers and how those meanings shape our perceptions of the "real world."

However, it would be a major mistake to assume that if meanings are present in a program, viewers must automatically adopt them. Just because a program offers a particular vision of the world does not guarantee that viewers will agree with that vision—in fact, most of us actively engage with programming, accepting some ideas, rejecting others, and even making our own meanings, which may not be evident to another viewer. As chapter 9 suggests, viewers engage with programming in ways outside of industrial control—whether through sabotaging *Big Brother* or creating fan websites celebrating reality contestants. Many critics mistakenly assume that viewers simply adopt the meanings presented on the face of a program—in the case of reality television, the genre is often condemned for celebrating greed and dishonesty with the assumption that viewers watching these programs embrace and wish to emulate such behaviors. But for many fans of reality television, these behaviors are mocked, not celebrated—for instance, the cutthroat techniques, pithy slogans, and often random results of *The Apprentice* may be viewed as an unintended satirical indictment of contemporary business ideals, not simply a celebration of Donald Trump's excessive wealth. Do viewers of *Fear Factor* necessarily view the show's disgusting and dangerous stunts as laudable, or might many people watch the show to mock contestants for performing public acts of self-humiliation? We cannot judge how meanings are received by viewers simply by the programs themselves or by the industry's intention in airing them. Instead we must view the multiple ways viewers incorporate television programming into their everyday lives.

The economic logic explored in these chapters focuses on television as first and foremost a commercial machine driven by profit motives. Certainly this view is often accurate, but it has notable limits. As discussed throughout, the television industry falls short of the ideals of a free market economy in a number of ways. Concentration within the television industry stifles competition, minimizing the effectiveness of market logic to guide central economic relationships—monopolization of cable markets leads to unresponsive pricing, vertical integration leads networks to prioritize their own productions, cable MSOs provide privileged accessed for the channels for which they have an ownership share, and so forth. The exchange that most resembles a free market economy is the advertising exchange, as agencies and distributors set prices and purchase

FEAR FACTOR

Fear Factor (NBC, 2001–06): One of the more sensationalistic and criticized reality shows, *Fear Factor* forces contestants to undertake risky and repellant tasks, such as eating live cockroaches or jumping out of a helicopter, to earn a cash prize.

slots primarily in response to supply and demand. However, the benchmark that is used to measure the desirability of time slots for ads is unresponsive to market forces—the vast majority of viewers have virtually no say in expressing their demands and viewing preferences, as ratings create a symbolic measure of viewing that accounts for the practices of only a tiny sliver of television households. Thus to argue, as many do, that commercial television simply follows market pressures is to ignore the numerous gaps in the system in which open competition and supply-and-demand pressures simply do not exist.

Even when television does follow market logic, such economic analysis cannot fully account for the broader range of practices and meanings tied to television creation and viewing. Most creators of television do not enter the industry to make money, as the creative side of the industry is highly risky and unlikely to produce wealth. Creators typically enter the television industry because they have talents to share, messages to convey, and stories to tell. Likewise, even though industry executives are motivated primarily by profit, often their personal tastes and interests can run counter to strict economic logic, as with Fox's three-season commitment to *Arrested Development* despite poor ratings. These goals and actions cannot be accounted for solely by strict market logic, as many creators and producers work within the medium seeking more than monetary rewards. Reality television certainly was born of a desire to make hit programming that could efficiently serve the goals of advertisers and distributors, but particular programs have additional motivations beyond profit, such as the mainstreaming of gay representations on *Queer Eye*, the racial experiment of *Black White*, or the social exposé of the reality documentary *30 Days*. The market model is invaluable as a partial explanation for what appears on television, but it is too narrow to account for all programming and strategies of the television industry.

Another economic perspective is overtly critical in its analysis of the commercial industry, viewing the medium as a tool of commodification that treats viewers as goods to be bought and sold. This perspective, often termed **political economy** among American media researchers, questions the social and political impacts of the commercial television industry. A political economy perspective argues that there are social and political costs incurred by commercial television: American society is awash in hypercommercialism, as every product, experience,

ARRESTED DEVELOPMENT

Arrested Development (Fox, 2003–06): An innovative cult sitcom that struggled in ratings but was beloved by critics, *Arrested Development* pushed the norms for television comedy with complex serialized plotting, fast-paced editing, and sexual innuendo. Although it was never a broadcast hit, the show generated enough of a cult following on DVD that a feature film version is in the works as of 2008.

lifestyle, and choice is surrounded by advertising and marketing muscle, leaving little terrain untouched. For political economists, by participating in this system as viewers, we turn ourselves into products to be sold to advertisers, treated as market segments more than individuals or communities. In reality television, this hypercommericialism is pervasive through product integration and the consumerist values embedded within many reality shows.

Although a political economy critique is a useful corrective to the celebratory rhetoric of competition and choice often offered by the industry, it has its limits in explaining how television can transcend economic motives and practices. Political economy has a hard time accounting for the legitimate pleasures involved in consuming television and the creative goals of producers—if all television were simply a process of commodification, why would anyone submit to such a system and gain pleasure from watching television? A political economy critique tends to treat all programming as equal in its meanings and impact, and assumes that viewers take in messages without much deliberation or resistance. There is no doubt that the economic system of television does encourage safe formulas over creative risks, consumerist affirmations rather than social debate. But we need to understand how even a program with clear economic origins, such as *All in the Family* or *M*A*S*H*, can offer creative innovations and engaging viewer experiences beyond the commodity exchanges that structure the industry.

It would be a stretch to view reality television primarily as a vehicle for social uplift or creative expression, but it is just as extreme to view it solely as a tool for profitability and consumerist degradation. For many observers of and participants in the television industry, economic forces are the central and overriding fuel to explain how American television works, generating programming decisions, impacting viewers, framing public interests, and setting technological norms. Understanding the machinery for profit and critiquing commodification are two useful complementary perspectives on television, but they are limited in how they better our full understanding of the medium. Economic arguments need to be supplemented with cultural, social, political, and aesthetic analyses, as presented throughout the rest of this book. One key alternative to the commercial drive of television is discussed in the next chapter: television as a democratic institution used to promote the public interest and citizenship.

FURTHER READING

Many books on television advertising are focused more on "how-to" goals, but a few provide more historical and critical perspectives. Stuart Ewen, *Captains of Consciousness: Advertising and the Social Roots of the Consumer Culture* (New York: Basic Books, 2001), and Michael Schudson, *Advertising, the Uneasy Persuasion: Its Dubious Impact on American Society* (New York: Basic Books, 1984), both offer important critical analysis of American advertising industries. Joseph Turow, *Breaking Up America: Advertisers and the New Media World* (Chicago: University of Chicago Press, 1997), and Matthew P. McAllister, *The Commercialization of American Culture: New Advertising, Control, and Democracy* (Thousand Oaks, Calif.: Sage Publications, 1996), focus on market segmentation and media integration, and their impact on advertising.

An important exploration of ratings and concepts of audiences versus viewers can be found in Ien Ang, *Desperately Seeking the Audience* (New York: Routledge, 1990). Philip M. Napoli, *Audience Economics: Media Institutions and the Audience Marketplace* (New York: Columbia University Press, 2003), offers a more economically focused perspective on the audience exchange; while Eileen R. Meehan, *Why TV Is Not Our Fault: Television Programming, Viewers, and Who's Really in Control* (Lanham, Md.: Rowman & Littlefield, 2005), argues from a highly critical perspective against the logic of ratings.

Reality television has been explored by a number of recent books—the best range of coverage is in Susan Murray and Laurie Ouellette, eds., *Reality TV: Remaking Television Culture*, 2nd ed. (New York: New York University Press, 2008); while Annette Hill, *Reality TV: Factual Entertainment and Television Audiences* (London: Routledge, 2005), offers a viewer-centered account of the genre. For a strong representative of the political economy approach to media, see Robert Waterman McChesney, *The Problem of the Media: U.S. Communication Politics in the Twenty-first Century* (New York: Monthly Review Press, 2004); David Hesmondhalgh, *The Cultural Industries*, 2nd ed. (Los Angeles: SAGE, 2007), offers a clear critique of the limits of that approach.

NOTES

[1]Cy Schneider, *Children's Television: The Art, the Business, and How It Works* (Chicago: NTC Business Books, 1987), 19.

[2]See James Twitchell, *Adcult USA: The Triumph of Advertising in American Culture* (New York: Columbia University Press, 1996).

[3]Ron Becker, *Gay TV and Straight America* (New Brunswick, N.J.: Rutgers University Press, 2006).

[4]Steve Rendall, "The Ratings Mirage," *Extra!*, April 2004, http://www.fair.org/index.php?page=2005.

[5]Gitlin, *Inside Prime Time* , offers a detailed account of this example. See also Mark Alvey, " 'Too Many Kids and Old Ladies': Quality Demographics and 1960s U.S. Television," in *Television: The Critical View*, ed. Horace Newcomb, 7th ed. (New York: Oxford University Press, 2007), 15–36, for a more nuanced discussion of this history.

[6]See Jeffrey S. Miller, *Something Completely Different: British Television and American Culture* (Minneapolis: University of Minnesota Press, 2000), for an account of such adaptations.

[7]See Susan Murray and Laurie Ouellette, eds., *Reality TV: Remaking Television Culture* (New York: New York University Press, 2008), especially chapter 7, for more on the economics of reality television.

[8]See Ernest Mathijs and Janet Jones, eds., Big Brother *International* (London: Wallflower Press, 2004).

CHAPTER 3

SERVING THE PUBLIC INTEREST

The previous two chapters present television as an industry designed to benefit private interests: media corporations, advertisers, marketing consultants, and television producers. This is the dominant way television is understood within the United States, and its function as a privately owned profit-making industry drives nearly every aspect of the medium. For most Americans who have never known any other system of television, the commercial essence of television may seem natural and inevitable, but the American system is actually quite unique, an exception to the model that most other nations use to structure television. Most countries follow a model of public service broadcasting (PSB), where television is run by public nonprofit institutions or the government, designed to serve public interests of citizenship, education, and cultural enrichment. This approach to broadcasting, typified by the British Broadcasting Corporation (BBC), has remained central in most countries even as commercial broadcasters and cable and satellite channels have challenged public service broadcasting through the growing reach of transnational corporations and conglomerates.

In the United States, the public service role of broadcasting has typically been marginalized, as commercial broadcasters assert that they are able to serve public interests while still making a profit. Yet television still serves a crucial role in defining American democracy, engaging and informing its citizens, and shaping national culture. Public broadcasting and noncommercial television alternatives perform some of these roles, while others are addressed by commercial news and public affairs programming. This chapter explores the public service roles of American television, examining the ways in which the medium intersects with governance and regulation, in an effort to chart out how we might consider television a facet of American democracy and judge its successes and failures.

REGULATING THE AIRWAVES: TELEVISION AND THE FCC

For many policymakers and critics, the term **regulation** is a red flag, suggesting government intervention into free market capitalism; such critics often celebrate **deregulation** as the way for markets to flourish without governmental mandates or restrictions. Certainly this distinction between regulation and deregulation has been crucial within the history of television, as calls to regulate or deregulate broadcasting have been offered by politicians and activists hoping to reshape television to fit differing visions of the ideal role for the country's central communication medium. Various pro-regulation advocates have campaigned for stricter policies on indecent content, balanced political coverage, or local corporate control, while deregulatory critics argue that all of these concerns would be better served by less rather than more government intervention. At its most extreme, calls for deregulation echo 1980s FCC chair Mark Fowler, who wanted to see communications technologies regulated no more than any other manufactured device, memorably calling television just a "toaster with pictures."

However, framing government's role in broadcasting within the binary of regulation and deregulation is a mistake—the distinctive properties of television as a medium require some form of regulation in order for television to function as either an industry or public service. If there were no governmental controls over broadcasting, anyone could set up a transmitter to broadcast television or could jam another station's reception via high-power signals flooding across the country, leading to a chaotic clutter of transmissions that could effectively make over-the-air broadcasting and satellite service impossible. Regulation is what allows cable companies to charge for their services, as without such laws anyone could run a line from another person's apartment or house to receive cable free of charge. Without regulations, companies would lack the exclusive rights to distribute a program—anyone could make copies of programming and redistribute it without permission from or payment to the creators. In other words, regulations set the ground rules for private media companies to do business and make profits: complete deregulation would be quite bad for the business interests who typically promote the term *deregulation*.

In trying to understand the roles of government policies and laws in American broadcasting, we should avoid thinking of regulation in opposition to deregulation, as full deregulation is not an option. Rather, we should consider what types of regulations serve what ends, and how any regulatory system favors particular interests over others. Deregulatory advocates such as Fowler are really pushing for certain regulations to remain in place while others are lifted, in a combination that best serves private broadcasting corporations. The real debate is between the competing forces of private and public interests, contrasting the commercial goals of industry with the potentially democratic goals of citizenship and access to the airwaves.

Public Airwaves and Competing Interests

In the United States, the chief agency regulating and overseeing television is the **Federal Communications Commission** (FCC). As with many aspects of television, the medium's regulatory framework was inherited from radio. In the 1910s, the new medium of radio was largely unregulated, with amateur broadcasters using the technology in a variety of ways independent of corporate and governmental interests; the airwaves themselves were seen as a common public resource, not owned or controlled by any user or institution. Yet in the late 1920s, the government responded to growing concerns that a cluttered spectrum of radio signals was competing for reception to the point that interest in the new medium was declining. Therefore, in 1927, the government created the Federal Radio Commission—an agency that in 1934 would become the FCC—in order to regulate the airwaves via a licensing system that is essentially still in place today.

The core responsibility of the FCC is to issue **broadcast licenses** to radio and television stations, providing them exclusive rights to use the public airwaves to transmit signals at a particular frequency and power. The airwaves remain a public common resource, although private broadcasters are granted rights as **trustees** to use their allocated airwaves at no cost for a limited time— today's licenses last eight years before broadcasters must apply for renewal, again at no cost. Throughout the creation of the legislation forming this system in the 1920s and 1930s, nothing explicitly mandated or suggested that licenses should be used for commercial goals, and the free licensure can be seen as leveling the playing field to allow nonprofit and noncommercial broadcasters equal access to the airwaves without needing to pay a steep price. However, the FRC and later the FCC granted licenses for the most valuable range of the radio spectrum to commercial broadcasters, on frequencies with stronger signals and geographic reach; early licensing decisions regularly privileged commercial stations with ties to the growing national networks NBC and CBS over nonprofit or independent requests. The effect of this preferential licensing process was to create commercial broadcasting as the default national system—nonprofit and noncommercial broadcasting accounted for approximately half of radio stations in the mid-1920s, but shrunk down to an ignored and often absent role in most regions by the mid-1930s.[1]

How did corporate commercial stations gain such an advantage over non-commercial broadcasters in the FCC's licensing process? The primary rationale used by the FCC to decide whether to grant, renew, or deny a license was, and still is, how the station serves the "public interest, convenience, and necessity," a provision written into the laws authorizing broadcast regulation. Often abbreviated as the **PICAN standard**, this guideline mandating that broadcasters serve the public interest is purposefully vague, not stipulating exactly how radio or television broadcasters should best meet public interests. The public service broadcasting systems emerging in Britain and Canada in the 1920s and 1930s offered one model for defining the public interest: educating and informing citizens for democratic participation, while offering cultural enrichment and diversity in programming to serve all audiences, including minority and specialized interests outside the majority taste. Under this definition, public interest is defined as the "public good," to be determined by the policymakers guiding institutions such as the BBC; this model has been critiqued by many skeptics, both from within PSB countries and from those with more commercial models, for fostering an elitist cultural role for broadcasting, and ignoring the tastes and desires of viewers who might disagree with official definitions of a common public good.

The American broadcasting model has regarded the concept of the "public interest" in quite different terms than public service broadcasters. Under fierce pressure from the commercial media's trade organization, the **National Association of Broadcasters** (NAB), the FCC, in the 1930s, embraced a definition of public interest as "that which interests the public." According to commercial broadcasters, listeners and viewers define their own best interests, and a profit-driven commercial system allegedly maximizes such interests by rewarding popular programming and services through increased advertising revenue. This model, tied to the myth that broadcast ratings function as a democracy, discussed in chapter 2, overturns the claims of elitism tied to public service broadcasting by conceiving radio, and later television, as corporate-facilitated populism, reflecting consumer interests and tastes through free-market ideals. While the FCC has never formally endorsed this commercialized notion of the public interest, the majority of the agency's policy decisions and license renewals, well as the frequent practice of FCC commissioners serving in lucrative executive positions within commercial broadcasting after leaving the FCC, all are evidence that the dominant definition of the public interest in American broadcasting regulation fits well with the interests of private media corporations over a broader notion of the public good.

This commercialized notion of the public interest is not simply the product of effective lobbying or FCC commissioners wishing to secure future employment with media corporations. One explanation for why the commercial American system emerged and has remained in place without much protest is because it fits with commonly held American ideals about the role of corporations, government, and public resources. Traditionally, American political thought has been grounded in liberalism, a belief in protecting individual rights and freedoms over shared group interests—liberalist thinking guided the Bill of Rights, and defined government's primary role as protecting individual rights and property, rather than administering common social goods or collective rights. Classic liberal economics encouraged small businesses as stimulating competition and entrepreneurship, and thus large corporations and centralized governments were often seen as an enemy to liberal individual rights and a thriving economy. In the early twentieth century, a revised philosophy emerged to address shifting ideas toward big business and government—this model of **corporate liberalism** redefines the federal government and corporations as cooperative facilitators of traditional liberal ideals, rather than their enemies. As corporate liberalism emerged as a model for balancing the competing interests of business, government, and individuals, it functioned as more than a political or economic theory, but seeped into public consciousness as an appropriate way to conceive of American society and economics.

The emergence of American commercial broadcasting followed many concepts tied to corporate liberalism. In this model, major corporations such as NBC and CBS worked collaboratively with the federal government to set policies and regulatory structures over the airwaves, an approach consistent with corporate liberal ideals for private administration of public resources. This partnership between corporations and governments was seen by many in the 1920s as the most effective way to stimulate the economy and serve the public, meeting the nation's needs through the mechanisms of the economic market. Corporate liberalism embraced the belief that for-profit corporations are more effective at administrating bureaucratic and technological systems than nonprofits or governments—a nationally endorsed and subsidized public authority comparable to the BBC was seen as less appropriate and efficient for managing a broadcast network than corporations such as NBC, and thus private corporate control was assumed to be the default system appropriate for an industry and technology as complex as broadcasting. The role of the public under corporate liberalism is primarily as consumers, fitting into the economic system by benefiting from its products and services. Thus the idea that "the public interest is what interests the public" was completely consistent with broadly circulating and widely held ideals of the cultural moment when the FCC set the stage for corporate dominance of public airwaves. While there was certainly substantial resistance to this model of broadcasting by some, the majority of Americans following the debates seemed content with entrusting the stewardship of public resources to the private profit-seeking hands of broadcasters.[2]

In issuing and renewing broadcast licenses, the FCC focuses its regulatory authority on local television stations, not national networks—as discussed in chapter 1, networks contract with local stations as affiliates, providing programming to be broadcast to the station's region over the frequency licensed by the FCC. But the FCC is able to influence and pressure network policies in a few indirect ways. Since affiliates are dependent on their broadcast licenses to stay in business, the FCC can threaten affiliates with fines or turning down renewal applications if they believe they have not been serving the public interest, and affiliates often put pressure on networks to shape programming and scheduling choices to meet their local needs. More directly, networks each own some of their affiliates, the O&Os discussed in chapter 1, and thus the FCC regulates the transmission of the networks' broadcasting system through licensing these network-owned stations.

Licensing television stations came to the forefront in recent years with the emergence of digital television systems. In the 1990s, Congress and the FCC developed a process to migrate television broadcasting from the analog system in place since the medium's origins to a digital broadcasting model, a technological development discussed more in chapter 11. For many activists and critics of the American broadcast system, the shift to digital was seen as a potential opportunity to correct the system, increasing opportunities for more public involvement, and to reverse the tides of commercialism and market concentration typifying television. However, the **Telecommunications Act of 1996, the largest revision to American media policy since the 1930s, allocated digital channels to existing television stations at no cost and with no opportunity for debate or competition.** The effect of this legislation and FCC policymaking is to keep the long-established model of national network commercial broadcasting in place, with minimal competition from outsiders or alternatives coming from nonprofit or noncommercial organizations. Additionally, many have criticized the government for giving away the rights to a huge spectrum of the airwaves, valued at the time at $70 billion, as a subsidy to the commercial broadcasting industry—in comparison, the FCC auctions off licenses to wireless telephone companies for millions of dollars.

While the FCC has often been critiqued as a "toothless watchdog" in its lack of firm oversight of broadcasters meeting public interest requirements, there are moments when the FCC has been more hands-on in encouraging particular policies and corporate behaviors. In the late 1940s, the commission published specific public interest guidelines for radio and early television broadcasters in a report nicknamed The Blue Book. These well-publicized guidelines—including a reduction in advertising time, increased airing of locally originating programming, and the inclusion of minority perspectives—were never formally endorsed as policies or used as standards for issuing licenses or renewals. While numerous FCC commissioners have pushed for holding broadcasters to higher standards, television licenses have virtually never been revoked or denied renewal based explicitly on a station's failure to meet the public interest; most FCC statements about public interest obligations function as threats for potential scrutiny or fines, rather than enacted policies that result in loss of licenses. Some FCC actions concerning educational television, discussed more in chapter 10, have asserted a more active role in maintaining the public interest in the name of serving children as a "special" type of audience.

One of the most noteworthy moments in the history of broadcast regulation was FCC chair Newton Minow's speech "Television and the Public Interest," delivered to the annual NAB convention in 1961. FCC chairs typically delivered encouraging and appreciative remarks to the NAB, but Minow, who had only recently been appointed by President Kennedy, gave a bitingly critical speech condemning the quality of television as a "vast wasteland" and challenging broadcasters to drastically improve the state of the medium through increased diversity and choices in programming. Explicitly rejecting the argument that the public interest was what interested the public, he implored broadcasters, "It is not enough to cater to the nation's whims; you must also serve the nation's needs." No formal regulations or license challenges followed, but Minow's attack on television programming, especially its weak coverage of public affairs, escapist tendencies in entertainment, and overly commercialized address toward children, put the industry on guard and stimulated some additional attention to educational, documentary, and social issue programming.

A decade later, a more direct FCC regulation challenged network domination of television, looking to improve the amount and quality of locally produced programming that might serve public interests ignored by the national network oligopoly. Along with the Fin-Syn rules discussed in chapter 1, the FCC passed the **Prime Time Access Rule** (PTAR) in 1970, mandating that stations could broadcast no more than three hours each night (except Sunday) of network programming or off-network reruns. PTAR and Fin-Syn both encouraged independent producers and local stations to produce programming that offered something distinct from well-established network routines and formulas. While Fin-Syn effectively led to a robust independent production market in the 1970s, PTAR did little to stimulate locally centered programming; instead of local production, stations filled the "access hour" (7:00–8:00 P.M. on the coasts) with first-run syndicated game shows and tabloid news shows such as *Entertainment Tonight*. The FCC eliminated the rule in 1995 due to the perceived weakening of network control in the multi-channel era, although networks have not reclaimed the access hour for national programming, with affiliates airing syndicated programming, both first-run and off-network, before networks begin scheduling at 8:00 P.M. on the coasts.

The PTAR and Fin-Syn policies point to one of the ways the FCC has traditionally been most active in regulating broadcasting: restricting the concentration of ownership and industry control by trying to encourage competition. In issuing or renewing broadcast licenses, the FCC examines what other licenses a company holds to avoid overconcentration within the industry and encourage diversity of ownership. The standards for restricting concentration have shifted since the beginning of television—initially, no company could own more than seven stations, and firm restrictions on **duopolies** banned a company from owning more than one station within a single market or **cross-ownership** of a newspaper and television station in the same region. These restrictions have loosened since the 1980s, with a cap in place limiting a single company from owning stations reaching more than 35 percent of American television households and loosening the duopoly ban for major cities in the 1996 Telecommunications Act. The expansion of ownership limits has led to more consolidation within the industry, with networks such as Fox and CBS and large station groups such as Sinclair and Hearst each owning more than thirty stations, including multiple stations in a single market. Advocates of this reduction in ownership regulation suggest that the rise of cable competition in the multi-channel era provided the increased diversity and market competition that ownership caps were meant to encourage, although it is important to note that many cable channels are also owned by the same media conglomerates dominating local station control.

These debates over media consolidation and concentration came to a head in 2003—the FCC proposed further loosening of the ownership cap to 45 percent of the television market, eliminating cross-ownership bans, and relaxing the duopoly rule to allow one company to own two stations in all markets, and up to three in the largest cities. Unlike most media regulation measures, which receive little press or public engagement, the 2003 revisions generated an outcry among many activists, flooded the FCC email servers with complaints, and forged a coalition of groups protesting the policies across the political spectrum, from liberal advocacy organization MoveOn.org and consumer rights groups to the right-leaning National Rifle Association and conservative churches. The FCC passed the controversial policies with a split vote of commissioners, but following unprecedented public outcry, Congress intervened to roll back the regulation; the courts subsequently overturned most of the FCC provisions, requiring the commission to devise a clearer rationale for the policies. While the difference between 35 percent and 45 percent of audience share does not noticeably change the landscape for concentration and competition, a lesson of the 2003 actions was that the American public had grown more active and engaged in media policy, unwilling to allow the FCC to set the terms following the industry lobby without significant public involvement and oversight.[3]

Although the American public had never been so engaged with media policy before 2003, a landmark case decades earlier highlights the social importance of broadcast regulation and public interest. In the height of the civil rights movement in the late 1950s and 1960s, television station WLBT in Jackson, Mississippi, followed editorial policies practiced by a number of southern broadcasters—they produced and aired pro-segregationist programming, blacked out network news or documentaries highlighting civil rights protests, and even preempted network programs featuring African-American performers, such as NBC's *The Nat King Cole Show*. The Jackson chapter of the NAACP and local churches challenged WLBT's license to the FCC, which repeatedly ruled in favor of renewing and maintaining its license for over a decade. It took an appeal to the courts by the NAACP to require the FCC to punish WLBT's owners, finally transferring control of their license to new owners in 1971. The case established an important precedent that the viewers of a station have legal standing to challenge a broadcasting license to the FCC, formally highlighting the public's role in the process of television broadcasting as more than just passive consumers. While no other broadcaster has become involved in such a contentious struggle over its public interest obligations, the WLBT case stands as a testament to how important a television station can become in a community to represent a powerful perspective on the world.

This discussion of licensing and public interest requirements applies only directly to broadcast television, as cable and satellite services do not require broadcast licenses and thus are regulated differently. The cable and satellite industries face some specific technical regulations, such as guidelines for satellite signals and cable system architecture, and must follow laws and regulations concerning all American industries, such as antitrust and labor laws. The FCC does regulate wired communications systems, including telephone and cable television, but the regulatory system focuses on cable systems as transmission companies, rather than the cable channels providing programming; such regulations include the "must-carry" and retransmission policies discussed in chapter 1. Cable systems typically negotiate with local and state governments to create franchise agreements allowing use of public resources to string cable wires, often in exchange for supporting local public, educational, and governmental programming, as discussed later in this chapter. But both cable and satellite systems face fewer direct regulations on content and public interest service than broadcasters, leading many broadcast stations to complain of undue burdens from the FCC, a claim that seems quite questionable given the FCC's typical lack of enforcement of public interest mandates.

Regulating Content

The FCC's regulatory authority focuses on the structure and system of broadcasting, and is concerned with issues of licensure and ownership. But for most people, government regulation of broadcasting raises thoughts of **censorship**, prohibiting what can be presented on television. The FCC is specifically forbidden from acting as a prohibitive censor, with federal law explicitly placing broadcasting within the realm of free speech. However, censorship can be understood more broadly than just prohibitions on speech; we can look at a wider notion of **content regulation** that helps shape what is allowed and encouraged on television versus material that is discouraged or punished. Through the concept of content regulation, we can see how the FCC and the television industry create guidelines and limits on acceptable content, developing important cultural norms without explicit prohibitive censorship.

Neither the FCC nor any other governmental agency acts as a proactive content regulator, as material cannot be submitted for approval before broadcast, nor will the government monitor broadcasts for unlawful content. Instead, the FCC serves as a reactive content regulator: anyone can file a complaint with the FCC about content found to be objectionable, and the FCC investigates and judges received complaints. If the FCC rules that a broadcaster has violated its standards for appropriate use of the airwaves, the commission will typically issue a fine against that broadcaster. Fines range from a low of $7,000 to a high of $325,000 for each incident on a station, and thus a network program can generate millions of dollars in total fines levied against each of its local affiliates. Fining television broadcasters has increased significantly in the wake of the 2004 Super Bowl broadcast discussed in this book's introduction. The FCC issued only two citations against television broadcasts in the ten years before 2004, while there have been more than ten since the Janet Jackson incident, along with a tremendous increase in the number of complaints filed with the FCC, most of which are coordinated by conservative interest groups such as Focus on the Family and Parents Television Council.

While the FCC maintains no explicit list of content that might trigger a fine, the commission is charged with regulating three main content categories: obscene, indecent, and profane content. Obscenity is considered sexual content appealing solely to "prurient interests," with no legitimate social value, a category the Supreme Court has ruled applies to hardcore pornography and is exempt from First Amendment protections. It is illegal to broadcast or transmit obscene content, whether by over-the-air, cable, or satellite systems, and doing so can result in both FCC fines and criminal prosecution. Thus even explicitly adult programming offered by subscription or pay-per-view cable services such as The Playboy Channel or Spice can feature only "softcore" pornography to avoid potential obscenity prosecution, although the boundaries between hardcore and softcore pornography are somewhat fluid and open to judicial interpretation and specific community standards.

The more common category of FCC content regulation is indecency, a concept referring to material that "depicts or describes, in terms patently offensive as measured by contemporary community standards for the broadcast medium, sexual or excretory organs or activities."[4] Clearly there is a great margin for judgment here, as the FCC must examine any complaint to assess what "patently offensive" might mean in the context of a particular set of community standards. Indecent expression is protected by the First Amendment, but can be limited by FCC regulations such as the safe harbor—the period between

6:00 A.M. and 10:00 P.M., during which there are potential child viewers—while allowing indecent broadcasts in the late night and overnight hours. In practice, broadcasters rarely broadcast indecent material even during the permitted late-night hours, as showing explicit sex and nudity over the airwaves would certainly create a public relations backlash with viewers and sponsors. Cable channels, especially premium channels, often feature potentially indecent content, but the FCC has refrained from issuing fines to cable, citing the optional nature of cable subscriptions and the legal gray area as to whether the FCC has the authority to directly regulate cable content.

The third category of regulated content is **profanity**, or language deemed sufficiently offensive to be regarded as a nuisance. Like indecency, profanity is regulated following safe harbor policies, although fines are rarely issued for passing profanity in broadcasts. The key regulatory precedent on profanity stems from a 1970s court case against a radio station broadcasting comedian George Carlin's routine about the "seven dirty words you can't say on television." Although Carlin's list of words was not drawn from FCC policy, the routine did effectively set the parameters for what language was deemed profane and thus disallowed during daytime hours. In the wake of the 2004 Super Bowl incident, the FCC increased its punishment of both indecency and profanity complaints, although a 2007 court decision ruled that the FCC had overstepped its authority by fining broadcasters for "fleeting expletives" spoken in a live awards show, asserting that profanity must be frequent and repeated to warrant punishment; this decision is under appeal at the time of this writing. But even in its more activist mode of the mid-2000s, the FCC issues relatively few citations and fines over content, leaving most of the decisions over appropriate content to private broadcasters and their customers, as both advertisers and viewers can reject programming they feel is inappropriate.

FCC content regulations help shape broadcaster decisions over what to schedule and produce, leading to an array of self-censoring practices by networks, stations, and cable channels. As discussed in chapter 1, all networks and channels have an internal standards-and-practices division to review content and recommend changes to prevent the airing of material that might draw FCC action, consumer complaint, or advertiser backlash. Self-regulatory standards-and-practices decisions impact both the production processes before programs are aired and the reediting or overdubbing of purchased programming, especially theatrical films or foreign imports. In the classic network era, the NAB created a broadcasting code containing guidelines with specific content regulations for member stations; since the mid-1970s, the NAB code has been replaced by individual network or channel policies rather than an industry-wide set of standards. The television industry usually takes a proactive stance concerning potentially indecent or profane content, as it wishes to avoid outside regulation or bad public relations. However, programmers will occasionally seek to push boundaries of previous content norms to generate publicity, appeal to new audiences, or spice up a stale genre or program, as with *All in the Family*'s taboo-busting content in the 1970s or *NYPD Blue*'s incorporation of mild nudity and profanity in the 1990s. The television industry often manages a careful balancing act between alienating or angering some viewers, sponsors, and regulators, and appealing to new audiences through innovative and groundbreaking programming, with such risks often coming from less established sources such as Fox in the 1980s or cable channels in the 1990s.

Another mode of content regulation involves a partnership between the television industry and the FCC. After threats of increased governmental content regulation in the mid-1990s, the television industry created a set of **parental guidelines** or content ratings (not to be confused with Nielsen ratings) to categorize the content of programming based on its appropriate audience and type of content. The ratings, including TV-Y for youth, TV-PG for parental guidance, and TV-M for mature, are modeled after the film industry rating system, although they include greater specific labeling of potentially objectionable content, such as V for violence, S for sexual situations, and L for language. Producers, networks, and channels self-designate each program's label based on a shared list of guidelines overseen by an industry-sponsored review board. The FCC mandates that televisions manufactured since 2000 contain the **V-Chip** technology, which allows viewers to block programming based on rating categories. Additionally, various systems such as DBS satellite receivers, cable boxes, and DVRs contain parental locks to prevent access to programs deemed unsuitable for children. Although this ratings system is designed to balance broadcaster freedom with increased viewer control, critics have suggested that the networks and channels do not always apply ratings consistently or accurately, raising skepticism about the effectiveness of such a self-regulated model.

Although television's content regulation concerns primarily material viewed as potentially harmful to minors, such as sexual images and profanity, other, less sensational facets of content are regulated. As discussed in chapter 2, the Federal Trade Commission prohibits false claims in advertising, and television broadcasts are subject to libel laws banning slanderous representations. Equal-time policies mandate that any airtime received by one political candidate must be offered to competitors—a policy with unusual ramifications when Arnold Schwarzenegger ran for governor of California, as his films could not be shown on California television without allowing other candidates hours of free airtime. Similarly, actor Fred Thompson's bid for the Republican presidential nomination in 2008 complicated the status of *Law & Order* reruns featuring Thompson; NBC decided not to air any reruns over broadcast stations, but TNT continued showing episodes featuring the actor, arguing that equal time mandates apply only to over-the-air broadcasters, not cable channels.

One of the most controversial examples of content regulation was the FCC policy known as the **fairness doctrine**. Starting in the 1940s, the FCC ruled that broadcasters, as public trustees, must avoid broadcasts presenting singular perspectives on controversial issues. To allow stations the ability to present programming with an editorial perspective, the FCC ruled that broadcasters needed to schedule airtime for contrasting opinions and positions. As part of the deregulatory actions of the FCC in the 1980s, the fairness doctrine was eliminated; Congress subsequently attempted to pass laws mandating the policy to the FCC, but were vetoed by both presidents Reagan and Bush, and some lawmakers continue to push for a return of the policy into the 2000s. The most notable effect of the elimination of the fairness doctrine was on radio, as the allowance of unbalanced editorializing enabled the rise of conservative talk radio in the 1990s.

What are the implications and impacts of the fairness doctrine and its elimination? On the one hand, the logic of requiring broadcasters to use the public airwaves to present a range of perspectives is a noble idea, working to avoid the dominance of one position on key public issues. But the effect of the fairness doctrine was to discourage explicit editorializing by broadcasters, even decreasing journalistic attention to potentially controversial issues for fear of FCC reprisals—thus the doctrine arguably led to broadcasting fewer perspectives on issues rather than more. Additionally, the logic of treating issues as two-sided can be overly simplistic, as most complex topics have more than just two competing perspectives, and often some positions on issues might have more factual merit than others that must be presented for the sake of "balance." For instance, someone could contend that a television documentary on global warming would need to give equal time to arguments that the phenomenon is not the result of human activities, despite the overwhelming consensus of the scientific community. While today journalists claim to have internalized the goals of fairness and balance through their reporting, many critics have argued that without explicit mandates for multiple perspectives, broadcast journalism has lost its effectiveness in informing and educating American citizens. These issues of fairness and objectivity will be returned to in the next chapter within the broader context of television journalism.

Copyrighting Programming

Most regulations of television are overseen by the FCC, which serves as the guardian of the public interest while facilitating private control of the airwaves. But one key aspect of governmental regulation outside of the FCC's scope helps shape television and allows private interests to profit from broadcasting and cable systems: copyright. While copyright policies are so widespread and broadly followed as not to be commonly regarded as an explicit regulation, it is crucial to understand how copyright impacts television programming and how its policies are being challenged in the era of digital convergence, potentially transforming

BATTLESTAR GALACTICA

Battlestar Galactica (ABC, 1978–79; Sci Fi, 2003–09): The original network series, a short-lived science fiction program produced after the success of *Star Wars,* retained a small cult following for decades. The recent critically acclaimed cable series reimagines the original, using the story of a human fleet on the run from a robot race to comment on contemporary political issues, such as the Iraq War and terrorism.

the entire business model of the media industries. Copyright policies are an aspect of media policy where the industries have consistently lobbied for more regulation rather than less, undercutting the assumption that regulation always harms business interests and deregulation furthers them.

Copyright policies are grounded in an explicit clause in the U.S. Constitution authorizing Congress to grant exclusive rights of a work to its creator for a limited term. These rights grew significantly in the twentieth century, notably extending the term of copyright repeatedly and expanding the purview of copyright to include derivative works and to prohibit technological means of unauthorized copying. For new television programs today, every show and episode is copyrighted by its production company for a term of ninety-five years, which grants the production company exclusive rights to license or sell the program or adaptations and excerpts of its content for almost a century. These protections effectively allow producers and distributors to offer exclusive access to programming, enabling the commercial system of television broadcasting. One important limit on copyright protection is that it protects the specific expression of an idea but not the idea itself, a legal distinction that allows for television's logic of imitation discussed in chapter 1. Hence, copyright law requires a producer to obtain the rights to remake a program such as *Battlestar Galactica* using the same title and characters, but permissions are not needed for a show such as *America's Got Talent* to mimic the basic format and concept of *American Idol*.

While rights holders have the ability to restrict access to their copyrighted material, television producers obviously want their material to be seen and consumed, not just remain under lock and key. Copyright maintains a balance between the owner's right to control the terms of how a work is consumed and the public's ability to view and make use of that work. A provision in American copyright law allows for **fair use** of copyrighted material without permission or payment, provided that such use is limited to small portions of a work, noncommercial uses, educational, critical, or satirical purposes, or other defenses against copyright litigation. Fair use is designed to be a somewhat ambiguous and flexible defense against rights holders suing users for copyright infringement, not a clear-cut set of rules to follow or avoid. Some cases are fairly straightforward—for instance, nearly every image from a television program used in this book is copied under fair use to support the book's educational and critical mission, and satirical programs such as *The Daily Show* regularly reuse news footage without permission as fair use to critique and parody the news media. Other uses are more borderline, as with a blogger embedding a clip from television news to illustrate a point about current events, or a YouTube user posting a television clip to start a conversation about the clip's content. In practice, fair use is only a defense against litigation, so most users are reluctant to risk enormous lawsuits at the hands of global corporations seeking to protect their copyrights, and thus they relent when pressured by media industries or avoid potential infringement charges altogether.

One key legal decision concerning copyright significantly shifted the future of American media. In the mid-1980s, the Supreme Court ruled in a close 5–4 decision that the use of a VCR to copy and "time-shift" a television broadcast for personal use fell under fair use provisions and thus was not an infringement of copyright. This decision, widely known as the **Betamax case**, led to the growth of the VCR technology and a broad array of video-copying and -recording possibilities, discussed in chapter 11. Not all copying practices are protected by the Betamax case, as online file-sharing and tape-trading do not constitute personal fair use, but the Betamax case allowed technology companies to create and sell devices enabling both infringing and non-infringing uses. Today, recording broadcasts, time-shifting, and the use of recorded material in classrooms or for critical commentaries are all fair uses exercised daily across America, even though the television industry has tried to push for policies to restrict such uses. Specifically, the industry has lobbied for regulations that would restrict copying of digital broadcast materials even when the user is following fair use provisions—in 2003, the FCC mandated that televisions include a system called the **broadcast flag**, which would allow broadcasters to stipulate and restrict how digital transmissions could be copied, but the policy was overturned by the courts due to the FCC overstepping its authority. As of this writing, the industry is working to lobby Congress for a similar policy to be mandated by federal law.

Copyright is one of the legal areas that reinforce the industrial consolidation and limited competition described in chapter 1. Ultimately the "products" owned by television producers are the copyrights to their programming; being able to charge for the right to broadcast and distribute programming is the chief way producers make money and participate in the industry. Rights to broadcast and use programming are typically priced at levels that make them inaccessible to competitors outside the television industry, setting the bar too high for most new entries to participate in the internal dealings of the industry, as well as favoring internal rights sharing within a corporation to create the synergy discussed in chapter 1.

Television programmers and distributors also often create reciprocal agreements for sharing footage without clearing copyrights or paying royalties—for instance, sports broadcasters and cable channels regularly allow each other to use highlights from each other's programming in a mutual exchange. However, new competitors might find it difficult to get comparable access to sports footage at the risk of encroaching on the market of established broadcasters; such protections even apply to noncommercial uses of footage, as broadcasters and sports leagues have cracked down on users posting highlights on online video sites without obtaining permission or paying royalties to broadcasters. Sports leagues, broadcasters, and home video distributors often overstate their copyright privileges—every baseball and football broadcast states that its descriptions and accounts of the game cannot be retransmitted without league consent, a legalistic claim that has little backing in copyright law, just as warnings at the beginning of most DVDs deny legal fair use rights. In general, media industries aggressively assert their copyright privileges, both in rhetoric and litigation, leading to an environment where most people assume that rights holders can dictate the terms of everyday use more than is legally guaranteed, an aspect of regulation that directly impacts fan practices, discussed more in chapter 9.

The issue of copyright and television has become more central in the digital convergence era for a number of reasons. As television programs have become more marketable, with DVDs and downloadable content, as discussed in chapter 11, the value tied to a program has shifted. In the classic network era, a television program's economic value was generated solely from transactions within the industry, between producers, distributors, advertisers, and transmitters. Although arguably a viewer watching a program via a shared VHS might result in lowered ratings and thus affect advertising revenue, the ratings system is so restricted that the vast majority of viewer behaviors had no direct impact on the industry's revenue. This changed somewhat with premium cable channels, as sharing recordings of HBO programs clearly undercuts the subscription revenue model. Today, viewers can purchase copies of programs on DVD and through video-on-demand, and can download episodes via iTunes or other services, making the potential losses of illicit copying even more tangible to rights holders. With the rise of easily accessible digital distribution technologies such as online file sharing or streaming video, the industry regards every viewer watching an illicitly obtained copy as potential lost revenue from DVD or download sales, a position put to the legal test in 2007 when Viacom sued YouTube for $1 billion for playing host to more than 150,000 allegedly infringing video clips.

The industry's crisis in digital copying corresponds to similar issues faced by the music and film industries, but television's response has been different; it has generally avoided lawsuits against users for illegal downloading. In part the television industry's comparative inaction against downloaders has been due to a wish to avoid the negative backlash that occurred with the music industry's campaign against its own customers, but it also stems from television's different business model—as discussed in chapters 1 and 2, television programming has long been seen as "free" by viewers, with the advertising exchange not resulting in direct consumer spending for television. Since VCRs and other recording technologies have allowed legal time-shifting of seemingly free content, it doesn't seem substantially different to viewers to download a missed program from a file-sharing system versus having recorded it on a DVR or viewing it on a network website. While the industry regards such downloading as illegal, the rhetoric of the music industry framing downloading as piracy or theft seems less appropriate for a television program that is already widely available at no direct cost. Thus the industry has been willing to offer free access to programming via network websites, with embedded advertising, or has allowed for low-cost downloading with greater technological simplicity than that offered by file-sharing programs, possibilities explored in more depth in chapter 11.

THE NONCOMMERCIAL ALTERNATIVE: PUBLIC TELEVISION IN AMERICA

Commercial interests dominate American television far more than any other national broadcast system, but there are noncommercial alternatives in the United States. While public alternatives have never risen to the central role that public service broadcasting serves in most other countries, public television has been an important aspect of American television for decades, providing innovations and alternatives that have influenced commercial television and generated strong commitment from many viewers. Public television has also served as the focus of heated debates over the role of the government in broadcasting, the public's identity as citizens or consumers, and the opportunities for everyday people to take part in television as a democratic medium. Although public television has always operated on the margins in America, its impacts have been felt more broadly throughout the television landscape.

The Rise of the Public Broadcasting System

Public television was quite marginal in the early years of American television, as commercial broadcasters dominated the rush for station licenses in the 1940s and 1950s. The FCC did allocate hundreds of frequencies for educational television (**ETV**) stations in the early 1950s, with universities and other nonprofits receiving licenses to establish broadcasting facilities. However, few universities had sufficient resources to invest in expensive production and transmission equipment, and thus many ETV stations never survived the decade, with commercial broadcasters buying out ETV licenses. Surviving ETV stations generally used their facilities as a "university of the air," broadcasting lectures and other instructional programs with low production values to small audiences, but most of the country was left unserved by ETV. The Ford Foundation was the chief funder of ETV's early efforts, underwriting **National Educational Television** (NET) in the 1950s to connect ETV stations and share programming, but the system made little impact during its first decade.

The growth of public television was fueled by the rhetoric of Newton Minow's vast wasteland speech—as Minow was condemning the public interest records of commercial broadcasters, the Kennedy administration urged the growth of noncommercial alternatives. NET grew somewhat stronger in the early 1960s, expanding its programming to more than strictly instructional shows by airing elite cultural performances such as opera and classical theater, British imports, and public affairs documentaries and talk shows to serve as "an oasis in the wasteland" of television. Commercial broadcasters in the 1960s held mixed opinions about the potential of NET and public broadcasting—a thriving public broadcasting system could be a new competitor for network television, but it could also serve public interest mandates sufficiently as to allow commercial stations to avoid airing low-profit public affairs programming. Under the corporate liberal perspective still dominant in the mid-1960s, public broadcasting was seen as an approach that could never effectively interest the public as fully as profit-seeking networks would, and thus it was always confined to the margins of the television schedule.

The reformist policies of 1960s embraced public broadcasting as filling an underserved niche—the 1965 Carnegie Commission on Educational Television pushed for a partnership between private foundations and government to build a stronger infrastructure of public television, a development enacted in the Public Broadcasting Act of 1967. This law created the **Corporation for Public Broadcasting** (CPB) as an administrative agency to distribute and administer government and foundation funding to local public broadcasting stations. CPB was designed to serve as a politically independent agency, with secured long-term funding outside of the political appropriation process similar to other public service broadcasting systems. However, under the Nixon administration the independent system was never fully enacted or funded, forcing the CPB to apply for annual federal funding and answering to politicians judging the quality, tone, and approach to its programming, a structure that would lead to years of controversies and debates.

The structure of CPB was designed to fund local stations, keeping public broadcasting rooted at the local level rather than forming a national network comparable to commercial broadcasting. However, the costs of programming a noncommercial station were prohibitive for most, and the **Public Broadcasting Service** (PBS) was formed in 1969 to interconnect local public stations and share programming resources, taking over the role of NET. Unlike commercial networks, PBS does not actually produce or procure programming, but rather shares programming provided by one member station with others across the nation, with the service administered in conjunction between CPB and affiliated stations. Although any station can generate programming for PBS, the vast majority of programs come from the major urban stations with the strongest funding bases, such as WGBH Boston, WNET New York, KCET Los Angeles, and KQED San Francisco. Additionally, CPB was directed by the government in the late 1980s to create a new production service to help fund and promote independent productions that had struggled to find space on PBS; these efforts created the Independent Television Service (ITVS) in 1991, which supports programming about or produced by minority or underserved populations, such as those featured on the documentary program *Independent Lens.*

The architects of public television in the late 1960s were trying to provide an alternative to the commercial broadcasting system via programming that was unlikely to emerge from the networks. One of the challenges of this strategy is that public broadcasting has always served as the default home to programs with low popularity, as commercial broadcasters have cornered the market on genres with mass appeal. In other national public service broadcasting systems, public broadcasters such as the BBC air programs with marginal or limited appeal alongside popular hits such as the soap opera *EastEnders* and the sci-fi show *Doctor Who.* In the American system, public television programs are typically regarded as things that people *should* watch rather than what most want to watch. Educational programming has always been a staple, although PBS shifted in its late-1960s emergence more toward daytime early-childhood programs such as *Sesame Street*, discussed in chapter 10, and away from the university-level lectures found on ETV.

While educational programming has always been central on PBS, other important genres include how-to programs such as *The French Chef* and *This Old House*, science shows such as *NOVA* and *Cosmos*, performing arts programs such as *Great Performances* and *Austin City Limits*, and history documentaries such as *American Experience* and *The Civil War.* In the classic network era, PBS was the primary place for viewers to see such programming, although commercial cable channels, Discovery, TLC, The Food Network, History Channel, and Bravo, have all thrived in offering the niche genres that were once unique to PBS. Additionally, PBS generated enthusiasm for British imports, bringing BBC dramas to *Masterpiece Theatre* and offering Americans their first glimpses of *Monty Python's Flying Circus* and *Mystery!.* Public television also became well known for presenting public affairs and documentary programming that was more in depth, investigative, and often critical of dominant corporate and political interests than that found on commercial channels—shows such as *Bill Moyers Journal* and *Frontline* established PBS as both a source of in-depth investigative journalism and an object of scorn from conservative critics.

In the 1970s, PBS became known for highbrow British imports, as well as the over-the-top comedy mocking highbrow British culture on *Monty Python's Flying Circus.*

Although conservative voices have often had a place on PBS shows such as *The McLaughlin Group, Firing Line,* and *Wall $treet Week,* public television's reputation for liberal bias has impacted its government funding by making it an object of right-wing attacks.

Public Broadcasting's Continuing Controversies

American public television has been at the center of many political controversies, with critics coming from both the left and the right wings of the political spectrum. Conservative critics regarded PBS skeptically from its inception, as the Nixon administration attempted to eliminate the service before it was even fully established and succeeded in making its governmental funding precariously limited and tied to the political budget process. Much of this conservative skepticism stems from the very idea of a public system competing with private interests: according to many conservatives, following a corporate liberal mentality, the free market enterprise of private commercial broadcasting is guaranteed to serve the public interest by showing the American public what they want to watch. Additionally the type of programming often offered by PBS fits into what conservatives have regarded as the purview of "liberal elites"—not only the left-leaning journalism of Bill Moyers, but the high cultural realms of symphony, theater, and British culture that, to many conservatives, smacks of "East Coast liberal elitism" force-feeding American viewers the equivalent of healthy "green vegetable" television, rather than the network programs that most viewers seem to prefer. However, the very market forces that such conservative critics of public broadcasting hail as democratically serving the public interest often produce a high level of sexual content and profanity that many conservative voices typically condemn, while PBS has far stricter internal standards of content regulation toward potentially indecent content than most networks and cable channels.

The conservative resistance to public television came to the forefront in the mid-1990s after Republicans gained control of Congress. House Speaker Newt Gingrich targeted public television as an outdated relic in the multi-channel era and repeated charges of East Coast liberal bias, suggesting that taxpayers should not be forced to pay taxes for television they do not watch. Gingrich's campaign to defund CPB was resisted, in part by defenders framing the issue as Republicans trying to eliminate Big Bird and Barney—even though PBS's successful educational shows were the least threatened type of programming, as they generate significant revenue from merchandising. The controversy over funding public television should be grounded in the context of how little money CPB actually gets from the federal government: its 2006 appropriation was $396 million, a scant portion of an overall budget exceeding $2.7 trillion and representing around $1.30 of public funding per American. Conservative attacks on public broadcasting often use the rhetoric of cutting governmental spending, even though cutting CPB funding would do little to reduce taxes or spending; the broader resistance to public television fits more within a general opposition to state-sponsored broadcasting and objection to the content and tone of PBS programming.

The 1990s saw conservatives fail to dismantle public television through defunding, but in the 2000s their strategy shifted toward changing its operations from within the system. Kenneth Tomlinson, a conservative journalist appointed by President Bush as CPB's board chair in 2003, attempted to counter perceived liberal biases at PBS through a number of controversial actions. Tomlinson launched a secret investigation of NOW with Bill Moyers to demonstrate the show's "liberal bias," used inappropriate political considerations in hiring decisions, and illicitly raised funds to create a conservative program, The Journal Editorial Report. These and other questionable activities led to a federal investigation charging Tomlinson with politicizing CPB in violation of a number of laws and policy, which resulted in his resignation in 2005, although a number of policies and decisions attempting to make public television embrace more conservative politics remained in place. Academic research into the political content of PBS's programming has found that as a whole, its public affairs coverage privileges business and governmental sources similarly to commercial news broadcasts, and that claims of liberal bias seem substantiated only for particular programs, which are outweighed by other more conservative-slanted shows—as discussed more in chapter 4, ideas of bias and balance on television journalism are more complicated than critical slogans tend to acknowledge.

While federal funding for public television has served as a political battleground, actual funding of public television comes from a range of sources, with less than 20 percent of revenues coming from the federal government. State and local governments provide support to their local stations, accounting for around 20 percent of national budgets, while universities and colleges provide funding and institutional support for a number of stations across the country, especially for educational programming to be used in schools on many stations. Approximately one quarter of all public television funding comes from "viewers like you," with memberships and pledges from dedicated viewers during regular funding drives providing crucial support for PBS and local stations. Some PBS programs and productions are able to generate substantial revenue from video sales, companion books, and other media tie-in products. Such auxiliary revenue is especially important for children's programming—for instance, Sesame Workshop, producer of *Sesame Street, Dragon Tales*, and other PBS programs, receives over 40 percent of its budget from product licensing, a facet of children's television discussed more in chapter 10.

Another more controversial funding source, accounting for around 15 percent of public television revenues, is **corporate underwriting**, a term for charitable support of programming that some critics suggest comes too close to commercial sponsorship. In the early years of PBS, a corporate underwriter received brief special thanks before or after a program, but throughout the 1990s these acknowledgments expanded into high-production-value videos lasting up to a minute highlighting a company's brand image and social engagement—a form of promotion that many suggest is essentially advertising. As PBS has traditionally served as a refuge against commercialism and corporate influence, left-leaning critics have decried the gradual rise in these pseudo-advertisements on public television. Additionally, corporate underwriters typically support programming from the early stages of its development, and it becomes easier to produce some genres over others—underwriters typically favor uncontroversial educational and culturally uplifting programs rather than investigative journalism, documentaries highlighting social problems and inequities, or programs serving minority interests.

For many supporters of the ideal of public television, this corporate influence has undermined the very freedoms from commercial pressures that CPB was created to offer; such critics point to the limited governmental support of CPB as an intentional policy that forces underfunded public television stations to embrace corporate partnerships. Activists looking to reinvigorate public television call for an independent nonpolitical funding mechanism, such as a small

Even though *Austin City Limits* airs on non-commercial PBS, its corporate underwriting from Budweiser resembles a traditional advertisement, raising the question of how public television truly differs from commercial broadcasting.

sales tax on the sale of television sets, fees for FCC-issued broadcast licenses, or a tax on advertising sales, and converting CPB into a public trust that would be immune from political maneuvering.[5] Additionally, public television advocates envision more local and community engagement, allowing public television to serve as a venue not just for viewers to receive noncommercial alternative programming, but also for communities to create programming and have their voices and perspectives heard via the public resource of the airwaves. These goals of public engagement and participation have seen only occasional successes with a few local stations, although a more active and participatory culture of public television has emerged around cable television.

Public Access Television and the Local Alternative

Public broadcasting is not the only noncommercial alternative in American television. As cable penetration rose in the 1970s, the FCC required that cable systems provide channels and support for noncommercial programming for three purposes: public access, educational programming, and governmental service, a category often abbreviated as **PEG access**. Governmental services air public meetings and hearings, such as city council sessions or school board meetings, while educational channels typically show content provided by local educational institutions, including student-created programming and educational material. **Public access** is the broadest category, serving as an open avenue for anyone in a community to produce and distribute noncommercial programming without censorship or restrictions, aside from obscenity, copyright, and libel laws. Cable systems designate one or more channels for PEG functions, run by a community **access management organization** (AMO), and providing financial support through a surcharge on cable subscriptions. While in 1979 the Supreme Court struck down the FCC's mandate as overreaching its authority, PEG access gained sufficient support that most local and state cable franchise agreements started mandating PEG channels as part of their contracts, and Congress passed laws enabling such requirements in the 1980s.

PEG access television is primarily community-based and local in focus, defined as noncommercial and unconcerned with ratings. Governmental channels seek to provide citizens the opportunity to watch public meetings from their homes, offering far more coverage of local governance and community issues than other broadcast media. Educational channels are tied directly to local schools, colleges, and universities, allowing a community to benefit from educational materials and student productions. Both of these functions offer programming designed to address viewers as citizens and residents of a local community, be it a major urban center or a rural township; however, because PEG channels require a cable subscription, many residents are not served by these community resources.

The public access function of PEG channels is the most controversial and transformative of television's cultural role. Public access channels treat viewers as potential producers, with AMOs offering free or low-cost access to, and training in, video production technology. Many AMOs serve as community media centers, offering outreach to local schools and civic groups, and participating in the media literacy efforts discussed more in chapter 10. Because of the democratic nature of open public access, the quality and content of programming varies greatly—some programs seek to mimic traditional formats such as sitcoms, musical performances, or talk shows, while others explore more experimental possibilities in both content and format, with nearly all programs operating on minimal budgets and with low-end production values. Although a few producers have used PEG as a stepping stone to broadcasting careers, most public access programmers are primarily interested in reaching out to a small community of viewers and taking advantage of the "electronic soapbox" that public access allows. For some critics of traditional broadcast television, public access is the only example of using television as a truly democratic medium, encouraging active use of the technology to both consume and produce mass media in a public open-access dialogue.

Although PEG channels are local in scope, serving only the subscribers of a single cable system, public access producers and AMOs have tried to use networking technologies to distribute and share programs more broadly. Activist producers in the 1980s founded Deep Dish TV Network to redistribute content via satellite to AMOs across the country, allowing programming such as

Public access programming, like *Paper Tiger Television*, embraces low-budget production values, but can offer sophisticated ideas and commentary on the mainstream media.

the media criticism series *Paper Tiger Television* to gain a national following. In the 1990s, Free Speech TV developed a similar strategy, growing into a national distributor of programming to PEG channels and establishing a regular channel on Dish Network's DBS system. These efforts, which typically focus on left-leaning activist documentaries and talk shows that are otherwise absent from the commercial airwaves, allow public access to serve as an alternative mode of television to engage viewers as citizens rather than consumers.

The future of PEG access is uncertain in the digital convergence era, as cable companies are lobbying to reduce PEG funding by changing their regulatory and contractual obligations. The expansion of digital broadcasting and cable has made channels more available and plentiful, leading some supporters to hope that PEG access becomes more widespread and available, perhaps through over-the-air or satellite transmissions. But the rise of online video, inexpensive video cameras, and desktop video editing has made the creation and distribution of video content much more accessible and commonplace than when the PEG movement was developing. In an era when nearly anyone can post a homemade video to the world on YouTube, is there still a need for local public access channels? Some supporters point to PEG's educational and governmental services as inherently local, and thus poorly served in the global clutter of online video, while others highlight the community media function of AMOs as serving a broader role than just video production and distribution.

The only certainty is that the roles and functions of community television will be debated and revised in the coming years. The potential of public access to address television viewers as active democratic citizens points to the focus of the next chapter: television's journalistic function and role in electoral politics.

FURTHER READING

The debate over broadcast regulation and democracy is a vital area of scholarship. C. Edwin Baker, *Media, Markets, and Democracy* (Cambridge, UK: Cambridge University Press, 2002), provides a key overview to the issues; while Robert W. McChesney, *The Problem of the Media: U.S. Communication Politics in the Twenty-first Century* (New York: Monthly Review Press, 2004), offers a highly critical perspective following a political economy approach. Thomas Streeter, *Selling the Air: A Critique of the Policy of Commercial Broadcasting in the United States* (Chicago: University of Chicago Press, 1996), offers a historical perspective rooted in the idea of corporate liberalism.

Issues of content regulation typically explore censorship beyond just television. Marjorie Heins, *Not in Front of the Children: "Indecency," Censorship, and the Innocence of Youth* (New Brunswick, N.J.: Rutgers University Press, 2007), is a detailed critical history of censorship across media. Heather Hendershot, *Saturday Morning Censors: Television Regulation Before the V-Chip* (Durham, N.C.: Duke University Press, 1998), offers an important history of television censorship aimed at children. Copyright policy has been a crucial research area in recent years; Siva Vaidhyanathan, *Copyrights and Copywrongs: The Rise of Intellectual Property and How It Threatens Creativity* (New York: New York University Press, 2001), provides a historical account of American copyright; while Lawrence Lessig, *Free Culture: How Big Media Uses Technology and the Law to Lock Down Culture and Control Creativity* (New York: Penguin Press, 2004), provides an activist's approach to fair use and digital issues.

For more on public broadcasting in America, see William Hoynes, *Public Television for Sale: Media, the Market, and the Public Sphere* (Boulder, Colo.: Westview Press, 1994), for a critique of corporate and political pressures; Laurie Ouellette, *Viewers Like You? How Public TV Failed the People* (New York: Columbia University Press, 2002), offers a cultural approach to the rhetoric behind public broadcasting. Laura R. Linder, *Public Access Television: America's Electronic Soapbox* (Westport, Conn.: Praeger, 1999), provides an overview of PEG television; while Megan Boler, ed., *Digital Media and Democracy: Tactics in Hard Times* (Cambridge, Mass: MIT Press, 2008) explores the role of community media in the digital era.

NOTES

[1]Robert W. McChesney, *The Problem of the Media: U.S. Communication Politics in the Twenty-First Century* (New York: Monthly Review Press, 2004), 40.

[2]Thomas Streeter, *Selling the Air: A Critique of the Policy of Commercial Broadcasting in the United States* (Chicago: University of Chicago Press, 1996).

[3]McChesney, *Problem of the Media.*

[4]"FCC Factsheet on Obscene, Indecent and Profane Broadcasts," available at http://www.fcc.gov/cgb/consumerfacts/obscene.html.

[5]See Citizens for Independent Public Broadcasting, http://cipbonline.org.

CHAPTER 4

TELEVISED CITIZENSHIP

Both the regulatory structure of broadcasting and the institutions of public television are designed to ensure that the public interest is central to the practices of television broadcasting. But how do television stations and channels attempt to serve the public interest? Arguably every genre could serve the public interest by engaging and entertaining the public, especially under the corporate liberal interpretation of consumerist "public interest." But two crucial types of programming specifically address a broader concept of serving the American public as citizens. One format, educational television, is discussed more in chapter 10. The second type of programming is what we normally consider the result of television's role in a democracy: journalism and public affairs programming. How does television news serve the public interest, informing citizens and fulfilling the role of the press imagined by the United States Constitution? And how can commercial systems of the for-profit television industry reconcile with the demands of robust and independent journalism?

TELEVISION JOURNALISM:
NEWS FOR PUBLIC AND PRIVATE INTERESTS

As with most aspects of television, we must turn to radio to understand television news; but to truly understand the role of journalism in American culture, we need to look back even farther. The American press is embedded in the country's origins, and a key document for studying journalism is the U.S. Constitution. The **First Amendment** seems on its surface only to prohibit government interference with freedom of speech or the press, but its historical context expands our understanding of media's role in American democracy. The newspapers of the eighteenth century were typically local publications with explicit political positions, with a large number of differing newspapers serving a range of readers within any region—this forum of competing partisan publications functioned as an **adversarial press**, willing to disagree and argue with government and economic leaders in the service of creating an engaged and informed citizenry and of fighting potential tyranny. For the framers of the Constitution, freedom of the press meant not only freedom from government censorship, but also a free and open arena of competing ideas and publications, and the freedom for citizens to have access to a variety of positions via the press. Although such freedoms were not directly mandated by the Constitution, early American media policies explicitly encouraged a robust and diverse press through postal subsidies and government publishing contracts to support the print industry, all working to make the press an explicit component of the American political system by engaging citizens through public debate and an open forum of competing ideas.[1]

By the time radio broadcasting rose to prominence in the 1920s, the press had become more commercially driven and less diverse, with newspapers consolidating into national chains and wire services, most cities featuring no more than two daily papers, and significant barriers in place to new publishers entering into any market. The press in the early twentieth century was primarily advertising-supported, often embracing sensationalist and tabloid forms to gain readership. Additionally, journalism had shifted away from a model of partisan advocacy and explicit political engagement, and toward a professionalized code of objectivity and nonpartisan reporting. Rather than a number of different journalistic sources offering varying perspectives on any issue, readers found that a smaller number of papers covered the same stories with similar approaches, with purported objectivity, less of an adversarial attitude toward the powerful, and a goal for conveying information instead of engaging in persuasion—the most common variation between papers was found in the level of seriousness of tone and willingness to create sensational headlines to generate controversy and spur sales. Instead of an adversarial press questioning the powerful and offering a range of positions, twentieth-century journalism was more frequently a **consensus press**, speaking in concert with the vested interests of government and corporate leadership. It was this model of objective, nonpartisan, and commercial for-profit consensus journalism that was adopted by radio, with many early stations owned by newspapers and reporting provided by services such as the Associated Press.

Newscasts became a staple of network radio in the 1930s and 1940s, with journalism helping broadcasters fulfill the FCC's public interest mandate. Radio journalists crafted their programming to fit the strengths of the medium by offering features unavailable to print journalism. While often broadcasters read material directly from print sources, as on-air journalists were initially called "news readers," radio newscasts used the live nature of broadcasting to report incoming news faster than print could respond. Additionally, newscasts in the 1930s used on-location reporters to take listeners to the scene of key events, such as Europe on the eve of World War II, and broadcast the voices of politicians and world leaders whom most Americans had only ever read about, creating a type of immediate emotional engagement that print could not match. President Roosevelt used radio to great advantage in the 1930s, conducting "fireside chats" with listeners over the airwaves and effectively bringing his political messages directly into the homes of American citizens. Radio journalism fostered these qualities of liveness, immediacy, intimacy, and the ability to transport listeners to another world, all of which would be adopted and exploited by television news.

The Rise of Television Journalism

As television emerged in the 1940s, the networks quickly converted their radio news divisions to serve television as well. Since on-location reporting via video was not technologically feasible, early network news relied primarily upon licensing film footage shot by newsreel companies, which had supplied news footage for cinemas in the 1930s and 1940s. Short daily newscasts, such as NBC's *Camel News Caravan*, mixed still images and newsreel footage over the voice of a newscaster reading stories, a slow-paced model that did not play to the potential strengths of television's liveness and intimacy. But as radio declined in popularity throughout the 1950s, the news divisions of television networks became more prominent in representing the public interest face of national broadcasting. Most news in television's early years fit into the pattern of the objective, consensus press, although there were some memorable exceptions.

One of the most notable moments in television journalism occurred in the medium's early years. Edward R. Murrow had established himself as a star reporter for CBS Radio during World War II, with a persona known for eloquent celebrations of democratic ideals and human rights. He came to television in 1951, as the host and co-producer of CBS's *See It Now*, a prime time public affairs show with an in-depth account of a new story each week presented with a mixture of live in-studio commentary and self-produced on-location filmed segments. Murrow notably brought viewers on location to the Korean War front in 1952 and provided in-depth coverage of the 1952 presidential election, but both *See It Now* and Murrow are best remembered for engaging with the anti-communist movement known as the Red Scare.

Murrow hosted episodes of *See It Now* challenging anti-communist attacks against an Air Force officer and the ACLU in 1953, but he wanted to

SEE IT NOW

See It Now (CBS, 1951–58): An early example of prime time television news with host Edward R. Murrow exploring one topic in depth each week, the show typically covered uncontroversial issues with depth and seriousness. *See It Now* is best remembered, as dramatized in the film *Good Night, and Good Luck*, for a series of controversial episodes addressing the Red Scare and attacking Senator Joseph McCarthy's tactics for promoting anti-communism.

engage directly with the chief politician leading the Red Scare, Senator Joseph McCarthy. In March 1954, Murrow and his producer, Fred Friendly, aired a blistering condemnation of McCarthy, featuring numerous audio and film clips of the senator's contradictory and inflammatory speeches and concluding with Murrow's eloquent commentary calling upon Americans to denounce the politics of fear and accusation. CBS agreed to air the show only after Murrow and Friendly offered to pay for the airtime themselves instead of the show's normal sponsor Alcoa; although McCarthy and his supporters denounced the broadcast, general viewer response was overwhelmingly favorable. Shortly after Murrow's

Edward R. Murrow challenged Senator McCarthy by drawing upon clear evidence from newspapers, audiotape, and filmed accounts of McCarthy's own words and contradictory claims, a rare example of television news taking an adversarial and controversial stand.

broadcast, ABC preempted its daytime schedule to air live coverage of the Senate's Army-McCarthy hearings into alleged communist infiltration of the U.S. Army—the ratings for these broadcasts were much higher than expected and stand as one of the first examples of a live televised **media event** capturing the attention of the American public. While most moments in television history do not rise to this level of notoriety or political import, Murrow's broadcast and ABC's live coverage highlighted the power of television journalism to engage and persuade the American public, as many cite these broadcasts as the turning point in the Red Scare.

Murrow's adversarial Red Scare broadcasts were not typical of early television news, but they did represent many of the ideals and goals of television journalists. News divisions were established as separate and distinct from the entertainment divisions of networks, with a clear mandate to foster positive public goodwill and fulfill public interest requirements. While network news divisions did compete among each other, the networks' corporate management did not regard news divisions as potential money makers. Typically companies sponsored public affairs and news programs to boost their reputations for investing in the public good under the single sponsorship model discussed in chapter 2. Additionally, there was a clear dividing line between the journalistic division of a network and the commercial wing—a divide journalists sometimes refer to as the separation of "church and state"—in order to ensure that news coverage was not influenced by the agendas of the sponsors or greater corporate goals. While there were certainly instances of commercial pressures impacting television journalism in the 1950s, the assumed central role of early television's independent news divisions was to inform and educate American citizens following the norms of objective, professional-consensus journalism of the day.

The 1960s saw a distinct growth of network news divisions in cultural prominence and industrial importance. In the wake of Newton Minow's push for increased social responsibility on television, discussed in chapter 3, public affairs programming became more prominent in network promotion and scheduling. Notably the early 1960s saw a series of high-profile prime time **documentaries** probing social issues, such as the CBS Reports investigation into migrant farm workers, called "Harvest of Shame," and the NBC White Paper report "Sit-In," one of the earliest examples of television coverage of the civil rights movement. Most television documentaries of the era were less adversarial to established national values, as one of the primary themes of such programming was building a consensus around cold war politics and America's aggressive foreign policy positions against Soviet expansion. Throughout the 1960s, television news became America's central authority and trusted source for national public affairs, with networks establishing regular nightly half-hour broadcasts behind star anchormen such as CBS's Walter Cronkite and NBC's team of Chet Huntley and David Brinkley. While newscasts and documentaries rarely reached the ratings levels of popular prime time entertainment programming, they were regarded as shaping the national consciousness by defining what issues were worth covering and establishing television as the authoritative medium for national news.

Television's central role was highlighted in November 1963 in the wake of President Kennedy's assassination. In the immediate aftermath of the shooting, networks preempted nearly all programming to provide live information, tributes, and commentaries for four days leading up to the funeral, an enormous technological hurdle in the days before satellite feeds. The coverage of the media event surrounding President Kennedy's death highlighted particular elements unique to television journalism. The combination of audio and visuals allowed for a profound emotional and human connection, with one of the signature images of Cronkite removing his glasses to wipe away tears in a rare moment of lost composure, a gesture that encapsulated the shock and grief of the nation. Television's ability to take viewers to specific locations through live broadcasts was underscored unintentionally with NBC's live coverage of Jack Ruby shooting Lee Harvey Oswald days after Kennedy's assassination. The simultaneous nature of live broadcasting could be seen in the clustering of viewers around their television sets, with a peak audience of over 90 percent of televisions tuned in to coverage at a given moment. The Kennedy assassination stands

CBS news anchor Walter Cronkite, the symbol of stoic journalistic objectivity, needed time to steady his emotions while reporting President Kennedy's death in 1963, an image that stands in for a nation in mourning via a media event.

as the defining television media event, although later moments, such as the 1969 moon landing, the Watergate hearings, the Challenger space shuttle explosion in 1986, the O.J. Simpson chase and trial, and the attacks of September 11, all evoke similar responses of shared national engagement and public ritual through television journalism.

Television news coverage in the 1960s not only helped bring together the nation through media events, but also worked to divide and fracture public opinion concerning controversial issues. The civil rights movement garnered little television coverage in the 1950s despite landmark court decisions and major public protests, but the 1960s saw more attention from television newscasts. Two broadcasts from 1963 stand out as crucial in swaying public opinion concerning civil rights—Martin Luther King, Jr.'s famous "I have a dream" speech was broadcast live during daytime on all three networks and excerpted during the evening news, helping to establish King, one of America's most eloquent and charismatic speakers, as a nonthreatening face of the civil rights movement to a majority of white viewers. In the same year, footage of a Birmingham, Alabama, civil rights protest turning violent showed white police removing young black protesters from the streets with fire hoses and police dogs—these emotional images highlighted the violence faced by African-Americans, who responded with stoic bravery and a lack of retaliation. Together, these and other moments from civil rights coverage played to television's strength of reaching out to viewers emotionally and through intimate interpersonal appeals, helping to push many viewers toward growing support for civil rights legislation.

Television coverage of the Vietnam War, hailed as the first "television war," similarly engaged viewers with both emotional and rational appeals. Television reporters had unprecedented access to the armed forces and delivered filmed reports of military action and in-the-field profiles with little governmental interference. Early coverage of the war in the mid-1960s kept with American television's general support of cold war foreign policy, framing most stories around official U.S. policies and supportive profiles of troops; similarly, coverage of the growing antiwar movement framed mostly young protesters as deviants, radicals, and potentially unpatriotic. As the war effort started to appear less successful and the antiwar movement gained traction within broader public opinion in the late 1960s, the television coverage shifted as well, featuring more images of war carnage, explicit violence, and voices of dissent from both America and Vietnam. It is debatable whether public opinion drove the shift in coverage, or if the media's shifting take on the war guided public opinion, but the two certainly reinforced each other. Television journalism typically tries to present perspectives matching and reinforcing the presumed consensus values and assumptions of its audience, a process referred to as **indexing** the news. In 1968, during a special report, Cronkite called the Vietnam War a "stalemate," a proclamation that many critics regard as the crucial tipping point in crystallizing widespread public disapproval for the war, and highlighting the power of the news to guide and shape public opinion in the classic network era.

Even as network news ascended to become the central medium for Americans to engage in current events, the format was regularly critiqued for the limitations imposed by the nightly half-hour schedule. Issues were inherently covered briefly, without time for extended debate or discussion, and with a tendency to reduce speeches to short sound bites. Networks supplemented these nightly broadcasts with prime time documentaries, although these expensive and low-rated programs grew less frequent by the late 1960s, and Sunday morning political talk shows such as *Meet the Press*. Additionally, PBS began its own newscast in the mid-1970s, *The MacNeil/Lehrer Report*, which focused more on discussing issues from multiple perspectives than presenting on-location features and reporting.

But the most well known and influential supplement to the nightly news was the **news magazine**, a prime time show featuring a few longer stories with more depth than possible in half-hour newscasts. The format was pioneered in the late 1960s by CBS's *60 Minutes*, which offered an innovative format by emphasizing the narrative structure and emotional dimensions of news stories— correspondents presented clear personalities rather than the detached authority typical of anchors, stories highlighted villains and heroes framed within brief morality plays, and topics were personalized through emotional profiles and heart-wrenching situations. Many traditional journalists decried the format as overly dramatic, manipulative, and sensational, saying that it led with emotion

The iconic stopwatch at the start of *60 Minutes* has signaled the standard for the news magazine genre for thirty years.

60 MINUTES

60 Minutes (CBS, 1968–present): The most influential and successful news magazine, this long-running series provided an emotional, narrative basis for extended news stories, a formula that eventually resulted in high ratings and led to a boom in the genre in the 1980s and 1990s. *60 Minutes* remains one of the most revered and respected programs on television, although its audience has shrunk and shifted to older demographics in the multi-channel era.

rather than facts, but the show frequently featured more in-depth investigative reports than other television journalism.

60 Minutes moved throughout the schedule for years, but by the late 1970s it found itself in its now long-standing place on Sunday evening and in the top twenty of the weekly Nielsen ratings. Per television's logic of imitation, ABC latched onto the hit by starting *20/20* in the late 1970s and the late-night *Nightline* in the early 1980s, expanding the reach of network news divisions; NBC would successfully join the news magazine competition with its series of *Dateline* programs in the 1990s. The rise of the news magazine marks a crucial shift in the industrial understanding of television journalism—if television news of the 1950s was seen as a necessary cost of doing business to boost network image and fulfill public interest requirements, by the late 1970s the news divisions were seen as potentially profitable facets of a network schedule. News magazines were a low-cost alternative to prime time entertainment, and networks would use such programs as schedule fillers, while encouraging news divisions to produce more entertaining stories appealing to younger demographics. One path toward such ratings success was innovated by Fox as it debuted in the mid-1980s with tabloid-style **infotainment** programs such as *America's Most Wanted* and *A Current Affair* rather than creating its own news division. Although network news divisions maintained their journalistic goals and independence from entertainment divisions, they found themselves under internal pressure to boost ratings with reduced staffing, as well as external competition through the rise of cable news in the 1980s.

Twenty-Four-Hour News in the Multi-Channel Era

When CNN was launched in 1980, it appeared to most observers of the television industry as an act of supreme folly. Cable television was still a marginal system in less than 20 percent of American television households, and most critics were skeptical both of an audience's appetite for twenty-four-hour news coverage and of a channel's ability to deliver nonstop trusted journalism on cable's comparatively low budget. However, owner Ted Turner was committed to the project, investing the profits from his successful "superstation" WTBS, which had expanded from a local Atlanta UHF station to be carried on growing cable systems throughout the country, into the upstart Cable News Network. Like many cable ventures of the early 1980s, CNN generated large financial losses and skepticism from established media professionals, but it weathered initial hardships to launch a second channel, CNN Headline News, in 1982, and by 1985, it was turning a profit and reaching thirty million American homes. Turner continued to expand his operation by opening numerous international bureaus, luring established journalists and hosts to the channel, and offering international versions of the channel for distribution around the world. Along with other early cable innovators The Weather Channel and ESPN, CNN proved that there was a distinct market for an aspect of the traditional television news schedule to be expanded into a twenty-four-hour channel and allow viewers to tune into coverage on their own schedule.

CNN's big breakthrough was undoubtedly its coverage of the Gulf War in 1991. While networks had correspondents on location with live satellite feeds, their coverage was squeezed into the evening news or brief special reports. CNN turned nearly its entire schedule over to war coverage, airing every available detail, from military press briefings to footage of bombing runs, with its coverage peaking at a share of over 10 percent of the television audience,

CNN built its reputation on its large news-gathering infrastructure, international focus, and ability to deliver news at an instantaneous pace.

numbers previously unheard of for cable. However, taking a lesson from the relatively unrestricted coverage of the Vietnam War, the U.S. military greatly limited press access to the war; information was doled out to pools of reporters, and the military demanded clearance of stories in the name of security. The military also heightened its choreography of its briefings and crafted presentations to offer compelling stories of American successes, Iraqi human rights violations, and high-technology "precision bombing" campaigns with minimal civilian losses—the media presented such claims unchallenged, in keeping with the dominant national narrative of American superiority and righteousness, but months after the war, independent investigators found that much of the material presented by the U.S. military was deliberately misleading or incorrect, such as overstated bombing success rates and understated civilian casualty rates. While the Gulf War demonstrated the ability of television to offer war coverage with unprecedented moment-to-moment detail, it also revealed the nature of such reporting as overly reliant on official sources, focused on compelling and potentially misleading action footage, and offering reassuring narratives at the cost of complexity and accuracy.

Network news responded to the growth of CNN by reasserting its own values of authority and trustworthiness—the 1980s and 1990s saw remarkable stability with the consistent presence of anchors Dan Rather, Peter Jennings, and Tom Brokaw, all vying for Cronkite's former spot as America's most trusted voice of journalism. News magazines continued to be important facets of prime time programming, and so-called "soft" news programming in morning shows such as Today and Good Morning America expanded the reach of network nonfiction programming. Networks tried to compete with CNN on its own terrain by launching cable news channels in the 1990s—some have been successful, such as CNBC and MSNBC, while others were short-lived, such as CBS Eye on People, which was sold after two years to Discovery Channel and renamed Discovery Times.

While Fox never offered broadcast network news, it did emerge as an important player in television journalism through Fox News Channel, which was launched in the mid-1990s with a self-proclaimed mission of objectivity in the face of what many saw as a biased liberal news media. The contested issues of bias and balance are discussed more later, but Fox's contributions to television news go beyond political slant, with a number of innovations that influenced the channel's competitors and changed the face of journalism. Fox News offered a highly graphic style, with digital images and text keyed over visuals using techniques discussed in chapter 5; Fox's visuals often use images of American icons to reinforce the channel's self-proclaimed patriotic identity. The channel also operates with far fewer reporters and bureaus than CNN or network news, relying more on in-studio personalities to offer opinions on the news rather than actively reporting it. By foregrounding news **pundits** instead of journalists, Fox

News costs far less to run than its competitors, and its success has led to the growth of pundit-based programming on CNN, MSNBC, and network news. Pundit news emphasizes conflict and confrontation, typified in the style of *The O'Reilly Factor* and *Hannity & Colmes*, which adds entertainment and drama to the news, although many critics suggest that such entertainment comes by sacrificing accuracy and depth. After its inception, Fox News quickly achieved high ratings, especially among older demographics outside of major cities, as the channel seemed to serve viewers who were dissatisfied with the conventional model of network and cable news. But despite Fox's success, it is important to remember that the ratings for news channels are still a fraction of network broadcasts; even as network news ratings shrink, the nightly broadcasts still serve as the primary news source for the largest number of television viewers.

Television news has long been critiqued for not offering sufficient investigative and critical reporting into key issues, focusing instead on sound bites and scandals. The rise of twenty-four-hour cable news might suggest a cure for such problems: With sufficient time and resources to do in-depth reporting and expanded coverage of issues, a cable news channel could devote a portion of its airtime to cover marginalized topics with an unprecedented degree of detail and investigative focus. Most critics believe that the opposite has been true, with cable news leading to even more sound bites and scandal coverage, rather than fewer. Why would this be true? Arguably, cable news is at its best in the face of a media event worthy of twenty-four-hour coverage; thus in the aftermath of

Fox News's *O'Reilly Factor* typifies the channel's reliance on pundits, heavy use of graphics, and opinion-driven confrontational rhetoric over journalistic reporting.

September 11 or Hurricane Katrina, cable news could devote hours to the tales of hundreds of victims and rescue workers, providing multiple angles on complex and vital stories. But in the absence of such an important story, cable news tends to elevate mundane issues into hyped scandals, such as celebrity crimes or alleged sprees of shark attacks, and turn serious issues into sensationalist events. Despite the large number of hours to be filled on cable news, channels tend to cover a fairly small number of stories with tremendous frequency and cost-saving repetition. Often when one channel elevates a story's importance, others will follow immediately, in a process termed **pack journalism**; as channels jockey for ratings positions, television's logic of imitation extends down to the level of selecting news stories.

The social costs of pundit-driven pack journalism might have been felt most powerfully in the run-up to the Iraq War. After the attacks of September 11, journalists across all media found themselves in consensus mode, hoping to reaffirm and reinforce national unity and shared ideals. In their coverage of the strike against Afghanistan, media followed governmental requests without debate, avoiding images of antiwar protestors or anything else that might raise doubts about the military mission. CNN even stopped showing shots of Afghani civilian victims after advertisers and politicians complained that such images might undermine the war effort. As the Bush administration began to build a case for attacking Iraq, few journalists investigated or even questioned claims that later proved to be false, such as the presence of weapons of mass destruction or alleged Iraqi ties to al Qaeda and the 9/11 attacks. Instead, network and cable news offered dozens of pundits repeating Bush administration claims and rosy predictions for a quick and painless war, and featured almost no antiwar commentators—such pro-war messages were aired with such repetitive frequency that they functioned almost as advertisements selling the war as a product.

Journalists who did investigate these claims found a number of holes in official positions. A few print journalists offered alternative, more critical and skeptical analysis during the run-up to the war, but they were almost never featured on television, where the sense of public pro-war consensus guided coverage to virtual identical reporting across channels. When television news did feature critics or politicians critical of administration claims, they were attacked as unpatriotic or worse by pundits, judgments that look quite misguided in hindsight. MSNBC even fired its highest-rated host, talk show pioneer Phil Donahue, for being too critical of the Bush administration's plans for Iraq and for featuring antiwar guests. The media coverage before the war and during its first year offered the unusual scenario that the most critical and probing television coverage of these issues appeared on the comedic "fake news" program *The Daily Show with Jon Stewart.*

While a number of print and television journalists have since apologized for failing to investigate and criticize claims leading to the Iraq War, the model of consensus journalism is still in place—pundits and commentators speaking out against the war began to find a consistent place on television only in 2006, on shows such as MSNBC's *Countdown with Keith Olbermann*, once public sentiment had clearly turned against the war. Television news generally presents stories consistent with what they believe Americans wish to hear, rather than probing for factual accuracy or exploring diverse perspectives on issues.[2]

The Debates over Bias

The logic of network and cable news today is directly tied to notions of **media bias**. For many critics and commentators, the question of bias involves partisan politics, imagining the press to be overtly supportive of left- or right-wing positions. For decades, conservative critics and politicians have perceived the news media as highly liberal, harkening back to Murrow's attacks on McCarthy and Cronkite's turn against the Vietnam War. Accusations against the so-called "liberal media" intensified in the 1980s within the Reagan administration, with conservative activists working to define mainstream journalism as inherently liberal and biased against conservative positions, and with a well-funded movement to build conservative media alternatives such as talk radio and right-wing newspapers. There has been a concerted effort among many conservative politicians and critics to repeat the charge of "liberal media" so frequently as to make it seem self-evident and true—the actual evidence of liberal bias is far less conclusive than the chorus of voices making the accusations would have people believe.

Many of these accusations of a biased liberal media are based on studies showing that the voting patterns and political affiliations of professional journalists skew toward the Democratic Party in greater numbers than the general population. These studies have been interpreted as clear evidence of liberal bias, but the evidence is not definitive—critics tend to equate Democratic affiliation or voting for President Clinton with labels such as "leftist," even when the Democratic Party moved to the center of the political spectrum in the 1990s and Democratic politics are far more centrist than the left-leaning parties in other democratic countries. Other studies of journalists' policy positions suggest that they may actually be more conservative than typical Americans on economic issues, supporting free trade, corporate deregulation, and market-based policies favoring business interests. Additionally, many media companies have actively recruited conservative pundits and journalists to counter this alleged imbalance, making the claims of staffing bias less relevant in recent years.[3]

However, the focus on the political positions of journalists is misleading at a broader level—individual journalists have far less personal influence on the choice of perspectives and topics of stories than the institutional systems of corporate media that publish and broadcast the news. As television news became increasingly seen as a source of potential profit in the 1970s, news directors faced more pressure from the media corporations to present stories that would both generate ratings and please sponsors. As media conglomeration increased in the 1980s and 1990s, news divisions found themselves part of global corporations whose sibling holdings might potentially find themselves on the negative side of a news story, such as General Electric's environmental record or Disney's questionable labor practices. Although few journalists claim to have been explicitly ordered to stifle controversial reports about their corporate parents or potential sponsors, they suggest that it is an assumption in newsrooms that generating negative publicity for their parent corporations and sponsors will not be rewarded. Journalists know that it becomes difficult to advance within the hierarchy of television news if you get a reputation for angering the corporations that own and fund the media, and thus understandably they tend to shape their journalistic choices to fit into their institutional systems and advance their own careers.

One clear perspective emerging from this system is a **corporate bias**, with the news media framing issues to fit with the perspective of business interests. Such shaping is not maintained through overt internal directives, but by a more passive system of priorities. News media shape public opinion through the selection of what stories are told and what are omitted—television news covers economic issues through the viewpoint of business interests, focused on the stock market, the triumphs of CEOs, and tales of successful profits and entrepreneurial inventions. While entire channels such as CNBC and Bloomberg Television focus on the corporate perspective on the economy, television news coverage of labor movements and the economic concerns of average Americans is mostly absent, except when presented as a threat to corporations via a strike or labor action. Working- and middle-class economics are often reduced to consumer spending, with sales figures during holidays or other periods used as a marker of broader economic health, rather than considering measures such as wages, savings, or consumer debt. Likewise, stories of corporate crimes or environmental damages rarely get the attention paid to more frivolous celebrity scandals, natural disasters, or sensationalist crime stories. The selection of stories and perspectives triggers a process termed **agenda setting**, framing what is viewed as newsworthy and what is ignored by the news—a shorthand notion of agenda setting is that the news doesn't tell us what to think, but it tells us what to think *about*. If viewers are unaware that a story or perspective even exists, they cannot begin to contemplate how it might fit into the larger context of the news they are receiving. Although it is certainly not an overt editorial objective of most journalists, the system of television news sets the agenda to focus on the corporate world as the center of American economics, a perspective echoed in the other genres of television discussed more in chapter 7.

Corporate bias emerges from the systems of journalism, not necessarily the beliefs of individual journalists. Another bias emerges from how journalists report the news, a perspective that might be called an **official bias**. As the press became more conglomerated and shifted models from adversarial, partisan journalism to consensus, objective reporting, journalists put more weight on official sources: the voices of government, military authorities, business executives, and other leaders. If an official source such as the White House press secretary asserts that something is news, journalists follow suit by reporting the story, granting government officials their own agenda-setting power. Both the Reagan and Clinton administrations used this power shrewdly, channeling presidential charisma into photo opportunities and public speeches that would instantly become newsworthy and shape the coverage on that evening's news. By yielding some of their story-selection power to governmental officials, journalists could claim more objectivity and lack of bias by simply reporting the actions of powerful leaders. Official sources also emerge as key voices on interview programs, with political leaders making the rounds on Sunday morning talk shows to reinforce their perspectives on the news and set the agenda.

This reliance on official sources has led to a number of consequences. Because journalists need access to high-ranking officials, they have become less adversarial and willing to challenge powerful leaders for fear of being shut out of interview opportunities or potential leaks of developing news. If an official source is unwilling to comment on a story, a practice common to the Bush administration in the 2000s, it can be difficult for a reporter to get the story on the air for fear of it being viewed as unsubstantiated, a problem that particularly limits investigative journalism that challenges official leaders. Additionally, in the rush to appear as unbiased and objective as possible, journalists have refused even to correct inaccuracies of official statements—instead of fact-checking the powerful, journalists turn to other officials to offer adversarial positions, and quote both sides without judgment or offering factual context. Thus in the run-up to the Iraq War, a number of journalists refused to contradict Republican claims that members of the press knew were inaccurate, to avoid being perceived as liberally biased, and instead relied upon Democratic politicians to offer a contrary "opinion" on the facts, a position that most Democrats would not take for fear of appearing "unpatriotic" in the face of a consensus push to war.[4] At its worst, this bias toward official sources turns reporters into passive conduits for governmental press releases and spin, undercutting the adversarial role of the press envisioned by the Constitution and presenting opposing sides of an issue as inherently equal, regardless of facts or context.

A third bias stems from the medium of television itself. As discussed more in chapter 11, the medium of television can convey particular meanings and evoke responses beyond its content. Television news conveys information through audio and moving image visuals, with occasional on-screen text and graphics. When compared to print journalism, it becomes clear that television's format tends to communicate differently and its particular features create what might be considered a **medium bias**. Print journalism is well suited for offering detailed, factual, and analytical material that can be consumed at a reader's own pace, conjuring images of people and places in the mind of the reader. Television's strength is conveying presence and intimacy, emotional connection and authenticity—it is far less effective at presenting complex arguments or offering factual details to be referenced beyond a passing moment in a broadcast, at least given how American television's formal qualities have developed and are typically used. While both print and television journalists construct their pieces as stories, emphasizing narrative elements of heroes and villains, key events and confrontations, television's visual mode highlights the emotional dimensions of storytelling, as popularized by *60 Minutes*, rather than the rational and analytical tone of print. These distinctions should not necessarily be understood as making one form more valued or legitimate than another—emotional engagement and rational analysis are both important elements in understanding current events—but this medium bias shapes how television news operates.

Television's medium bias benefits public figures with charisma and strong emotional presence, and hurts those whose appearance or tone is less engaging. A classic example is the first televised presidential debate between candidates Kennedy and Nixon in 1960: Kennedy appeared youthful, charismatic, and appropriate for television, while Nixon, an older figure, was allegedly sweating due to a fever and had refused to have proper makeup applied. A public opinion poll conducted after the debate, albeit one with questionable methodology, suggested that radio listeners felt Nixon had equaled or bettered Kennedy, while television viewers overwhelmingly thought Kennedy had won the debate. Even if the medium split was not the core reason for this difference, certainly Kennedy emerged as the first made-for-television president. The power of images to sway viewers emotionally was marshaled by President Reagan's staff in the 1980s—the administration regularly designed "photo ops" for the press to capture footage of President Reagan surrounded by patriotic symbols, or framed as an everyday American eating jellybeans or working on his ranch. Newscasts used this footage as "wallpaper" to run over stories about the president, but the emotional power of the images outweighed any critical policy analysis that journalists offered as the analytical content of the story, with the visual and emotional identification trumping reporter's rational and analytical language.[5] Similarly President Clinton's talk show appearances playing saxophone made him appear more sympathetic and accessible, creating a lasting image that would help him remain charismatic to many Americans throughout subsequent scandals.

For some critics who decry the effect of television on American democracy, this medium bias is evidence that television reduces all politics and current affairs to matters of shallow celebrity and glossy surfaces. While this tendency is certainly commonplace and potentially dangerous, we should not ignore the

Images like Ronald Reagan lifting weights are not news per se, but television news regularly used them to wallpaper reports about the President, conveying the emotional perception of Reagan's energy and vitality regardless of the content of the news story.

importance of television's emotional connection to the news. The images of post-Katrina New Orleans galvanized viewers and encouraged charitable giving, volunteerism, and activism in a way that a print version of the news from New Orleans might not have done. Murrow's attack on Senator McCarthy was effective not just because of the logical assembly of McCarthy's contradictions, but also because of the contrast between McCarthy's hot rage and Murrow's cool moral outrage. For many voters, the likeability of presidents Reagan or Clinton was not just the product of good media managers and crafted images, but was also tied to a sense of integrity and sincerity in their communication styles and manifest in their beliefs and actions. Even after the Iran-Contra scandal undermined Reagan's claims of integrity and Clinton's illicit affair cast doubt on his sincerity, many supporters still felt emotionally connected with these men through their televised personas and charisma, willing to forgive their crimes based on a sense of humanity conveyed through the media. While we must remember that its images are always carefully crafted and selected, television offers a more intimate connection both with leaders and with everyday people than previously possible in the news media, encouraging a sense of human interaction and presence that print cannot match.

If these three biases of television journalism—corporate, official, and medium—shape what we see and how television serves the public interest, how might we reconsider accusations of political bias? While it is hard to substantiate that television as a whole has either an explicit left- or right-wing bias, particular broadcasters and channels certainly do convey a political agenda. Bill Moyers built his career on investigative journalism willing to question the powerful interests of politicians and corporations, placing him on the left side of the political spectrum, while most financial news programs convey a right-wing faith in free markets and reduced government regulation. Pundits have traditionally spanned the political spectrum, from conservatives George Will and Tucker Carlson to liberals George Stephanopoulos and Rachel Maddow. However, the vast majority of traditional journalists have been emphatically dedicated to notions of objectivity and nonpartisanship, only occasionally offering political positions when overwhelmed by a situation, as in Murrow's famous broadcasts. This landscape shifted significantly in the 1990s, making the idea of the media's political bias central in redefining the politics of television news.

When Fox News debuted in the mid-1990s, it had a partially obscured political axe to grind—founder and CEO Roger Ailes, who had previously been a political consultant for numerous Republicans, including Presidents Nixon, Reagan, and the first George Bush, drew upon decades of accusations against the "liberal media" to launch the new channel. Fox News branded itself as the only nonpartisan news channel through slogans "Fair and Balanced" and "We Report, You Decide," implicitly labeling competitors such as CNN and broadcast networks as liberally biased. Most research has suggested that Fox News skews far to the right of mainstream in its pundits, expert guests, story selection, and framing; and some individual Fox journalists have direct ties to Republican politics, including former Fox anchor Tony Snow, who left the channel to become President Bush's press secretary in 2006. However, Ailes insists that Fox is "commonsense" news in line with "average Americans," rather than a partisan channel, although he admits that the channel sits more to the right than its competitors. Rather than directly attack Fox's right-leaning content dressed in the guise of objectivity and balance, competing networks and other cable news channels embraced more punditry and conservative broadcasters in the wake of Fox's success, per television's logic of imitation, assuming that Americans wanted more conservative opinions and that the entire country's politics had shifted rightward.

However, we might consider another explanation for Fox's success. Much of Fox's ratings success comes from a niche of older, white, rural, and suburban viewers who watch a high amount of television, and who had previously found television news unsatisfying both in politics and tone. CNN and MSNBC's initial attempts to beat Fox at its own game of conservative punditry largely failed as that relatively small audience segment was already committed to Fox; MSNBC only found ratings success by shifting toward the left in the mid-2000s with overtly liberal hosts Keith Olbermann and Rachel Maddow, serving a partisan liberal niche otherwise unmet by television news, while CNN has branded itself as the nonpartisan centrist option. The audience share of Fox News is still a fraction of that of network news, representing a small but dedicated slice of the entire television news audience. Simultaneous to Fox's rise, another competitor to the mainstream news emerged as a popular alternative to a younger and more urban audience segment: *The Daily Show with*

Among their many contrasts, Fox News appeals to an explicitly rural and heartland vision of America...

...while *The Daily Show with Jon Stewart* emphasizes its edgy and urbane sensibility through comedy and satire.

> ## THE DAILY SHOW
>
> *The Daily Show with Jon Stewart* (Comedy Central, 1996–present): A satirical news program that has grown in importance in recent years, offering interviews with major political and media figures alongside comedic commentary on the news. As network and cable news came under attack for lacking journalistic integrity in the 2000s, *The Daily Show* became an unusual example of a news parody, often offering more critically engaged and fact-checked information than actual news programs.

Jon Stewart. Although *The Daily Show* does not embrace Fox's right-wing politics, claims of objectivity, or even the practice of journalism itself, these dual successes point to some common ground that has helped reshape journalism. Both Fox and *The Daily Show* aim to entertain audiences, either through the heightened drama of outrageous punditry or the wry humor of satire, embracing the emotional dimension of news that many journalists avoid in the name of objectivity. Both Fox and *The Daily Show* are willing to confront the powerful, and do not embrace the passive citing of competing experts to challenge a claim or official source. And both Fox and *The Daily Show* address their specific audience niches without striving for a broad national consensus opinion; they are willing to offer adversarial positions that counter more broadly held ideals to appeal to their core constituencies.

Of course Fox News and *The Daily Show* operate in distinctly different genres—one is a journalistic channel that its detractors claim is not actually real news via mocking labels such as "Faux News," while the other defines itself as fake news even though some supporters see it as one of the more accurate and insightful public affairs programs on television. And they clearly see each other as adversaries—*Daily Show* producers created the spin-off *The Colbert Report* as a direct parody of Bill O'Reilly and Fox News, while Fox tried to launch its own comedy news show, *The ½ Hour News Hour*, in 2007 as a conservative retort to Comedy Central, with recurring guest appearances from ultra-right-wing pundits Rush Limbaugh and Ann Coulter (the program lasted less than nine months). Depending on your own political opinions and beliefs, *The Daily Show* might appear to convey an accurate outlook of the world, while Fox News might seem hopelessly biased and damaging to the authority of the press—or you might feel the reverse. Both of these models of public affairs television coexisting on the cable schedule allows for the open expression of multiple positions and perspectives on the news, and encourages debate between positions, in order for viewers to see which is more appealing and accurate in framing our understanding of society.

These dual successes point to the importance and potential of the partisan press, and hark back to the function of journalism imagined in the Constitution. While the objective and professional-consensus model of journalism refuses to offer opinions, positions, or even facts on many issues, the partisan press and pundits dare to be adversarial and, at times, offer more investigative and factual material than so-called "serious news," with the clear effect of encouraging viewers to care passionately about news coverage and current events. One potential danger of the partisan press is that factual knowledge might suffer in the wake of opinion journalism. Research about this question is contradictory, showing that regular Fox News viewers were less knowledgeable about current events than the viewers of any other network or cable news outlet, but that regular *Daily Show* viewers were the most informed audience of all.[6] We might interpret these research findings as suggesting that people's knowledge about current events guides their choices in types of news, rather than the news promoting knowledge or ignorance. Many informed viewers seem to seek out the humor of *The Daily Show*, while some viewers who are less interested in current events may find the opinions of Fox News reassuring without challenging their political beliefs. Additionally, Fox's claims to objective, in-depth journalism do not fit with their practices of partisan reporting. Perhaps the key problem with Fox is not its lack of objectivity, but its refusal to own up to and embrace its partisan role.

For some critics, the answer to many of the failings of contemporary journalism would be a reinvigorated partisan press, with a commitment to investigative and factual reporting supporting opinion-driven coverage, a wider range of positions than just liberal or conservative, and an acknowledged political position beyond claims of objectivity or balance. Such a return to adversarial partisan journalism seems to have a market appeal in an era of narrowcasting, but might be a difficult shift given the corporate and official biases of television journalism. It is hard to imagine how a truly adversarial press might obtain corporate sponsorship and support by the media conglomerates that control television, as investigative critical journalism that challenges the status quo goes against the institutional basis of the commercial television industry.

Local News and Everyday Sensationalism

Unlike nearly every other television genre, journalism is not exclusively programmed by national networks or cable channels. The local basis of broadcasting stations is most apparent in local newscasts, which are a staple of most network affiliates and a few nonaffiliated stations across the country. Local news is one of the few types of programming not provided through network feeds or syndication, with stations featuring regular newscasts in early mornings, midday, early evening, and late night. Even though ratings have declined in recent years due to more competition from cable and online sources, local news remains quite profitable for stations, accounting for approximately 45 percent of station revenue on average, even though news fills only an average of just under four hours of each day's schedule.[7] But how does local news operate and impact our understanding of television's role in serving the public interest?

Local news has been a part of the broadcast schedule since the earliest years of television, when the well-funded VHF stations offered local newscasts to help distinguish themselves from UHF competitors, who could not generally afford the start-up costs of news studios. But it was not until the mid-1970s that local news began to resemble today's newscasts. The introduction of portable video record-ers and videotape editing systems enabled a model of **electronic news gathering** (ENG), with reporters traveling on location to cover the stories of the day. By the 1980s, professional-grade **camcorders** combined camera and taping technologies at a price affordable to local stations, and live relays using mobile microwave or satellite transmission systems allowed reporters to broadcast live from around a sta-tion's region. All of these technologies helped spur a rapid growth in the amount of local news featured on the schedule, and in reporters' abilities to cover a wider range of stories. By the 1980s, the format of local news was firmly in place, with regular segments on weather forecasts, local sports results, and clear genres of news stories including political, crime, arts, and feature reporting.

Since local news is such a profitable portion of a station's operation, the competition for audience share is fierce within most markets. The choices that stations make to appeal to audiences fit with many of the biases and tendencies of national network and cable news, with some particular features more unique to local broadcasts. With the rise of ENG and live reporting, newscasts began to emphasize the emotional and visual appeals enabled by television, seeking out stories with a visual hook to pull in audiences. Rather than stories of local poli-tics, investigations of community reforms, or informational features on a region's central institutions, local television news adheres to the mantra of "if it bleeds, it leads"—stories of public safety, violent crimes, accidents, disasters, car chases, and fears of potential threats are the staples of local newscasts, with titillating teasers airing to promote that night's most sensational stories throughout the day. Labels used to promote newscasts, such as "Eyewitness News" or "Action News," highlight the visual sensationalism that local news tries to capture, with an escalating race between stations to offer the most visceral and emotionally compelling presentation of local events. Critics of media sensationalism have studied how local news tends to provoke more fear than knowledge about sto-ries, potentially contributing to an inflated sense of actual crime and violence patterns in a community, discussed more in chapter 9. There is little doubt that local news has been successful in drawing a consistent audience across demo-graphic groups, as around two thirds of Americans cite their local news as their major source of news, and viewers typically find local news more credible than network options.[8]

Local news also demonstrates the impact of official and corporate biases. Economic reporting focuses on local businesses in typically positive ways, and relies upon business and government leaders to frame stories. Within many local stations, especially in smaller markets, news managers are frequently pressured by advertisers and their sales departments to shape stories to be more sympathetic to sponsors, either through "puff pieces" celebrating a local business initiative or by avoiding stories that might reflect poorly on the sponsor. While many local stations have found that viewers want to see more in-depth stories on a wide range of topics and investigative reporting, over the past decade news divisions have faced both significant budget and staffing cuts and growing numbers of news hours to fill per week, making it increasingly difficult to devote resources to reporting complex issues in-depth. In the face of tight budgets that need to be stretched to fill more hours, local newscasts often follow cheaper and simpler formulas—location footage of crime and accidents, statements from officials and press conferences, hyped stories to provoke emotional engagement, and a narrow focus excluding many parts of a local community. The emotional and violent hooks of local news are profitable and seem to increase ratings, even if viewers complain about too much sensationalism and too little breadth of coverage.

Although local news has traditionally been produced by local stations, some components of newscasts have more national origins. For network affiliates, local news can build on network programming, such as providing the local angle on a topic of that evening's network programming, whether an environmental story featured on news magazine *20/20* or the dangers of crimes featured on *CSI*. Stations owned by networks or large station groups often share news stories or interviews concerning a regional or national topic, with station groups distributing segments to its numerous stations. A more ethically questionable practice involves **video news releases** (VNR), short segments that resemble news stories presented by a reporter, but are created by public relations firms to promote a client or its agenda. In a cost-cutting attempt to maximize profits and fill increasing news schedules, local stations will air VNRs as if they were actual news stories. Examples of VNRs include a piece on automobile safety devices produced for General Motors and a story about the importance of life insurance funded by Allstate. VNRs found themselves in the spotlight in 2005 when it was revealed that the U.S. government had funded, produced, and distributed VNRs presented as journalistic news stories in support some of its policy initiatives, including the education bill No Child Left Behind and proposed changes to Medicare. While trade organizations representing public relations firms and broadcast journalists state that VNRs should be aired with statements of disclosure citing the source of the footage, researchers have found that most stations who use VNRs do not clearly mark the stories as public relations promotions rather than actual journalism, a practice prompting a FCC investigation resulting in fines in 2007.[9]

So do local newscasts adequately serve the public interest? Local news encompasses such a broad range of practices that it would be impossible to generalize. Certainly many local stations are meeting the desires of many viewers, with local news being seen on average as more credible and less biased than national networks or cable. For most Americans, local television news is the primary means by which they stay informed about their community, but research suggests that the vision of the world conveyed by local news paints a more violent and dangerous picture than reality, and that the news is shaped by corporate and official interests in ways that remain invisible to most viewers. The trend moving away from local origination of stories is particularly concerning, as the American model of broadcasting is designed to have a local orientation especially for public interest programming. We can see additional concerns surrounding both local and network news through a detailed analysis of election coverage, with clear evidence that television has dramatically transformed American politics.

POLITICS FOR PROFIT: TELEVISION AND AMERICAN ELECTIONS

The highest-profile intersection between television and American democracy is the medium's role in electing government representatives. From airing debates to profiling candidates, television has become the central means for voters to learn about candidates and shape their decisions, making an effective media strategy one of the key requirements for political success. Elections are also extremely profitable for the television industry: the 2006 campaign cycle generated over $2.1 billion in revenue for televised political advertisements, making politics the second largest sector of the advertising market, trailing only the automobile industry. We must examine these dual roles of television in electoral politics—public interest provider of information and private interest broker of airtime—in tandem to understand the medium's ultimate role as a democratic institution and to assess its relative impacts on American democracy.

Television's potential for shaping American politics became evident in the medium's first decade, with the presidential campaign of 1952 setting key precedents. Republican candidate for vice president Richard Nixon was one of the first politicians to use television's medium bias for political gain—Nixon had been accused of financial misdeeds involving unreported political contributions, and presidential candidate Dwight Eisenhower was under pressure to drop Nixon from the ticket. But Nixon took his case directly to the American people via television, buying airtime for a thirty-minute prime time speech defending his financial dealings; the speech is most memorable for Nixon's admission that the one unreported political gift he received was his family dog Checkers, and he refused to return it. This broadcast, referred to commonly as the "Checkers speech," swayed public sentiment toward Nixon and helped demonstrate the emotional and personal connections possible through television, a mode of address that Nixon would have trouble mastering later in his political career.

The second innovation from 1952 was the emergence of televised political advertising. Democratic candidate Adlai Stevenson was reluctant to run campaign ads, saying that Americans should not have their politics "sold like detergent." Instead, he bought airtime to run full campaign speeches at 10:30 P.M.; however, the eloquent yet long-winded Stevenson frequently ran long, and stations cut off his speeches before completion. Eisenhower was far less accomplished as a speaker, but his advisers devised a strategy to connect the candidate to television viewers: he filmed a series of twenty-second commercial spots called "Eisenhower Answers America," featuring a seemingly average American asking questions about key issues and Eisenhower responding through stilted and awkwardly scripted answers. For today's viewers, the spots appear amateurish and likely to generate mocking scorn more than identification or praise, but in television's early years, Eisenhower's ad campaign reached viewers and generated enthusiasm through the candidate's direct address to American voters. After 1952, it would become impossible to run a major political campaign without packaging candidates through short commercial spots.

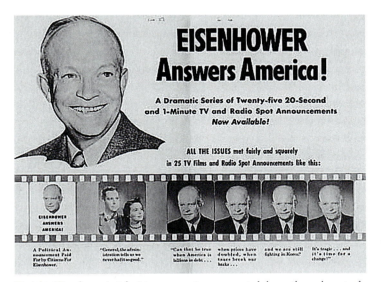

Dwight Eisenhower's television campaign, promoted here through a trade magazine ad, highlighted his engagement with everyday Americans, allowing him to appear more in touch with voters and setting important precedents for campaign advertising.

Political advertising follows most of the strategies used to sell products discussed in chapter 2. Many ads, especially early in a campaign, focus on brand awareness, establishing name recognition for a candidate and creating positive links about a candidate's experience, character, and qualifications. Many commercials in this vein can be considered **image ads**, offering visions of the candidate in his community, playing with his children, and interacting with average Americans in frequently patriotic settings. Such ads work to reinforce upbeat emotional associations for voters and hope to evoke positive visual imagery whenever a voter thinks about the candidate. When analyzed rationally, image ads offer little real information—after all, do voters really question whether a candidate actually loves his family, cares about his community, or supports America? Image ads are all about implicit persuasion, building positive associations with a candidate at the emotional level. Successful image ads include President Reagan's "Morning in America" reelection campaign in 1984, and candidate Clinton's self-defining video "The Man from Hope" in 1992.

Another genre of political commercial is the **issue ad**, similar to boosting knowledge of a consumer product. Although many critics praise issue ads as the most rational and serious way to educate voters about candidates, there are very few pure issue ads; most link a candidate's policy position with a particular image and set of emotional appeals. For instance, an ad touting a candidate's healthcare reform plan will typically use visuals to convey the politician's compassion, willingness to tackle tough issues, or toughness in standing up to special interests. Other issue ads function more to contrast candidates' positions on the issues, a strategy that frequently bleeds into attack strategies. With the rise of campaign websites, more detailed policy positions have migrated online, where candidates can offer specific proposals and control their image more directly, as well as solicit contributions, sign up volunteers, and create virtual communities.

Concrete discussion of policy issues is most common in the controversial style of **attack ads**, where campaigns critique opponents' records and proposals. Often attack ads offer the most direct comparison between candidates, although they are obviously slanted to favor one side and misrepresent competitors. Negative ads focusing on a candidate's record typically take specific votes out of context, claim contradictions between policies or votes that might be more complex than they appear, and oversimplify positions into starker differences between candidates. For instance, in 2004 Senator John Kerry was regularly characterized as a "flip-flopper" for changing positions on issues, an accusation Republicans used to raise doubts about his integrity and leadership ability—but such accusations can be made about nearly any politician with a significant record, as many votes are on complex omnibus bills that contain policies and amendments a candidate might not endorse. Kerry's campaign was unable to fight these accusations, and the Bush campaign effectively defined Kerry's character as untrustworthy and unprincipled through attack ads.

Many attack ads are less focused on a candidate's record than on creating negative emotional associations with an opposing politician or entire party. One of the most famous attack ads was offered in President Lyndon Johnson's 1964 campaign against Barry Goldwater. In an effort to frame Goldwater as too volatile and extremist to lead the country, the "daisy ad" superimposed a young girl picking petals off a daisy with a countdown to a nuclear bomb explosion, ending with the tag line "the stakes are just too high for you to stay home." Democrats paid to air the ad only once before Republican protests led Johnson's campaign to pull it from the air, but the ad itself became news, replayed as a topic of analysis during network news and making the front cover of *Time* magazine. The daisy ad both raised the emotional stakes for negative campaigning and proved that a productive side effect of a controversial ad was free airtime and publicity when the ad became newsworthy. While few attack ads today rise to the irresponsible inflammatory level of the daisy ad, most use production techniques to engage voter's emotions. For instance, competitors are often shown in unflattering black-and-white images with ominous music, while the sponsoring candidate is warmly portrayed in color and with a pleasing soundtrack.

Negative campaigning is a controversial strategy that public opinion polls suggest is unpopular with voters, but research demonstrates that it works. Negative ads are quite successful in defining a candidate's positions and character, as well as emotionally affecting voters. Candidates try to remove themselves from the negative tone of such ads, and recently most negative campaign ads are paid for by either the political parties or outside interest groups. In 2004, the most notable presidential attack ads came from activist groups such as MoveOn.org on the left, Swift Boat Veterans for Truth on the right, allowing the candidates to appear to rise above the fray of negative campaigning. Another side effect of intense negative campaigning is frustrating voters and making them disinterested in politics. While it might seem that this would be a negative outcome for politicians, some candidates can benefit from lower voter turnout in specific elections, and critics suspect that campaigns purposely ratchet up negative ads to suppress voter interest—a strategy that might benefit one candidate, but certainly hurts democracy.

Campaign advertising is by far the most costly aspect of a political campaign, with the bulk of spending going to creating and placing television commercials on the air in local markets. **Political media consultants** are a key part of this process, mimicking the role of agencies in traditional advertising by managing the process of strategizing, producing, test marketing, and buying airtime for campaign ads—all for a huge payday, with consultants earning over $1 billion in the 2004 campaign. Activists and a few politicians have suggested that the huge costs of political campaigning, especially funding broadcast ads, leads to government corruption and undue influence from major donors and the special interests that help fund campaigns, ranging from labor unions to major industry lobbyists. **Campaign finance reform** has emerged as a challenge to established political practices, with regulations and laws pushing back against the influence of money in politics. One of the big impacts of these reforms has been the creation of political organizations known as 527 groups, such as MoveOn or Swift Boat Veterans, to create attack ads apart from parties or campaigns, a tactic that runs counter to the reformist goals of recent legislation.

One potential avenue for governmental reform strikes at the very heart of television's broadcast structure. Reformers from both political parties have proposed legislation that would require stations using the public airwaves at no cost to fulfill their public interest obligations by offering free airtime to candidates. Under such a proposal, candidates would receive vouchers to purchase advertisements from local stations, funded by a spectrum usage fee, as well as from stations providing longer time slots for more detailed speeches or presentations. Broadcasters have lobbied strongly against such proposals, as they would result in a huge loss of revenue from the lucrative political advertising market. Additionally, the corporate liberal mind-set of most policymakers suggests that such a major overhaul to the campaign and broadcasting system is unlikely, especially since such reform would overturn the very system that elected the incumbent legislators. The courts have a mixed record on the question of whether regulating campaign advertising violates First Amendment rights of broadcasters and politicians, with some rulings supporting reformers and others overturning regulations. It is important to note that when compared with other democracies around the world, the United States is one of the very few countries where highly profitable advertising is the centerpiece of campaigning, another example of American broadcasting serving as an exception to typical practices throughout the world.

Although political advertising dominates electoral politics and serves to frame candidates in the public's mind, television news also devotes a good deal of time to electoral politics—both network and cable news, in covering national races, and local news on state politics, focus a great amount of coverage on elections. But the type of coverage focused on elections is more controversial. The majority of election coverage is focused on politics more than on policies—typically, television news and talk shows frame campaigns in terms of the game of elections, highlighting who is winning or losing based on polls, and examining the day's events for their political impact. Television reporting spends much less time analyzing the policy positions of candidates, investigating their campaign claims, or providing broader contexts or comparisons relevant to the issues and how they might impact voters and viewers. This focus on the electoral contest, often called **horse race coverage**, looks more at campaign strategies, analyzing speeches and political ads not for what they say about governing, but for the underlying political motives and impacts of a politician's strategies.

A good example of how television news frames elections as horse races can be found in the televised presentations of debates. For many voters, debates are an important opportunity to hear policy positions, see candidates think on their feet responding to unexpected questions, and compare the ideas and personas of their potential officials. Television coverage shifts the pre- and post-debate discussion to questions of competition: Who won and lost? Who had the best sound bites or put-downs? What will voters think? Such discussions always rely on pundits and campaign officials to frame and spin the debate performances, often placing the actual issues being debated in the background, behind the questions of competitive politics. Televised debates are frequently moderated by pundits and journalists, and increasingly their questions have shifted away from policies and more toward horse race issues such as electability and scandals. Likewise, television coverage of major debates often use focus groups to measure voter response to the debates, rating candidates' performances like a new product or television pilot in the quest to handicap the race. Even when recent debates have tried new formats to engage voters more directly, such as the town hall format of the 1990s or YouTube-submitted questions in 2007, the television coverage focused less on the interesting issues raised by ordinary Americans and more on which politicians played the game most effectively.

Why do the media focus their coverage on the game of politics, and what are the social impacts of this strategy? As with most aspects of television, the causes and effects of such practices are complex and overlapping. One key reason for the focus on the contest rather than the content of politics is the sense that competition makes for more entertaining and engaging coverage, and thus boosts ratings. Since commercial news competes for audience numbers, the desire to entertain rather than educate audiences makes financial sense and fits the industry's concept of "what interests the public." Additionally, the logic of pack journalism, objectivity, and official bias supports this trend, as news divisions follow each other and allow the candidates to define the topic of the news without investigating their claims beyond presenting competing official or expert voices about any issue. Horse race coverage is cheaper to develop, requiring pundits more than investigative reporting, and journalists based in Washington find the competitive aspects of politics more within their expertise than complex policy initiatives. Finally, the medium bias fits well with the competitive emotional excitement of winners and losers rather than the informational and potentially, though not necessarily, dry and detached focus on policy analysis, turning politics into more of a televised sport than an informative civics lesson.

One additional incentive for horse race coverage is particularly problematic. Broadcasters and cable channels are not only in the industry of producing news—even more so, they are in the business of selling advertising. Since political advertising is such a lucrative source of a station or cable channel's revenue, it helps the business side of television to create an atmosphere conducive to selling political ads. By focusing on competitive politics, television news helps generate interest in campaigns, especially early in races, and allows the politicians and parties to frame the issues for voters. It goes against the interests of politicians for journalists to contradict their ads or provide in-depth analysis undermining campaign promises; television news often avoids this mode of reporting, in part to avoid upsetting their "clients" of political campaigns. For campaign finance reformers, an additional argument for de-commercializing politics is that it might help improve the quality of reporting covering elections.

The social impacts of horse race coverage are quite important, demonstrating one way that television journalism falls short of its public interest potential. Numerous studies have shown that Americans lack significant knowledge of current events and that U.S. voter turnout numbers are much lower than in most other democracies. If television truly is the country's primary information source, it seems clear that the medium is not succeeding in either educating or motivating citizens to participate in democracy. Voters regularly complain of "election fatigue" as journalists start horse race coverage earlier in each campaign, or suggest that they feel too uninformed to participate effectively in elections. While perhaps the horse race approach yields some short-term ratings gains for broadcasters, critics suggest that the long-term impact decreases citizen engagement and interest in politics, which further drives the need for broadcast journalists to try to entertain audiences through competition and scandal, fueling a cycle of political apathy and sensationalism.

One potential effect of horse race journalism is that it might impact election results themselves, guiding voters to make their choices to successfully handicap the contest. In the Democratic primaries in 2004, John Kerry swept most states, including surprising early wins in Iowa and New Hampshire. Analysis of voter polls suggested that one of the major reasons Kerry emerged as the Democratic nominee was that voters thought he was the most "electable" candidate. More than his stance on the issues, many Democrats seem to have voted for Kerry because they saw him as the strongest candidate to bet on in a horse race with President Bush. We can see this as a strong instance of agenda setting, with the media shaping the public opinion not to favor any particular candidate, but to frame the election in the terms of competitive campaigning rather than issues-based governance.

Television's treatment of electoral politics sits at a crossroads between the public and private interests structuring American broadcasting. The commercial imperative of nearly all American television forces journalists to shape their coverage to maximize ratings, cut down costs, and avoid conflicting with their sponsors, including the campaigns and political parties themselves. Most individual journalists certainly believe their work as operating in the public interest, and wish to inform and inspire Americans to be engaged citizens in a participatory democracy. However, journalists work within a system where there are numerous barriers to models of reporting that might better serve public interests: standards of objective disengagement, limits on adversarial approaches, and the need to deliver consistent ratings all privilege the mode of journalism most common on American television today.

It will be interesting to see how the rise of online video, as on YouTube, might alter these norms by providing citizens direct access to both politicians and stories about elections that might not otherwise make the evening news. An often-cited example of the impact of online video was in the 2006 Virginia Senate campaign. During a campaign speech, Senator George Allen, a popular incumbent and potential future Republican presidential candidate, berated a young volunteer for his opponent's campaign and called him "macaca," a term many viewed as a racially insulting reference to a monkey. The volunteer, a college student of Indian descent, was videotaping the event; while such footage would have been unlikely to make it onto television, it soon appeared on YouTube and generated thousands of views and links from blogs. The story trickled up into newspapers, magazines, and television news, raising key questions about Allen's racial attitudes and integrity, and marked the turning point in the campaign that ended in his defeat. The YouTube clip showed the strengths of video in conveying emotional realism and authenticity, but functioned outside the private interest motivations and structures of television.

Many critics see television news at a point of crisis in recent years, with competing challenges from online video and journalism, as well as from more established innovations such as Fox News and *The Daily Show*. No matter how television's news and public affairs transform, it is vital to remember the foundational role that the press is designed to play in American democracy, and that the system of broadcasting itself was structured to serve as a trustee for the country's shared resource of the public airwaves. As a viewer, a producer, a citizen, or an outside observer, it is crucial always to ask how American television might be succeeding or failing in its duty to serve the "public interest, convenience, and necessity," and how we might demand more from the trustees of this invaluable public resource.

FURTHER READING

Much of the research on television news is distinctly critical of its impact on democracy—for instance, see James Hamilton, *All the News That's Fit to Sell: How the Market Transforms Information into News* (Princeton, N.J.: Princeton University Press, 2004), and Robert W. McChesney, *The Problem of the Media: U.S. Communication Politics in the Twenty-First Century* (New York: Monthly Review Press, 2004). Robin Andersen, *A Century of Media, a Century of War* (New York: Peter Lang, 2006), explores various news forms in covering wars, while Peter Dahlgren, *Television and the Public Sphere: Citizenship, Democracy, and the Media* (London; Thousand Oaks, Calif.: Sage Publications, 1995), offers an overall critique of television journalism.

For key historical moments, Thomas Patrick Doherty, *Cold War, Cool Medium: Television, McCarthyism, and American Culture* (New York: Columbia University Press, 2003), provides a strong account of television and the cold war; Michael Curtin, *Redeeming the Wasteland: Television Documentary and Cold War Politics* (New Brunswick, N.J.: Rutgers University Press, 1995), covers 1960s documentaries; and Richard Campbell, *60 Minutes and the News: A Mythology for Middle America* (Urbana: University of Illinois Press, 1991), analyzes the essential news magazine. For more recent developments, see Piers Robinson, *The CNN Effect: The Myth of News, Foreign Policy, and Intervention* (London: Routledge, 2002), about the impact of cable news; and Jeffrey Jones, *Entertaining Politics: New Political Television and Civic Culture* (Lanham, Md.: Rowman & Littlefield, 2005), for an account of political satire.

Television's impact on electoral politics gets a good overview in Shanto Iyengar and Jennifer McGrady, *Media Politics: A Citizen's Guide* (New York: W.W. Norton, 2007), and Thomas A. Hollihan, *Uncivil Wars: Political Campaigns in a Media Age*, 2nd ed. (New York: Bedford/St. Martins, 2008). For more on political advertising, see Michael M. Franz, et al., *Campaign Advertising and American Democracy* (Philadelphia: Temple University Press, 2007); http://www.livingroomcandidate.movingimage.us/ is an excellent online database of presidential advertisements.

NOTES

[1]See McChesney, *The Problem of the Media*.

[2]See Eric Alterman, *What Liberal Media? The Truth About Bias and the News* (New York: Basic Books, 2003); and "Buying the War," *Bill Moyers Journal* (PBS, 2007).

[3]McChesney, *Problem of the Media*, 102–107.

[4]This use of official sources instead of fact checking is discussed by journalists in "Buying the War.".

[5]See "Illusions of News," *The Public Mind*, PBS, 1989.

[6]Pew Research Center for the People and the Press, "Public Knowledge of Current Affairs Little Changed by News and Information Revolutions," April 15, 2007, http://people-press.org/reports/display.php3?ReportID=319.

[7]Statistics for 2005 found in *The State of the News Media 2007*, The Project for Excellence in Journalism, http://www.stateofthenewsmedia.org.

[8]Ibid.

[9]Diane Farsetta and Daniel Price, "Still Not the News," Center for Media and Democracy, November 2006, http://www.prwatch.org/fakenews2/execsummary.

SECTION 2

Television Meanings

American television is certainly shaped by the commercial and public institutions discussed in the previous four chapters, but for most people, television refers to the programs we watch. How do these programs communicate and express ideas? How do the meanings of television programming relate to American culture? To explore these issues of meaning, expression and content, the next four chapters turn to the analysis of television **texts**. For cultural critics, a text is any bounded communication system that can be analyzed, from a novel to a billboard, a piece of music to a painting. Texts need not be grounded in language, as visual and aural expression convey meaning and can express ideas. Television programs are clearly texts for the purposes of analysis, offering a range of meanings expressed through visual, sonic, and linguistic cues. To understand the textual dimension of television, we can draw upon critical traditions from the study of film, literature, visual art, music, and theater, while recognizing that television has its own particular modes of expression and cultural norms.

The textual aspect of television can be best understood by following a useful but somewhat artificial division between the **content** of programming, or the meanings offered by television, and the **form** of expression used to express those meanings. Note that this distinction is certainly blurry, as all content depends on form, and form expresses content. Chapters 7 and 8 focus on questions of content and meaning, considering how television texts represent the world in particular ways that can connect with and shape American culture. Chapter 5 offers an overview of the formal attributes of television that are used to express such meanings, provoke emotional reactions in viewers, and shape our vision of the world seen via the television screen, while chapter 6 focuses on the ways television tells stories and employs specific genres to engage and communicate with viewers. Together, these four chapters should provide a solid foundation for understanding the complex and sophisticated ways that television functions as a medium to communicate both entertaining diversions and core cultural values.

CHAPTER 5

MAKING MEANING

Why study the form of television programming, which is typically understood to be sufficiently obvious as to be accessible to any viewer? Examining the formal practices of media allows you to think like a creator, understanding how programs are made from the perspective of the producers. This is obviously a useful approach if you wish to work in the television industry in any capacity. But it is also insightful for everyday viewers of television, as being aware of formal elements allows for a more sophisticated understanding of programming. Just as learning the intricacies of any sport's rules and techniques helps you appreciate an exceptional athletic performance or game plan, knowing how television programs communicate enables a more nuanced appreciation of texts that are particularly effective, compelling, or aesthetically ambitious. Formal awareness also allows for a heightened critical perspective on the creation of meanings. Understanding the formal structures texts use to communicate with viewers helps us unpack the ways an advertisement persuades us, a news broadcast shapes our perspectives, or a drama portrays the world. Formal analysis is a crucial tool of a media-literate viewer.

One important issue runs throughout our discussion of television's form: the question of realism. Viewers regularly judge a program on whether it feels true to real life, expecting content to be believable and to relate to their world. But realism is a tricky issue, as all television is inherently unrealistic: television provides a partial and skewed representation of the three-dimensional worlds it portrays on a two-dimensional screen. We rarely actually want to see a program that realistically portrays every detail of real life, such as long commutes, mundane conversations, and uneventful days. We expect programming to be informative and entertaining more than realistic, so producers regularly portray a version of the world that is more engaging than reality, even if it strives to feel realistic and true to life.

We might consider a difference between realism in content, which is discussed in chapter 7, and realism in form. The formal practices of television are distinctly unrealistic as well; we rarely experience our world with background music, superimposed captions, and fades to black before cutting to commercials. Some aspects of television's form are understood to be more realistic, a style better termed **naturalistic**. We typically view naturalistic form as representing the real world without any manipulation, as with reality television or news interviews, but such naturalistic style actually follows a particular set of highly artificial conventions of moving image production that we only comprehend as realistic. Other formal practices are more **presentational**, overt in their use of technology and video conventions to represent the world; when a program is presentational in form, we rarely forget we're watching television, but a naturalistic style invites us to lose ourselves in the story. Of course, conventions change over time, so a silent film of the 1920s or a black-and-white television show of the 1950s may have been seen as naturalistic upon release, but such techniques would call attention to themselves as highly presentational choices today.

Realism in form and content are often not tied together. Most sports programming is quite realistic in its content, as it presents real athletes competing in unscripted events, but presentational in its form, with frequent use of graphics, replays, voiceovers, and direct address to the cameras, reminding us that we are watching a television program. A science fiction program such as *Star Trek: The Next Generation* might present an unrealistic world of androids, light-speed travel, and psychic aliens, but the form it uses to show that world is quite naturalistic—conventions of narrative, camerawork, staging, editing, and music all follow norms that make us forget we're watching a fictional world, as viewers are drawn into a fantasy that is presented as if it were real. Understanding the techniques of creating meanings through television's form allows us to better grasp how fantasy can be presented with such a compelling sense of realism.

MODES OF TELEVISION PRODUCTION

Like all facets of television, formal attributes of texts are tied to historical developments that cut across technological, institutional and cultural practices. Television developed in the 1940s with preexisting institutional structures drawn from radio, as the same networks and regulatory structures carried over

STAR TREK: THE NEXT GENERATION

Star Trek: The Next Generation (syndicated, 1987–94): Updating the 1960s classic science fiction series, this was the most successful of the *Star Trek* series, gaining strong ratings in first-run syndication and reigniting the devout *Trek* fanbase. *Next Generation*'s success led to three spinoff series, and four feature films starring the new cast, as well as inspiring a number of acclaimed and successful science fiction series in the 1990s.

from radio into television. Similarly, most early television programs were adaptations of established radio titles, with networks bringing radio programs such as *The Ed Sullivan Show, Stop the Music*, and *The Goldbergs* to television to help build the new medium. The networks were invested in making television into "radio with pictures," to continue their control over these media, but the addition of pictures was a significant shift in the creation of programs. Even if the stars and premises of radio hits could be imported to television, producers needed to think how best to incorporate the new visual dimension to radio programs; to solve this problem, early television turned to two other media as visual influences on television's radio foundation: cinema and live theater.

Television's **modes of production** emerged out of the early years of television programming, with each mode drawing differently on the technological and cultural legacies of radio, cinema and theater. Each mode of production offers its own set of technological practices and aesthetic norms, and all models that emerged in the early 1950s remain in practice to this day, tied to specific genres and cultural functions of television. Other production modes have developed since the 1950s, with the emergence of newer technologies of videotape and digital video.

Multi-Camera Live Studio Production

Throughout the 1930s and 1940s, radio and cinema coexisted as dominant media central to American culture. Each had distinct cultural functions and aesthetic tendencies. Going to the movies was a special event, and thus Hollywood embraced entertaining spectacles that would draw in a paying audience. The recorded nature of film led to carefully constructed repeatable texts that could be viewed as a fully realized art form. Radio, besides lacking film's visual dimension, also had particular strengths as a medium. As a domestic format, radio became part of the texture of everyday life, with many households listening throughout the day while involved in other activities. Radio programming was nearly always presented live, with the knowledge that you were hearing information or a performance at the same time as the entire country, and thus programming was often timely and attuned to a particular moment. Radio was also ephemeral, as what you heard would generally never be heard again in that exact performance, leading to an emphasis on continual production of new programming rather than film's focus on producing a smaller number of texts with a longer shelf life.

As television emerged as a new form in the 1940s, producers faced a dilemma: clearly the institutional base for television was drawn from radio, but the formal dimensions of presenting moving images and sounds via a screen had been well established by film. In favoring the associations tied to the radio medium, early television creators emphasized the experience of live, simultaneous viewing of programming over the more controlled, long-lasting recordings of motion pictures. Recorded material, whether in the form of radio recordings or telefilms, was disdained as violating the very nature of broadcasting, which was assumed to unite the audience in the shared simultaneous experience of a unique live performance, as discussed more in chapter 11. Not coincidentally, live programming fit well with what television networks could offer exclusively—simultaneous access to national programming—and thus the networks emphasized the mode of production that best ensured their continued economic control of the television medium, instead of allowing for the possibility of more local broadcast control.

So how did the emerging television industry adapt radio programming for the screen? For some genres, producers could simply place cameras in front of the radio announcers and performers to show musical performances, comedy routines, and newscasters as offered by radio variety and news shows. But scripted dramatic and comedic performances needed more than just a camera capturing actors speaking into microphones. Scripted entertainments turned to the live theater as the key precedent for how to represent a live performance visually. To establish a set of norms for how to present a live television program, the industry devised a system of **multi-camera live production** that the majority of early television programs followed.

The television industry in the 1940s was based in New York City, much like network radio and the major theatrical companies, which further helped to differentiate television from the California-based film industry. Television production followed the theatrical model of presenting a performance in real time on a stage. However, instead of limiting access to an audience in the same building, cameras would capture the action to broadcast it live to millions of viewers in their own homes. Live television production took place within **television studios**, buildings customized to make the complex practice of broadcasting programming efficient and routine. Although they have changed significantly since the 1940s, television studio production still follows the same basic setup and design as in the medium's earliest years.

The basic setup of a television studio starts with a stage area for performers to present a program's content, whether it's a scripted drama, musical performance, or a news anchor reading headlines. Staging of programming typically follows norms of theatrical presentation, with sets, props, lighting, costumes, makeup, and performers often framed by a stage with curtains. Many early television genres directly referenced live in-studio audiences, with announcers and performers acknowledging the theatricality of the performance by addressing both viewers and studio audiences in front of the curtain. Scripted dramas and comedies might not acknowledge the audience explicitly, but they still followed the basic theatrical convention of a performance space separated from an audience space, whether in-studio or at home.

The chief difference between television and theatrical performances is the use of technology to broadcast material around the country. Studios feature multiple cameras, typically three, which visually capture the performances, along with a series of microphones to transmit audio. Early cameras were quite large and limited in their visual flexibility. They were mounted on large wheeled pedestals to enable them to be moved while shooting and be repositioned in relation to the action; contemporary cameras are far more compact and offer

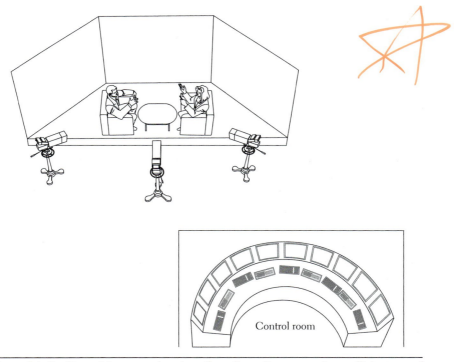

Figure 5-1 Studio multi-camera shooting allows for audience reactions, efficient use of time, and live broadcasting, but has little control over mistakes or flexibility of camera angle or location.

excellent resolution, but they still are wheeled around studios on pedestals by camera operators in a manner similar to the 1950s. Live studio cameras do not record video directly, but transmit video signals to a **control room** via wires. Likewise, all microphones, whether wireless lapel mics or overhead booms on poles, feed into an **audio mixer** to process sound signals.

Both the audio mixer and control room work to mix the multiple inputs coming from the studio into a single stream of video and audio to be broadcast. For audio, a sound editor mixes the various microphones and other sources, such as recorded music, effects, and prerecorded voices, into an **audio mix** that focuses viewer attention and conveys the necessary content from the performance. The control room uses a **video switcher** to select which of the cameras will be broadcast, choose how to switch between shots using dissolves or other effects, and add additional video sources such as graphics, titles, and prerecorded footage. Through this process of **live editing**, video and audio are combined and transmitted to the station or channel, which transmits the program out over the airwaves.

Live television broadcasting retained the air of vitality that typified the radio era, as viewers were invested in watching programming in their homes that they knew was being performed in New York as they watched. The spontaneity and risk of live broadcasting was one of the medium's appeals, as viewers reveled in the improvisatory humor of Milton Berle recovering from mistakes on *Texaco Star Theater*, or the thrill of musicians performing in the moment. Live broadcasting certainly had its risks, as mistakes and technical difficulties could turn programs into disasters and disrupt the expensive plans of the producers and networks. But the cultural norms of radio carried over to television's early years to privilege live broadcasting as more respected and legitimate than recorded programming.

One of the chief drawbacks of this live system was that the material was not recorded through this process. Videotapes were not widely used until the late 1950s, so the only way to record live programming was through a **kinescope**, a low-quality system in which a film camera would shoot the program directly from a television screen receiving the live signal. Kinescopes were important for networks trying to cope with the multiple time zones throughout the United States—typically, live programming would be rebroadcast for the West Coast three hours after the initial live broadcast, leading to a lower-quality image throughout the Pacific time zone. Many kinescopes were discarded after being broadcast, making archival records of early television quite inconsistent.

Nearly every form of television in the late 1940s was broadcast live, as filmed options were regarded both as too costly and of questionable quality. Some theatrical films were aired on television, but early televised films were most commonly British imports or marginal independent American companies outside the mainstream film industry, as Hollywood initially positioned itself as a hostile competitor to television. The theater industry was much more cooperative with television, as much of early television's creative talent worked in theater.

SATURDAY NIGHT LIVE

Saturday Night Live (NBC, 1975–present): The long running live late-night sketch comedy show has consistently pushed boundaries of network standards, with the "Not Ready for Prime Time Players" skirting censors in the 1970s, and has established comedic catchphrases and trends through recurring sketches for decades. While the show has gone through dry spells, cast members have had a strong record making the transition to successful film and prime time television careers.

An important type of programming in the 1940s and 1950s was the **anthology drama**, which offered a unique stand-alone play presented live each week via a sponsor-named program such as *Kraft Television Theatre* or *Goodyear Television Playhouse.* Typically these programs featured teleplays from prominent writers such as Paddy Chayefsky and Rod Serling, and starred Broadway actors in critically praised social dramas such as *Marty* and *Requiem for a Heavyweight.* Since each week presented an original story, with new casts, often elaborate sets, and extensive rehearsal time to perfect staging for live broadcast, they were quite labor- and money-intensive as compared to ongoing series. Thus the prestigious genre declined in prominence throughout the 1950s, as networks looked to offer more cost-efficient and less risky programming.

Today, multi-camera live production remains a key component of the television industry, serving as the dominant means of production for numerous genres. Since liveness is most crucial for timely current events, this mode of production is common for news, public affairs, sports, and event programming in which such immediacy is valued. Channels such as CNN, Fox News, ESPN, and the Weather Channel present mostly live programming, although throughout their live broadcasts they feature many prerecorded segments of sports highlights, on-location news features, and interviews. Occasionally, scripted programs will use a live broadcast as a stunt to generate ratings, as programs including *The West Wing, ER, The Drew Carey Show,* and *Will & Grace* have featured special live episodes. *Saturday Night Live* remains an exception on American television, offering regularly scheduled live entertainment programming that celebrates spontaneity and unpredictability over careful control. But since the 1950s, the vast majority of entertainment programming has been recorded via film or videotape.

Single-Camera Telefilm Production

Live studio production was the preferred mode for early television, aligning the new medium with radio and theatrical influences, but filmed television programs, or telefilms, date back to the medium's early days. Telefilm production was modeled after the film industry's well-established factory-style system of production, and offered particular advantages to television producers willing to take the financial risks tied to the more expensive telefilm mode. Not surprisingly, telefilm production was centered in Los Angeles, taking advantage of the technological and talent base of the film industry. Once telefilm became a viable alternative to live production in the mid-1950s, film studios moved to their central position in producing television programming that they still maintain today.

The basic model of telefilm production exchanges the efficiency and immediacy of live production for increased control and flexibility in shooting and editing. Live studio production was seen as ideal for genres that benefit from immediate audience response, such as music and comedy, and that foreground a theatrical or limited internal setting. But narrative genres popular on radio and in film, such as detective shows and Westerns, and nonfiction documentary productions need the flexibility of outdoor and multiple locations that in-studio production cannot effectively offer. Thus the earliest telefilms were for these genres, offering locations and action sequences typically unavailable in live productions.

A telefilm follows the production model of Hollywood filmmaking. In a live studio shoot, multiple cameras capture the action, with a director selecting between the angles in real time. Telefilms use a single camera to shoot a scene from a particular angle—often in multiple takes to ensure adequate quality of performance and visuals—and then retake the same scene with a different camera setup. A typical dialogue scene will film a take of the action from a distance to cover the entire scene, called a master shot, and then set up shots with facial closeups of each major character, leading to at least three camera angles and a corresponding sound recording for each shot. The production process thus takes much longer, as each camera setup must reset lighting and microphones, and every scene must be performed multiple times from each angle. Single-camera shooting can employ some routines for efficiency, as typically scenes are shot out of order to make the best use of cast members and specific sets or locations, instead of following the script's temporal order.

The postproduction process is even more time consuming, as reels of film must be developed and then edited together into a continuous sequence and synchronized with sound. Since labor is one of the most costly elements of any media production, single-camera production is far more expensive than the live model, which was one of the chief reasons for the emerging television industry to prefer the less financially burdensome live mode of production. Yet telefilm has its own particular appeal, which led a number of producers to establish the Hollywood standard as a viable and commonplace mode of television production.

Beyond the flexibility in genre and location shooting that telefilm offered, a filmed production ensured more control in the quality of the product—multiple

Figure 5-2 Single-camera shooting provides greater control of location, angle, and prevention of errors, but is far more time-consuming and costly than multi-camera shooting, offering little possibility of live audience reactions or spontaneity.

takes and postproduction editing eliminated the potential of a technical difficulty or blown performance undermining an entire program. Producers relished the control of image, editing, tone, and pacing that single-camera production offered, ensuring that the program matched the creator's vision with fewer risks than live production. The flexibility of camera and sound setups with single cameras allowed for more creativity in visual style, potentially enabling directors to mimic the look and feel of Hollywood films.

But the chief rationale behind the adoption of telefilm production was the durability of a high-quality program beyond the initial live broadcast. The image resolution of a telefilm was far superior to that of a kinescope, meaning that programming could be shown across time zones and multiple times without a loss in quality. Some of the earliest telefilm productions were for syndicated programming, which by definition could not be produced live; each local station scheduled programs on its own, so no live programming could be syndicated.

The biggest breakthrough program to popularize telefilms on a major network was the crime drama *Dragnet*, based on a popular NBC radio drama. *Dragnet*'s producer and star Jack Webb insisted on visualizing the show via telefilm, to capture its documentary-style visuals, multiple locations, montage editing with frequent voiceover narration, and on-location portrayal of Los Angeles.

Dragnet's early use of telefilm production allowed for outdoor and on-location shooting, enabling greater authenticity for the crime drama, as well as lucrative high-quality reruns.

Producing the show through his own Mark VII production company, Webb bankrolled a pilot shot in the L.A. City Hall to the objections of NBC, which was invested in the common notion that filmed programming would not be viewed as legitimate. The show became an instant hit after its 1951 debut, residing near the top of the ratings throughout the 1950s and establishing the norms for the television police drama.

Dragnet also demonstrated the chief economic strength of telefilms. When Webb placed the show on hiatus in 1954 to shoot a feature film version, NBC decided to air repeats of earlier episodes in prime time. The success of these reruns, which looked as good as their initial broadcast due to the telefilm model, paved the way for reruns of filmed programming serving as a lucrative source of income for both networks and producers. Telefilm programming thrived in syndication, compensating producers for the greater economic risks of the costly production model with potential long-term revenue unavailable for live programs. Because of these economic incentives and the cultural legitimacy that *Dragnet* gave telefilms, filmed programming became more common throughout the 1950s, eroding the assumed superiority of live television in the eyes of many viewers, critics, and industry leaders.

Single-camera telefilm remains one of the most common modes of production in contemporary television. Nearly every prime time dramatic program uses this form today, as medical programs, crime shows, family dramas, science fiction

DRAGNET

Dragnet (NBC, 1951–59, 1967–70): One of television's earliest hits adapted from a radio drama, *Dragnet* set the norms for the cop show through its focus on urban locales and crime-solving procedures, as well as innovating telefilm production techniques and the use of reruns. The 1960s version returned to the air with its 1950s sensibility still intact, promoting a strict law-and-order mind-set in the face of hippies and youth counterculture.

shows, and fantasy programs all capitalize on the high-quality visual control and longevity of telefilm. Although most sitcoms are produced in studios, a number of single-camera telefilm sitcoms, such as *The Andy Griffith Show*, *M*A*S*H*, and *Malcolm in the Middle*, have sacrificed the instant audience response of studio production for the visual flexibility of single-camera production. The mid-2000s saw the rise of single-camera sitcoms, with cult hits such as *Scrubs*, *Arrested Development*, and *The Office* using the more variable production model to offer variety from the traditional studio show. Other high-budget short television productions employ the single-camera telefilm model, most notably advertising and music videos, which cost far more per minute than typical scripted programming, but maximize production values and control of images and sound through telefilm.

Multi-Camera Telefilm Studio Production

The two basic production modes started in the early 1950s each offer particular creative and economic incentives. Live studio production drew upon radio and theatrical traditions to offer the spontaneity, immediacy, and economic efficiency of live performance. Single-camera telefilm enabled more creative flexibility and control, with a guarantee of a high-quality artifact to use for multiple time zones and reruns inspired by Hollywood filmmaking. One of television's earliest hits, *I Love Lucy*, innovated a hybrid of these two modes that established an alternative that played to each strength and soon became the norm for sitcoms and other in-studio genres.

Lucy came to television much like other early programs: CBS wanted to bring star Lucille Ball from radio to television. Ball made a number of demands that CBS resisted, including co-starring with real-life husband Desi Arnaz (whose Cuban ethnicity dismayed the network), producing the program in Hollywood instead of New York, and shooting the show on film. CBS agreed to these demands only if Ball and Arnaz assumed greater financial risk and bankrolled the more expensive production costs. The couple created Desilu Studios

> **I LOVE LUCY**
>
> *I Love Lucy* (CBS, 1951–57): Television's first smash hit sitcom, *I Love Lucy* offered innovative representations for its era, including a cross-cultural marriage and a housewife trying to escape the home for the bright lights of show business. But its most lasting innovation was its multi-camera telefilm production method, allowing high-quality reruns to air for decades.

to finance the program and fortuitously negotiated full ownership of the program, ensuring a windfall from future syndication revenues.

Although *Lucy* has had tremendous impact through its long-term popularity and creative influences on future sitcoms, the show's greatest effect on television production was its innovative use of a multi-camera telefilm model. The show was performed in a television studio in front of a live audience, following the basic setup of live broadcasting. But instead of sending video signals to the control room for live editing, each of the three cameras recorded the action on film, while the audio was mixed to tape. The show would then be edited in postproduction like single-camera telefilms, with an editor choosing from among the camera angles and synchronizing visuals to sound. While certainly not as time-consuming as single-camera production—as the multiple cameras could adequately cover a scene in a single take—this production mode was still more costly than live production due to postproduction labor and the cost of film.

Multi-camera telefilm offers tremendous benefits for producers. In the short-term, the system allows for retakes and editing around mistakes to avoid the risks of live broadcasting, while the potential long-term rewards for syndication revenues of a high-quality telefilm are vast, outweighing the increased production costs. For comedy performances, this system is particularly useful as it allows for more control without losing the immediacy of performing in front of a live audience. Sitcoms followed *Lucy*'s lead throughout the 1950s, adopting this production mode and reducing the reliance on live broadcasting for scripted programming. Thus by the late 1950s, virtually no scripted prime time programs were broadcast live, as they all were produced on telefilm via either a multi-camera mode for comedy or single-camera mode for drama. Few unscripted programs were filmed, although there were exceptions such as *You Bet Your Life*, a comedic game show starring Groucho Marx that used a multi-camera telefilm mode to censor out risqué ad-libbed comments and to tighten the show's comedic pacing.

Videotape's Transformation of Television Production

While the basic systems of television production established in the 1950s remain in use today, a number of technological innovations have transformed and altered these practices. Most notably, the emergence of **videotape** as an alternative recording technology to film changed all three modes of television production considerably. Videotape emerged in the 1950s as a means of making magnetic recordings of visual and audio television signals in real time; early systems were cumbersome and limited in their storage capacity and image quality. The first main use of videotape for the television industry was as a replacement for kinescopes, allowing for a live network broadcast to be recorded for a West Coast feed with better resolution and no film developing. By the late 1950s, videotapes were used by all three networks to replay live broadcasts for the West Coast and create archival copies, although the size and fragility of the tapes made them still inferior to telefilm for rerun and syndication purposes. Local stations adopted videotape as a cheaper means of local production, allowing them to augment programming procured from networks and syndicators. Videotape has greatly improved in image quality over the years, although it still offers a different image quality compared to film, with more color saturation and less subtlety in lighting and contrast.

Live-to-tape programming provided a production model that balanced the low cost and efficiency of live production with the repeatability of telefilm. A program could be shot in a studio following all of the protocols of live production, but instead of sending the final video and audio mix out over the airwaves in real time, the signal would be recorded on videotape for future broadcast. This system became popular throughout the 1960s for genres where efficient and timely production was important, but where liveness was not an essential quality of the broadcast, such as talk shows, variety programming, soap operas, game shows, and educational programming. These genres typically lack the potential for long-term revenue through syndicated reruns as with sitcoms, thus discouraging the cost of multi-camera telefilm production. This live-to-tape system, or live editing, is still the most common production model used for unscripted programming, allowing talk shows such as *The Tonight Show* to tape each afternoon for late-night broadcast, or game shows to shoot multiple episodes each day of production.

An early limitation of videotape was its poor system for editing, as the manual splicing of tape was often inaccurate, difficult to do, and risked damaging tapes and playback equipment; thus any program needing extensive postproduction editing would be shot on film until the late 1960s. Once technology for easier electronic editing of videotape emerged in the late 1960s, videotaped programs that employed editing grew more frequent; most notably, *Rowan and Martin's Laugh-In* was a big hit in 1968 with a cut-and-paste style of fast-paced

THE TONIGHT SHOW

The Tonight Show (NBC, 1954–present): This long-running program established the genre of the late-night talk show, with comedic monologues and sketches combined with celebrity interviews and musical performances. While notable hosts Steve Allen, Jack Paar, and Jay Leno all left their mark, the show is best remembered for Johnny Carson's decades in the host's chair from 1962 to 1992, when he was the unchallenged king of late night.

ROWAN AND MARTIN'S LAUGH-IN

Rowan and Martin's Laugh-In (NBC, 1968–73): This hit sketch comedy show combined a fast-paced editing style, psychedelic visuals, repeated catchphrases, and topical one-liners to appeal to young baby boomer viewers.

editing that would have been impossible prior to electronic videotape editing, and cost-prohibitive on film. Likewise the rise of electronic editing allowed for prime time sitcoms to shoot live to tape with additional editing as needed, typified by *All in the Family* and other sitcoms produced by Norman Lear in the 1970s.

Videotape impacted the production of live television as well. Television sports have always been presented live whenever possible, but videotape allowed for the addition of the **instant replay** as a component of live coverage, where individual camera angles could be replayed in slow motion. Many commentators note that the emergence of instant replay in the early 1960s allowed for the growth of football as a popular sport, as the single-camera wide-angle perspective typical of most live sports coverage was particularly confusing for viewers watching football on a small screen. Videotape also allowed for the incorporation of sports highlights into nightly newscasts and later programs such as ESPN's *SportsCenter*, which arguably transformed how games were played, as players strove for individual achievements and projected larger-than-life personalities to be featured on nightly highlights, rather than focusing on team goals.

Television news was also transformed by videotape, adding to the live presentation of anchors reading headlines in studios; in the 1950s and 1960s, all on-location footage was shot on film, necessitating a costly and time-consuming editing process that bristled against the immediacy and timeliness of live reporting. Mobile video cameras and recorders emerged in the 1970s, enabling the ENG production discussed in chapter 4. Reporters and producers could shoot on location, interview outside of studios, and quickly edit the footage together in the same day, which led to the efficient production of news stories that remains commonplace today. By 1980, hardly any local or network news divisions used film, as videotape had become the norm for producing pre-made stories to incorporate into live broadcasts. Thus even though genres such as news and sports are typically broadcast live, much of the footage seen on these programs is actually taped.

While telefilm remained the most common means for network single-camera scripted production, the emergence of portable video recording allowed other unscripted genres to employ videotape as with ENG. Videotape enabled more cost-efficient documentary productions, which was particularly useful in the low-budget world of public television and emerging cable channels, including the public access programming discussed in chapter 3. Early reality programming of the late 1980s followed suit, with shows such as *Cops* and *Rescue 911* using the cheap flexibility of videotape to shoot on location, and setting the stage for the more widespread reality boom of the 2000s. In recent years, the emergence of high-definition video technology has begun to supplant film as the sole option for scripted programming, as some network dramas shoot on HD video, offering visual resolution comparable to film, as discussed more in chapter 11.

Likewise multi-camera studio production still uses both telefilm and videotape as recording media. Multi-camera telefilms remain in use for sitcoms that target more of an upscale audience, such as NBC's 1990s programs *Seinfeld*, *Frasier*, and *Will & Grace*, as the high-quality image conveys a sophisticated tone. Most studio sitcoms are shot by multi-camera video systems, with live editing augmented by postproduction video editing; again, the emergence of high-definition video cameras is beginning to supplant conventional video and telefilm as the norm within television production.

These basic production modes account for nearly everything appearing on American television, with the notable exception of animated programming, which follows an alternative mode of creating images via drawing or computers. These modes of production are more than just technological and institutional systems, as they have a direct impact on the style and meanings offered by television programming. A live-edited videotaped sitcom such as *All in the Family*, *Roseanne*, or *Everybody Loves Raymond* focuses on limited settings, character relationships, and longer scenes played out in front of the cameras and a live audience; typically these types of programs emphasize domestic life and the community of a family or workplace. Telefilm sitcoms such as *The Office* or *My Name Is Earl* typically employ more editing, varied locations, and multiple storylines that are controlled and paced through postproduction editing. Even an in-studio telefilm production such as *Friends* or *Frasier* tends to use the production mode to expand the show's focus outward from the central locale of the main characters.

This is not to suggest that the mode of production determines the meanings and style of any program, as producers can employ any production model in creative and atypical ways. But the decision to shoot on video or film, in studio or on location, is more than an economic choice: each of the modes of production detailed here offer particular norms and possibilities that impact the meanings made by television programming. The particular visual and audio elements that comprise a text highlight how all meanings emerge as a synthesis of technological, institutional, creative, and cultural practices employed in producing a television show. Understanding how a program is made is crucial to our understanding of what that program means.

THE ELEMENTS OF TELEVISION STYLE

The concept of **style** is useful in examining texts from all media, and points to the formal characteristics that help express meaning independently of a text's content. For literature, you might analyze a poet's use of rhyme and meter, or a novelist's use of metaphor. A painting's style might be found in its brushstrokes or the use of perspective, while a photograph's style can reside in its framing and composition. Style is not exclusive to creative or artistic media, as a newspaper story uses stylistic features of voice, tone, and address to help frame its particular way of reporting content. Thus for television, style refers to the variety of formal elements that are used in all genres to communicate meanings and elicit responses from viewers; any text uses these elements together to create an overall stylistic system that can be analyzed. **Stylistic analysis** can serve many functions: it can allow us to appreciate the artistry and creativity offered by a program, highlight how particular meanings are encoded within a show, explain the emotional impact programming has on viewers, and teach us how television techniques shape the way we view the world represented on-screen.

Television's stylistic elements most closely parallel film, as motion pictures established a set of norms for using moving images and sounds to convey meanings and tell stories within its fifty-year history prior to television's emergence. Not only does television draw directly on film's stylistic techniques, but its critics use concepts developed in film studies to analyze the elements of television style. Thus the following overview of television's five main stylistic techniques—staging, camerawork, editing, sound, and graphics—employs the vocabulary established by film scholars to analyze movies, but highlights the particular ways that television uses style in a distinct manner that sets it apart from film.

Staging

In virtually all television programming (with the exception of animation), content is conveyed via images and actions occurring in front of a camera, a facet of television style called **staging**.* For an average scene within a fictional program, this would encompass the set, props, lighting, costume, makeup, and actor movement and performance—in other words, everything that takes place in front of the camera. Each element of staging is a conscious choice by the producers, with dozens of technical and creative staff members working to ensure that everything that will appear on screen conveys the program's meanings and tone. Every element of staging is visually accessible to viewers, but typically we ignore how sets, costumes, and lighting are carefully controlled aspects of a television program working to shape the meanings and impacts of all shows.

All of these elements apply to nonfiction and unscripted programming, too, as the staging of newscasts, talk shows, reality programming, and game shows all convey meanings and help elicit particular reactions by audiences; the sets, lighting, and personal appearances featured on different programs help set each program's tone. Staging need not be fully planned, as on-location shooting of a news story still captures elements that are played out in front of a camera: field producers carefully choose where to place the camera to best show the events and images they wish to portray, and often make changes to the environment to best convey the intended message. Even when the events in front of the camera can be seen as authentic real-life behaviors, the elements presented on-screen can still be best understood using the specific facets of staging.

Consider the difference between the staging of two popular game shows, *The Price Is Right* and *Who Wants to Be a Millionaire*. Both programs are clearly part of the game show genre, with similar presentations of ordinary people competing for prizes through a rule-based contest, but they have quite different tones as conveyed by their visual styles. *The Price Is Right* is shot in a brightly lit studio, with a set featuring colorful visual décor and elaborate props tied to the quirky games featured on the show. While longtime host Bob Barker dresses formally in a suit, the show's spokesmodels typically wear skimpy outfits and sometimes join the show's announcer in over-the-top skits wearing clownish costumes, lending a frivolous and theatrical quality to the program. Contestants follow the casual tone of the show by dressing in everyday outfits or choosing unusual costumes to stand out from the crowd, while the show's producers encourage them to scream and jump around when chosen to participate in the game. All of these

---

* This book's use of the term *staging* is similar to the concept of *mise-en-scène* discussed by film scholars; however *mise-en-scène* is a somewhat elusive, contested term, and may be less applicable to the broad range of television productions, including sports, news, and game shows.

The bright colors and casual demeanor of *The Price Is Right* directly contrasts with…

stylistic elements convey a festive tone to the program, making it a celebration of the consumer goods and games of chance featured throughout.

Who Wants to Be a Millionaire is comparatively more formal, reserved, and serious in its staging. The set is quite bare, with a metallic, high-tech design emphasizing the contestant on the hot seat positioned in the center of a circular audience looking down on the action. Lighting is focused on the contestant, with the audience in dim shadows and lighting effects used to accent the dramatic impact of a question and answer. Host Regis Philbin is outfitted in designer suits, and contestants dress and act in a reserved and dignified manner. The show's staging works to convey an air of respectability and business-like seriousness, with none of the carnivalesque elements of *The Price Is Right*. Clearly the two programs' content furthers these distinctions, as *Millionaire* asks challenging factual questions, while most of the games on *The Price Is Right* reward luck or the less culturally valued knowledge of consumer pricing. But it is important to realize how much of any program's meaning is conveyed by how it looks, not just what is said.

For fictional programs as well, staging conveys information about the show's setting and tone. Sets, props, and costumes are carefully designed to provide visual markers about the characters and how they live—contrast the working-class milieu of sitcoms such as *Roseanne* and *My Name Is Earl* with the upper-class settings of *Frasier* and *The Fresh Prince of Bel-Air*. Every element presented within the frame of a shot potentially can convey meaning to viewers, so production designers spend a great deal of time creating a consistent staging that

…the formal, dark, and metallic tone of *Who Wants to Be a Millionaire*, showing the power of set design, lighting, and props to impact a show's tone and style.

THE PRICE IS RIGHT

The Price Is Right (CBS, 1972–present): One of television's longest-running series, *The Price Is Right* encourages audience participation in its often goofy games based around consumer knowledge. Host Bob Barker was the face of the program for thirty-five years, generating a surprisingly devoted fanbase across generations.

effectively sets the tone for the program. Often a program's staging is designed to be as naturalistic as possible, but even the attempt to recreate a real-life setting can result in choices that use artificial and constructed techniques to portray real life.

Television series face particular challenges concerning staging when compared to films: while a film needs to craft a set to convey all information and reactions over a compressed two-hour narrative, television series typically design sets that might last throughout a multi-year series. Thus design elements must both instantly convey a mood consistent with the narrative, and create a long-term space in which a story will grow over a number of years. A good example of this possibility comes from sitcom *Everybody Loves Raymond*: in the kitchen of Raymond parents' house, an oversize wooden fork and spoon hang on the

EVERYBODY LOVES RAYMOND

Everybody Loves Raymond (CBS, 1996–2005): A popular comedy notable for its excellent cast and cynical tone, this show shifted the family sitcom dynamics away from the kids, focusing instead on the conflicts between the couple and the husband's overbearing parents living across the street from each other in Long Island, New York.

wall. Throughout the series, these are unmentioned background set elements that convey the family's love of food and tacky décor. But in the show's seventh season, the episode entitled "Baggage" highlighted the fork and spoon from the background, providing an anecdote about how they hang in the kitchen as a remnant from a stubborn fight dating back forty-five years. Thus staging must provide both background setting and allow for narrative developments in long-running television series.

Because a successful series will inhabit the same setting for years, designers tend to downplay spectacular sets that might overshadow dramatic action. The goal of most television design is to create an inhabitable and believable space that can host a show's human drama and comedy, and portray a fictional world that viewers welcome into their homes each week. Television sets, props, and costumes can become such ritualized parts of American culture that they turn into icons worthy of museum display. After long network runs, the signpost from *M*A*S*H*, *Star Trek*'s phaser, Archie Bunker's chair from *All in the Family*, and *Seinfeld*'s puffy shirt are all displayed at the Smithsonian Institution as important artifacts of American cultural history.

Settings can be constructed in a television studio or soundstage, or be shot on location. For reality programs, news stories, and documentaries, on-location shooting is a must, bringing real-life locations to the screen; however, producers do not simply set up a camera and shoot whatever they see, as typically interviews and planned events are shot in a carefully controlled locale that is deemed to best convey the facets of "reality" being portrayed. Likewise many reality shows take place in so-called real locations that are little more than inhabitable soundstages, such as the houses featured on *The Real World* or the sparse landscape of *Survivor*. Most people appearing on reality shows have their appearances controlled by producers as well, with specific costume and makeup decisions helping to define how the audience will differentiate among characters in an unscripted scenario.

Fictional programming can also use on-location settings to convey a realistic sense of a place, as in *The Sopranos* shooting in New Jersey, or to stand in for a locale beyond the parameters of a studio, such as the beach setting of

Baywatch. Travel programming—whether the documentary footage featured on the Travel Channel, the round-the-world reality competition of *The Amazing Race*, or a fictional on-location drama such as *Route 66*—highlights the ability of television to offer visual representations of the world. It has been a long tradition throughout television history for programs to feature a locale as a central facet or even character in a program—*Dragnet* began every episode with a montage of Los Angeles and the line "This is the city," while Baltimore is best known to television viewers as conveyed through the fictionalized lenses of *Homicide: Life on the Street* and *The Wire*. Location shooting allows both fictional and nonfictional programming to transport viewers to a broad array of locales, which can be a chief appeal of television as a "window on the world" within your own home.

Lighting also can impact a program's mood and tone. Typically, programs shot live or on videotape have little variety in lighting, as video cameras require a high-level of lighting saturation and register little contrast between light and dark; thus most sitcoms, soap operas, and unscripted programs use lighting primarily to illuminate the action, not convey tone. Filmed programs can use lighting more creatively, as programs such as *The X-Files* and *Angel* have used limited dim lighting to emulate the tone of *film noir* and to stimulate emotional responses of suspense and horror. Within studios, lighting can work to highlight particular facets of the stage and downplay others, as in *Millionaire*'s dimly lit audience, which focuses attention on the contestant and host, while 1950s anthology dramas used more pronounced lighting effects to create transitions through live broadcast, as influenced by the genre's theatrical ties.

The element of staging that we are typically most aware of are the actions of the people in a program, whether the performances of actors in a drama or the behavior of journalists, contestants, or participants in unscripted programming. Performances certainly involve sound as well as staging, as dialogue delivery is often one of the most notable aspects of an actor's role, but the physical gestures, movements, and presence that performers bring to television texts is a crucial aspect of any show's staging.

One noticeable element of most television programs is the physical appearance of performers. From newscasters to sitcom actors, music video dancers to spokespeople in commercials, the people who appear in television tend to be highly attractive by conventional beauty norms, as discussed more in chapter 8. When performers deviate from such cultural norms, programs tend to acknowledge such body types as abnormal, as in the working-class mockery of the ideal sitcom family on *Roseanne* or even the title of *Ugly Betty*. This extends to reality television, where most contestants are chosen in part for their looks and charisma, even on programs such as *Survivor* and *The Amazing Race*, where such attributes are not needed to succeed in competition. Certainly the beauty imperative for television performers stems from the commercial desires of advertisers to create a fantasy world for viewers to watch longingly. But it is important to recognize how for many programs the physical attractiveness of on-screen performers is a chief appeal that draws in viewers.

Performances for most television personalities, however, extend beyond their beauty; the staging of television is dependent on the people who inhabit the sets, wear the costumes, and use the props. Any television performer must convey particular meanings to viewers beyond just what he or she says. A successful newscaster's appearance, gestures, and way of looking into the camera should convey trustworthiness, integrity, and command of the material—assumed qualities in newscasters made apparent by their absence in the fiction parody of the moronic anchor Ted Baxter on *The Mary Tyler Moore Show*. Such norms do depend on specific presentational modes—newscasters on morning shows such as *Today* act more casually than evening anchors, and journalists on pundit programs such as *Hardball* display more emotion and opinion than aloof and detached anchors. Likewise, historical contexts can shift the typical style of newscasters, as the measured, dry tone of 1950s newsreaders John Cameron Swayze and Douglas Edwards would appear out of place on contemporary newscasts.

Fictional programming clearly relies on performances to engage viewers and sustain narratives. Dramatic actors strive for emotional engagement and sufficient charisma to captivate viewers. Sitcom stars must be able not only to deliver lines humorously, but to project enough warmth and likeability to encourage viewers to invite their characters back into their homes each week—unless performers can create engaging characters who are charismatic but unlikable, as achieved by *Seinfeld*. The chief goal of most television performers meshes with the commercial goals of the television industry: to create performances that compel viewers to return for the next episode. Whether this is achieved by establishing integrity, warmth, desire, or compassion, a television performer works to create a compelling bond with viewers through both vocal and physical performances.

Television acting styles can vary by genre and historical era. Typically dramatic programs embrace a **naturalistic performance** style, creating characters that appear believable and true-to-life. The goal of a naturalistic performance is to convey a clear and consistent inner motivation and emotional life of a character, enabling audiences to engage with the melodramatic plots experienced over the course of episodes. Dramas that feature acclaimed performances, such as Andre Braugher on *Homicide* or Allison Janney on *The West Wing*, are typically hailed for the naturalistic realism and humanity conveyed by the actor, as well as for the effective writing and directing. Even sitcoms can embrace a naturalistic mode of performance, with subtle humor coming through the understated characters' experiences on programs such as *Taxi*, *Cheers*, and *M*A*S*H*.

Many comedies offer a more **antinaturalistic performance** style, with ties to theatrical presentations that acknowledge the audience. Variety stars such as Milton Berle and Carol Burnett employ this style, inviting viewers to laugh at their over-the-top antics that are clearly designed to be nonrealistic and exaggerated. Specific performers on sitcoms, such as Jack and Karen on *Will & Grace,* or entire programs such as *Married...With Children,* have embraced this cartoony presentational mode of performance, inviting audiences to laugh at what is clearly an extreme performance rather than a robust, realistic one. Dramatic programs can employ antinaturalistic strategies, with dry emotionless performances denying a character's emotional life; *Dragnet* pioneered this strategy, which lives on somewhat with contemporary procedurals such as *Law & Order.* Likewise, soap operas embrace a more melodramatic and emotional performance style than prime time dramas, working against assumed naturalistic criteria but instead following the expectations of soap fans.

It is tempting to lay out criteria for what makes a good television performance, but these are highly dependent on genre—a compelling performance on a daytime soap opera might appear over the top if placed in a prime time crime show. All genres, and even specific programs, define their own particular performance styles and techniques, depending on how they fit into the overall text. Regardless of what performance style a program employs, the ongoing nature of series television encourages consistency in tone to maintain the appeals that engage an audience for that particular program.

The elements of staging, from performance to set design, are the most apparent facets of television texts—these on-screen elements are what we are most likely to remember across episodes. Except for when they are added via special effects or animation, the images we see on screen are captured from a reality presented in front of television cameras. Whether it is a staged performance on a constructed set of a spaceship or a real-life encounter shot on the street, the images that comprise a show's staging work to engage viewers' attention through their ties to real life and their ability to evoke emotional response. But the means by which we see these images are highly constructed, both through the creation of staging through production choices and the work of cameras and editing that brings the images to the screen.

Camerawork

If staging creates a real image to be shown on the screen, camerawork is the technique that captures that image for viewers. Even in a highly naturalistic documentary program, camerawork involves numerous choices that shape the meanings of and emotional responses to the stylistic elements played out in front of the camera. Shooting on video or telefilm is a physical process involving cameras and with a range of techniques, all of which can alter what we see and what it means. To understand how camerawork frames and shapes our televised vision of real and fictional worlds, we need a detailed vocabulary of techniques used to record images on film and video.

THE LARRY SANDERS SHOW

The Larry Sanders Show (HBO, 1992–98): One of HBO's first original fictional series, this critically acclaimed reflexive sitcom explores the behind-the-scenes life of a late-night talk show. Star Garry Shandling mocked his own experiences on talk shows, as the series featured regular celebrity cameos making fun of their own star personas with a dry, subtle sense of humor.

One key variable is the **recording medium** used to shoot images. As discussed previously, the difference in image quality between videotape and film is significant, with film offering a more muted tone than the bright coloring of videotape. Within these two forms, different film stocks and videotape formats can offer a broad range of image quality, with varying contrast, graininess, sharpness, and color tone. A program may use multiple recording media to signify different elements of a story: a dream sequence might employ a tinted or brighter image, or flashbacks may use black-and-white footage. Some programs employ both videotape and film. *The Larry Sanders Show,* an HBO show portraying the behind-the-scenes drama of a late-night talk show, uses video to signify the on-camera portions of the fictional talk show, while filmed sections represent behind-the-scenes footage of the characters. No particular film stock or recording medium has innate meanings, but the choices of image quality made by the producers convey certain assumptions, especially in contrast to other programs or sequences.

Camerawork can also alter the **speed** of motion in a given sequence, with different uses for fictional and nonfictional media. Traditionally film cameras could shoot a scene in fast or slow-motion mechanically, although today film and video speeds are more likely to be changed via digital effects in postproduction. In fictional programming, fast motion is most commonly used as a comedic device to compress action and express chaotic movement; time-lapse motion can compress action quite dramatically, showing the growth cycle of a plant or a sunrise in a matter of seconds in both nonfiction and fictional programs. Slow motion is a common device in fictional programming for dream sequences, intense action, emotional reactions, and other instances that demand a heightened sense of drama and engagement. For nonfiction, slow motion is commonly used to analyze movement in depth, as in a sports replay or analysis of news footage. Although altering motion speed is not a technique that evokes realism, it can be used quite subtly in a manner by which viewers will see the emotional or analytical effect as naturalistic in tone.

Cameras capture images using **lenses**, which can be altered to change visual elements in a number of ways. One key variable is **focal length**, which alters the degree of magnification and depth of an image—a long focal length makes objects appear closer to the camera than they truly are, while shorter focal lengths can create the illusion of objects appearing farther from the camera. Lenses with long focal lengths, also called **telephoto lenses**, are often used to capture images from far away when cameras cannot get close enough physically to the action, as with sporting events, concerts, or political speeches. **Wide-angle lenses** use short focal lengths, causing "fisheye" distortion with objects close to the camera, but allowing a broad panorama of a crowd scene or landscape. Many cameras allow for varying focal lengths via a **zoom lens**, altering the image magnification throughout a single shot.

Different focal lengths also alter visual **perspective**, or the spatial relation between elements. A longer focal length compresses depth in an image, leading to a flattened perspective, where objects can appear closer to one another than they truly are. Shorter focal lengths increase the depth of a shot, creating the illusion of a deeper space within the frame. Television typically uses this expressive potential far less than film, partly because the smaller screens offer less resolution for image depth, and partly because studio shooting allows for little physical depth in staging compared with on-location or soundstage film shoots. Some telefilm programs do explore depth and perspective as creative

An extreme example of a wide-angle lens is the "fisheye" effect from a peephole, seen here in an episode of *Seinfeld*.

A long telephoto lens makes the squadroom in *Hill Street Blues* seem even more cramped and crowded.

The long telephoto lens from center field to home plate reduces the sense of depth on a baseball field, making the distance between pitcher and batter seem shorter than 60 feet, but allowing much more detailed visuals than with a normal focal length.

elements—*Hill Street Blues* used long lenses to shoot inside a crowded police squad room, creating a claustrophobic, densely packed image. But in most unscripted programming, altered perspectives are a by-product of the use of focal lengths to capture subjects within the frame, not an aesthetic goal.

A rack focus shifts viewer attention from Dwight...

...to Michael, within the pseudo-documentary style of *The Office*.

Another lens variable is **focus**. The camera operator can control what elements in the frame are clear or blurry. Depending on a lens's focal length and the amount of available light, a camera setup has a potential **depth of field**, the range of distance from the camera in which images can be in focus. Shorter lenses offer more depth of field, allowing for heightened depth of an image with foreground and background elements in focus. Television more commonly uses a narrower depth of field and longer lenses, leading to limited planes of

> ## THE OFFICE
>
> *The Office* (NBC, 2005–present): An American remake of a beloved British sitcom, *The Office* uses documentary-style filming to portray life in a Scranton, Pennsylvania, paper sales office. The show's popularity was fueled by online and DVD sales that surpassed its limited broadcast ratings, developing a cult audience that embraced its uncomfortable brand of "cringe comedy."

> ## LATE NIGHT WITH DAVID LETTERMAN
>
> *Late Night with David Letterman* (NBC, 1982–93): An ironic take on the late-night talk show, Letterman exposed production machinery such as control rooms and stage managers, along with reflexive commentary on the genre's conventions, such as Stupid Pet Tricks. When Letterman was passed over to replace Johnny Carson as the new host of *The Tonight Show*, he moved to CBS to start *Late Show with David Letterman* and compete directly with Carson's replacement, Jay Leno.

the image in focus at any moment. *Hill Street Blues* offers a crowded image, but only the central figures are in focus, allowing viewers to pick out the key action from the chaos. With most television, however, the primary goal of camerawork is to keep the action in focus and to use camera choices to convey content with direct clarity, not to highlight visual composition or experiment with depth and focus.

One technique used frequently in dramatic television is the **rack focus**. When a shot has a narrow depth of field, part of the image will be out of focus. Over the course of a continuous shot, the camera operator can alter the focal plane to shift what part of the image is sharp and clear, effectively guiding viewer's perception by changing focus from one character to another. Because this device requires a carefully planned camera and staging setup, it is rare to see it in unscripted programming, although the effect often appears unplanned and typical of the pseudo-documentary style, such as on *The Office*. However, most manipulations of focus and depth are used subtly in television, guiding viewer perception and creating emotional responses without being readily obvious to casual viewers.

A more overt and noticeable facet of camerawork is **framing**. All action in front of the camera is framed by the camera, which conveys a visual relationship to the staging. Although we rarely think about it, one of the most powerful facets of camera framing is defining the boundary between **onscreen and offscreen space.** Some offscreen space is within the world of the staged program, such as a character leaving their living room to enter the kitchen—we may not visually follow them in this sequence, but the storyworld continues out of the frame. Much offscreen space is outside the realm of the story, with the lighting grid, cameras, and live studio audience remaining forever out of the frame of a sitcom. A vital function of camerawork is to define the boundary between what we do and do not see in any sequence, often sustaining the illusion of a fictional storyworld and masking the machinery of production. Rules about offscreen space can be broken for innovative results. In the early 1980s, *Late Night with David Letterman* broke the norms of the talk show by revealing the cameras, control room, and backstage, offering a more ironic and reflexive version of the genre.

Framing defines our visual proximity to the staged action, with a range of options available to the producers. Proximity is typically labeled using three basic types—long shot, medium shot, and closeup—with variations straddling the types (medium-long shot) or on the margins (extreme closeup). While there is no hard-and-fast rule as to what defines the boundary between these terms, each shot has a set of typical uses and conveys particular meanings within a television program, illustrated here with *The Wire*. One common shot within television programs is the **establishing shot, an extreme long shot** that sets the scene from a distance. This can be a shot outside the bar on *Cheers*, a survey of

This establishing shot locates a scene from *The Wire* on the docks of Baltimore and offers a grey, grim tone.

THE WIRE

The Wire (HBO, 2002–08): One of the most acclaimed series in television history, *The Wire* shifted the police drama by focusing equally on the criminal drug gangs being pursued by the Baltimore police, and expanded its scope to examine a range of urban institutions including the shipping docks, city government, public schools, and daily newspapers across its highly serialized five seasons. The program was also notable for its predominantly African-American cast countering an array of television stereotypes.

the audience on a talk show, the view outside a prison before a news story on a criminal, or an overhead shot from a blimp at a sporting event. Establishing shots help ground the program in a particular location and set the mood for the show, neglecting details in a scene in exchange for a sense of the entire place.

Long shots offer more details of a scene, but still provide a sense of the space in which the action is taking place. Typically long shots show people's full bodies and are often used to show multiple people moving in a shot—Carla serving drinks on *Cheers*, talk show guests entering the stage, prisoners working, or athletes running on the field. Long shots are a staple of most programs shot in

An interior long shot places this scene from *The Wire* in a poorly lit police station, conveying Detective McNulty's isolation.

A medium shot of Stringer Bell, from *The Wire*, establishes a conversational distance from the character.

studios, such as sitcoms, game shows, talk shows, as well as many telefilmed dramas and on-location programming such as sports, documentaries, reality shows, and special events. A long shot of a scene is often termed the **master shot**, capturing the entire staging and performance.

While long shots can highlight the relationship between people in the frame, the limited size of television screens can make it difficult to read the facial features and gestures that convey emotions. Dramatic programs use **medium shots** to show characters together with more attention to visual details and subtle performance cues, framing people from their waists to above their heads. Medium shots are commonly used in unscripted programs as well, framing a news anchor, a game show contestant, or an interview subject on a talk show. The proximity of a medium shot is sufficiently close for the viewer to register a character's facial expressions without appearing to invade that character's personal space, mimicking the distance between two people in a typical conversation in real life.

Conventional medium shots include the **two shot**, where two people converse close together within the frame, and the **three shot**, featuring three characters. A specific type of medium shot comes from soap operas—in a framing sometimes called a **two shot west**, conversing characters both peer into the space beyond the camera, with one person standing in front of another. By showing the audience both characters' facial expressions, but not allowing them to see each other's reactions, we can visualize the expressions of duplicity and secrets that form many of the narrative pleasures of the soap opera genre.

This two shot west from *The Young and the Restless* allows viewers to see the emotional reactions of both characters in the midst of a conversation, highlighting the relationship drama focus of the soap opera genre.

Closeups are a key part of television's visual repertoire, as they allow a high degree of intimacy and emotional expression. **Medium closeups** frame from the person's chest to the top of his head, while closeups fill the frame with a person's face. Medium closeups are more common, as they provide facial detail without feeling overly intrusive. A full closeup is usually reserved for moments of intimacy and intensity in dramas, or for shots conveying interrogation or scrutiny in an interview or reality program. Television's small screens have traditionally made closeups more common than in films, although this can vary by genre— soap operas use far more closeups than sitcoms, as they tend to convey more emotional intimacy and intensity.

The most intimate option is the **extreme closeup**, which allows an isolated detail, object, or body part to fill the screen. Commonly used to highlight a piece of evidence or object contributing to the narrative, extreme closeups often feel quite artificial—*CSI* relies on extreme closeups of bodies so intimate that they dive under the skin. Unscripted programs use extreme closeups to isolate details for scrutiny—an athlete's bandaged knee, a criminal's handcuffs, an ingredient being used on a cooking show. Each type of shot proximity offers different potential to producers, allowing viewers to visualize a scene or details in ways that follow typical conventions or that violate norms for creative and expressive possibilities.

Other variables in camera framing are less commonly altered. Most television programming uses a standard **camera height** at eye level to the staged action, making it more noticeable when a camera looks up at a character from a **low angle** or down from a **high angle**. Potentially a camera can be **canted** at an angle to the action, providing a disorienting slanted perspective. Though rarely

As emotions rise, *The Wire*'s Stringer Bell is framed in a close-up to heighten the intensity of the scene.

The Wire uses extreme close-ups both to highlight the technologies of surveillance, and the intent eyes of the police monitoring criminals.

used, these camera techniques can express a sense of visual expressivity through creative angles, or sometimes arise through unplanned reactions in unscripted shooting of action for a documentary or reality program. But all techniques that define the frame of a television image impact how we perceive the world portrayed on the screen and require consideration to comprehend how formal attributes construct a televised image.

The final facet of camerawork is **camera movement**. While film and video cameras are often mounted on tripods to increase stability, they still allow cameras to move and pivot, reframing shots as they are being captured. Some movements are created by pivoting the camera on a stationary tripod—cameras can **pan** horizontally, mimicking the motion of turning your head left or right. A mid-court camera at a basketball game continuously pans back and forth within a long shot to follow the ball, while a dramatic shot of the police entering a crime scene might pan around the room to capture the cop's survey for evidence. Cameras can also **tilt** up or down to show the height of a subject: a gradual rise to reveal a new skyscraper on a news program, or a tilt down to reveal a patient's condition on a medical drama.

Most cameras are quite mobile, mounted on wheeled pedestals in studios, on moveable dollies, or held by a camera operator. Moving cameras are called both **dolly** and **tracking** shots, referring to the devices used. Dolly shots can wheel in any direction, reorienting the frame of the staged action. Cameras will often dolly in toward the actors as a scene develops in intensity, an effect that can be achieved either through actual camera movement or zooming lenses. Soap opera cameras are almost always reframing shots through gradual movement and zooming to heighten emotional engagement. Quick movements in an action sequence can add intensity and excitement, while slower movements often will lend a subtle emotional effect.

Less commonly, cameras can move vertically in a **crane shot**, rising off the ground or down from the air while mounted on a mechanical crane. More commonly used in telefilms, cranes are usually used at the beginning or ending of scenes, to transition to and from long shots establishing the place of the action. Sports cameras can be mounted on remote-controlled cranes, tracks and pulleys, allowing for a range of motion to capture the action in ways beyond the capacities of a human camera operator.

Many programs use **hand-held** cameras to shoot the action in a flexible manner. Hand-held camerawork, long a staple of documentary and news footage, tends to be less steady and jumpier than with mounted cameras, as camera operators need to capture unplanned action on the run. Hand-held cameras are also used for scripted programs, with crime dramas such as *Law & Order* adopting the unsteady look to convey a sense of gritty realism and spontaneity, with pans and zooms done quickly as if in response to an unplanned event, rather than as actually rehearsed on a soundstage. Often a program employing hand-held camerawork will purposely feature out-of-focus moments or mistaken framing, a style used to add realism to the fictional world. This documentary style has become more commonplace in recent years with reality programs and even sitcoms such as *The Office*.

THE WEST WING

The West Wing (NBC, 1999–2006): A rare example of a political drama succeeding on television, *The West Wing* combined a robust visual style with snappy dialogue, exceptional acting, and attention to complex political issues. The show reached one of the most upscale audiences in prime time, making it a favorite for advertisers trying to reach viewers who otherwise watched little television.

Not all hand-held cameras are unsteady. A device called the **Steadicam** straps the camera to an operator, using gyroscopes to ensure a smooth gliding effect even as the cameraperson walks. *ER* uses the Steadicam to swoop around operating tables, providing a smooth perspective on a chaotic environment. *The West Wing* employs the technique of a "walk and talk" scene, where a Steadicam operator follows characters walking through the halls of the White House in a constant discussion framed by a steady two-shot—at times the camera may change its attention to another character in the halls, maintaining a long take of a dialogue sequence with visual pacing to match the snappy dialogue. Steadicams are rarely used in unscripted programming, aside for shooting concerts or other staged events.

The broad range of techniques comprising camerawork—from framing to focus, camera movement to depth—all position viewers in relationship to the staging. For the bulk of television forms, it might appear that the job of the camera is merely to show the staged action clearly, as with a newscast, sitcom, sporting event, or game show; but every type of shot involves a number of choices that impact how we see the images portrayed and what meanings we take away from them. Even if you never pick up a video camera yourself, a better understanding of the techniques used to capture moving images makes you a more critical and attentive viewer as to how each shot of a television program helps shape your perception of that program and of the world represented on the screen.

Editing

Producers use staging and camerawork to create shots that capture action. The third key element of television style puts those shots together into a larger program: **editing**. Editing has a tremendous impact on constructing the meanings, tone, and impact of any program, even though the majority of television programs are edited in a manner that appears almost unnoticeable to casual viewers.

Editing is a highly unnatural way of viewing the world. It is hard to imagine a situation in which your visual perspective changes places or time frames within a split second, yet this is the effect of every edit in television and film. Viewers learn how to understand this jarring effect at a young age, as nearly every sequence on film and television follow a basic system of **continuity editing** that becomes so ingrained that it feels natural. By itemizing the elements of continuity editing, we can see how it constructs particular perspectives on the televised world that are worth examining critically.

In a multi-camera live or live-to-tape production, edits are made while the action is occurring, while for telefilm or single-camera videotape productions, editing is done after the fact, during postproduction. Programs using postproduction editing can present shots together to appear like continuous action, even though they were actually shot in different places and at different times. The effect of the continuity editing system, established by filmmakers in the early twentieth century, is to create the illusion that an edited sequence presents action that is occurring in continuous time and space, as with a multi-camera studio shoot.

The basic unit of editing is the **cut**, an instant switch from one shot to another. The term derives from traditional cinematic practices where two strips of film were physically cut and pasted together. Video editing and contemporary film editing via digital technology avoid physical cutting, but the effect and terminology remain. A cut typically reframes the visual perspective on any action significantly, altering the proximity of the camera to the action, the angle used to shoot the staging, or both. An edit where the shots do not sufficiently reframe the action is called a **jump cut**, which typically jars and disorients viewers by breaking continuity.

In any edited continuity sequence, the goal is to create a seamless flow between cuts and establish a uniform, coherent sense of the staged space and linear time. A number of norms have been established to reinforce continuity. Within any sequence, typically all camera angles are located on the same side of the action, a practice knows as the **180-degree rule**—an imaginary line runs between the main characters in a scene, with all camera angles located within a semicircle, or 180 degrees on one side of this **axis of action**. By keeping all camera angles on the same side of this axis, the sequence maintains a consistent **screen direction** and avoids disorienting cuts that may confuse viewers. A shot from the other side of the axis would reverse the relationships between the characters and the direction of their eye lines.

Although this system of continuity editing was developed for single-camera cinema with postproduction editing, the effect resembles a scene shot with multiple cameras all simultaneously capturing the action. In a multi-camera studio shoot, the cameras all stay on the same side of the action for practical reasons—so cameras do not capture each other during shots, and so the studio audience does not see the cameras onstage. In a single-camera shoot, the cameras typically observe the same shooting patterns, even without these practical concerns.

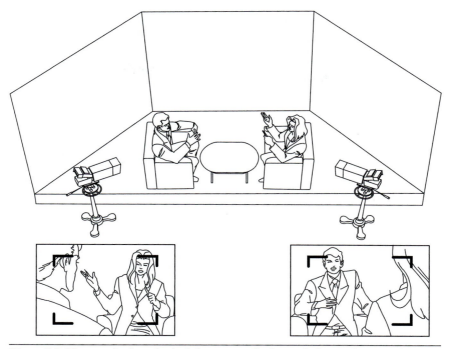

Figure 5-3 The standard method of shooting and editing dialogue alternates between close-ups of two characters, framed by medium shots that establish the characters' relationship in space.

A continuity sequence typically uses a limited repertoire of specific shots. The first shot usually will establish the relationship between the figures within the space of the staging, framing the action using a long or medium-long shot. The sequence then cuts between isolated shots of the specific characters, framed in medium closeup or closeup, often with the other character in the side of the frame to reinforce the staging; the back-and-forth editing between closeups in a dialogue is termed **shot/reverse shot**. Often as a sequence progresses in dramatic or comedic intensity, the isolated shots will increasingly dolly or zoom inward, to fill the frame with each character's face. Sequences will return to the long shot when staging shifts, reestablishing the relationship between the characters in the space. Typically, a continuity sequence concludes with the long shot to reinforce the scene and the relationship between characters.

Continuity editing is not used solely in scripted programs. News stories follow principles of the continuity system to create consistent screen direction and convey spatial relations. Interviews are commonly edited using shot/reverse shot, with shots of the subject and journalist alternating in sequence. Such sequences provide the illusion of a continuous timeline between shots, but often shots of the interviewer are taken after the interview, as the single video camera must

These four shots from *Sex and the City* show a continuity sequence from two-shot...

...to medium close-up...

be repositioned to shoot the journalist for what are called "pickups"—a practice satirized in the film *Broadcast News*, as the reporter reshot his reactions to the interview and faked crying to garner sympathy. Continuity editing reinforces the sense that on-screen action occurred in the sequence and space that it appears on-screen, even when it has been shot out of sequence or in multiple locations.

…to reverse medium close-up…

…to final two-shot to close the scene.

Multi-camera shoots do not need to create an illusion of continuity, as each camera captures the action simultaneously. A live edit, either to videotape or via live broadcast, still follows basic continuity norms in shooting and camera selection, as soap operas and sitcoms observe the same editing style as filmed dramas. In a multi-camera telefilm shoot, as commonly used for sitcoms, cameras capture continuous action but are edited together in postproduction following single-camera strategies. Even though the mechanics of editing are quite different for live edits, single-camera shoots, or multi-camera telefilms, the results in the final program are typically quite similar, following the continuity system and ensuring maximum comprehensibility for viewers to follow the space and time presented on-screen.

Editing is not limited to continuous sequences, as edits often relocate viewers in time and space by shifting scenes between sequences. Such transitional edits rely on techniques besides straight cuts, commonly with **fade-outs** to a black screen (especially preceding a commercial break), **fade-ins** from black (for returning from breaks), and **dissolves** from one shot to another, with both images briefly overlapping. Such gradual edits, which are still viewed as fairly naturalistic, are typically understood to signal shifts in time and/or space; it would be quite unusual for a fade or dissolve to be used in the midst of a continuity sequence. Less naturalistic are **wipes**, in which a line or other shape passes through the screen, replacing the image with another shot. Wipes call attention to themselves, and thus are typically used only for programs or sequences in a highly presentational style, such as children's programming, sports, or opening credit sequences.

Direct cuts can relocate viewers in time or space, but usually in tandem with other devices to signal such a transition. Cutting between two distinctly different images, such as a brightly lit outdoor scene following a dim interior, will probably be understood as a transitional edit, while also creating a more jarring response than with a dissolve or fade. Sound and graphics are quite effective in signaling transitions, as discussed in the next sections. Although most edits strive for coherence and clarity, often editing can work to temporarily disorient viewers, engaging them to deduce the relationship between two shots to build suspense and mystery. On *Alias*, the heroic spies might discuss a vague plan to recover some information, followed by a cut to an undetermined location; it takes viewers a few moments to figure out who is in this new locale, and what their plan might be, adding to the narrative pleasure through suspenseful uncertainty.

Editing between sequences typically condenses the time frame presented. While any given scene typically covers a continuous series of events, the next scene will often represent another moment: that night, the next day, or the like. This condensation of time by omitting intervening moments is an **ellipsis**, used in nearly all scripted programs—*24* is a noteworthy exception for presenting a continuous twenty-four-hour story (aside from commercial breaks). Transitions can also present simultaneous action, cutting to a sequence occurring at the same time in another location via **cross-cutting**, a technique used to create suspense or thematic parallels between different sequences. Transitions can also signal a **flashback** to a previous moment in the story, moving backward in time to provide earlier story information or reflect on past events.

Scripted programs typically signal temporal shifts clearly to ensure comprehension, guiding viewers to maintain coherent story chronology. Unscripted programming, such as reality television, documentaries, and news stories, will often mix the chronological order and pacing of real events without signals, leading to the illusion of continuity even when it did not really exist. A news story about gun control might show images of a protest and a gun show. Viewers will typically assume these events are temporally linked, even if they may have been shot in distinctly different times; they were edited together not to mislead but to visualize the relative sides or convey a position on the issue. A reality show may edit moments from a fight between participants together with "confessional" interviews discussing the relevant people, leading viewers to believe that the interviews were responding to the fight, when they were actually shot two days beforehand. As viewers, we are well trained to watch for continuity, so unless told otherwise, we regularly assume continuous action, a tendency that producers can exploit.

Editing is primarily used to further continuity of action and tell a clear story, but it also generates emotional reactions and thematic meanings. More than any other form of television, music videos use editing as an expressive device, pacing edits to establish a **rhythm** that can follow or provide counterpoint to the music's beat. While many videos tell a story, they typically cut between multiple threads of action, including musical performance, dance sequences, and narrative. Many times the edits between threads are not related in time or space, but provide thematic resonances or graphic parallels. Such editing strategies are experienced less as comprehensible action and more as evocative pleasures tied to a video's pacing and emotional responses.

Rhythmic editing certainly matters in other genres. One of the most powerful devices available to producers is the decision not to edit a shot. A single shot with a lengthy duration is termed a **long take** (not to be confused with the proximity of a long shot). Long takes highlight unedited continuity, and often foreground engaging performances, allowing viewers to become immersed in intense action without any disruptions. They also offer a bit of "showiness" to producers, as they present a challenge to maintain consistency in performance, staging, and camerawork—"stunt" episodes of *Mad About You* and *The X-Files* have been shot with single takes between each commercial break, leading to numerous impressive long takes lasting over ten minutes.

More frequent cutting can also convey rhythm in a range of programming, as rapid rates of editing are typically used in action sequences to increase excitement and tension. Often the pace of edits across a continuity sequence will become more rapid as emotions rise and camera framing moves in closer. Editors use the rhythmic and graphic elements of editing as powerful elements that guide viewers' emotional responses, even though editing itself is a facet of a program often not consciously noticed by casual viewers. At one extreme, music videos in the 1980s employed such a rapid pace of editing, often with a focus on graphic imagery and rhythmic responses more than coherent continuity, that many critics and producers refer to the "MTV style" as representative of any fast-cutting sequence, a trend that has spread across television genres and into films. For more traditional programs, editors or live directors plan shot selection and pacing to best convey both coherent action and emotional impact, whether for a chase on a cop show or an interview on a news magazine. Editing is a variable that always impacts how we perceive the world represented on-screen.

One important stylistic element to consider in analyzing any sequence is a combination of staging, camerawork, and editing: the choice of what is not seen on-screen. Producers always choose what to show and what to omit in a program; often the omissions are powerful choices, able to create suspense, mystery, ambiguity, or even deception. A news editor might omit showing a gruesome image, a camera might frame a shot hiding an actor's face offscreen, or a director might choose not to stage a significant confrontation between characters. In each case, the choice not to visualize something impacts the meanings and tone of the sequence. To be a critical viewer, you must consider not only why images are presented as they are, but also why certain images are left unseen.

Graphics

A number of television's visual elements cannot easily be categorized as staging, camerawork, or editing. The last visual element of television style is **graphics**, the creation or manipulation of images using non-photographic techniques. Graphics techniques span many different practices within television programming, and are used in most genres to convey information and create compelling visuals that exceed the possibilities of photographic representation.

The most graphic-intensive type of programming is **animation**, in which the entire visual world is created non-photographically. Most commonly, images are drawn onto transparent **cels**, and then shot frame by frame on a film camera, a technique used by animated programs such as *The Simpsons* and *SpongeBob SquarePants*. In recent years, **computer-generated animation** has become more popular, with all images created and animated digitally, a technique used on diverse programs such as *South Park* and *Dora the Explorer*. Other types of animation create the illusion of motion using clay figures or objects, as in *Robot Chicken* or *Gumby*.

Even though animation does not use the other techniques of visual style to capture images, it often mimics the effects of staging, camerawork, and editing: animated images shift to resemble a camera pan or zoom; sequences follow principles of continuity editing; characters are drawn to mimic human performances and appearance. The norms of visual style common to live-action programming are typically emulated within animation. Even though there is no technological rationale for following such practices, viewers are trained to expect certain norms of visual style regardless of the show's mode of production.

Graphic images can be incorporated into traditionally shot programming, creating a hybrid of animation and live-action forms. While this technique is much more common in films, given the expense of creating naturalistic **computer-generated images** (or CGI), science fiction and horror programming uses such techniques to create fantastic creatures or complex effects. The high-budget short forms of music videos and advertising tend to be more adventurous in using animation and CGI as creative elements in conjunction with staged action. Many visual effects and innovations common to cinema are used frequently in commercials and videos, where visual spectacles attempt to cut through the promotional clutter.

Digital imaging is also used to alter the visual elements captured by cameras. On reality programs, people's faces will be digitally blurred if they do not consent to appearing on-camera, and signs for non-sponsored products are blurred out if they do not pay for product placement. Image manipulation can obscure accidentally shown cameras or microphones within the frame, or even "touch up" the appearance of performers to make them more (or less) attractive. Digital processing can be used to alter the image to resemble old film footage, changing the color tint or adding "dirt" to the screen, or bathe a shot in an unusual color scheme to change the mood. In the digital age, staging and camerawork are only the first step in defining what appears in the frame of a given shot.

A much more common use of graphics involves overlaying material onto an image. Through a process called **keying**, graphically generated visuals can be placed atop a video image; keying dates back to early television, preceding the digital era, and can be used in both live edits and postproduction. The most common use of keying is to overlay text in front of an image: title and credits running over a video sequence, captions translating foreign languages, or an identification tag labeling the program, channel, or speaker seen on-screen. Images can be keyed as well, as with inset pictures hovering over the shoulder of a news anchor introducing a story.

The rise of digital technology has led to an increase in the complexity of keyed images, especially in sports and newscasts. A segment on one of the twenty-four-hour news channels might have numerous layers of graphics at any moment, with images behind the anchor, multiple inset graphics, text captions, and numerous crawls at the bottom of the screen offering headlines, stock prices, and sports scores. This leads to a distinctly different mode of watching the news from traditional newscasts: watching an image with multiple streams of information favors a wandering eye scanning for key words in headlines and stories. Critics argue that such visual clutter undermines the analytical function of journalism, as viewers glance for quick "factoids" rather than digesting an entire story. Such an argument suggests that stylistic choices can unintentionally

LIVE

EXTREME WEATHER

CNN TROPICAL STORM FAY 3:00p ET

BRITISH CHAMBERS OF COMMERCE: UK FACES "DISTINCT F

The use of keying has become more cluttered in recent years, as in this CNN telecast with split-screen, keyed weather map, overlayed news crawl, and other graphic information creating a densely packed screen.

impact the cultural function of television programming and how viewers make sense of information.

One specific use of keying is a **chroma key**: the action is staged in front of a single-color backdrop (typically green or blue), which is electronically replaced with another image. Most commonly, chroma key is used for weather reports, as the forecaster stands in front of a colored screen to be keyed with a series of maps. This technique can be used for special effects, too, such as when actors are placed in environments via the superimposition of images.

Graphics can also be used to combine multiple video signals on one screen. A **split-screen** image is often used in interviews, especially when the participants are not in the same location. Multiple screens are also used in sports broadcasting, allowing viewers to observe multiple games, or combine replays with ongoing action. Typically these uses of keying and multi-screen graphics are found in live-edited programs such as news, sports, and events, enabling viewers to visually consume multiple streams of information simultaneously, although filmed shows such as *24* use these techniques for dramatic effect.

Fictional programs use graphics and keying in a more limited manner. Most programs use some sort of title sequence and credits that key text over images, often with credit sequences that establish the mood or tone for a series. The spooky imagery layered in the credit sequence for *The X-Files*, the stark animation conveying a businessman falling from a skyscraper on *Mad Men*, or the casual titles keyed over a montage of comedic scenes for *Friends* all clearly establish each program's tone, genre, and setting. Often programs will use keyed captions to signal scene transitions, marking the time and place of the new sequence to guide viewers through the narrative. But split screens, graphic boxes, and frequent textual captions are quite rare in scripted programming.

Television's use of graphics highlights the way programming signals realism to viewers. Most graphics techniques break the illusion of realism conveyed by continuity editing and naturalistic staging; split screens and captions call attention to television as a presentational medium. Thus programming that seeks to create a naturalistic and immersive fictional world typically minimizes the use of graphics. Nonfiction programs such as news and sports use a presentational mode that acknowledges that it is a television program, and thus use graphics frequently to maximize the various techniques that can convey information to viewers. Thus even though graphics typically signal an artificial and presentational mode, they are most commonly used in programming presenting real rather than fictional worlds.

Sound

Television conveys content using two of our senses: vision and hearing. Yet most analyses of television's style and form focus on the visual qualities of the moving image; we call ourselves "viewers" not "listeners," after all. **Sound** is a crucial element of television's form, however, with a number of specific techniques and terms that help deepen our understanding of the medium's power to communicate with and impact viewers through sound.

We can categorize sound on television into three basic types: voice, music, and environment. **Vocal sounds** are clearly a staple of television programming, present whenever people are talking. Most commonly, **dialogue** presents the speech of multiple people interacting, whether it be in a scripted drama or an unscripted discussion on a talk show. Dialogue is most connected to written programming, as many programs have notable styles of speech, such as the snappy patter of *The West Wing*, or particular characters known for their vocal performances, as with the deep nasal tone of *Everybody Loves Raymond's* Brad Garrett. The combination of written dialogue and vocal performance is typically how most scripted series establish characters, advance narratives, and keep viewers engaged in programs. Unscripted dialogue, such as interviews and reality show exchanges, is often edited to follow patterns of scripted dialogue to maximize clarity and flow between participants, and often performers will try to follow dialogue norms in nonfiction programs, as in the forced casual "chat" between newscasters on local news programs.

A less common vocal presentation is a **monologue**, where one person speaks alone. Monologues in fictional programs are rare, as they either use a contrived way to maintain naturalism, such as a character speaking on the phone or into a tape recorder, or will explicitly break from realism, as in the commentaries delivered into the camera on *The Bernie Mac Show* or *Malcolm in the Middle*. Soap operas sometimes use soliloquies, that is, characters speaking to themselves to express their emotional states, but this device is typically viewed as too artificial or stagy in other fictional genres. Nonfiction programs in a presentational style feature monologues much more frequently, as a newscaster talks directly to the camera, a commercial shows a spokesperson extolling a product, a comedian performs a stand-up routine on a talk show, or a politician gives a speech. Reality programming uses the "confessional camera" to give participants an opportunity to reflect in isolation via monologues, which are typically intercut with the actions being discussed. Monologues, such as graphics, break the illusion of realism and thus are used sparingly in fictional programs trying to create a naturalistic storyworld.

A final use of vocal sound is **voiceover narration**, where we do not see the voice speaking on-screen. Some voiceover serves solely an introductory function. NBC's newscast opens with an announcer intoning "This is NBC News," while *Law & Order* opens every episode with a introduction starting, "In the criminal justice system, the people are represented by two separate yet equally important groups." Other programs have ongoing narration, setting the scene, signaling transitions, and explaining relevant information. Early television used such narration frequently as a holdover from radio programming, typified by *Dragnet's* narration by main character Joe Friday, as he walked viewers through police procedurals as if he were reading from an incident report. More recent use of voiceover narration in fiction tends toward offering comedic commentary, as on *Scrubs* or *Arrested Development*, or using a narrator to establish the show's storybook tone, as on *Pushing Daisies*. Nonfiction programming often uses narration to explain footage, as with nature documentaries or news stories. Narration can provide alternative interpretations and additional information to supplement the visuals and dialogue occurring within a scene.

The second main type of television sound is **music**, which can serve a variety of functions and roles within a program. Music can clearly intersect with voice, as characters or soundtrack singing can function like monologues or dialogue, with lyrics conveying information about the show's narrative—although very few scripted programs aside from children's shows have embraced the convention of theatrical and film musicals, with characters regularly breaking into song. But music itself can convey a great deal apart from its use of words. One common use of music is a program's **score**, the musical soundtrack that can define a scene's tone, mood, and genre. A score can quickly establish a sequence as belonging to a specific genre, such as horror, soap opera, or comedy, almost regardless of the visuals. Scores are often original compositions, typically orchestral instrumental music designed to convey emotional content. Shows often have a composer create a library of core musical themes that are used throughout a series, rather than fresh new scores for each episode.

Television also licenses existing music, such as popular songs that highlight a show's mood or a character's personality. This practice became popular in the late 1970s and early 1980s with shows such as *WKRP in Cincinnati* and *Miami Vice*, using rock music to appeal to a youthful audience. The rise of music videos in the 1980s fed into this practice, with visual sequences with minimal dialogue designed around a musical selection, mimicking the visual style of MTV. Soundtracks of songs featured on programs have become a common ancillary market for teen-oriented television series such as *Dawson's Creek* and *The O.C.*, which feeds into the cross-media holdings of conglomerates such as Time Warner discussed in chapter 1. As MTV began airing programs beyond music videos more frequently in the 1990s, music remained a central component and was featured prominently in reality shows such as *The Real World* and cartoons such as *Beavis and Butthead*.

One particularly important use of music in television is opening **theme songs**, which often come to stand in for the program as a whole. It is hard to think about shows such as *The Andy Griffith Show*, *The Jeffersons*, or *The Muppet Show* without humming their catchy theme songs. Some theme songs are instrumentals, setting the mood of diverse shows such as *Taxi*, *The Simpsons*, *Six Feet Under*, or *Mission: Impossible*, while others use lyrics to convey a sense of the show's tone, as in *All in the Family*, *Cheers*, or *Malcolm in the Middle*. Lyrics can also provide a basic overview of the show's basic narrative situation, as in the songs from *The Beverly Hillbillies*, *The Brady Bunch*, *Gilligan's Island*, and *The Fresh Prince of Bel-Air*. Many programs adopt existing music as their theme songs: *The Sopranos* and *Friends* took fairly obscure pop songs by bands A3 and The Rembrandts, respectively, transforming them into iconic songs tied to these hit series. Other series adopt well-known pop songs for their themes, such as *CSI's* use of "Who Are You?" or "With a Little Help from My Friends" on *The Wonder Years*. Original themes can also become popular hits, as theme songs from shows such as *Dragnet*, *Hill Street Blues*, *The Greatest American Hero*, and *Miami Vice* were all hit singles following their television debuts.

Some programs feature live music throughout. Variety programs and late-night talk shows feature both in-house bands and guest artists playing music onstage, while musical-themed shows of today (MTV's *TRL*) and yesterday (*American Bandstand* and *Soul Train*) highlight bands and singers performing their current hits. Nearly all genres use music as part of their overall presentation, if only as a transitional device on a news program segueing into or out of a commercial break. Even though playing background music is not a sign of naturalistic presentation, it often feels odd to viewers for a program not to have music as an element; for instance, the unusual episode of *Buffy the Vampire Slayer* entitled "The Body" (where a main character dies suddenly) gained much of its unsettling power by eliminating music from the soundtrack entirely. Likewise, *The Wire* is notable for using background music only in its

BUFFY THE VAMPIRE SLAYER

Buffy the Vampire Slayer (The WB, 1997–2001; UPN, 2001–03): One of television's biggest cult hits, this series offered an unlikely mixture of horror and teen drama, overlaid with witty dialogue and complex serialized plotting to appeal to viewers outside of its network's original target teen demographic. The show's success led to spin-off *Angel* and inspired UPN to take over distributing the program after negotiations for the sixth season stalled with The WB.

season-ending montage sequences, and otherwise only featuring music coming from sources from within the narrative world, like radios and nightclubs.

The third type of sound source commonly found in television is **environmental sound**. While vocal and musical sound are specific types of expression, sounds coming from the environment can range widely from incidental traffic noise in the background of an on-location shot, to a carefully designed sound effect mimicking a spaceship's roar on *Star Trek*. Environmental sound rarely has as direct an impact on viewers' comprehension and emotional responses as voice and music, but it can strengthen a sequence's naturalistic or presentational quality. In both live-editing and postproduction sound editing, the mix between music, voice, and environmental sound works to convey a sense of a sequence's naturalism, spatial dimensions, and mood.

When a scene is being shot, microphones are positioned to capture the primary sound sources from the staging, but often a microphone is dedicated to capturing **ambient sound**. This can range from the incidental sounds of footsteps and props being used in a studio shoot, to the crowd noise at a sporting event. Ambient sound adds to the naturalistic sense of a location, creating a richer environment. Often it will be added to a sound mix to artificially enhance a naturalistic scene, such as adding sounds of birds to an exterior shot or the sound of typewriters clicking on newscasts of the 1970s. Even silence in a particular scene includes ambient sound, with a "room tone" recorded to avoid the sterile absence of pure silence.

Sound effects are specially crafted sounds designed to mimic the sounds that would be created in the environment depicted on-screen. Some effects work to provide sound to an artificial element, such as a CGI monster on a horror show, the movement of a graphic logo on a twenty-four-hour news channel, or the howling wind of a fictional hurricane. Often sound effects can be added to heighten the impact of staged actions, as in the sounds of shooting guns, taking photographs, or slamming doors. A sound effect added in postproduction might actually sound more naturalistic than the sound recorded during the shoot. At times, a well-made sound effect might be more convincing and emotionally engaging than an image in conveying a narrative element, as in an off-screen shooting, an unknown creature, or a car crash.

All three types of sound sources on television can be further understood using the crucial distinction between diegetic and nondiegetic sound. **Diegetic sound**, which comes from the world represented on-screen, includes dialogue, noises within the scene, and music that is heard within the staged action. **Diegesis** refers to the world represented in a program, and thus all sound heard by characters is diegetic. Diegetic sound is typically used to convey information about what is presented in the show's staging, whether it is the fictional world of a hospital on *ER* or the questions and answers on a game show. We know what is happening by listening to voices and noises coming from that world. **Nondiegetic sound**, which only the audience can hear, cannot be heard by characters on-screen, and thus originates outside the world represented on-screen. The most common forms of nondiegetic sound are soundtrack music or voiceover narration, typically added in postproduction editing or mixed into the action during a live edit.

Voiceover narration can blur the boundary between diegetic and nondiegetic, depending on the source. Nondiegetic narration comes from outside the storyworld via an external narrator with no connection with the staged action, such as Rod Serling's framing narration on *The Twilight Zone* or Ron Howard's satirical commentary on *Arrested Development*. Some narration functions as the **internal voice** of a character, such as J.D.'s running thoughts on *Scrubs* or Carrie's commentary on *Sex in the City*, but is shared only between the audience and one character—these sounds are diegetic as they are part of the storyworld, even though they are limited to one character. To complicate things further, some narrators may be viewed as **extradiegetic**, existing in the storyworld but not emerging directly from the on-screen action. Examples of extradiegetic narration include Mary Alice's commentary from beyond the grave on *Desperate Housewives* and the retrospective voice of Kevin reminiscing on *The Wonder Years*. Typically, narrators outside the storyworld are perceived as more reliable and less subjective than internal monologues of characters or nostalgic reflections tinged with interpretation, but all narration pulls a program toward a more presentational rather than naturalistic style.

Music can also straddle the boundary between diegetic and nondiegetic frames. Music is typically part of the nondiegetic soundtrack, working to set the mood and tone of a scene but not entering into the story. When music is diegetic, a program usually reveals its source visually, as with a band playing in a bar or someone turning on a stereo; this is needed because viewers typically expect musical accompaniment to function nondiegetically. Programs can play with this boundary creatively—*Gilmore Girls* features a town troubadour who plays music commenting on the action, a diegetic representation of a typically nondiegetic element.

GILMORE GIRLS

Gilmore Girls (The WB, 2000–06; The CW, 2006–07): A dramedy focused on a mother and teen daughter who are also best friends, the show contrasts life in a quirky small New England town with the upper-crust world of private schools and Yale University with an attention to class differences in America. The program emerged with support from the Family Friendly Programming Forum, designed to encourage more programming with cross-generational appeal, and its fast-paced, witty dialogue saturated in pop-culture references set it apart from typical teen dramas in drawing both adult and young viewers.

Environmental sound is nearly always diegetic, as it refers to the world represented on-screen. A form of nondiegetic environmental sound unique to television is the **laugh track** for many sitcoms. Either the immediate response of a live in-studio audience or a recording of laughter added in postproduction, this laughter is presumably not heard by the characters, even though the actors can hear a live audience. Compare this type of sound with the audience responses on talk shows, variety shows, and sporting events—in these genres, applause, cheers, and laughter are clearly heard and shared by the on-screen personalities, who often directly address a crowd and respond to their reactions.

For viewers, television sound serves many functions. Most centrally, it conveys information through vocal expression, the primary use of language within television. Sound also guides our attention in a scene, pointing viewers to particular visual elements, as in a sportscaster highlighting a play or investigators discussing a piece of evidence central to the story on *CSI*. Sound can also be used in contrast to visuals: satirical programs such as *The Daily Show* can criticize public figures by simultaneously showing visuals contradicting their statements, or a fictional program can use music in counterpoint to visuals to create emotional tension or ambiguity.

Music and environmental sound also guide our emotional reactions to a sequence, as the choice of score and sound effects directly shapes how we perceive and respond to what is seen on-screen, often without our realizing that sound has affected our reaction. Sound can convey a rhythm to a scene, often in conjunction with visual editing, which can trigger emotional responses such as excitement, suspense, or sadness. A common technique is the **musical montage**, which rhythmically edits a number of visual sequences over a song that signals an emotional response—a technique common both to sports highlight sequences and to dramas signaling an emotional peak or development in a relationship.

Sound often works in conjunction with editing to signal transitions between sequences, with a musical cue swelling or changing abruptly to indicate our shift from scene to scene, or a voiceover narrator explicitly signaling a new location or time. A more subtle technique is called a **sound bridge**, in which the audio and video in an edit are staggered: the next scene's sound is heard before cutting to the new shot, or the first scene's sound lingers over the new image. Sound bridges, as well as sound **cross-fades** similar to the visual dissolve, are part of the continuity system, creating a naturalistic sense of seamless flow between sequences. For nonfiction programming, sound editing is often used to maintain continuity in a news story or documentary sequence, even if the sound and image are from different sources.

Sound has particular importance in television when compared with film. It is hard to imagine a situation in a movie theater when you might watch the image but not hear the sound, or inversely listen without watching (aside from a particularly gory moment in a horror film). Whereas film assumes a constant integration of sound and vision, television viewers often separate these two sensory streams. The remote control's mute button allows viewers to eliminate the sound track easily, commonly during advertising breaks or while in the midst of other conversations; certain viewing situations also call for silent television, as in loud public places such as bars or airports. Viewers also look away from the screen while immersed in another activity, such as checking email on a computer or going into a nearby room, relying on the continued soundtrack to keep them alerted as to what is happening on-screen.

Although we shouldn't overstate the frequency of such separations of sound and image, they are much more common for television than film. Producers recognize this potential and often create programs that can withstand the separation of image from sound. Advertisers strive to create commercials that can still persuade while muted or when only heard from the next room, and sports and newscasts use extensive graphics to visually update scores and headlines. Sound can be used to hail viewers' attention, with an exciting sports call or dramatic music cue pulling our eyes back to the screen. Producers recognize that television typically competes for attention in a busy household full of distractions, and thus they use both sound and visual cues to maintain continuity and clarity for viewers—especially through commercial breaks.

This chapter on television's style offers a litany of terms and techniques that might be confusing to readers lacking experience creating videos. However, being attuned to the techniques that producers employ to create television makes you a more critically engaged and informed viewer, able to see the nuances and subtleties that producers use to convey meaning and create desired responses in viewers. Watching a program and paying attention to camerawork or editing widens the scope of what you notice, and potentially deepens your appreciation of the complex system of communication offered by every minute of television. Whether you use this awareness to enjoy programs more fully as sophisticated creative works, or to uncover manipulative and potentially deceptive techniques that may have previously gone unnoticed, being a formally aware viewer is a crucial skill in an era of media saturation.

FURTHER READING

There has been less critical analysis of television's formal dimensions than other areas of research. Jeremy Butler, *Television: Critical Methods and Applications*, 3rd ed. (Mahwah, N.J.: Lawrence Erlbaum Associates, 2007), offers the best overview of televisual form for beginners. John Thornton Caldwell, *Televisuality: Style, Crisis, and Authority in American Television* (New Brunswick, N.J.: Rutgers University Press, 1995), explores the history of television style and production, focusing on the 1980s. Greg M. Smith, *Beautiful TV: The Art and Argument of Ally McBeal* (Austin: University of Texas Press, 2007), offers a detailed aesthetic analysis of one innovative series.

Production-centered studies can offer accounts of the ways meanings are conveyed through sound and vision, such as Todd Gitlin, *Inside Prime Time* (Berkeley: University of California Press, 2000), Laura Grindstaff, *The Money Shot: Trash, Class, and the Making of TV Talk Shows* (Chicago: University of Chicago Press, 2002), and John Thornton Caldwell, *Production Culture: Industrial Reflexivity and Critical Practice in Film and Television* (Durham, NC: Duke University Press, 2008). A strong outline of these production practices can be found in Elana Levine, "Toward a Paradigm of Media Production Research: Behind the Scenes at *General Hospital*," *Critical Studies in Media Communication* 18, no. 1 (2001): 66–82.

CHAPTER 6

TELLING TELEVISION STORIES

The various elements of television's style explored in chapter 5 can convey an almost infinite range of information and emotional material, but the vast majority of television programming focuses on one common goal: telling stories. Narratives are the central form of all scripted television genres, from sitcoms to science fiction, cartoons to soap operas. Unscripted programming also uses narrative structures and conventions to present compelling accounts of an athlete's rise and fall, to heighten the drama of a game show competition, to tell the confessional tale of a talk show guest, and to structure a news story. This chapter explores how television narratives work, and considers how genre categories help shape our experience with a broad range of stories.

THE FORM OF TELEVISION NARRATIVE

Television storytelling might seem to be a simple practice: a writer devises a fictional tale and then writes a script for the show. But television storytelling is comprised of a broad array of elements, and thus we need to look carefully at the practices involved in crafting narratives. The process of storytelling includes much more than the writer, too, with all of the formal elements discussed in chapter 5 used in tandem to create compelling narrative worlds and to communicate a story to viewers. Understanding how television stories are structured, and the range of devices that can be used in their telling, greatly improves our ability to critically engage with and analyze nearly all types of television programming.

Characters and Events

All narratives comprise two key elements: characters and events. Any story involves characters who participate in the action, and events that comprise the narrative's forward movement; virtually any narrative can be summarized by recounting the events that occur and the characters who engage in the action. While we recognize characters and events as the core building blocks of narratives, particular facets of these storytelling elements deserve more consideration.

In nearly all programs, **characters** are the people featured in the narrative. In certain instances, characters may not be people—*Lassie* features a dog as a main character, just as *Mr. Ed* focuses on a horse, while cartoons regularly feature animals, aliens, cars, and sponges as characters. But in each of these cases, the nonhuman character is imbued with some aspect of humanity, such as Mr. Ed's ability to talk or Lassie's skill at rescuing her family. A central element of characters is **agency**, the ability to undertake actions and make choices with narrative consequences; watching characters react to ongoing narrative developments is a main way viewers engage with television stories.

Certain characters fulfill particular functions in a narrative. One key role is the **protagonist**, the hero at the center of a narrative. Typically in many films and novels, one primary protagonist anchors a narrative, with a central goal that carries the story forward. This is most common on self-contained narratives such as made-for-TV movies or anthology dramas. Ongoing series typically present an **ensemble** of central characters, each of whom may serve as protagonist for a particular episode. Even a series with a strong central protagonist, as in the title characters of *Buffy the Vampire Slayer, House M.D.*, or *Frasier*, the protagonist is typically part of a team of central characters who comprise an engaging ensemble. It is rare to have a single protagonist in an ongoing series, with exceptions such as *The Fugitive* or *The Incredible Hulk* standing out with their plots of individual heroes on the run.

In the self-contained narratives of films and novels, characters can serve as **antagonists**, to act in opposition to the protagonist as a villain or adversary. Television series might feature antagonists in single episodes, as in the criminal on police drama, but ongoing narratives rarely have such clear villains. Soap operas famously feature villains who later become heroes (as well as the reverse), and prime time serials often embrace such ambiguous characters whose

LASSIE

Lassie (CBS, 1954–71; syndicated 1971–73): A beloved long-running family drama about a boy and his dog, a collie named Lassie, and their adventures, the show represents a model of wholesome, family-oriented programming that many associate with the 1950s.

MR. ED

Mr. Ed (CBS, 1961–66): The story of a talking horse who would speak only to his owner, *Mr. Ed* is typical of a cycle of high-concept fantasy sitcoms from the 1960s that used fantastic or outlandish ideas to distinguish themselves from typical 1950s fare.

THE O.C.

The O.C. (Fox, 2003–07): A teen drama focused on wealthy residents of Orange County, California, *The O.C.* combined soap opera style plotlines with witty pop culture banter to generate a dedicated teen audience before fading in later seasons. The show notably featured obscure independent rock music that led to a number of popular soundtracks.

alliances and motives are always shifting, such as Arvin Sloane on *Alias*, *The O.C.*'s Julie Cooper, or Ben Linus on *Lost*. On comedies, antagonists are typically humanized and allowed to coexist with the ensemble, as with Ted Baxter on *The Mary Tyler Moore Show* or Dwight Schrute on *The Office*. Even *Taxi's* Louie DePalma, who might be the least sympathetic regular character ever to appear on a network sitcom, was portrayed with sufficient charm and heart to make him part of the ensemble.

Television narratives tend to foreground changing **relationships** between characters more than focusing on a singular protagonist goal or conflict with an antagonist. This is partly due to the ongoing nature of a series, where it would be difficult to maintain the narrative drive of a single goal or personal conflict. Additionally, viewers can grow to know television characters with much more depth than possible in a single film, and thus the characters' relationships become more defined and central to the ongoing series narrative. Even series

> ## TAXI
>
> *Taxi* (ABC, 1978–82; NBC, 1982–83): A sitcom about New York City cab drivers created by veteran producers of *The Mary Tyler Moore Show*, *Taxi* had a darker and more cynical tone than typical comedies of its era, with a strong cast and wry sense of humor. Producers from *Taxi* went on to create the more successful *Cheers*, which shared a similar tone and focus on atypical characters for a sitcom.

that focus on single stories in each episode—for example, crime procedural *Law & Order*—develop in-depth characters and establish relationships between characters as an ongoing source of viewer interest. Programs in all genres can generate long-term viewer investment by creating compelling relationships between characters, and develop shifting alliances and underlying emotional connections over a long-term narrative.

Unscripted programs also use characterization to present people and relationships. News and sports programs regularly frame subjects as heroes and villains, using various production methods to guide viewers' interpretations of the people represented on-screen, such as camera framing, music cues, and lighting. Reality programs expend a great deal of effort in casting participants whom producers imagine will be compelling characters on a show, and pair personalities that they anticipate will create dramatic relationships, whether hostile or romantic. Talk shows shape their productions to portray guests as vivid characters and highlight relationships, using reference points from the world of scripted narrative. Viewers interpret real people using the narrative traditions of characterization, looking to real-life characters as the source of entertaining human drama.

Characters are only one component of a narrative; when trying to summarize an episode of a television series, the behavior and relationships of characters is often secondary to the basic question of "what happened?" The narrative **events** comprising an episode are central to storytelling, and generally when we think of a program's narrative, such specific actions are the most memorable aspects of the show. Nearly any event can be significant in terms of narrative, but usually an event must trigger some change in a character's status to be dramatically significant, whether within a relationship (a husband is caught in a lie to his wife), professional situation (a police officer accepts a bribe), or even as a matter of survival (a spy is captured by an enemy). Many narrative events are comparatively minor, offering details about a character that are significant but not central to the episode's main story.

Narrative events have a particular logic of **cause and effect** that viewers assume to be guiding the story; we assume that all main events presented in the narrative are related to one another in a chain of causality. When we see two characters commit a crime or kiss, we expect that this event will trigger another narrative action: the criminals might be arrested or the lovers might be discovered by a romantic rival. If the plot does not follow up on the consequences of an event, it may feel unsatisfying to viewers or seem to lack narrative significance. Part of the pleasures of watching narratives can be the act of tying together seemingly disconnected narrative threads, as on *Seinfeld* when Kramer unexpectedly injures a whale while golfing on the beach, forcing George to confront his own earlier lie about being a marine biologist.

Nonfiction shows often frame events using a causal logic as well. Reality shows typically stage events in order to maximize dramatic and causal impact, with high-stakes competitions and opportunities for personal conflict. A sports profile will suggest that an athlete's success or failure was caused by a previous rivalry or injury, or news interviews will attempt to discern the reasons why a politician made a particular policy decision or chose a certain career path. Newscasts use causal logic in telling an individual story—the latest poll shifted because of a candidate's successful debate—but the newscast as a whole lacks cause-and-effect relationships between stories: we don't think that the candidate's debate had any effect on the next story about a region rebuilding after an earthquake or the weather forecast. To fully understand how nonfiction programs present the real world using the tools of fictional narrative, we need to explore the related concepts of story and plot.

Story and Plot

Scholars who study narrative, from literature to film to television, have offered an important distinction between two familiar terms that are commonly used interchangeably: story and plot. On any fictional narrative program, many events occur and characters respond with particular actions—doctors treat patients injured in a car accident on *ER*; Claire and Cliff teach Theo a lesson after he gets poor grades on *The Cosby Show*. We do not see the accident or Theo failing a test on-screen, but these events clearly occurred within the show's fictional world, triggering the events we do see. The **story** of a television narrative consists of all events and characters within the world of a show, whether they are shown on-screen or not.

A program's **plot** is the way the story is told, consisting only of events shown on-screen, and the particular choices used to present that material, such as chronological order, omission of key details, and retelling events from multiple perspectives. Plot also includes nondiegetic material that guides our understanding of the story, such as musical scores, captions, and voiceover narration. When watching a narrative program, viewers are presented the plot via the elements of television style: each viewer must connect the dots between events shown

THE COSBY SHOW

The Cosby Show (NBC, 1984–92): A groundbreaking hit sitcom that portrayed a financially successful African-American family and built upon the comedic appeal of star and producer Bill Cosby. The show helped NBC rebound from years of weak ratings and established Thursday nights as the network's stronghold for many future seasons.

on-screen to construct the story within his or her mind, a process called **narrative comprehension**. The car accident and failed exam are part of the story, but they are not part of the plot; we know they happened because we can put together the clues given to us in the plot, such as dialogue, props, and events that require some missing cause.

In order to follow a narrative, we need to recreate the story being told by the plot. The act of narrative comprehension is an automatic process that all television viewers learn to follow, much like viewing continuity editing as a naturalistic presentation. Each television narrative constructs a **storyworld** or diegesis, a consistent universe in which all of the story elements, characters, and events are taking place—even material that is never revealed within a program is part of the storyworld, such as the cause of the *ER* accident or the topic of Theo's failed exam. Viewers regularly make inferences and fill in gaps to create a consistent and coherent storyworld from the plot; often the sign of a poorly told story is when the plot lacks consistency or requires far-fetched leaps of the imagination to make sense. Even programs that present storyworlds that are obviously unreal demand internal logic and consistency; we expect shows such as *Battlestar Galactica* or *Terminator: The Sarah Connor Chronicles* to avoid contradicting themselves, even though we accept the presence of robots masquerading as humans as not mirroring the real world.

How does this distinction between story and plot apply to unscripted programming? For news, sports, reality programs, talk shows, and game shows, the storyworld is our real world; the tennis matches, interviews, trivia contests, and elections presented on television all really happened. But these programs apply the techniques of storytelling to real-world events to create compelling narratives, turning the messy real events into a streamlined plot. People are presented as characters, highlighting past events and personality traits that might cause later narrative actions—a rivalry between players, a personal tragedy to overcome, a strong motivation for success. Editing a news story or reality show selectively presents events, focusing on those with the greatest causal impact while omitting those that do not seem to move the story forward. Reality programs rely so much on editing to narrate stories that the Writers Guild has tried to unionize reality editors by highlighting how they construct narratives much as writers do. Unscripted programming takes real-world events and turns them into plots, a process of narration that applies to both fictional and nonfictional television; as viewers, we should be aware of how plots are always partial presentations of the storyworld, a process that can be especially manipulative or deceptive when the storyworld is real.

Narration and Narrators

The process of taking story material and conveying it as a television plot is called **narration**, the act of storytelling itself that presents the story via a medium. Some aspects of narration apply to every medium, as with how story information is paced and selected, while others are unique to a particular form, such as the use of moving images and sound to communicate story to viewers. Understanding the choices and processes used to narrate stories highlights how both fictional and nonfictional programs construct a particular vision of their storyworlds using the techniques common to television.

When the creators of a program have a story they wish to tell, they must make a series of choices as to how to narrate that story using television's formal techniques. Every choice impacts the plot construction and potentially shapes the effectiveness of the program. One important decision involves the **range of story information** presented by the plot. At one extreme is **unrestricted or omniscient narration**, in which any story material can be presented without regard to what main characters know or experience. Most soap operas offer unrestricted narration, potentially sharing story information and even internal thoughts about every character within the large ensemble; many sitcoms, dramas, and reality programs similarly use unrestricted narration.

At the other extreme of the spectrum of story information is **restricted narration**, where all story information is filtered through the experiences of one or two main characters. A classic example is *Dragnet,* in which follows the process as the police construct the crime story; thus in procedurals, including contemporary examples such as *CSI, House M.D.,* and *Medium,* we are often restricted to learning story information alongside the main characters investigating the relevant events. Restricted narration might also place limits on narrative space rather than characters—sitcoms such as *Barney Miller* or *Cheers* stage nearly all the action in one central location, so all narration occurs within the space of the police precinct or bar, respectively, regardless of which characters in the ensemble are present.

Few shows are exclusively restricted or unrestricted, but occupy a middle ground that may change throughout the course of an episode. A program such as *Veronica Mars* shares some features with restricted procedurals, as Veronica typically investigates some mystery that is revealed to the audience following

VERONICA MARS

Veronica Mars (UPN, 2004–06; The CW, 2006–07): A cult favorite about a teenage girl who works as a private detective, *Veronica Mars* emphasizes the class conflicts in a fictional California city between wealthy, white elites and working-class and ethnic teenagers. The program uses voiceover narration and complex narrative twists to resemble film noir style mixed with a teen drama.

her own discoveries, and her investigation is framed by her voiceover narration. But as in many mysteries, at times the audience can know more than the characters, as when Veronica is about to stumble into a dangerous situation. Or the character may know more than the audience, as when she has planned some scheme that we discover as her victims experience it. Additionally, some scenes focus on other characters in the ensemble and present story information that Veronica does not know, expanding the range of narrative information beyond the restricted perspective of the protagonist.

Charting the amount of information a narrative provides to viewers versus what characters know helps explain how plots can trigger emotional reactions. When a show creates suspense, surprise, or mystery, it usually withholds particular story information from viewers, leading us to make mistaken inferences or faulty assumptions in constructing the story. Crime shows typically wait to reveal the events causing the investigation until the end of a program, encouraging viewers to try to solve the mystery based on clues doled out over the course of an episode. Ongoing series can reveal story information that makes us rethink the plots of previous episodes and revise our ongoing assumptions; *24* revels in such plot twists, revealing characters to be duplicitous at the end of a season, forcing viewers to rethink everything presented throughout the series.

Not only can narration control the range of information conveyed to viewers, but programs also present different degrees of **depth of story information**. Most typically, television programs offer **objective narration**, presenting the external storyworld via what characters do and say. Some techniques move toward more **subjective narration**, presenting story information from the perspective of a particular character. Subjective narration can be achieved through camera angles representing a character's own vision, or **point-of-view shot**, or through sound that is clearly filtered through what a character is hearing, inviting us to experience the story through the eyes and ears of the character; such subjective techniques are uncommon, typically used to show a character who is experiencing the world differently, as with a character who is hallucinating or has lost hearing.

SIX FEET UNDER

Six Feet Under (HBO, 2001–05): A quirky drama about a family running a California funeral home, the show highlighted HBO's ability to push boundaries in representing sexuality and drugs beyond the limits of broadcast television. *Six Feet Under* features a groundbreaking representation of an interracial gay couple, as well as one of the most acclaimed series finales in television history.

MEDIUM

Medium (NBC, 2005–present): A crime drama with a paranormal twist, *Medium* focuses on a psychic and her work in the Phoenix, Arizona, district attorney's office, in balance with her home life as a mother of three.

A more common use of subjective narration offers **mental subjectivity** by giving viewers access to a character's internal thoughts: voiceover narration, dream sequences, flashbacks, and visual fantasies all take us into the mind of a character, helping us to experience story information that no other character shares. Such devices can provide comic moments, as featured on *Scrubs* or *My Name Is Earl*; character depth, such as characters' conversations with dead people on *Six Feet Under*; or significant plot points, such as the psychic dream sequences on *Medium*. Such subjective devices tend to make a program more presentational in style, calling attention to the techniques of television production and breaking away from naturalism. This directly contrasts literature, in which realist novels offer subjective immersions into the consciousness of characters with the same naturalistic tone they use to describe objective settings and actions.

One device straddles the boundary between objective and subjective narration: a character speaking directly to the camera is called **direct address**. Most fictional programs rely on a naturalistic theatrical convention termed the **fourth wall**, in which the performers do not acknowledge the audience (or cameras), pretending that a wall exists between the stage and the audience. When a character directly addresses the camera, he breaks through the fourth wall and thus shatter the naturalistic illusion. Some shows, such as *Moonlighting* or *Northern Exposure*, use direct address only occasionally as a self-aware gag, while others such as *Malcolm in the Middle*, *It's Garry Shandling's Show*, and *The Many Loves of Dobie Gillis* use it regularly throughout the series. It can be unclear whether such a direct address is a moment of subjective narration, offering a

MALCOLM IN THE MIDDLE

Malcolm in the Middle (Fox, 2000–06): An acclaimed and popular single-camera sitcom about a dysfunctional working-class family with a genius teenage son, the show uses an over-the-top cartoony style and direct address to the camera to highlight the absurdities of the family's life.

DESPERATE HOUSEWIVES

Desperate Housewives (ABC, 2004–present): A comedic soap opera about a group of female friends in the suburbs, the show was an immediate hit with its combination of mystery, melodrama, and broad comedy.

glimpse into the character's consciousness that we both see and hear, or an non-naturalistic objective moment in the life of someone who has a constant audience with a camera. For reality programs using confessional cameras or scripted programs framed with the presumption of a documentary film crew recording the events, as on *The Office*, these moments of direct address are clearly part of the objective storyworld, but offer some internal insights beyond interactions with other characters.

Direct address and character voiceovers can serve a specific function in a narrative: as a **narrator** responsible for telling the story. Most television programs do not use the device of an explicit narrator except through voiceover narration. As discussed in chapter 5, narrators can be diegetic characters whose internal monologues guide us through the story (as on *Grey's Anatomy*) or external figures who omnisciently present the narrative (as in *Arrested Development*)—or creative combinations of internal and external roles, as with Mary Alice's narration from beyond the grave on *Desperate Housewives*. Often narrators are presented using a **framing device**, which serves as a bracket at the beginning and end of episodes to introduce and conclude the narrative. The retrospective comments of Kevin looking back on his childhood on *The Wonder Years* frames the program as nostalgic recollection, but rarely intrudes into the ongoing story. External narrators can frame a story as well, as in the opening and closing announcer commentary on *Soap*, which simultaneously summarizes the action and humorously mocks the over-the-top storylines.

Nonfiction programs use narrators much more frequently. Documentaries often use voiceover narration to provide commentary and analysis, reframing

THE WONDER YEARS

The Wonder Years (1988–93): This dramedy uses voiceover narration to tell the story of the main character's youth in the late 1960s and early 1970s, viewing the generational conflicts of the era through the eyes of a child.

SOAP

Soap (ABC, 1977–81): An outlandish and risqué sitcom mocking soap operas, *Soap* was one of the first prime time series to use serialized plots and regular cliff-hangers. The show generated controversy before its debut for its portrayals of a gay character, adultery, and sexual innuendo, creating publicity that helped it receive strong ratings.

footage of animal behavior or a village ritual into a coherent story by emphasizing character, causality, and continuity. News stories also use narrators, as reporters typically use voiceover to guide viewers through the story and emphasize the narrative dimensions of the factual footage. Both documentary and news narrators might be diegetic characters, whose presence enters into the world portrayed via interviews and shots of the reporter, or nondiegetic figures who remain fully apart from the action, a technique often called "voice of god narration."

Even programs that do not feature explicit narrators still narrate. All programs that tell stories use narration to convey a storyworld as a plot to be experienced by viewers. The process of television narration involves all techniques that the medium uses to communicate, from explicit devices of voiceover and captions to more subtle practices such as camera angle and set design, as explored in chapter 5. Each stylistic choice made by producers impacts how the story will be presented and what viewers will take away from the program. Studying how television tells stories requires us to be aware of how all elements of television style work together as a formal system that conveys narrative information in particular ways.

Narrative Time

One vital way that television narration can present story information is through the manipulation of narrative time. Narratives are inherently time based, as we follow a chain of events occurring over a certain period. We might consider three different temporal streams within all narratives regardless of medium. **Story time** is the timeframe of the diegesis, how time passes within the storyworld. Story time typically follows realist conventions of straightforward chronology and linear progression from moment to moment. With exceptions such as science fiction time traveling or magical clocks freezing time, we assume that characters experience time in a moment-to-moment progression as in real life, and thus we construct our imagined storyworld following realistic temporal rules.

Very few narratives represent time passing on-screen strictly following story time, however. **Plot time** is the time frame as told within a given narrative, how time is presented on-screen. Editing skips over many moments of story time, providing ellipses in plot time through omissions and shifts forward that seem commonplace. Plot time is the most variable element of television storytelling, as producers use a wide range of techniques to construct a continual story through the selective presentation of on-screen moments from the storyworld. The act of narrative comprehension involves mentally rebuilding a continuous storyworld out of a fractured and sometimes jumbled plot time.

Finally, there is **screen time**, the temporal framework used in telling and watching the story. Film and television strictly controls screen time, as watching a one-hour program typically takes the same time for all viewers. Recording and playback technologies can alter the individual experience of screen time, allowing for pauses, replays, and fast-forwarding through a program on video, but screen time is generally a constant and scheduled flow in the experience of watching television. When a program presents story material, screen time flows along with plot time, but the commercial breaks and episodic scheduling freezes plot time while the screen turns to other material. At the end of a program's season, screen time may wait for three months or more before returning to the show, but story time might be paused on a mysterious cliff-hanger or could resume the narrative two years into the future. *Buffy the Vampire Slayer* innovatively rejoined the storyworld each fall as if the summer had passed in the storyworld, mirroring story and screen times, but few shows follow such chronology. Screen time can also influence story via the seasonal shift of a program. Many series follow the time of year that episodes air, with specific episodes for holidays such as Christmas or Halloween, a specific time scheme that loses meaning when a show is watched in reruns or on DVD.

The three streams of story, plot, and screen time can be manipulated by creators in interesting ways to create compelling narratives. One key variable is **narrative order**: assuming a continuous chronology of story time, narratives can present the plot out of sequence. Common reordering devices include **flashbacks**, in which we see the past events on-screen, and **retelling** past events, as characters reveal past story information without actually showing the events. Genres such as mysteries use reordered plot time to create suspense, waiting until the end of the narrative to disclose the inciting incident that diegetically occurred near the beginning of the story, typically revealed by the detective

BOOMTOWN

Boomtown (NBC, 2002–03): A short-lived but critically acclaimed crime drama, *Boomtown* innovatively portrays a criminal investigation from a range of shifting individual perspectives, including detectives, beat cops, emergency technicians, lawyers, and reporters.

narrating the crime story, a flashback replaying the events, or a combination of both. Some programs manipulate plot time more experimentally, presenting story events using jumbled chronologies. *Boomtown* innovatively narrated a conventional crime story by presenting a reordered set of sequences, each representing the restricted perspective of a police officer, lawyer, emergency technician, or criminal involved in the case. *Lost* is renowned for its play with narrative time, incorporating flash-forwards, flashbacks, time travel, and a range of other devices to create complex temporal systems. Such narratives with complex plot order require more active and attuned viewer attention to comprehend the action and assemble proper chronology.

Plots can also vary **narrative frequency**. In the storyworld, an event occurs only once, but it can be told multiple times in a program. This might be a repeated flashback of a memory that haunts a main character, or a recall to events occurring in previous episodes. Opening credit sequences will often include such flashes of earlier narrative moments to capture a program's mood and scenario. Most programs present story events multiple times to ensure viewer comprehension via **story redundancy**, especially if new events depend upon knowledge of earlier episodes. An increasingly common nondiegetic redundancy device is starting a program with a "Previously On" recap showing scenes from earlier episodes; nearly all television narratives include some redundant repetition of previously told narrative material within dialogue and visual representation within the story itself. Some programs use frequency to create ambiguity and tension—both *The West Wing* and *Alias* have started episodes with a moment of tension or suspense, with a keyed caption cuing a chronological shift backward (for instance, "72 hours earlier"), and the rest of the episode leading back to this original moment in the plot, repeating it and resolving the crisis. A distinctive plot device, typically called "the *Rashomon* effect," after the influential 1950s Japanese film, offers multiple subjective flashbacks on one event, with each character recalling a distinctly different version of the story—a storytelling technique that has been featured on episodes of diverse programs ranging from *All in the Family* to *The X-Files*, *Magnum P.I.* to *Diff'rent Strokes*.

A third variation using time in television storytelling is **narrative duration**, altering how long any given event lasts within the program. Typically any scene in a fictional program plays out in "real time"; the duration of a two-minute conversation is the same for story time, plot time, and screen time. Edits between scenes can shorten story duration, providing ellipses to condense the story into the plot's limited telling. Montage sequences offer even more notable condensation, typically reducing a long process of a romantic courtship or character's task to the length of a popular song. As discussed concerning camerawork, slow and fast motion can increase or delay the duration of a story for emotional effects or narrative efficiency. More subtly, a program can cross-cut between two or more simultaneous sequences to create suspense and tension, a process that typically lengthens the plot duration of a deadline story, as with those involving a ticking bomb or a medical emergency.

An innovative example of the creative potential of television's narrative time is *24*, a show whose very name indicates an awareness of the temporal strategies of storytelling. The show is most notable for allegedly unrolling in "real time"—each hour-long episode presents one hour of story material, with each of the season's twenty-four episodes tying together into one very busy day in the life of a counterterrorist organization. Thus it would seem that the three temporal streams of story, plot, and screen times are all presented uniformly. However, the show is actually less precise and straightforward than this. Each episode does present a simultaneous hour of story and screen time, but the story and plot pause for a week of screen time until Fox schedules the next episode. Additionally, each commercial break inserts a gap of a few minutes in story time, with the presumption that nothing of narrative significance occurs within such breaks—although the show does occasionally "cheat" by freezing story time during commercial breaks or while presenting another character's plot. These temporal differences are more notable on DVD—without advertising, the program presents closer to forty-five minutes of plot and screen time while representing an hour of story time. The show also uses split screens extensively to present simultaneous action across space, which effectively doubles plot time in the course of a sequence. The program *24* also opens with recaps that repeat previous events outside of the strict chronological sequence. Finally, the program uses captions regularly to demarcate the precise moment during the story's twenty-four-hour cycle, further calling attention to its temporal structure. The program's popularity, especially in DVD viewing, suggests a heightened awareness of the role of narrative time among contemporary viewers, who flock to a show that highlights its own storytelling mechanics.

Nonfiction programming uses temporal strategies in somewhat similar ways to fictional shows, although the norms of production and viewer expectations are quite different. Certainly live programs depend on a sense of seamless continuity, even though instant replays in sports alter both frequency and duration in violation of a live sensibility. Edited nonfiction such as news stories nearly always condense and reorder segments, and reality programs regularly arrange hours of

24 uses multiple split-screens and keying of a clock to convey the complex simultaneous action in its unique narrative format.

raw footage into episodes that create the illusion of sequential time and causal logic. Viewers understand that such programs are not presenting an unmediated reality, but the expectation is that such temporal alterations will stay true to the general content of the real world if not the exact chronological details, an expectation that is not always upheld. The processing of narrative time in both fictional and nonfictional television is a nearly automatic ability for viewers, even when they are presented with complex variations such as *Lost* or *24*, but it is worth making the process more conscious to note both the creative potentials of television storytelling and the ability of editing to manipulate and even deceive viewers into imagining a seamless story or real world.

Narrative Modes and Plot Structures

Television's stories follow many norms used across media, while also employing their own particular systems for the unique aspects of series programming. Most television stories follow the basic narrative structure typical of all media: a beginning state of **narrative equilibrium** or peace is ruptured by a **complicating action**, and then resolved to a changed state of equilibrium. Both Hollywood films and television programs typically follow a **three-act structure**: the first act presents and then disrupts a situation, the longer second act prolongs and complicates the disruption, and the third act resolves the conflict and restores equilibrium. Some programs follow these norms quite similarly to the cinematic medium. **Made-for-television movies** are stand-alone narratives that mimic the scope, length, and structure of films. Some stand-alone narratives have multiple episodes in the form of **miniseries**, such as *Roots* or *V*; miniseries begin with the intention to resolve the story over a small number of episodes, typically airing over a week or two. More commonly in contemporary television, fictional narratives are presented as ongoing series, with original stories offered in each episode designed to run as long as ratings ensure profitability for the distributor.

Television series treat their underlying narrative structure in various ways. Series fiction might be viewed on a continuum concerning how stories are presented across the series. On one end of the spectrum are the stand-alone narratives of **anthology series**, in which each episode offers an independent storyworld. Beyond the anthology dramas of the 1950s, most American anthology series are science fiction and horror shows such as *The Twilight Zone, The Outer Limits,* and *Tales from the Crypt*. Episodes of an anthology series are united by a shared title and often a host, who introduces and frames each episode's story, but the stories are unique and typically take place in freestanding and unrelated storyworlds. Such stand-alone plots commonly follow basic narrative structure, although the genres of science fiction and horror frequently conclude without reestablishing equilibrium. Anthology series productions are typically more costly than the efficient production of continuing series, and lack the popular familiarity of ongoing series, and thus are rare in contemporary television.

A more common structure for contemporary programs are **episodic series**, which present a consistent storyworld, but each episode is relatively independent: characters, settings, and relationships carry over across episodes, but the plots stand on their own, requiring little need for consistent sequential viewing or knowledge of story history to comprehend the narrative. In American television, this has been the most common model for prime time television, as situation comedies and dramas have followed episodic norms in crafting a familiar storyworld with plots that commence and resolve within each episode, and thus may be viewed in any order. Frequent markers of change in episodic series stem from the birth and growth of children, and additions or subtractions to the cast of characters. We can place the episodes of *Bewitched* in a rough order based on daughter Tabitha's age (as well as its shift to color and the recasting of Darrin Stevens). Yet there are minimal narrative differences between these various episodes, as we do not need to know Tabitha's infant backstory to appreciate her toddler mishaps.

Episodic programs offer a compact violation and restoration of the underlying situation. Although the specific form that a narrative disruption may take depends on genre conventions—crimes on cop shows versus family squabbles on sitcoms—the basic structure of episodic programs transcends genre. The conclusion of any episode returns the characters to the equilibrium of their

BEWITCHED

Bewitched (ABC, 1964–72): A popular fantasy sitcom about a witch who marries a human, the show has been viewed as a proto-feminist commentary on female power and the struggle women face in giving up their careers for marriage and motherhood. While the political undertones are noticeable, the show was best known for its amusing special effects and comedic dynamic between cast members.

HOUSE M.D.

House M.D. (Fox, 2004–present): A hit medical drama, *House* approaches medicine more like a crime procedural, with a team of diagnosticians investigating a mystery disease each week. The show is notable for its main character, Gregory House, an antihero whose difficult personality makes him a compelling foil for the other more sympathetic doctors, and the award-winning performance by lead actor Hugh Laurie.

given situation; any lessons learned or characters changed will likely be forgotten or ignored in subsequent episodes. While an episode's plot will be resolved, the underlying situation forestalls complete equilibrium that would undermine future narrative complications. Lucy may be foiled in a particular attempt to break into show business on an episode of *I Love Lucy*, but she'll try again the following week; no final resolution of her desires is achieved, even if each episode does provide some degree of closure. While the police on *NYPD Blue* or *Homicide* might solve one episode's case, crime continues to plague their cities to guarantee future stories. Episodic programs present closure of each week's self-contained, straightforward plotlines—singular criminal or medical cases, family or office mishaps, individual character conundrums—as any conflict must be solved quickly, but not conclusively enough to upset the basic narrative situation. Many episodic programs adhere to a **procedural** structure, where the self-contained episodes follow the process by which a narrative enigma is solved through police work, legal maneuvers, or medical investigation, typified by recent dramas such as *C.S.I.*, *Law & Order*, and *House M.D.*

Serial narratives are on the other end of the narrative spectrum. Serials were for many years confined to the genre of the daytime soap opera in American television, although in other countries prime time serials have been more common, such as Latin American *telenovelas* or British "kitchen sink" shows. By the 1980s, serial form had entered prime time in America, through family dramas (*Dallas* and *Dynasty*, so-called prime time soaps), crime shows (*Hill Street Blues*), and medical dramas (*St. Elsewhere*). The key feature of serial narration is continuing storylines traversing multiple episodes, with an ongoing diegesis that demands viewers to construct a storyworld using information gathered from their full history of viewing, which for some soap operas can go back decades. Serial programs do provide closure of storylines, but rarely in the same episode in which the plot was introduced. When storylines are resolved in serials, they are often replaced with even more suspenseful or engrossing narrative enigmas—the resolving third act morphs into a disruptive first act of a new plotline. The three acts of any story rarely correspond to the structure of a single serial episode, with carryover of a lengthy second act across weeks or months of a series.

A mixture of serial and episodic forms, called **episodic serials**, employ **narrative arcs**, multi-episode plotlines that run across a series but eventually are resolved. Arcs can be as brief as two episodes, in the common formulations of a "two-parter" in a typical episodic series, or might run throughout an entire season or beyond. One of the many innovations of *Buffy the Vampire Slayer* was its use of singular arcs for each of its seven seasons, structured around a specific villain threatening the town of Sunnydale. A model of season-long arcs has been adopted by subsequent programs such as *24* and *Curb Your Enthusiasm*. In contemporary programming, story arcs are a typical storytelling device for television narratives, with procedural dramas and conventional sitcoms even incorporating minor arcs concerning character relationships or ongoing problems. Thus television series can be structured using norms from four **narrative modes** across a spectrum illustrated in Table 6.1: stand-alone anthologies, self-contained episodes, episodic serials using arcs, and full ongoing serials.

This spectrum of narrative form is complicated by the storytelling structure within each episode; most television shows feature multiple storylines per episode. Some procedurals contain only one story each episode, as with the focus

Table 6-1 Television narrative forms can span a broad spectrum of modes varying by story structure and ongoing continuity.

Narrative Mode	Made-for-TV Movie	Miniseries	Anthology Series	Episodic Series	Episodic Serial	Serial Narrative
Examples	*The Day After, Brian's Song, Recount*	*Roots, Band of Brothers, John Adams*	*The Twilight Zone, Masterpiece Theatre, Mystery!*	*Law & Order, Everybody Loves Raymond, House M.D.*	*Buffy the Vampire Slayer, Veronica Mars, Seinfeld*	*Days of Our Lives, The Wire, Lost*

THE X-FILES

The X-Files (Fox, 1993–2002): This innovative series focuses on a pair of FBI agents investigating paranormal mysteries, with a long-term conspiracy arc involving aliens and government cover-ups. The show became a surprise hit after weak first-season ratings, generating a cult fanbase, spawning two feature films, and influencing many future programs to explore innovative techniques of television storytelling.

MURPHY BROWN

Murphy Brown (CBS, 1988–98): A behind-the-scenes sitcom about a television newsmagazine, the show notably centers on the assertive, explicitly feminist title character, with storylines tackling political culture and contemporary issues. The program's notoriety peaked in 1992, when Vice President Dan Quayle condemned Murphy's decision to have a child as a single mother, prompting a rebuttal episode that mocked Quayle, a debate that played a part in that year's presidential election.

on a singular case in *Dragnet* or *Law & Order*, but typically an episode will feature at least two or three different storylines, called the **A plot**, **B plot**, and **C plot**. A plots focus on the central narrative conflict, usually featuring the main character and taking up the largest portion of the screen time, while B and C plots offer thematic counterpoint, contrast, or resonance with secondary characters. Much of the balance between plots is specific to different genres. Soap opera episodes feature four to six plots, often without clear hierarchies among them, while other genres often balance their focus between workplace and domestic plots, or events versus relationships.

In addition to specific plotlines in an episode, many series will present ongoing **runners**, established issues in the storyworld that rarely trigger explicit narrative events and main plotlines. Runners are frequently tied to character relationships, or a character's ongoing situation involving employment or other goals. Thus on *The X-Files*, the potential romantic relationship between Mulder and Scully was a runner, factoring into many episodes briefly, but rarely emerging as a significant plot point in an episode. For comedies, runners can be ongoing gags, such as the never-ending stream of secretaries hired by the title character on *Murphy Brown*. Runners establish continuity within the storyworld, and are often points of focus and pleasure for fans, but do not function as fully serialized plotlines such as the mystery, conflict, and relationship arcs typical to television series.

The main structural difference between episodic and serial narratives is the status of events at the end of a given episode. Serial programs refuse full resolution of most plotlines within any episode, typically ending episodes with at least one unresolved cliff-hanger designed to stimulate viewers to tune in to the next episode. Episodic programs usually wrap up all major plot points by the end of each episode, enabling the series to be viewed in any order. Core narrative conflicts that define the series usually remain across episodes—for instance, *Bewitched* never resolves the underlying conflict between Samatha's supernatural witch powers and her attempts to live like a normal human—but the particular plots that such conflicts create are wrapped up by the end of each episode. For episodic serials, most episodes resolve at least one plotline, while leaving others dangling; the degree of seriality varies depending on whether the plots left open are central A or B plots, or more minor C plots. Such mixed programs, which are typical of contemporary complex narratives such as *Buffy*, *Scrubs*, *Battlestar Galactica*, and *The Sopranos*, maintain a degree of unity and closure for each episode while foregrounding arcs and serialized plots that require viewers to watch the series in order to fully comprehend the story.

Television storytelling is faced with many specific structural limitations when compared with the more flexible formats of other media such as film or literature. There are few mandates for how long a book should be, how to structure chapter breaks, or how characters might evolve over the course of a story. While films typically run around two hours, a specific film's exact length and story pacing can be flexible. Commercial American television is far more constrained. Programs are almost always designed to fit precisely into thirty- or sixty-minute schedule blocks, and networks and channels demand regular commercial breaks that segment shows and reduce actual running times to twenty-two or forty-five minutes. Television programmers have established narrative norms using commercial breaks to structure plots, providing markers for suspenseful moments and signaling **act breaks** within the story. Producers realize that a commercial break offers viewers a chance to surf channels or turn off a program, so they aim to end each act with a compelling narrative hook to sustain the viewer's interest throughout the break; this is especially important in the pre-credit sequence segment called the **teaser**, which strives to capture viewers for the rest of the program using a particularly exciting enigma or amusing taste of the episode. In recent years, the rise of successful original programs on channels without advertising breaks, as on HBO and Showtime, has given producers more freedom to experiment with structures and violate norms of act breaks and program length. But typically, the institutional constraints of commercial television help structure how stories are narrated, forcing creators to follow strict guidelines and narrative routines.

The realities of creating an ongoing narrative through the collaborative enterprise of television production can also force unplanned story developments.

When an actor decides to leave a program or has a significant change of health, as with John Spencer's sudden death midseason on *The West Wing* or Jennifer Garner's pregnancy during *Alias*, writers must restructure narrative arcs and story plans accordingly, a challenge a serial novelist like Dickens never had to cope with. Likewise, network mandates to boost ratings or fan reaction to particular characters or stories can alter long-term plans that writers might have for a television series, highlighting the fact that television storytelling must juggle numerous pressures to maintain an ongoing storyworld while attempting to craft coherent and consistent episodes comprising a larger narrative arc.

These institutional pressures on television storytelling constitute **extrinsic norms** that range beyond any one program. The entire television medium follows certain norms such as series format and regular scheduling. Other extrinsic norms are restricted to particular genres, such as soap operas saving the most exciting story material for Friday's installments, or crime procedurals presenting and resolving a given case over the course of one episode. While these rules can be broken, viewers notice when the story deviates from such narrative norms. All narrative forms can establish **intrinsic norms**, too, storytelling practices that get established as typical within that particular text. Television series narration lends itself to establishing intrinsic norms typical to a given program that will repeat across episodes. For instance, *Six Feet Under* begins every episode with a "death of the week" to be handled by the family's funeral home. Intrinsic narrative norms allow a series to establish its own style and train viewers to expect such patterns. As *Six Feet Under* progressed as a series, the show played with viewer expectations and anxieties through misdirection as to who would die in the initial segment, creating particular viewing pleasures unique to the long-form series narrative model of television.

Nonfiction programming can adopt some of the narrative structures and storytelling strategies of fiction to engage viewers and present the real world. Newsmagazines can be thought of as anthology programs, presenting multiple stand-alone stories each episode, while twenty-four hour newscasts are more serialized, offering ongoing accounts of unfolding action narrated in a manner to keep viewers returning for more developments. Reality programs certainly adopt storytelling strategies common to soap operas and serial dramas, with footage edited to foreground relationship tensions and drama while highlighting the impact of each action across the community of participants. Using such strategies to tell real stories should not be viewed as inherently dishonest—although sometimes editing techniques do explicitly deceive viewers—as nonfiction traditions such as history and biography always aim to present the past as a compelling narrative. But critical viewers should always be aware how formal narrative techniques in both fictional and nonfictional forms selectively present and construct their worlds in ways that are never transparent representations, whether of an imaginary storyworld or of real life.

In analyzing the narrative strategies of a television series, we need to be careful about how to consider the text to be examined. At times, a narrative can clearly be a single episode, but often shows need to be looked at in the context of a multi-episode arc, a whole season, or even an entire series, depending on the specific questions being asked by a critic. Understanding the narrative strategies of television programs also requires attention to the specific genre norms that have been established over the course of television history, as each category of programming has its own practices for telling stories and creating meanings.

TELEVISION GENRES

Genres, or types of television programs, could be considered as part of nearly all six facets of television explored in this book—ranging from an industrial strategy as with the account of reality television in chapter 2, to a component of everyday life, as with the discussion of children's television in chapter 10. Although genres are important to television as more than just part of textual form, television scholars have most commonly considered them as formal elements, along the lines of style and narrative. To understand the range of ways that genre matters for television, we can survey different approaches to genre analysis and how they treat television programming as parts of generic systems.

Why Genres Matter

Drawn from literary and film studies to distinguish between major types of narratives, television genres have become important for television critics, creators, executives, and audiences. Genre studies have intersected with major trends in critical television studies, drawing upon many theories and approaches tackled throughout this book. Even at the level of everyday viewers or *TV Guide*, categorizing programming into genres such as science fiction or soap operas is a central component of how television is understood and experienced.

The origins of genre studies date back to the classical era, as Aristotle distinguished between major dramatic categories of epic, tragedy, and comedy. As newer media create new narrative models, genre categories have become more specific. Literary studies have shifted in the modern era to consider genre fiction as a facet of popular culture, considering categories such as romance and mystery as key popular genres. Film scholars took up this approach, examining the underlying structure and cultural meanings of important film genres such as Westerns and musicals. As television developed into our most prevalent storytelling medium, genre categories such as the sitcom and game show became part of a broader generic vocabulary.

Genres may be defined by a broad range of criteria; one common way focuses on narrative structure. Thus the mystery genre requires a crime, which the detective hero investigates and eventually solves to restore balance in the storyworld. Likewise romances and thrillers depend on their common narrative structures focusing on relationships and suspenseful events, respectively. Another important way genres can be defined focuses on setting and iconography. Westerns might have a variety of plots that can resemble detective stories or romances, but they are all set in a similar era and locale, featuring horses, guns, and frontier décor. Thus medical shows, legal dramas, science fiction stories, workplace comedies, and espionage programs are all distinguished by their common set of locations, character types, and iconography. Other genres may be categorized by their intended audience reaction: comedy tries to make us laugh, while horror strives to scare us.

Television adds a particular wrinkle into these differing modes of categorization. Unlike film and literature, the television schedule regularly features both narrative and non-narrative programs, fictional and unscripted shows. Thus the talk show genre is certainly not categorized by its narrative structure, intended emotional reaction, or setting. But what makes a talk show distinct? A key aspect of genre categorization that applies to both scripted and unscripted programming is a reliance on particular **genre conventions**. Some of these conventions are tied to narrative (as with the plot device of overheard misunderstandings typical of many sitcoms), while others are rooted in the setup of a given genre (game shows featuring prizes and contests of luck or skill). Thus a talk show might be identified by a number of conventions such as the empathetic (or confrontational) host, a participating studio audience, guest experts or celebrities, and sensationalist issues. But there is little uniformity in what types of conventions are relevant across genres, as important conventions such as setting or intended emotional affect in one genre may have no relevance in another.

These different criteria for categorization are usually understood easily; once viewers see enough of any genre, they can identify the common ground without even noticing inconsistencies between genre categories, as we soon learn to identify typical traits as part of a general set of conventions. But problems can arise with these various modes of categorization. How might genre critics examine a program such as *The X-Files*? The narrative typically follows detective story structure, but the setting draws upon science fiction traditions, while the audience reaction often invites horror and occasionally comedy. Does the show belong to all of these genres? Or is it a program that makes genre categories irrelevant? In some ways both are true—like many programs, *The X-Files* mixes genres to a point that we can't look at it as a pure case of any one genre, but it still draws upon genre traditions to play with the form and formulas that are commonplace across television. To understand some of the show's more creative moments, it is important for viewers to be familiar with the conventions of horror, detective shows, and science fiction that *The X-Files* employs in original ways.

Although their cases typically track alleged alien invasions, werewolves, or mutants, *The X-Flies* follows the norms of detective procedurals overlayed with science fiction and horror conventions.

This points to one of the most vital functions of genre within television: as **routines** for producers and programmers to more efficiently create and schedule television shows. As discussed in chapter 1, shortcuts to manage production and promotion practices are essential; genres provide a shorthand set of assumptions and conventions that producers can use to make a new program familiar to audiences and easier to produce. Genres often serve as baseline formulas for producers, creating a core set of assumptions and patterns that make the production of so many hours of original programming more efficient and streamlined. Producers face the tension between originality and similarity, needing to rely upon formulas to make programs accessible and recognizable to fickle audiences, while still making shows original enough to be distinguished from the pack. When a group of similar shows achieves popularity at a given moment, **genre cycles** can emerge, with particular types of shows saturating the airwaves—examples include spy shows of the 1960s, prime time serials of the 1980s, and the reality boom of the 2000s.

Some critics look at this facet of television genre dismissively, pointing to the formulaic nature of television programming and devaluing its creativity and originality. The opposition between genre and originality might be a false choice, however. Many of the finest works of popular culture have been rooted in genre traditions, from Sherlock Holmes detective stories to Alfred Hitchcock's cinematic thrillers. Such is true for television, too: classic sitcoms such as *The Dick Van Dyke Show*, detective dramas such as *The Rockford Files*, and science

TWIN PEAKS

Twin Peaks (ABC, 1990–91): A short-lived but groundbreaking drama that mixes mystery, soap opera, horror, and comedy via the surrealistic style of film director David Lynch, *Twin Peaks* is one of American television's most unique series. The show had a burst of popularity as viewers pondered the mystery of the murder of Laura Palmer, but ratings declined after an anticlimactic mystical explanation; its legacy lives on through boundary-pushing programs such as *The X-Files* and *Lost*.

fiction such as the multiple *Star Trek* series all accept the conventions of their genres and explore the creative possibilities within generic boundaries. Even programs that seem to rebel against strict genre categorization, as with *The X-Files*, use the conventions of their multiple genres to elicit and often contradict audience expectations. Thus a celebrated innovative program such as *Twin Peaks* does not dismiss genres in exchange for some idealized original creative vision, but rather plays with the assumptions and conventions of soap operas, detective dramas, and supernatural horror to highlight the limits of formulas, while still embracing some of their conventional pleasures. It is hard to imagine television programming that operates entirely outside of the system of genre, not because all television is formulaic and unoriginal, but because genre categories are immensely useful and pleasurable to both the industry and audience.

The question of what meanings genre categories have for audiences and their broader cultural contexts has been the focus of much genre analysis from a variety of critical positions. Chapter 7 explores the social functions of genres in more depth, considering whether programs shape the way we see the world or respond to our own preestablished cultural needs. There is no doubt that one of the defining features of genre programming is repeatable and familiar formulas—thus for television viewers, watching a genre can serve as a **ritual** activity that provides a comfortable and predictable experience, reinforcing certain repeated meanings. For most viewers, programs within a genre offer a degree of familiarity that fulfils particular tastes and desires. Many viewers define their own viewing by genre, becoming fans of specific genres such as sports, news, science fiction, and mysteries, a facet of viewing discussed more in chapter 9.

If genre texts are defined by specific conventions, then genre categories also contain a set of commonly held **generic expectations** for viewers to guide their viewing practices. A program's genre helps signal to audiences how they are expected to react to a show: a person falling off a cliff might be tragic in a family drama, suspicious on a police show, or comedic in a cartoon. Viewers often judge the success of a program based on how well the show fits their genre

M*A*S*H

*M*A*S*H* (CBS, 1972–83): A single-camera telefilm sitcom about an army hospital in the Korean War, *M*A*S*H* ran for more than three times as long as the war itself. Initially the show was an antiwar satire with outlandish humor that commented on the Vietnam conflict from a historical distance, but it was transformed into more of a "dramedy," with serious overtones and character development, concluding with the most-watched television series episode ever.

expectations, such as a comedy making them laugh or a mystery creating suspense. Many genres evoke a sense of **generic realism**, a set of form and content norms that viewers can expect to be followed within a particular program, and thus feels "real" to a viewer. A cartoon character can get back up from a fatal fall even when the same accident would cause death in other genres; our expectations for the rules of the storyworld depend on our expectations of generic realism. It can be jarring when such rules are broken, a technique used to dramatic effect in examples such as the *Buffy the Vampire Slayer* episode presented as a musical or the *M*A*S*H* episode structured as a documentary newsreel. But typically viewers expect a program to follow its own intrinsic narrative norms and codes of generic realism, ensuring that what we see meets the expectations we bring to the program each episode. Most successful programs clearly establish their generic expectations and fulfill viewer desires by following genre norms and conventions consistently.

Genre analysis can fall into a common trap: it is easy to overstate the uniformity of any genre category. Genres are used as shorthand to highlight the similarities between shows—and thus gloss over differences—but genre programs can often be misread as more consistent and uniform than they actually are. Looking at a genre historically is one way to correct for to this mistake. The evolution of the American police drama demonstrates the wide range of differences possible within this seemingly uniform category. Programs produced in the 1950s, such as *Dragnet* and *Highway Patrol*, highlighted a fully functional criminal justice system effectively upholding law and order with little personality or conflict, with a spare visual style and focused narrative asserting the authenticiy of the programs' messages. By the 1970s, the conventions of the maverick cop bucking an unyielding system to more effectively dole out justice in unconventional terms found its way on to programs such as *Baretta* and *Starsky & Hutch*, along with a muddier visual style and ambiguous narrative structure. The genre mixing of *Hill Street Blues* in the 1980s incorporated melodramatic serial storytelling into the show's gritty vision of urban crime, humanizing both

HILL STREET BLUES

Hill Street Blues (NBC, 1981–87): One of television's most acclaimed series, this police drama incorporated serialized narrative, intertwined plotlines, and relationship dramas along with a messy and complex visual style that gave it a level of realism and authenticity atypical for television at the time. While it struggled in the ratings for years, its critical appreciation and numerous awards sustained the show for years, with its influences still felt today.

HOMICIDE: LIFE ON THE STREET

Homicide: Life on the Street (NBC, 1993–99): A bleak police drama set in Baltimore, *Homicide* was beloved by critics and a small cult audience, but struggled every year for renewal due to weak ratings and disinterested advertisers. The show boasted a diverse and talented cast and refused to glamorize crime or police work, making it one of television's most downbeat but emotionally engaging programs.

the individual officers and the system itself. The 1990s returned to more procedural concerns, with *Law & Order* and *Homicide: Life on the Street* focusing on the casework of humanized police, while questioning simplistic divisions between criminal and legal behaviors. All of these programs clearly belong to the police drama genre, yet they offer widely divergent meanings, conventions, and assumptions as to what the police drama says about its cultural context and how it uses textual form to convey meaning. Genre analysis must consider the historical evolution of genres, rather than thinking of genre categories as ahistorical unchanging definitions, although even a single moment in history might contain a more diverse group of programs than easily classified by a set of genre norms.

One way of thinking about genres is to consider how they operate as **cultural categories** themselves, rather than as shorthand for their collected programs. Thus instead of examining the evolving meanings and form of police shows, we might look at how the television industry, critics, and audiences have made sense of the category "police drama" throughout different contexts—whether police dramas are assumed to be critical or supportive of social norms, tied to real-life cases, functioning as escapist fantasies, or appealing to a mass audience versus a specific niche of viewers. Obviously these cultural assumptions filter into programs, as producers shape their work to convey their take on the genre, and successful programs then reshape the assumptions linked to genre categories. But genre categories can be shaped outside of the process of production, too. The cartoon genre has shifted throughout television history via scheduling practices on Saturday mornings in the 1960s and channel branding through the creation of Cartoon Network in the 1990s. As a set of assumed meanings and values, the cartoon genre changed from a mass-audience component of theatrical film bills in the 1940s, to a lowbrow, highly commercialized kids-only genre in the 1960s, to a hip, nostalgic facet of Americana in the 1990s, even when the actual cartoons themselves were consistent, as with Bugs Bunny shorts created in the 1940s.[1] The study of television genres can look beyond just programs categorized by genre labels to consider how the categories themselves are constituted, challenged, and changed by audiences, industries, and critics.

There is no doubt that genre remains an important facet of television programming and practices to this day. Many programs incorporate **genre mixing** to appeal to broad audiences and explore innovation by combining unlikely categories. For instance, *Buffy the Vampire Slayer* mixes teen dramas and supernatural horror, allowing their themes to reinforce each other—as in an episode where a mundane competition for the cheerleading squad heats up after a witch sabotages rivals using magical spells. Even through such fantastic metaphors, genre norms and expectations remain central in the minds of creators and viewers, with the assumptions and expectations of teen dramas and horror playing off each other creatively. The rise of narrowcasting has highlighted genres as branding mechanisms to label channels unified by their dedication to specific genres, from news (CNN) to music videos (MTV2), sports (ESPN) to science fiction (Sci Fi). New technological developments, such as digital program guides incorporated into cable, satellite, and digital video recorders, allow for genres to be used as a searching and sorting mechanism for users to find desirable programming, reinforcing the continued importance of genres as an organizing principle for both the television industry and audience. Genre categories and programming remain useful for producers, critics, industries, and audiences, and continue to play a key role for the development of television into the twenty-first century. Taking a closer historical look at four television genres—soap operas, game shows, situation comedies, and talk shows—points to the range of ways that genre matters.

Soap Operas

Probably no genre is as intimately linked with the television medium as the **soap opera**. Soap operas exist at the crossroads between the mundane and the sensational, the repetitive and the original, the commercially contrived and the emotionally sincere, and domestic life and the wider world. The name of the genre, which might be the only genre label that mocks the type of program it categorizes, stems from the genre's early history on radio when such shows were initially known as "daytime dramatic serials." The term *soap opera*, coined by press accounts of the popular genre in the late 1930s, was a scornful combination of the high-art aspirations and melodramatic excesses of opera with the mundane household products sold by the sponsors that produced the programs. The name stuck, suggesting that fans and creators of soap operas recognize that the genre is always regarded skeptically in comparison to more legitimized forms of entertainment and art—but despite their condemnation, soap operas can be (and are) appreciated by millions of viewers on their own terms. Soap operas may be the world's most popular genre, with Latin American *telenovelas* and other soaps from around the globe saturating most national television systems; within the United States, soaps have thrived as a staple of television's daytime schedule.

Soap operas emerged on radio in the early 1930s as part of daytime programming specifically targeting female audiences, an assumption that has remained in place to this day even though a good percentage of viewers are male. The programs began as daily fifteen-minute shows scheduled each afternoon, presenting continuing stories in the life of a central character, and proved to be a highly popular form among its target audience of female homemakers. The genre proliferated on radio throughout the 1930s and 1940s, transitioning to television in the 1950s and expanding to thirty- and sixty-minute time slots airing each weekday afternoon. Broadcast live in the 1950s, soap operas have been shot live-to-tape since the 1960s, following a consistent style of domestic settings, facial closeups, demonstrative performances, and emotionally coded music to highlight the genre's melodramatic tone. Unlike most other fictional genres, soap operas air new episodes year-round with no reruns (aside from those that air on newer cable channels such as SoapNet). Although soap operas have had periods of low ratings, they remain a constant in network schedules, with some programs, such as *Guiding Light* and *As the World Turns*, lasting more than fifty years on television. Soap operas remain fairly popular today, especially via technologies such as VCRs and DVRs, which viewers use to time-shift daily episodes to watch at their convenience.

The basic structure of the daytime soap opera has changed little over the past fifty years. The genre's serialized narrative mode is its core formal attribute, highlighting how each story event impacts a community of relationships across the fictional world. Soap operas feature large ensembles of characters, often centered on a family, town, or institution such as a hospital; in their ensembles, characters are interrelated through a complex and multifaceted web of relationships stretching back decades in viewer memories. Characters can come and go, sometimes recast via dramatic devices such as major reconstructive surgery or returning from death after years of absence, but the network of relationships and community remains intact, forming the focus for long-term viewers who recognize each character's changing place in the larger narrative system.

In any given episode, soap operas offer little forward motion within narrative events, but the dramatic interplay between characters is quite nuanced and complex for viewers with long-term investments in the storyworld. Soap operas prioritize relationships over events—thus even when a major event happens in a soap opera, the question of "what happened?" is often secondary to "how does it affect the community of relationships?" A typical episode will feature four or five different plotlines, with each typically focused around a conversation between two or three characters confronting an issue of emotional significance. Shifting between these storylines over the course of an episode, the dialogue offers a good deal of redundancy by recapping previous events and reminding viewers of relevant relationships.[2]

This repetition serves to catch up viewers who have missed previous episodes or even part of the current program, but it also highlights a central narrative pleasure of soap operas—savvy viewers notice the way each narrative action triggers important reactions in characters and relationships. Even if viewers are witnessing the seventh retelling of the previous week's big narrative event, they are gleaning information about how this event impacts each character who learns about it, accumulating nuance in direct proportion to the amount of long-term **backstory** knowledge any viewer possesses to make sense of these ongoing tales. As such, the narrative events themselves of serial dramas traditionally focus more upon relationship changes than the chains of cause-and-effect actions typical of procedural dramas or episodic sitcoms. When soap operas do feature narrative events such as murders, accidents, and grand schemes, they are typically narrated so that viewers focus upon the ripple effects it has upon the community more than suspense over what may happen next. This emphasis was altered somewhat in the early 1980s, when *General Hospital* embraced an espionage plot that helped the program reach record ratings, and led to a rise in action-oriented narratives in daytime soap operas.

One important development in the history of the soap opera is the incorporation of relevant social issues into the lives of characters. Beginning in the late 1960s and 1970s, soap operas countered the rising age of their audience by addressing timely issues of the day, tackling taboo subjects such as interracial dating, abortion, breast cancer, and rape—and later AIDS and homophobia—to appeal to a younger generation of viewers. While many critics who do not watch soap operas decry the genre as an escapist and even pathological vice for its viewers, the genre has often been more socially engaged and daring than much prime time programming, and its pleasures are much more complex and multifaceted than they might appear to an outsider without the deep background needed to decode the significance of any individual episode.

GENERAL HOSPITAL

General Hospital (ABC, 1963–present): A long-running daytime soap opera, *General Hospital* became the genre's most popular program in television history in the early 1980s with the high-profile couple Luke and Laura and a series of action-adventure plotlines that expanded the range of stories typically told on daytime. The series has continued to explore plots outside of its medical title, with significant attention to espionage, gangster, and serial killer storylines, alongside the more typical genre plots of romance and familial intrigue.

PEYTON PLACE

Peyton Place (ABC, 1964–69): One of the first examples of serialized programming in prime time, *Peyton Place* was an adaptation of a popular novel and film about relationships in a small town that helped launch the careers of young actors Mia Farrow and Ryan O'Neal. The show's initial popularity proved that audiences would watch ongoing stories in prime time, but its declining ratings left networks reluctant to imitate the show for another decade.

DALLAS

Dallas (CBS, 1978–91): A hugely popular series that launched a cycle of prime time soap operas in the 1980s and succeeded in global distribution, *Dallas* centered on a ruthless family of oil tycoons, showcasing their wealthy, materialistic lifestyle. *Dallas* is best remembered for its season-two cliffhanger, "Who Shot J.R.?" which encouraged more than 360 million viewers worldwide, and 90 million in the United States, to tune in for the answer at the start of season three.

While soap operas have persisted in daytime schedules, prime time programming has adopted many aspects of the genre's serial form. The first American prime time serial was *Peyton Place*, in the mid-1960s, which adapted a popular novel focusing on sexual intrigue in a small New England town; the show aired twice weekly on ABC, following soap opera narrative styles but shot on telefilm with established actors and rising stars. Despite ratings success in its first season, *Peyton Place* quickly fell out of favor, and networks abandoned prime time serials for more than a decade. The form was reborn first through the parodies of daytime soaps *Mary Hartman, Mary Hartman* and *Soap* in the late 1970s, and then the breakout success of *Dallas* in 1978. *Dallas,* and subsequent imitators *Dynasty, Falcon Crest,* and *Knot's Landing,* drew their ensemble casts, complex webs of relationship, and ongoing melodramatic storylines from soap operas, but compressed the narrative into weekly episodes and season-based scheduling as with other prime time series. Hence, even though these dramas, as well as newer examples of prime time serials such as *Melrose Place* and *Party of Five*, draw upon many conventions from the daytime soap opera, there is a distinct difference in the two forms' use of narrative structure, industrial systems, and viewer engagement. It is useful to separate the distinctive conventions and expectations of daytime soap operas from their use of serial narrative structure. Serial form has been adopted by many other genres across the prime time schedule, but the daily schedule, production style, and melodramatic tone remain distinctive to the afternoon series that are most tied to the pejorative but much beloved genre label of soap opera.

Game Shows

Like soap operas, **game shows** are often considered formulaic and forgettable filler on the television schedule, but they have played a key role in television history and have remained an important genre for the entire life of the medium. While soap operas have existed on daytime television schedules with remarkable continuity for more than fifty years, game shows have had a number of peaks and valleys in their popularity and place in American television. Game shows offer television's mixture of entertainment and commercialism in more explicit terms than most genres, and thus provide insight into the operation of the television industry and viewers' practices.

In the early days of television, game shows were known more commonly as **quiz shows**, with a successful tradition on radio in the 1930s and 1940s; the term *game show* became more common in the 1960s, in the aftermath of the quiz show scandals of the 1950s. Television quiz shows of the 1950s, many of which were adapted directly from radio hits, were popular in both prime time and daytime network schedules, serving as a relatively low-cost program that effectively promoted sponsors' products. Most game and quiz shows appeal to a broad range of viewers, with little focus on specific audience groups or market segments, although in the multi-channel era, specific niches have had their own game shows, as with MTV's *Remote Control* or Comedy Central's *Win Ben Stein's Money*. Nearly all quiz and game shows have been produced live or live-to-tape, as the unscripted action is captured in front of a studio audience, adding to the genre's economic efficiency.

Quiz and game shows can be broken down into a number of different program types or **subgenres** based on the mechanics of competition featured and the pleasures offered to viewers. Factual quiz shows present serious contests around questions of knowledge, rewarding trivial mastery and intellectual breadth—early hits *The $64,000 Question* and *Twenty-One* follow this pattern, as did later shows such as *Jeopardy!* and *Who Wants to Be a Millionaire*. Stunt game shows such as *Truth or Consequences*, *Beat the Clock*, and *Distraction* use questions and answers only as a pretense to subject contestants to outrageous physical stunts and challenges. Panel shows focus on celebrities working with contestants, often with the panel's comedic banter serving as the program's chief appeal, as on *I've Got a Secret*, *What's My Line?*, *The Match Game*, and *Hollywood Squares*. Games of skill often adapt well-known games or other challenges for competition instead of explicit tests of knowledge, including programs such as *Concentration*, *Tic Tac Dough*, and *Wheel of Fortune*. Some shows present specialty knowledge games, ranging from sports trivia on ESPN's *Stump the Schwab* to musical songs on *Name That Tune*, public opinion on *Family Feud* to consumer pricing on *The Price Is Right* and *Supermarket Sweep*. Social games focus on interpersonal relationships, as on *The Dating Game*, *The Newlywed Game*, and *Studs*, with prizes aimed at furthering romance. Games of chance such as *Let's Make a Deal* and *Deal or No Deal* require no skill to play, aside from assessing the odds in a high-pressure contest based on a random choice or event, but create drama out of uncertainty. These categories, as well as others, all fall under the broad category of game shows, as viewers recognize continuity across this broad range of program type and genre expectations.

The most significant event in the history of the genre was certainly the **quiz show scandals** of the late 1950s. In 1955, *The $64,000 Question* became a top prime time hit by drawing one innovation from scripted programming: creating ongoing "characters" by inviting contestants to return weekly to risk their winnings on new questions. Staging on the program was designed to maximize dramatic tension and seriousness, with record-setting prizes, bright lights to promote perspiring contestants, armed guards to create a high-security illusion, and bogus random selection by an early prototype of an IBM computer. Three years later, it was revealed that *$64,000* and other prime time imitators, including *Twenty-One* and *Dotto*, had drawn more than set design from fictional programs, as producers had been instructing contestants how to act during shows, shaping questions to heighten drama, providing answers to contestants they wished to see continue on the program, and pressuring contestants to fail on demand. These revelations prompted public outcry, cancellation of nearly all prime time quizzes, a grand jury investigation, congressional hearings, and legislation giving the FCC power to deny licenses to broadcasters of fraudulent quiz shows.

THE $64,000 QUESTION

The $64,000 Question (CBS, 1955–58): One of the popular big-money quiz shows of the 1950s, the program incorporated the popular innovation of bringing contestants back each week to create ongoing drama and intrigue. The show left the air in scandal when it was revealed to be a manipulated rather than honest competition, part of the broader quiz show scandals of the era.

How can we understand the scandalous reaction to these rigged quiz shows? At their core, the scandals were a case of conflicting genre expectations. Viewers watched these programs to be entertained, and thus they accepted the strategies being used to heighten drama and tension in set design, lighting, and game structure; however, the central genre expectation was that the game itself was pure competition. For viewers, quiz shows were most similar to sports, in which events are staged with artificial rules, but the results unfold from skill and luck; for producers, quiz shows were like staged dramas, aiming to entertain audiences and maintain ratings by any means necessary. After the scandals, producers adjusted their genre norms, still hoping for maximum entertainment, but stopping short of scripting the competition.

Devices like the isolation booth in *The $64,000 Question* created the illusion of intense drama and fair competition, despite the quiz shows being more scripted and planned than they appeared.

WHEEL OF FORTUNE

Wheel of Fortune (NBC, 1975–1991; syndicated, 1983–present): An extremely popular game show combining the word game Hangman with a roulette wheel, *Wheel of Fortune* began as a morning game show before expanding to become consistently the top-rated syndicated program in the evenings. Unlike companion program *Jeopardy!*, *Wheel* is less about showcasing contestants with trivia talents than highlighting everyday people who may not be particularly good at the game compared with regular viewers.

After the 1950s scandals, game shows moved out of prime time and minimized their high-stakes drama, focusing on a more casual tone in daytime and syndicated time slots. The genre flourished in syndication, as *Wheel of Fortune* and *Jeopardy!* have been early-evening staples since the 1980s. It wasn't until the surprise success of *Who Wants to Be a Millionaire* in 1999 that big-money game shows returned to prime time, with subsequent network hits such as *The Weakest Link* and *Deal or No Deal*. The game show has clear affinity with reality shows, as competitions such as *The Amazing Race, Fear Factor,* and *The Bachelor* are all comparable to game shows in their structure and pleasures. Although game shows rarely rival the popularity of other prime time genres, they are a consistent staple of the television schedule and appeal to a broad range of viewers. In the multi-channel era, Game Show Network emerged as a successful cable channel, airing a library of game shows throughout television history; the channel changed its name to GSN in 2004 and expanded its schedule to include reality programs, poker and blackjack competitions, video games, and other programs televising competitive games.

Game shows have always offered a broad range of appeal to viewers. Many shows invite vicarious participation, allowing viewers to play along with contestants—a pleasure extended with tie-in board games, computer games, and interactive websites. Some games employ this participatory mode by drawing contestants directly from the studio audience, as on *Price Is Right* and *Let's Make a Deal*. Other programs focus on humor and comedy, either through outrageous physical stunts or the comedic banter of celebrity panels or hosts, such as Groucho Marx on *You Bet Your Life* or Jimmy Kimmel on *Win Ben Stein's Money*. Regardless of their pleasures or place in the television schedule, game shows appeal to the industry due to their low-cost production and effective integration of sponsor promotion, and thus have remained a consistent genre throughout the history of television, watched by millions of viewers, even if overlooked by most critics.

Situation Comedies

Situation comedies, better known as **sitcoms**, are probably the most recognizable, prolific, and well known of television genres. Some of the most innovative and beloved programs throughout television history have been sitcoms, including *I Love Lucy*, *The Dick Van Dyke Show*, *All in the Family*, *The Cosby Show*, and *Seinfeld*. Likewise, some sitcoms, such as *My Mother the Car*, *AfterMASH*, and *Homeboys from Outer Space*, have been singled out as representing the worst television has to offer, with ridiculous premises, formulaic structures, or forced adaptations of previous hits. Many critics view sitcoms as typically formulaic and uncreative, with a few exceptions that break the genre's mold with innovation and creativity. A close look at the genre's history suggests that sitcoms offer a framework ripe for potential innovation that accounts for dozens of standout programs throughout the past six decades, with the genre changing and responding to shifts in American culture.

As with most television genres, sitcoms emerged from the radio industry of the 1930s and 1940s, although there were multiple forms of comedy programming on the radio schedule. One common form was the **variety show**, with comedians doing monologues or short skits interspersed with musical acts and other performances in a style drawn from vaudeville theater. This model lives on mostly through late-night talk shows such as *Late Show with David Letterman* or *Late Night with Conan O'Brien*. The model of **sketch comedy**, with scenes featuring stand-alone characters or situations that changed from sketch to sketch, was popular on radio shows such as *Abbott and Costello* and *The Bob Hope Show*. Such sketch comedies transferred to 1950s television via Milton Berle's *Texaco Star Theater* and Sid Caesar's *Your Show of Shows*. This model of comedy has remained on air with varying popularity; standout hits include *Laugh-In* in the late 1960s, *The Carol Burnett Show* of the 1970s, and the long-running *Saturday Night Live*, but situation comedies have been the dominant form of prime time comedy for most of television history.

Sitcoms were a staple of network radio schedules, establishing many of the genre conventions and expectations that persist to this day. Many popular radio sitcoms, including *Amos 'n' Andy*, *The Goldbergs*, *Beulah*, *The Adventures of Ozzie and Harriet*, and *The Life of Riley*, were adapted to television in the 1950s, creating a visual presentation for well-known radio stories. On both radio and television, sitcoms feature an established setting and small group of ongoing characters who each week encounter low-stakes comedic mishaps that are happily resolved by the end of the half-hour episode. Programs might present these storyworlds with a low-key naturalistic style, focusing on realistic characters in plausible scenarios (such as *The Cosby Show* or *The Mary Tyler Moore Show*), or using a more presentational over-the-top style, with exaggerated situations and broadly played performances (such as in *Married...with Children* or *I Dream*

THE GEORGE BURNS AND GRACIE ALLEN SHOW

The George Burns and Gracie Allen Show: (CBS, 1950–58): A popular early sitcom starring the married comedy team Burns and Allen, the show blended the fictional sitcom with direct address to the audience and reflexive gags such as Burns watching television to see what Allen was doing. Their humor, as developed previously on vaudeville and radio, focused on Allen's "illogic logic" and Burns acting as a straight man to sort out the resulting mischief.

of Jeannie). Both styles have resulted in popular and critically successful programs throughout television history. An early trend were sitcoms that blended fictional scenarios with variety show forms, as with *The Burns and Allen Show*'s host George Burns talking directly to the audience in front of the curtain before leaping into fictional scenes with his wife, Gracie Allen. This style has recurred in various forms, as in *It's Garry Shandling's Show*, which mixes a sitcom with a monologue-driven talk show, or in *Curb Your Enthusiasm*, which gives the appearance of documenting the (fictionalized) real life of star Larry David.

Sitcoms can be subdivided into two main types of programs, based on their central situation. **Domestic comedies**, or family sitcoms, focus on family life. In the early 1950s, shows such as *I Love Lucy*, *The Honeymooners*, *Burns and Allen*, and *I Married Joan* focused on childless couples and their neighbors, a trend that shifted in the mid-1950s to shows featuring parents and kids, such as *Father Knows Best*, *Ozzie and Harriet*, and *Leave It to Beaver*; on *I Love Lucy*, the Ricardos had a child in the second season, coinciding with Lucille Ball's real-life pregnancy. While children are common on family sitcoms, many shows, including *All in the Family*, *Rhoda*, and *Everybody Loves Raymond*, focus on the familial relationships between young couples and their parents. Domestic comedies generate conflicts from tensions between husbands and wives, as well as intergenerational battles, but they typically reaffirm the nuclear family and marriage as the stable foundations of American society. Many programs offer unconventional families as a revision of the typical nuclear family, such as *The Brady Bunch*, *Diff'rent Strokes*, *Full House*, or *Two and a Half Men*, but even shows that offer more critical looks at family life in turmoil, such as *All in the Family*, *Roseanne*, and *Malcolm in the Middle*, tend to reaffirm familial love and loyalty as beyond satire.

The second major type of sitcom is the **workplace comedy**, which focuses on a group of unrelated characters united by their profession and typically set in their office. The type of workplace can range broadly—from a cab company (*Taxi*) to a governor's mansion (*Benson*), a police station (*Barney Miller*) to a paper company's sales office (*The Office*). Probably the most common type of

THE MARY TYLER MOORE SHOW

The Mary Tyler Moore Show (CBS, 1970–77): Part of CBS's 1970s shift toward youthful urban audiences, this show focused on Mary Richards and her attempt to "make it on her own" in Minneapolis as a professional woman, and her friends and co-workers in the television newsroom where she worked. The program incorporated more subtle character-driven humor than most 1960s sitcoms, and offered a new set of representations for female characters that fit with a younger generation's sensibilities at the time.

workplace featured on office comedies are media companies, as on *The Mary Tyler Moore Show* (local television news), *WKRP in Cincinnati* (local music radio), *Murphy Brown* (network news), *Sports Night* (cable sports), *The Larry Sanders Show* (network talk show), *Just Shoot Me* (a magazine), *News Radio* (local talk radio), and *30 Rock* (network comedy)—a tendency unsurprising given the interests and experiences of television writers. Office comedies allow for more diversity of characters and potential for changing cast members than do typical family shows, although often the relationships between co-workers mimic the family dynamics common to domestic sitcoms, with the significant addition of romantic entanglements as a source of narrative conflict and character development.

Not all sitcoms fit clearly into either domestic or workplace models. Some programs find a balance between the two locales, notably *The Dick Van Dyke Show*'s integration of suburban family life with the main character's office life as a television comedy writer. Some mixed domestic/office sitcoms merge the spaces of work and home, as with *Newhart*'s married Vermont innkeepers or the boarding school on *The Facts of Life*, in which occupations and domestic life coexist. Most shows with this split focus treat one area as more central than the other—either a domestic comedy with workplace scenes (as with *Frasier* and *Bewitched*) or a workplace sitcom featuring one character's domestic life (such as *Welcome Back, Kotter* and *Murphy Brown*). Some programs, such as *Seinfeld*, *Laverne and Shirley*, *Bosom Buddies*, and *Friends*, focus on a group of adults bound by friendship instead of family or career, offering potential for new relationships and conflicts outside the clear confines of home or office—although often these shows make such characters roommates or neighbors to highlight the domestic life of single adults.

Sitcoms are ripe for genre mixing. A common mixture is the **animated sitcom**, which emerged in the 1960s with *The Flintstones*, a prehistoric remake of

THE DICK VAN DYKE SHOW

The Dick Van Dyke Show (CBS, 1961–66): A classic sitcom that blended domestic life in suburbia with behind-the-scenes looks at a network comedy program, the show is notable for its sophisticated tone and stellar cast.

THE FLINTSTONES

The Flintstones (ABC, 1960–66): A surprise hit animated prime time sitcom that later lived on in syndication for kids, *The Flintstones* set *The Honeymooners* in the Stone Age, allowing visual and verbal gags and puns about dinosaurs and geology. The program was a hit with teenagers, and helped launch the first wave of prime time animation in the 1960s, and established Hanna-Barbera as the most successful studio for televised animation.

THE HONEYMOONERS

The Honeymooners (CBS, 1955–56): Originating as the most popular running sketch on *The Jackie Gleason Show*, *The Honeymooners* ran as a stand-alone sitcom for one season but is still remembered as one of the classics of early television. Focused on a bus driver, a sewer worker, and their wives living in working-class New York, the show was part of an era that featured more ethnic and lower-class characters before the rise of the suburban sitcom in the late 1950s.

The Honeymooners, and became most popular in the 1990s with *The Simpsons, King of the Hill,* and *South Park.* Animated sitcoms allow for unrealistic gags, outrageous plot twists, and broad social satire that would be difficult to achieve in a live-action production. The **fantasy sitcom** was a popular cycle in the 1960s, with *Bewitched, I Dream of Jeannie, The Munsters,* and *Mr. Ed* combining typical sitcom conventions with a supernatural dimension, thus allowing for unusual comic possibilities and conflicts. Fantasy sitcoms have frequently

MOONLIGHTING

Moonlighting (ABC, 1985–89): A genre mixture of mystery, romance, and comedy, *Moonlighting* features Cybill Shepherd and Bruce Willis as a pair of witty private detectives. Beyond serving as a launching pad for Willis's successful film career, the show is best remembered for its self-aware reflexive tone satirizing television conventions and playing with genre norms.

reappeared on television schedules, with programs *Mork & Mindy*, *ALF*, and *Third Rock from the Sun* using aliens to inject comedic mayhem into typical sitcom formulas. Sitcoms can engage in **genre parody**, mocking the conventions of other genres—*Get Smart* mocked spy programs, *Police Squad* and *Sledge Hammer!* parodied cop shows, and *Soap* satirized soap operas, all within the framework of a weekly sitcom.

One particularly interesting genre mixture is the **dramedy**, crossing comedy and drama in a delicate balance. Dramatic elements have frequently been present in sitcoms, notably on early innovator *Room 222* and in later seasons of the long-running war sitcom *M*A*S*H*, but the dramedy mixture emerged as a fledgling genre cycle in the mid-1980s, drawing upon production methods, styles, and narrative forms from both comedy and drama traditions. *Moonlighting* was a notable popular innovation, incorporating explicit and reflexive comedy into an hour-long detective series, but subsequent half-hour dramedies such as *The Days and Nights of Molly Dodd*, *Hooperman*, and *Frank's Place* failed to connect with audiences despite critical praise. *The Wonder Years* was the only half-hour dramedy of the 1980s with a successful long-term run. Dramedies made a comeback in the 1990s, although hour-long dramas with comedic content, such as *Northern Exposure*, *Ally McBeal* and *Desperate Housewives*, have succeeded far more than half-hour dramatic sitcoms such as *Sports Night*, although *Sex and the City* might be thought of as a successful dramedy.

Most sitcoms are shot in a multi-camera studio mode, with a live audience providing feedback for comedic timing and laughter to cue viewers at home. Often broadcast live in the early 1950s, sitcoms soon shifted to *Lucy*'s innovative multi-camera telefilm system, and by the 1970s many shows moved to a live-to-tape model. Both modes of recording are commonly used today, with videotaped programs slightly more common. A few shows have employed a single-camera telefilm system, most notably *M*A*S*H* in the 1970s, which allowed producers to break away from the confines of studio sets and limited staging. Single-camera

SEX AND THE CITY

Sex and the City (HBO, 1998–2004): One of HBO's first hit series, this show focuses on the friendship between four professional women, their love lives, and their shopping habits. Although first notable for its sexual explicitness, the series remains popular for its blend of comedy and character drama along with its urbane sensibility.

SPORTS NIGHT

Sports Night (ABC, 1998–2000): A short-lived dramedy portraying life behind the scenes at a sports cable network resembling ESPN, the show was beloved by critics but never clearly fit network expectations for a comedy; creators and the network battled over the proper role for a laugh track and how to market the series. The production team went on to create *The West Wing*, a drama with a similar visual and dialogue style that achieved greater success within the hour-long drama format.

sitcoms became more common in the 1990s and 2000s, with hits such as *Malcolm in the Middle, My Name Is Earl,* and *The Office* making creative use of such production techniques. Most dramedies use single-camera production models.

A similar production shift involves laugh tracks. In the 1960s, even animated sitcoms such as *The Flintstones* used fake laugh tracks to cue audience reactions, but starting in the 1970s some producers resisted the use of such overt comedic signals. *M*A*S*H* used laugh tracks minimally, avoiding them altogether in operating room scenes and more dramatic moments, while dramedies of the 1980s avoided them. *Sports Night* began using laugh tracks at the network's insistence, although producers minimized their use throughout the first season and eliminated them entirely by the show's second season. Laugh tracks are still used in most studio-shot sitcoms, but rarely on animated or single-camera programs, allowing for a more subtle comedic tone.

Traditionally sitcoms have followed a limited narrative structure: a minor complication in the situation's equilibrium triggers comedic mishaps, which are resolved by the end of the episode, with no lasting impact into the next week. However, many programs stray from these norms and employ more varied structures and storytelling devices. Many shows refuse the return to equilibrium,

CHEERS

Cheers (NBC, 1982–93): A classic sitcom that survived two years of weak ratings to become a massive hit, *Cheers* portrays life in a working-class Boston bar to highlight characters and a setting atypical for television. The series incorporates some serialized plots, especially concerning romantic relationships, and an explicit focus on class conflicts to form an influential model of comedy, and inspired the highly successful spin-off *Frasier*.

whether allowing domestic conflict to persist on *All in the Family* or *Malcolm in the Middle*, offering no retreat from wartime on *M*A*S*H*, or presenting unresolved absurd situations at the end of *Simpsons* episodes. Character arcs are a common ongoing feature of sitcoms, as with Mary Richards's growing independence on *Mary Tyler Moore* or Kevin's maturity on *The Wonder Years*; *Cheers* added more explicitly serialized relationship plots through Sam and Diane's multi-season courtship, often with season-ending cliff-hangers, a tendency that many sitcoms like *The Office* have employed in recent years. *Seinfeld* uses complex interweaving plot structures that often deny resolution and culminate in farcical collisions of ongoing running jokes and references, a technique adopted by other shows such as *Arrested Development* and *Scrubs*. Contemporary sitcoms have much more variety in plotting and narrative structure than early examples of the genre, even though many critics still view the sitcom as a wholly formulaic genre.

At certain moments in television history, a cycle of sitcoms seems to directly address the social conditions at play in America. In the early 1970s, as discussed in chapter 2, CBS initiated a group of socially engaged sitcoms to target younger urban audiences, such as *All in the Family*, *Mary Tyler Moore*, and *M*A*S*H*. These programs tackled social issues more directly than in previous eras, although television programs are always in dialogue with their historical contexts. As explored in chapter 4, both escapist programs, such as *The Munsters*, and shows explicitly tackling issues, such as *Will & Grace*, can tie into the social issues of their day through commentary and satire. Genre critics need to be sensitive to how any genre can be socially engaged in a number of implicit ways beyond explicit representations. Thus the history of any genre responds to changing social norms and conventions, as with sexually frank sitcoms of the late 1970s *Three's Company* and *Soap*, but often in ways that make us reconsider notions of escapism or relevance, a topic revisited in chapter 8.

Talk Shows

When you think of a talk show, what type of program comes to mind? It might *The Oprah Winfrey Show*, which features experts or celebrities discussing issues concerning emotional struggles and ways for self-improvement. Or perhaps it would be more sensational programs such as *The Jerry Springer Show*, which highlight the most outrageous stories of marginal members of society for viewers to leer at. Maybe celebrity-driven interview programs such as *The Tonight Show* come to mind, with a series of celebrity guests promoting new projects interspersed with comedic banter. Or you might think of political talk shows such as *Meet the Press*, with pundits discussing current affairs and interviewing important experts and politicians. Talk shows are a broadly encompassing genre, including all of these program types, as well as call-in advice shows (*Loveline*), single-interview programs (*Larry King Live*), magazine shows with multiple interview and chat segments (*Live with Regis and Kelly*), and specialized interview shows (*Inside the Actors Studio*).

There are almost no genre conventions that apply to every talk show, but some are common across many examples of the genre. As per the name, **talk shows** focus on dialogue between people. Almost every talk show features a central host (or pair of hosts) with guests that change each episode. Topics might range broadly, but talk shows typically find themselves balanced between the poles of entertainment and journalism, either offering a lighter side to the news or discussing entertainment topics. Usually shot in a multi-camera studio with live editing to videotape or occasionally broadcast live, many talk shows feature their studio audience participating via questions and comments, or at least responding with laughter or applause—or chanting and screaming raucously on more sensationalist programs such as *Springer*. Most talk shows last an hour, although some can be a half hour; the genre rarely is aired in network prime time, but fills schedules in all other hours, including late-night, morning, daytime, and weekends, often in syndication and cable channels. Talk shows are a low-cost genre, with simple production values and few expenses aside from the host's salary and basic sets. They generate steady but not impressive ratings, with exceptional programs such as *Oprah* ranking as central texts in American television shaping national trends and tastes. Winfrey's program about mad cow disease allegedly triggered a significant decline in beef sales in the mid-1990s, and her book club catapults each selection on to the bestseller lists.

Like nearly every television genre, the talk show's roots reach back to radio, where interview programs and celebrity variety shows were a staple. Early television talk shows of the 1950s, such as *The Tonight Show* and *Person to Person*, set the conventions for celebrity interview programs and furthered the careers of hosts Steve Allen, Jack Paar, and Edward R. Murrow. *Today* established the

THE OPRAH WINFREY SHOW

The Oprah Winfrey Show (syndicated, 1986–present): As the host and pro-ducer of the most successful daytime talk show, Oprah Winfrey has cre-ated a devoted fanbase surrounding her serious treatment of social and personal issues, advocacy for literacy and reading through her influential book club, and focus on self-improvement and charity. The show's suc-cess has allowed Winfrey to become one of the media's most powerful figures, with a successful cable channel, magazine, book series, radio channel, and online portal.

THE JERRY SPRINGER SHOW

The Jerry Springer Show (syndicated, 1991–present): The epitome of the "trash talk" style, *Springer* features outlandish situations that typically generate physical and verbal conflicts between guests. Many critics debate how seriously to take the show, as some argue that it glamorizes deviant and abusive behavior, while others see it as an outlandish circus that is self-aware and purposeful in its excesses.

norms of the morning magazine program, mixing news, interviews, and how-to segments in a model that remains popular today, while *Home*, hosted by Arlene Francis, innovated the afternoon talk show aimed at women, blazing a trail for future female hosts such as Barbara Walters, Oprah Winfrey, Katie Couric, and Rosie O'Donnell.

The term *talk show* did not enter common usage until the mid-1960s, grow-ing in prominence with a number of key developments in the 1960s and 1970s. Johnny Carson's tenure as host of *Tonight* began in 1962. In his thirty years as the "king of late night," he established the model for late-night talk shows that continues today. Daytime shows such as *The Merv Griffin Show* and *The Mike Douglas Show* mixed celebrity interviews with casual public affairs discussions, running from the mid-1960s through the 1980s. The successful 1970s syndi-cated daytime program *Donahue* tackled often-sensational issues of the day with a participatory audience and empathic host; the show targeted the women's audience that Phil Donahue felt had been underserved in addressing serious social concerns.

The 1980s saw the rise of two major figures in the talk show. Oprah Winfrey brought her local Chicago talk show to syndication in 1986, with *The Oprah Winfrey Show* quickly supplanting *Donahue* as the top-rated daytime talk show.

DONAHUE

Donahue (syndicated, 1967–96): The pioneer of the issue-oriented daytime talk show, *Donahue* thrived for almost thirty years by tackling serious issues with an overtly emotional tone to appeal to a female audience. The show was eventually overtaken by *Oprah* and other more sensational programs, appealing to younger viewers.

Oprah combined *Donahue*'s issue-oriented focus with an overtly emotional appeal to women through revelations about her personal life, creating a form of "public therapy" that has remained highly successful for two decades; Winfrey's success brought about a stream of emotionally attuned issue-oriented imitators throughout the 1990s, such as *The Sally Jessy Raphael Show* and *The Geraldo Rivera Show*. In clear counterpoint to Winfrey's sincerity, David Letterman emerged as the new face of the late-night talk show in the 1980s through his NBC program *Late Night with David Letterman* before shifting to CBS in 1993. Letterman undercut the glossy decorum of Carson's *Tonight Show* with a self-deprecating irony, reflexive acknowledgment of the tools of television production through stunts like throwing pencils at the camera or bringing crew members on-screen, and winking celebration of mundane entertainments such as Stupid Pet Tricks and goofy contests like "Will It Float?" *Late Night* appealed to the youth audience through its absurdist humor and iconoclastic guests and musical artists, paving the way for the subsequent successes of hosts like Conan O'Brien, Jimmy Kimmel, Bill Maher, and Jon Stewart.

Talk shows in the 1990s were at the center of a cultural controversy involving a genre cycle derided as "trash talk," as daytime programs such as *The Ricki Lake Show* and *Springer* appealed to the youth audience with boundary-pushing sensationalism, in-fighting among guests, and a focus on typically unseen members of American society branded as "deviant" by many. The controversy flared following the so-called *Jenny Jones* murder of 1995—using a typical "surprise" structure, one *Jones* episode revealed to a male guest that a male acquaintance had a romantic crush on him, provoking the guest to later kill his admirer in a homophobic rage. Commentators and politicians crusaded to "clean up" talk shows, encouraging sponsor boycotts and asking local stations to weed out offensive programs. Many of *Ricki*'s imitators did leave the air quickly, but more in keeping with the normal saturation phase of genre cycles than from political pressure. "Clean" talk shows such as *The Rosie O'Donnell Show* and *The Ellen DeGeneres Show* followed with a low-key celebrity-driven format harking back to the 1970s, but so-called "trash" shows such as *Springer* remained steady fixtures, continuing to appeal to their core audiences.

THE JENNY JONES SHOW

The Jenny Jones Show (syndicated, 1991–2003): A talk show with decent popularity, *Jenny Jones* became notorious for inspiring the 1995 murder following the "secret crush" episode. The show lasted for years, although it became less sensational in the wake of the controversy.

Talk shows remain a diverse genre, with a wide range of formats, audiences, and topics coexisting across the television schedule. Some formats are granted a great deal of cultural respect, as public affairs talk shows such as *Face the Nation* help set political agendas and late-night talk shows highlight celebrity news and personalities. Daytime shows remain a point of contention, as critics debate whether such shows exploit people's emotions and parade unusual guests as televised "freak shows," or provide a public forum to showcase a broad range of voices that are otherwise excluded from mainstream television programming. While we cannot definitively label the genre as either a public service or exploitation, it is useful to consider the various ways viewers engage with specific programs rather than assuming that the texts themselves have singular straightforward meanings. As subsequent chapters explore, viewers can take diverse meanings away from programs, and thus any proclamations about the impact a genre may have on its audience needs to examine how people actually watch it. Research on talk show viewers has suggested that claims about both the genre's uplifting possibilities and its corrupting influences are overstated, as most actual viewers have more subtle engagement with programs than either polarized position might suggest.

Many more genres exist than the four examples explored here, from the broad genres of sports, drama, and advertising, to specific categories such as nature documentaries, cooking shows, and talent competitions. Every genre has its own industrial strategies, cultural meanings, and viewer practices, with many norms changing throughout its history. Individual programs often draw upon multiple genres, playing with categories to entertain and engage viewers, as well as to set themselves apart from competing shows. Genre is one of the main organizational strategies for television creators, distributors, and viewers, and thus needs to be considered whenever analyzing a television text and its cultural importance.

FORMAL ANALYSIS IN ACTION: THE CASE OF *LOST*

This chapter and chapter 5 introduce a number of specialized terms and a set of categories that provide a way to look at and discuss television programming with more specificity and depth than typical viewers might bring to the screen. These concepts are best understood in practice, rather than just as a glossary of techniques and strategies. To demonstrate how formal analysis of television programming can heighten our awareness of how shows make meaning and impact audiences, as well as to provide a framework for appreciating the creativity and artistry of television productions, this chapter concludes with an account of an innovative contemporary series: the prime time drama *Lost*.

ABC brought *Lost* to the air in the fall of 2004 with aggressive promotional strategies to try to create a hit, but the show was quite risky for the network and producers. The pilot cost a reported $12 million, one of the most expensive television episodes ever made. Additionally, the story of a plane crash on a mysterious island does not fit clearly into any established television genre. Critics anticipating a scripted version of the reality hit *Survivor* were clearly off-base. The cast contains a few television veterans, but no stars guaranteed to draw an audience by name alone. Reportedly there was such apprehension among ABC executives about the potential success of the series that they almost pulled the show from the schedule over the summer, afraid of being saddled with an expensive flop. But within a year, the show regularly placed in the top 20 on Nielsen's weekly ratings chart, performed strongly with youth demographics, released a top-selling DVD, spawned a vast number of websites dedicated to decoding the island's mysteries, won six Emmy Awards including one for Best Drama, and inspired a number of prime time imitators—the surest sign of television success. Looking closely at the show's formal practices can help explain its remarkable and surprising success.

When analyzing a show like *Lost*, which is still airing new episodes as of this book's writing, we are faced with a conundrum: how do we delineate the boundaries of the text? Must we wait until the entire series has aired before analyzing it? Certainly if the goal is to explain the overall structure of the series narrative, we cannot do anything but speculate until the entire series is completed. But we can look at an entire season, multi-episode arcs, and individual episodes as textual units to explore the show's narrative and style. Thus we will consider the first season and selected episodes to consider how the show creates meaning, and what innovations seem to elicit viewer pleasure.

The opening of *Lost*'s pilot illustrates how formal choices convey meanings and emotional responses to viewers, and sets the tone for an entire series. We can break the show's first nine minutes into three different sequences, or **beats**, each with distinct styles, tones, and narrative functions. The first shot, following the simple title shot with the word *LOST* floating on-screen, is an extreme closeup of a closed eye, which opens with a startling sound effect and an exaggerated iris dilation. Although it lasts only five seconds, the shot immediately signals that something unusual is happening, both in the storyworld and in how it is being conveyed to us. The image and sound are both non-naturalistic and create an

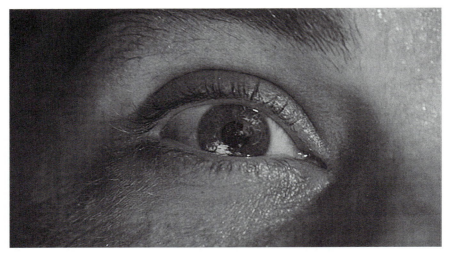

The pilot of *Lost* opens with an extreme close-up of an eye, provoking mystery and disorientation...

...then cuts to a point-of-view shot looking up in a forest, providing a little more narrative clarity.

eerie sense of mystery: Whose eye is this and where is this person? This sense of disorientation continues throughout the sequence, as we cut to a shot looking up at trees in a jungle from below, followed by a slowly swirling crane shot of a man in a suit lying on the jungle ground looking up. We then see shots of Jack Shephard (played by Matthew Fox) alternating with his visual point of view of the jungle and a dog wandering up to him. A closeup of a miniature liquor bottle he discovers in his pocket hints at a recent airplane experience. He hears a sound and sprints through the jungle, with disorienting jump cuts and violations of the 180-degree rule heightening the sense of confusion and the intensity of the action. Musical cues and non-diegetic sounds contrast loud pulses with quiet drones, ratcheting up the sense of anxiety and unease. Jack emerges from the jungle and on to the beach into a closeup; the camera pans in a counterclockwise circle along the beautiful beach, seemingly following his point of view, but Jack appears within the frame much earlier in the circle than we expect, jarring us out of his perspective and furthering the show's unsettling visual style.

This opening two-minute sequence creates both disorientation and identification, confusing us but grounding viewers in Jack's experiences to establish him as the protagonist, at least for the first episode. It makes us want to know more, too, generating suspense that is needed both for the show's complex narrative and for ABC's desire to generate audiences for a weekly series. While promotions had made it clear to potential viewers that the show was about the aftermath of a plane crash, this perplexing opening, placing us in an unknown locale with no establishing sequence to set the narrative stage, was a risky choice for producers. By focusing on this character's confusion and the odd presence of the dog in the jungle, we immediately get a sense that *Lost* will not follow standard television conventions, and that we must tolerate a degree of narrative confusion in trying to comprehend the action.

The next sequence revealing the wreckage is both harrowing in its raw emotional intensity, with corpses and people crushed by falling debris and sucked into plane engines, and spectacular in its high-budget special effects atypical of television. We discover the fate of Flight 815 along with Jack, witnessing the crash wreckage on the beach and realizing the gravity of the situation through his perspective. After following Jack across the beach with a long tracking shot revealing the extent of the wreckage and ensuing chaos, we experience the trauma of the aftermath in a four-and-a-half minute sequence with incredibly fast editing—the average shot lasts under two seconds—constantly moving hand-held-camera work, and high-impact sound effects, all of which generate a sense of intensity and anxiety more common to Hollywood action movies than to most television programs. This sequence uses telephoto lenses to flatten the depth of the crash scene, making it appear that wreckage and characters are closer together in order to heighten the sense of danger, while alternating long shots emphasizing the scope of the disaster with closeups highlighting emotional distress. During this sequence, we learn Jack's name and that he is a doctor, and we follow along as he saves numerous lives and takes command of the situation. We also glimpse almost all of *Lost's* thirteen other main characters featured in the season, although it will take much of the year to get to know them and their relationships in any depth.

This action sequence ends with Jack saving Claire and Hurley from being crushed by a falling airplane wing, followed by a moment of relative calm from

The high-budget post-crash set creates spectacle and action...

...as well as intense human drama in a moment of riveting crisis.

the explosions and traumatic injuries of the previous minutes. The third beat shifts to a calmer and more emotional tone—the music moves from pulsing action to a more elegiac lyrical style, as the cast and crew credits appear as keyed graphics in the lower part of the screen. The staging slows in pace, as Jack staggers through the crash site assessing the scene with relative calm, and the editing rhythm is greatly reduced, with only ten cuts over the next two minutes. Camerawork becomes steadier and more static, allowing us to view

The final shot of the opening sequence offers both calm and chaos, with the surviving hero framed by the wreckage and the dangling hand of a victim.

the wreckage and Jack's emotional reactions more clearly. The centerpiece of this sequence is a fifty-second slow zoom-in from long shot to closeup as Jack pauses to catch his breath and talk with Boone, framed by wreckage—but with the dangling arm of a corpse hanging above his head to subtly remind us of the grave situation. The emotional tenor of this sequence directly contrasts with the mystery and action of the first two sequences. In the first nine minutes of *Lost*, the show's style establishes the broad range of tones and viewer emotional engagements the series will offer, conveying information about the storyworld while helping to forge viewer expectations for what they will see throughout the series.

While *Lost*'s style is certainly a distinguishing aspect of the series, maximizing the beauty of its on-location Hawaii set with creative and ambitious camerawork, sound, and editing techniques, what the show has become best known for is its unconventional narrative content and structure. The creative mix of convention and innovation marking the show's stylistic choices carries over to *Lost*'s use of narrative structure and genre categories. In many ways, *Lost* follows conventions of television storytelling. It typically emphasizes moment-to-moment clarity and comprehension via the continuity system; it segments its stories into commercially divided acts with suspenseful act breaks; and each episode offers clear A and B plots with runners. As a large ensemble series—Jack is a central character, but not the singular heroic focal point presented by the pilot—*Lost* draws upon serial fiction conventions of charting the relationships within a community. Given that most of the survivors are complete strangers, much of the dramatic action involves developing new relationships in a high-stakes situation, as alliances, romances, and friendships are both developed and destroyed. The show uses suspense and surprise frequently, revealing major story developments in unexpected ways both to characters and to viewers—often in the last moments of an episode, for maximum suspense. But *Lost* is more notable for its innovations in genre and narration.

Nearly every television program is explicit in its genre identity, clearly branded by channel, promotional material, and narrative. At first, *Lost* appeared to be a disaster program, a genre seemingly unsuited for an ongoing storyline, with narrative focus on the castaways' struggles to escape from and survive in an isolated world. If this were the sole thrust of the narrative, it would probably be quite disappointing, as little could match the intensity and dramatic stakes of the show's opening moments. But within the program's first two hours, it becomes clear that the island is not what it seems, with a monster roaming the jungle, a sixteen-year-old distress signal from previous castaways, and a polar bear inexplicably living in the South Pacific—not to mention various other mystical and science fiction developments that have since been revealed. Ultimately the show's genre remains uncertain even after numerous seasons: Is it a supernatural thriller, a scientific mystery, a soap opera in the wilderness, or a religious fantasy (or all of the above)? Unlike previously celebrated genre mixtures such as *Twin Peaks* and *Buffy the Vampire Slayer*, *Lost* refuses to wear its genre references on its sleeve, preferring to force viewers to speculate on relevant generic frameworks, and then to confound our expectations through twists and reversals.

The program's most notable innovation is its unique storytelling structure. On one level, the compelling narrative questions and pleasures would appear to be predicated on the suspense of what will happen to the survivors: Will they get off the island or will the "Others" (the island's mysterious inhabitants) get them first? But the show created equally compelling narrative enigmas in the backstory of each character during the first season. What were Kate's criminal acts and motivations? How did John Locke become paralyzed and acquire his uncanny outdoorsman expertise? How did Danielle arrive on the island and what happened to her child? And why were these people brought together on this airplane and then unbelievably spared in the crash? While many detective stories lodge unknown narrative information in the past—who committed the crime?—*Lost* balances a large number of enigmas in both the past and future of its large ensemble of characters, often linking backstory mysteries with revelations about the island.

This storytelling scope is carried out in an innovative narrative structure, with nested flashbacks built into each episode. *Lost*'s flashbacks are presented without typical framing devices of voiceover reflection, a character telling another about his past, or transitioning with out-of-focus dissolves. Instead, flashbacks typically cut directly from a closeup of the relevant character with a subtle "whoosh" sound effect, an intrinsic norm that becomes familiar to viewers after a few uses. The pilot provides flashbacks on the plane before the crash from the perspective of three different characters, playing with narrative frequency by showing the same moment from the differing perspectives of Jack and Charlie. These flashbacks force us to reconsider what we have already seen on the island, as with Charlie's flashback that reveals his heroin addiction, which reframes his behavior. The flashbacks also help explain objects that are highlighted by closeups, such as Jack's liquor bottle and Walt finding a pair of handcuffs in the jungle, both of which are revealed during flashbacks to the plane.

Subsequent episodes use another structure for flashbacks: each episode foregrounds one character's backstory, interweaving past events prior to the doomed flight with the challenges of life on the island, to create parallel narrative threads that resonate in often surprising ways. By providing insights into the characters' pre-island lives, the flashbacks establish character depth and share restricted story knowledge with viewers that the other islanders lack. Often these revelations are quite significant, as with Locke's paralysis, Sawyer's criminal past, and Hurley's relationship with a series of mysterious numbers. Because we know more about these characters than anyone else on the island, the narrative creates suspense and mystery in the developing relationships among the castaways. The program's use of flashbacks is an intrinsic norm, as viewers come to expect flashbacks to function in particular ways and are surprised when they do not, as in season two's episode "The Other 48 Days," which tells a story parallel to the experiences shown by the rest of the series, but uses no explicit flashbacks. Later seasons feature even more narrative experimentations, including flash-forwards and time travel, pushing the boundaries of complex storytelling within the mass medium of commercial network television.

Lost also innovates at the level of narrative arc. The entire series is focused on answering the question posed by Charlie at the end of the pilot: "Where are we?" The island proves to contain many mysteries, most of which go unsolved episode to episode. Previous programs, such as *Twin Peaks*, *X-Files*, and *Murder One*, have structured a series around a central mystery, but viewers often were frustrated by the lack of revelations and seeming lack of a clear creative plan. *Lost*'s writers have noted that they learned from such programs, and have promised steady discoveries about the island while maintaining a multi-year plan for telling the complex story. The show offers smaller arcs that resolve pieces of the mystery, as with the first season's plots about Locke discovering a hatch and Claire's abduction. These multi-episode arcs often answer one question while posing even more mysteries, nesting moments of closure within the overall narrative enigma. The producers' achieved one of their storytelling goals in 2007, when they negotiated an end-date of 2010 with ABC; such a planned conclusion is atypical of American network television, but essential to the complex mode of storytelling featured on *Lost*, allowing the producers to map out revelations and twists over multiple seasons.

Lost is a clear product of the convergence era, as multiple opportunities for closely viewing episodes on DVD, DVRs, and computer downloads, as well as collective analysis on fan websites, allow for a heightened engagement with complex clues hidden within the show. Additionally, ancillary products such as tie-in novels and video games extend the show's narrative architecture, and built to a multimedia "alternate reality game," conducted in the summer of 2006, that revealed crucial narrative backstory to dedicated fans. It remains to be seen if the show can sustain its mysteries over the course of a long run, as few programs maintain such ambitious creative goals throughout numerous seasons and across media, but its first four seasons mark it as one of the most innovative programs in television history.

This formal account of *Lost*'s style, narrative, and genre can help us understand the various appeals the program offers. It certainly helps explain how the show succeeds in creating emotional responses in viewers, as suspense, sadness, joy, excitement, and laughter all result from the careful use of television's formal elements. There are no guarantees that effective use of style and storytelling will create intended emotional responses, of course, but certainly the vast majority of programs that emotionally engage viewers do so through their blend of formal strategies and compelling meanings. A gripping story narrated poorly usually will not compel viewers. Likewise detailed formal analysis can help us understand the complex processes of viewer tastes. Looking closely at programs you find particularly pleasurable can help you understand what storytelling and presentational forms resonate most with your own tastes, and perhaps with broader cultural values, too. Understanding television's form can increase your appreciation of the nuances of the medium, and make clear how programs can be engaging or boring, artful or manipulative.

Formal elements help explain how meanings are made, and thus offer a useful vocabulary for analyzing and appreciating the strategies creators use to communicate. But there are certainly questions about a show's meaning that formal analysis alone cannot address, issues raised by *Lost* as well as by all programs. For instance, how does *Lost*'s focus on the battle between scientific and religious worldviews, encapsulated by the episode entitled "Man of Science, Man of Faith," resonate with contemporary American debates over faith and science? What do the relationships between the multi-ethnic characters tell us about how race and nationality operate in American culture? How do the behaviors of the island's characters construct or subvert gender norms, such as the beautiful outlaw Kate or the domineering husband Jin? What messages does the sympathetic characterization of former Iraqi soldier Sayid send, especially given that *Lost* aired during the Iraq War? To answer these types of questions, we need to apply our formal vocabulary and heightened analytical senses to explore television as a site of cultural representation—the topic of chapter 7.

FURTHER READING

Television storytelling has been studied as a formal system, often by genre. Glen Creeber, *Serial Television: Big Drama on the Small Screen* (London: BFI Publishing, 2004), explores prime time dramas, while Robert C. Allen, *Speaking of Soap Operas* (Chapel Hill: University of North Carolina Press, 1985), explores daytime serials. Horace Newcomb, *TV: The Most Popular Art* (Garden City, NY: Anchor Press, 1974), is an important early account of television narrative across a range of genres. Helen Fulton, ed., *Narrative and Media* (Cambridge, UK: Cambridge University Press, 2005), provides a broad overview of the relevant issues and genres from a British perspective; and Nick Lacey, *Narrative and Genre: Key Concepts in Media Studies* (New York: St. Martin's Press, 2000), offers a theoretical introduction to these topics.

The importance and practice of television genre is explored in Jason Mittell, *Genre and Television: From Cop Shows to Cartoons in American Culture* (New York: Routledge, 2004). Specific genres have received more detailed study. In addition to Robert Allen's book referenced earlier, soap operas are explored in Louise Spence, *Watching Daytime Soap Operas: The Power of Pleasure* (Middletown, Conn.: Wesleyan University Press, 2005), and Robert C. Allen, ed., *To Be Continued—: Soap Operas Around the World* (New York: Routledge, 1995). Thomas A. DeLong, *Quiz Craze: America's Infatuation with Game Shows* (New York: Praeger Publishers, 1991), offers a comprehensive history of the game show.

Sitcoms are one of the most studied television genres. See David Marc, *Comic Visions: Television Comedy and American Culture* (Boston: Unwin Hyman, 1989); Joanne Morreale, ed., *Critiquing the Sitcom: A Reader* (Syracuse, NY: Syracuse University Press, 2003); and Gerard Jones, *Honey, I'm Home!: Sitcoms, Selling the American Dream* (New York: St. Martin's Press, 1993), as well as books and articles on individual programs. Talk shows have been explored provocatively by Julie Engel Manga, *Talking Trash: The Cultural Politics of Daytime TV Talk Shows* (New York: New York University Press, 2003), and Jane Shattuc, *The Talking Cure: TV Talk Shows and Women* (New York: Routledge, 1997). For a range of analyses of *Lost*, see Roberta Pearson, ed., *Reading* Lost (London: I.B. Tauris, 2009).

NOTES

[1]See Jason Mittell, *Genre and Television: From Cop Shows to Cartoons in American Culture* (New York: Routledge, 2004).

[2]See Robert C. Allen, *Speaking of Soap Operas* (Chapel Hill: University of North Carolina Press, 1985), for an influential account of soap opera narrative.

CHAPTER 7

SCREENING AMERICA

As suggested in chapter 5, all television texts use specific formal techniques to communicate meanings. What are those meanings and how do they relate to the broader world outside of television? This chapter considers how television conveys meanings to its viewers that help shape the way we think about our lives and social worlds. This is not to say that viewers accept anything appearing on television as true. As chapter 9 explores further, viewers engage with programming in many different ways, and rarely take all meanings television presents simply as truths to be mimicked and believed. However, there is no doubt that the meanings we see on television do influence us, and form the basis for many behaviors, beliefs, and attitudes.

How might we understand the relationship between the meanings conveyed on television and the real world? One instinct might be to say that there is no real relationship between what we see and how we live. Television is often considered an **escapist** medium, and thus its meanings may have little to do with the real world. Following this line of thinking, we watch television to escape our lives, and thus we do not take its meanings seriously beyond their entertainment function. This explanation applies best to certain types of programming, as shows like *Lost* and genres such as science fiction and soap operas present a world that seems quite different from most people's experiences. The escapist approach to television's meaning dismisses serious analysis of texts by claiming "it's just TV." Why take it seriously if we watch it as a form of escape? Not only does this approach fall short when considering news, sports, reality shows, and talk shows, which all clearly have a direct tie to the real world, but it also neglects the fact that many fantasy programs do offer meanings concerning serious issues, whether it's the gender politics of *Bewitched* or attitudes toward government in *The X-Files*. Clearly we cannot dismiss television's meanings as simply escapism, as there is always some resonance with real issues even in the most escapist show.

The opposite approach to escapism assumes that television is a direct **reflection** of our world: if it is on screen, it must be true to viewers' lives. It is certainly true that much of what we watch on television does directly address the real world, but this critical approach goes further to contend that viewers would reject programs that did not speak to their realities. This position is difficult to support for programs that are explicitly fantastic and unreal, but it also falls short for shows claiming to present reality. As already discussed concerning reality programs, sports, and news, television always shapes the world it represents through its selective presentation of actions and characters, and use of narrative structures to frame events through plots. This is not to say that nonfiction programs are explicitly deceiving audiences, but such representations are rarely as simple as a reflecting mirror. No matter how realistic a television program might appear, it always uses techniques that distort and alter our perceptions of that reality. The mirror metaphor is tempting, but ultimately too simplistic, ignoring the many ways television shapes the world it portrays rather than just transmitting it.

If we want to think of the television screen as a mirror, a more apt analogy is a funhouse mirror that alters and distorts images: some elements are enlarged and highlighted, while others shrink or disappear altogether. In this way, television does not reflect as much as **refract** the world, altering its appearance through its particular techniques and forms of conveying meaning. We can think of this process as **representation**: taking facets of the real world and presenting them on-screen, but altering their meanings through the act of televising them. Some representations intentionally differ from the real world, as in the manipulative way 1950s quiz shows dramatically staged their scripted contests to appear to be honest competitions. But even if producers strive to represent their subjects as accurately and honestly as possible, all television offers a partial and skewed perspective on the world shown on-screen; everything we see is shaped by the techniques of camerawork and editing, which highlight some aspects of the world while leaving others off-screen. Even when representations are accurate, the way television represents the world always shapes our perceptions more than how a perfect reflection would.

This chapter explores how to study television's representations of the world, considering how the meanings created by television programs construct particular visions of American culture and how they fit into broader contexts. The next chapter focuses on the question of identity, thinking about how images of groups on television shape our sense of self and community. Even though such representations do impact viewers, helping to shape the way we see the world and establishing cultural norms to be followed, we cannot assume that we automatically accept the meanings given to us. Just because television represents the world in a particular way does not mean that all people who consume these representations adopt them as truth; representations cannot fully determine how viewers make sense of their meanings. The process by which viewers make sense of the world represented on-screen is discussed in chapter 9, which focuses on the meanings themselves and how they fit into broader contexts of American history and culture.

REPRESENTING THE AMERICAN NATION

All meanings in television programming are representations, with particular distortions, selections, and omissions. Depending on your interests, you might look at how television represents any type of subject: you could analyze the representations of furniture or dogs if you wished. Such an analysis might yield insights into how television neglects to include large-breed dogs in programming, or misrepresents the number of households who have wicker chairs. However, most critics interested in representation focus on subjects that seem most important to defining norms in American culture, not just chronicling how television accurately or mistakenly portrays the world. One important type of representational analysis focuses on visions of American **national character**. Nearly all meanings shown on American television might be considered as representing the national character, contributing to a shared sense of America and what makes the country distinct. This mode of national representation also gains significance as American television circulates around the globe, forming the most widely seen set of images of the United States throughout the world. Some programming might be explicitly about nationhood, such as the PBS documentary *The Civil War* or the presidential fiction *The West Wing*, but even shows that make no claims to address political or historical roots of American society still convey meanings that can represent a shared national culture. Many different programs, from *Leave It to Beaver* to *The Price Is Right*, have been described as "quintessentially American." What might that mean? How can one see shows about a suburban family or pricing games as conveying something essential about the national character?

The Power of Ideology

To understand how a program can be viewed as expressing national identity, we need to consider a complex but important concept: **ideology**. At its core, an ideology is a set of shared values and beliefs held by a group of people. Traditionally, ideologies have been thought of as major political and economic systems and practices; thus we might talk about ideologies of capitalism versus socialism, democracy versus monarchy. Scholars of American culture have expanded notions of political and economic ideology to include ideologies of identity, exploring how a group might follow a common set of beliefs concerning their definition of gender, race, sexuality, religion, age, and other defining categories, as discussed more in the next chapter. Analyzing programming as promoting ideology is debated by scholars, with some dismissing the approach, while many other critics believe it is the best way to view television's cultural impact. Before discussing the limits of such an approach, it is instructive to explore an **ideological critique** of American television to see what it might tell us about its meanings.

The term *ideology* in a study of American cultural forms specifically refers to the **dominant** ideas at a particular historical moment. Instead of focusing on competing belief systems, cultural critics consider ideology as the powerful dominant values that pervade American society. Such values are certainly historically specific: at the turn of the twentieth century, dominant ideology rejected women's suffrage, while today a belief in voting rights regardless of gender is an uncontested part of American ideology. Because dominant ideology changes over time, often it is easier to see how media convey now-outdated ideological meanings in earlier eras; for instance, representations of African-Americans on 1950s television may strike us today as quite explicitly racist and demeaning, but they were more commonly accepted by many viewers decades ago, with such racism seeming less obvious, or at least less openly discussed, in a segregated culture. However, according to an ideological critique, ideological meanings are to be found in television programs of any era. It is useful to consider how televised ideologies of today shape how we look at our world.

One of the primary ways television functions as part of ideology is in presenting dominant meanings as part of a shared **common sense** that appears natural and universal. For instance, consumer capitalism is a primary component of American ideology that is conveyed in nearly every television program you might watch: business news celebrates sales figures as economic success; sitcoms show characters who achieve happiness by acquiring new consumer goods; home improvement programs define "improvement" via consumption; and *The Price Is Right* rewards contestants who have mastered the knowledge of the marketplace. Even shows that offer critiques of consumerism typically endorse the ideology ultimately. *The Simpsons* has mocked its own merchandising in numerous episodes, but undermines its critique by licensing a broad range of merchandise and promoting products including Butterfinger candy. Rarely are alternatives to this consumerist economic system presented on television, except as vilified and unexplained threats of communism tied to "enemy" countries as

THE SIMPSONS

The Simpsons (Fox, 1989–present): One of the landmark shows in American television history, *The Simpsons* was an unlikely hit, renewing prime time animation as a popular genre and helping establish Fox as a legitimate competitor to the Big Three networks. The show is simultaneously an effective family sitcom with lasting and memorable characters and a pointed parody of sitcoms that skewers a wide range of media forms, genres, and cultural trends, appealing to a broad age range and an entire generation that has grown up with the show.

with the representations of the former Soviet Union or Cuba frequently found in espionage dramas of the 1960s. It is quite rare to see a program present a positive representation of characters rejecting consumerism or stories of communities offering alternatives to capitalist lifestyles, even though such movements exist in America. This is not to fault American television for not offering anti-capitalist programming (although some critics argue that television should), but rather to point out the pervasiveness of the ideology of consumer capitalism on television, even in programs that seem to be escapist or even critical.

How do such ideological messages find their way into television programming? It is tempting to imagine a secret cabal of television executives planning to brainwash the masses into their way of thinking, but ideology does not need such coordinated conspiracies to be effective. In fact, the power of ideology stems from its ability to become internalized by all members of a society as naturalized common sense, not requiring forced indoctrination or explicit propaganda. If the creators of television programming live in a society that predominantly holds the shared ideology of consumer capitalism as a natural and unquestioned system, then the shows they create will likely reinforce such an ideology—which further spreads such thinking among viewers, who themselves may continue to spread the ideology through their own practices. This cycle of ideology reproduces itself through media circulation and consumption, and needs no central conspiracy to dictate ideological meanings.

Of course in commercial television, a system exists that does actively work to disseminate the ideology of consumer capitalism: as discussed in chapter 2, the advertising industry that funds commercial television is dependent on promoting consumerism. According to ideological critics, not only does each advertisement explicitly promote the ideology of consumer capitalism, but the programming surrounding the ads must reinforce, or at least avoid contradicting, such a message. Sometimes this reinforcement is explicit, as with product integration or the creation of merchandising tie-ins for programming. But more frequently, this ideological consistency is enforced tacitly. If television producers want their program to find a place on the television schedule, they must create a show that meets the approval of a network or cable channel, which in turn must be able to sell advertising during the program. As discussed in chapter 11, programming and advertising can be seen as weaving themselves together into a continuous flow of consistent meanings. A show that explicitly counters the ideology of consumer capitalism will likely be unable to secure advertising and distribution, as discussed later concerning the case of *TV Nation*; thus creators must shape their programming to more effectively mesh with the values of the commercial system in which they are working. Whether they explicitly recognize how their programs fit with ideology or accept such values as natural, the logic of the commercial system furthers a dominant set of meanings while marginalizing and stifling contrary positions.

Ideological critiques have pointed out many ways that television reinforces a belief system that treats consumer capitalism as an unquestioned part of our common sense. Newscasts devote a great deal of coverage to business news, which nearly always frames owners and stockholders as protagonists and defines economic success by rising stock prices and profits, not rising wages or community service. Coverage of workers is typically limited to labor disputes that often frame labor as making "demands" while management make "offers"—contrasting terms that highlight the seemingly commonsense way ideologies can shape the way we view the world. Financial news programs and cable channels such as CNBC and Bloomberg typically construct their audiences as belonging to the ownership class, even though far more Americans are working class. Not only does this help advertisers reach more upscale demographics, but it also helps cement the ideology that any American can own a piece of the stock market, and that the health of the economy should be measured by the success of owners, not workers. Furthered by pressures from the corporate television industry and advertising system, television news works to reinforce the logic of corporate capitalism as a healthy part of American life, a position that is not as simple or as universally endorsed as it might appear on television.

Fictional television also works to support economic ideology, both to follow the logic of the advertising-supported system and to present programs that fit with American ideological common sense. The vast majority of shows focus on middle-class and upper-class characters, with overrepresentation of professions such as doctor, lawyer, media creator, and business owner. Even characters who lack obvious economic success typically consume at a level beyond their means, as seen in the idealized apartments on *Friends* or the consumerist paradise of *Sex and the City*. The most common working-class profession on television fiction is police officer, but cop shows rarely discuss the economic realities of police work, or focus on detectives who live a more upscale lifestyle than "beat cops." Other working-class representations are uncommon, and rarely grapple

ROSEANNE

Roseanne (ABC, 1988–97): A hit sitcom featuring comedian Roseanne Barr, the program combines a socially aware focus on the struggles of working-class life and a sarcastic tone challenging the typical image of nuclear families. *Roseanne* challenged numerous stereotypes throughout its run, including groundbreaking portrayals of gay and lesbian characters, and a focus on overweight characters atypical of the beauty norms typifying American television.

with the economic realities faced by the majority of Americans. Programs such as *Roseanne* or *Malcolm in the Middle* stand out because of the rarity of fictional television portraying a family struggling to live from paycheck to paycheck. Certainly one of the appeals of television fiction is as an escape from the mundane struggles of viewer's lives. Who really wants to watch a show about someone who works two boring, low-paying jobs with no future prospects, even if it is more true to life than other series? However, as one of the primary ways that people see representations of their world, television does convey a distorted vision of the American economic landscape, one that reinforces a consumerist ideology, defining success and happiness via ideals that are structurally unattainable for the majority of viewers.

One of the chief powers of ideology is to define what is considered "normal" for a society. As discussed in chapter 4, one of the primary issues concerning the television news industry is how it defines the spectrum of American political opinion. Since the 1980s, journalism has shifted markedly to the right, with positions that would once have been seen as conventionally liberal now defined as radical, and those formerly considered far-right now within the mainstream of conservative opinion. This is not simply the work of television, of course, but as America's primary news medium, television journalism has great influence in setting the terms of the political debate. Ideological theory suggests that by making a position appear to be commonsense and natural, it becomes a **cultural norm**. People hear an opinion, and if they feel it is consistent with how they view the world, they accept it as a norm. Politicians are quite aware of this technique, and cleverly use the media to reiterate terms that help shape opinion. For instance, Republicans gained public support for their tax cut policies in the early 2000s by repeatedly referring to the "estate tax" as the "death tax" on television and in other media appearances, a strategy that helped shift one commonsense notion (that people inheriting multimillion-dollar estates should pay taxes on them) into another (that people should not have to pay taxes upon their death). Regardless of your opinion on taxation, this change of one key word makes sense only in connection with broadly held opinions about fairness and economic responsibilities, ideologies that Republicans used to overtly attempt to shift public opinion.

Ideology and Identification

One of the more controversial aspects of ideological criticism is the concept of **false consciousness**. For some critics, ideological messages on television and beyond spread a deceptive notion of how the world works, an ideology favoring the rich and powerful while deluding the majority of the population. According to this view, television pacifies viewers by providing escapist fantasies, encourages happiness via consumption, and saps people's will to make real political and economic changes that might give them more equality and power in the world. Under this approach, television is seen as a powerful dominating force that turns viewers into victims of ideological brainwashing.

Most critics reject such a totalizing idea of false consciousness for a few reasons; for one, it assumes that viewers are passive sponges who absorb every ideological message without question, that they are duped and brainwashed by the powerful rays of the television screen. Research on actual viewers—as well as the experiences of nearly everyone you know—suggests that people are much more selective and skeptical in their viewing, as discussed in chapter 9. If ideology were such an all-powerful force, how could critics recognize its deceptiveness and be able to identify false consciousness? Some critics argue that false consciousness is an inherently elitist concept, condemning the abilities of the very people it claims to support: average viewers who supposedly enable their own exploitation. Additionally, television does not present a consistent ideological message across the hundreds of hours of programming available each day, but rather it offers a range of contradicting and varying meanings. Thus as an explanation for how viewers consume ideologies, false consciousness is too blunt an approach, one that cannot account for the ways most people watch television.

Ideological critics have proposed some more subtle ways of thinking about how viewers consume ideology without being brainwashed or bullied into accepting ideas they disagree with. Some critics look at television as a one-way form of communication, lecturing us on how to think ideologically. This perspective is commonly used for understanding advertising that explicitly strives to mold our thoughts and behaviors, as discussed in chapter 2. However, this approach has a hard time accounting for why viewers want to accept messages contrary to their own interests or why they choose one program over another. A more nuanced approach suggests that television is more of a dialogue between the program and viewer. A show opens a conversation that can be deepened if a viewer pays attention and watches, or ended by provoking disagreement or

THE BOONDOCKS

The Boondocks (Cartoon Network, 2005–present): An animated sitcom on the Adult Swim scheduling block based on a popular comic strip, the series focuses on a black family living in a white suburb while emphasizing radical politics and an urban, hip-hop aesthetic. The series has generated controversy for its use of explicit racial language, especially surrounding the episode "Return of the King," which imagines Martin Luther King, Jr., surviving into twenty-first-century America.

700 CLUB

The 700 Club (syndicated, 1966–present): A long-running Christian talk show hosted by conservative figure Pat Robertson, *The 700 Club* has served as a popular outlet for right-wing politics and religion on local stations throughout the country as well as national cable channels Fox Family and ABC Family. The flagship of the Christian Broadcasting Network, the show has generated controversy for Robertson's inflammatory remarks against homosexuality and feminism, and for his calls for divine retribution against various American cities for policies he views as "anti-Christian."

causing the viewer to change channels. According to this approach, viewers need to be offered an entry into a program's meanings, not just brainwashed by ideology. One useful concept here is **hailing**. Much like calling for a taxi on a street, television programs call out to viewers by getting our attention and letting us know we are being addressed. When you watch a program that gets your attention and offers you what you want to see, you have been hailed: viewers see themselves in the show, either explicitly identifying with characters or accepting the premise as pleasurable or interesting. For ideological messages to be conveyed effectively, programs must engage viewers, hailing them to accept the show as speaking to them personally.

How do programs hail viewers? It is more than just grabbing our attention, which is obviously a goal of all programming. Hailing tries to make viewers feel that the worldview offered by a particular program fits with their own personal outlook—a strategy that might apply to a broad range of political positions, from the far-left *The Boondocks* to the far-right *The 700 Club*. But most programs are less overt in their political viewpoints, and thus must hail viewers by making them feel comfortable with the show's perspective and encouraging viewers to identify with characters or performers. This process of **identification** invites viewers to imagine themselves as part of the text's storyworld (or perspective on the real world) and to adopt an attitude consistent with its tone. For instance, we watch *The Price Is Right* and vicariously participate in the competition, imagining how we would do at the game and picking contestants to root for. By identifying with the program, we tacitly endorse its perspective on consumerism and overt celebration of merchandise. According to such ideological theories, when you give yourself over to the pleasures of a program through identification, you accept the ideologies promoted by the show and endorse its vision of the world as your own.

Game shows and reality programs embrace hailing and identification explicitly through vicarious participation, as viewers imagine themselves competing in the televised contests; other genres offer more subtle opportunities for ideological engagement. Medical dramas typically feature characters such as *ER's* John Carter or *Grey's Anatomy's* Meredith Grey, idealistic but naïve doctors who function as viewer stand-ins as they learn about the stresses and challenges of medicine. Family sitcoms offer many points of identification, all inviting viewers to imagine themselves as part of a given family by embracing their values and beliefs, whether it is identifying as a father, a daughter, or an uncle. Cop shows typically ask viewers to identify with the legal system itself, following alongside police who try to enforce the laws and solve mysteries to maintain public safety. Soap operas invite viewers to identify as part of a community, involved in the shifting web of relationships as we generate intense attitudes toward characters as friends or enemies. Westerns place viewers in the role of white settlers building cities, often with opposition from Native Americans and other groups opposing the country's nineteenth-century expansion. All of these genres encourage viewers to identify with characters to enjoy the pleasures of the program, but through the process of identification we begin tacitly to accept the show's underlying ideologies.

One of the more explicit links between ideology and genre is the spy program, which presents American secret agents as representatives of a common national interest. Especially popular in the 1960s with shows such as *I Spy*, *Mission: Impossible*, and *The Man from U.N.C.L.E.*, spy programs invite audiences to identify with agents as cunning and often alluring extensions of government power, reinforcing dominant ideologies within the context of the cold war. Although these shows can question national norms, even mocking espionage itself, as on *U.N.C.L.E.* and the parody *Get Smart*, ultimately viewers are asked to identify as American citizens, as the narratives reinforce dominant ideologies of patriotism and nationhood. The rebirth of the spy genre in the 2000s saw shows such as *24* and *Alias* pit threatening transnational conspiracies against a reassuringly effective government response masked in secrecy and bolstered by high-end technology. These programs offer narratives that justify extreme

THE MAN FROM U.N.C.L.E.

The Man from U.N.C.L.E. (NBC, 1964–68): A witty spy show that bordered on parody in its take on James Bond–style espionage, the program inspired a dedicated cult fanbase that lasted for decades after the show left the air. *U.N.C.L.E.*'s plots notably incorporate innocent civilians in espionage drama, and focus on the transnational agency U.N.C.L.E. rather than the domestic-based agencies of the CIA or MI-6 popular in other spy narratives.

I SPY

I Spy (NBC, 1965–68): A groundbreaking espionage program that incorporates witty banter and exotic international locales, the show is best known for launching Bill Cosby's television career and featuring the first leading dramatic role for an African-American actor on television, winning Cosby Emmy Awards for all three seasons.

measures of violence and torture to overcome the terrorism that threatens the American nation from both outside and within our borders, a clear echo of cultural anxieties in the post-9/11 climate.

News programs also invite ideological identification, addressing audiences as like-minded citizens with a wise anchor presumably imparting an impartial and accurate perspective on current events. Often newscasts foreground how a story might impact an "average viewer," even addressing viewers directly in promotional clips for upcoming stories—"what you learn may surprise you," "if you think you know everything about this election, you'll be surprised," "are you doing everything you can to protect your family?" Both with rational discussions of how news stories impact everyday life and emotional appeals to stimulate viewer interest, television news regularly uses techniques to make viewers feel as if they are the personal target of a story, encouraging viewers to identify with the newscaster and accept the meanings offered as natural common sense. Opinion journalism, as discussed in chapter 4, also asks viewers to identify with pundit hosts such as Bill O'Reilly or Keith Olbermann, and to view these personalities as personal stand-ins confronting issues on our behalf. By generating a sense of identification with news personalities, television encourages viewers to watch their programs regularly and accept their underlying perspectives as cultural norms.

POLITICALLY INCORRECT

Politically Incorrect (Comedy Central, 1993–97; ABC, 1997–2002): A come-dic political talk show hosted by Bill Maher, the program brought an odd assortment of pundits, politicians, and celebrities together as a panel to debate and mock contemporary issues; the show's most notorious moment came during Maher's outspoken critique of President Bush following the attacks of September 11, 2001. After cancellation, the show was reborn on HBO as *Real Time With Bill Maher* in 2003, taking advantage of the premium channel's commercial-free model and lack of censorship to offer more provocative and profane positions.

One particular strategy used by many television programs is to evoke a feeling of patriotism in viewers, addressing audiences explicitly as Americans. Television's patriotic appeals range from program titles—*American Idol, America's Most Wanted, Good Morning America, American Dreams*—to iconography, as with the flags, eagles, and red-white-and-blue color schemes used by many news and talk shows. News and public affairs programming assumes that all viewers identify as American and thus accept government positions as the result of a democracy. The United States is a tremendously diverse country, as over 10 percent of the population are immigrants, and Americans have a much broader range of personal and political beliefs than is represented on television; however, most programming presents a patriotic belief in a common American identity as shared by all audience members.

When such nationalist and patriotic ideologies are violated, the response can be striking. Shortly after the attacks of September 11, 2001, *Politically Incorrect* host Bill Maher criticized people calling the attacks "cowardly," suggesting that the American military launching cruise missiles from afar was more "cowardly" than the airplane attacks of 9/11, as the terrorists killed themselves in the attacks. White House press secretary Ari Fleischer responded to a reporter's question about Maher's comments by asserting that given the proximity to the attacks, Americans "need to watch what they say," a remarkable comment from a government founded on freedom of speech. While Maher's show remained on ABC for six more months before being cancelled, sponsor and affiliate withdrawals were clear indications of the penalties television programs and personalities could expect for straying from dominant notions of patriotism and ideology. This instance highlights the limits to the meanings seen on television as the industry avoids programs that can be viewed as challenging national ideologies for fear of political or advertiser backlash.

Hegemony and Creating Consent

The concepts of hailing and identification suggest that ideology is not force-fed to viewers, but is accepted and often sought out by them. The term **hegemony** describes how a dominant set of ideals is accepted by the populace at large. Rather than being coerced into following propaganda, under hegemony, people actively accept ideologies as part of their everyday lives. As ideologies resonate with how people view their world, those ideologies become accepted and embraced, creating **consent** for the ruling class's positions and belief systems. Hegemony refers to the process of leading by consent of the ruled, actively accepting ideologies as part of common sense. Television and other media help to create consent by promoting dominant viewpoints and furthering the underlying economic and political systems. Unlike with theories of false consciousness, people who consent to ideology do so not by being overtly deceived into misperceiving the world, but because they feel that acceptance of the dominant ideology is ultimately preferable to attempting to fight it.

A good example of hegemony in action is NBC's political drama *The West Wing*. The show has been both hailed and criticized as a "liberal fantasy," appealing to viewers who felt that President Clinton had been too moderate and offering an idealized sanctuary for loyal Democrats during the Bush administration. However, the show's construction of an ideal Democratic president—a popular bumper sticker in the 2000 election read, JED BARTLET IS MY PRESIDENT—mixes liberal policy initiatives with an underlying patriotic and militaristic ideology that typically is seen as more conservative and linked to Republican politicians.

President Jed Bartlet on *The West Wing* offers a liberal ideal who also embraces a patriarchal militarism, an example of hegemony in action.

President Bartlet regularly leads America into armed conflict when motivated by goals of peace-keeping and global justice, and the show tempers his intellectual side with a commanding presence and religious background: prior to becoming an economist, Bartlet was planning to enter the priesthood. Bartlet also serves as the supreme father figure on the show, both for his staff, who nearly all lack family ties, and for the fictionalized country as a whole. Ultimately the program celebrates overtly patriotic visuals and music, while romanticizing a patriarchal commander in chief and the militaristic power of the presidency. For the liberal viewers who embraced the show's intellectual subtleties and moral quandaries, these ideologies of militaristic patriarchal patriotism come with the package. The show hails liberals while asking viewers to consent to underlying ideologies more consistent with the interests of NBC's parent company, General Electric, than the platform of the Democratic Party.

Ideologies need not always be aligned with right-wing over left-wing interests, although the investments and priorities of television's corporate system tend to favor interests that further consumer capitalism. One interesting aspect of television's representational spectrum is how religious beliefs appear in programming. Some American television is explicitly religious in focus, whether on channels such as Christian Broadcasting Network and PaxTV, fictional programs such as *Touched by an Angel* and *Joan of Arcadia,* or televised religious services and appeals often termed "televangelism." However, most fictional programming presents characters and families who are overwhelmingly secular, with religion playing little role in their lives. This contrasts directly with the beliefs and practices of most viewers. Surveys from 2001 suggest that the majority of American families belong to a religious congregation and 80 percent of Americans identify themselves as religiously affiliated, with more than 75 percent Christians, compared with only 15 percent self-identifying as secular. Yet on fictional television, few characters are represented as belonging to a religious community or congregation, or as identified with a belief system. Jewish characters are the one overrepresented religious group, as Jews are far more common on television than in the real world, where they comprise less than 2 percent of the American population.[1] Not only are most television characters much more secular than in real life, but programming also represents much more overt sex and violence than many religious groups believe appropriate, leading many religious figures and organizations to condemn television programming as immoral and dangerous.

How can we explain this clearly inaccurate representation of the religious character, beliefs, and practices of Americans on television programming? According to many, it is reflective more of the beliefs of Hollywood producers than most Americans. Media creators are much more secular and often Jewish in background than the general population, and thus the world seen on television might be more representative of their lifestyles. Secular programming also

TOUCHED BY AN ANGEL

Touched by an Angel (CBS, 1994–2003): A popular drama about angels sent to Earth to assist humans, the show was one of the most overtly Christian network television programs in history, generating a strong fanbase among more religious and conservative viewers, which fit with CBS's general appeal to more rural and older viewers.

purposefully depicts a world designed to appeal to the younger and more urban audiences desirable to advertisers, who are less likely to identify themselves religiously than older, rural viewers. Additionally, religion is often seen as a potentially divisive belief system, alienating viewers who may not wish to watch a show focusing on a particular denomination, or potentially angering a religious group for misrepresenting their beliefs. Ultimately television's ideological choices are almost always motivated by what the industry imagines will be the most profitable audience to sell to advertisers. If religious programming were seen as a hook for attracting valuable audiences, then networks would certainly shift their shows to include more overtly religious characters. Commercial television typically favors the ideological belief system of consumerism over religion, as it reinforces the ultimate economic goals of the industry regardless of political and cultural meanings. This is not to suggest that religious Americans are inherently more conservative in either their politics or television tastes, but that for many Christians who do define themselves as part of the religious right, fictional television's marginalization of religion and overt representation of sex and violence can be read as presenting an ideological message hostile to a widely held belief system.

Alternatives to Ideology: Television as a Cultural Forum

Ideological critics argue that television presents a consistent and uncontested vision of the world, reproducing the interests of the ruling class and the corporate television industry. However, most television shows present a more mixed set of meanings than pure ideological propaganda. For public affairs programs, diverse perspectives are represented by debates, disagreements, and competing sources of authority, as discussed in chapter 4. In fictional narratives, the status quo is always shattered by some conflict or disruption, as dramatic action moves from equilibrium to complication and back to restored equilibrium. Typically the disruption, not the equilibrium, is the focus of the narrative. Thus a typical narrative shows characters in conflict and crisis, not just an intact family unit; doctors, lawyers, and businesspeople must always encounter problems, even if those problems are overcome before the final commercial break. Even on *Dragnet,* which presents a clear ideological vision of the police as a source of stability, safety, and justice, each episode features a crime that challenges the program's underlying ideology through a violation of its shared notions of normal, acceptable behavior and beliefs. How can ideological theories explain these moments challenging the dominant ideologies featured in most programs?

Ideological critics would point to the narrative resolutions of programs as reiterating dominant perspectives. Families and institutions are upheld and restored by the end of the episode, reasserting such norms as proper and natural. But instead of viewing television programs as monologues offering a singular ideological position, we might look at any show as a collection of differing beliefs, viewpoints, and perspectives on the world. According to some critics, these differing visions coexist within programs, offering a **cultural forum** in which diverse ideas can be heard and seen. Some of these perspectives present dominant ideologies, but others might offer alternative positions and ways of looking at the world beyond hegemonic common sense. The cultural forum model suggests that television programs, especially in the classic network era, seek to reach the broadest possible audiences; thus they must offer a range of viewpoints, rather than just one dominant perspective, in order to hail viewers and promote identification. For a program to appeal to a mass audience, it must grapple with significant social and cultural issues relevant to many viewers, and offer diverse meanings relevant across the American viewing public. The show might end by reinforcing ideological perspectives, but the process of debate and conflict allows for a broader range of meanings to circulate and potentially might even undercut the dominant ideological system. This forum model treats television programs as **cultural rituals**, as viewers return to repeated formulas and plots to work through social anxieties via the process of debate and conflict offered by fictional narratives.[2]

The cultural forum model draws upon an additional meaning of the term *representation*. In America's democratic system, representation is the way of participating in political life, as citizens are represented in government via elected officials. Although we do not vote for television programs as our political proxies, the forum of television is a place where the ideals and opinions of viewers are represented in the culture, with certain positions holding power over the national common sense and others relegated to a minority dissenting role. Some programs are quite explicit in offering a forum for debating social issues through this mode of representation. Nearly every episode of *The West Wing* features multiple positions on serious matters of national importance, with dramatic action stemming from the characters' attempts to balance competing interests and beliefs around topics such as the death penalty, drug enforcement, and healthcare policy. Other programs, such as *Ally McBeal* and *The Wire,* regularly

ALLY MCBEAL

Ally McBeal (Fox, 1997–2002): Fox's hit dramedy focuses on an inse-
cure female lawyer working for an eccentric firm and juggling romantic
and professional issues. The series became known for its brief fantasy
vignettes, overt attention to social issues, and contentious representation of a professionally successful but emotionally unhappy woman.

build plots around social issues, integrating political debate into dramatic
action. While such discussions strive to incorporate a diversity of viewpoints and
often celebrate the complexities of political debate, there are always limits and
boundaries to television's cultural forum—certain positions are left unspoken or
instantly dismissed in the narrative.

A classic example of both the possibilities and limitations of an explicit cultural forum is the long-running war sitcom *M*A*S*H*. Following the hit comedy film about the Korean War from 1970, *M*A*S*H* debuted on CBS in 1972.
Although it would be hard to miss the program's overall antiwar message, most
episodes express a mix of both ideological and opposing viewpoints, along with
limits to what can be debated in its cultural forum. *M*A*S*H*'s protagonist doctors, Hawkeye Pierce and his successive bunkmates Trapper John McIntire and
B. J. Hunnicutt, regularly express disdain for the army, its policies, and the very

The cultural forum of *M*A*S*H* pitted anti-war pranksters Hawkeye Pierce and
Trapper John McIntire against conservative rule-following Frank Burns.

The Beverly Hillbillies used the contrast between the opulent world of Beverly Hills and the wacky low-class Clampetts to highlight class differences and satirize both cultural spheres.

rationale for the war that their country is fighting. Opposing positions come from rule-touting majors Margaret Houlihan and Frank Burns, who provide a typically ineffectual voice for army logic and policy, and from visiting characters who often object to the doctors' chaotic insubordination and lack of respect. While Pierce and friends usually succeed in their battles against Burns and petty army rules, they always fail in their central protest to dominant ideology—at the end of every episode except the finale, they are still stuck in a war they object to. The show offers a forum debating many issues, but limits its actions and outcomes, as main characters never desert their unit, refuse to serve, disown their own beliefs in America, or question the underlying anti-communist framework of the war. *M*A*S*H* debuted in the final years of the Vietnam War, and offers clear parallels to antiwar sentiment common among many Americans, but uses the metaphor of Korea to discuss contemporary issues only within particular limits. Thus it is a show that offers a critique of military ideology, but frames the debate within limits that refuse to allow such resistant messages to overturn the dominant system.

Programs such as *M*A*S*H* are explicit in their political debates, foregrounding social issues within the scenario, plot, and dialogue, but the majority of fictional programming is seemingly escapist and apolitical. Do such programs offer a similar cultural forum? As discussed in the next chapter, representations of identity categories including race and gender are clearly present in all programming, and such representations can be examined both ideologically and as a cultural forum. But seemingly escapist programs can also offer a perspective

THE BEVERLY HILLBILLIES

The Beverly Hillbillies (CBS, 1962–71): One of the most successful sitcoms of all-time, *The Beverly Hillbillies* dramatizes and mocks class conflicts between a rural family living in a rich neighborhood after striking it rich in oil. The series was consistent with CBS's rural lineup of the 1960s and with their nickname of "Country Broadcasting System," leaving the air when the network shifted focus to younger urban audiences in the early 1970s.

on national identity and economic systems. For instance, *The Beverly Hillbillies*, a top-rated sitcom from the 1960s, can be looked at as a purely escapist program. The show portrays the comedic exploits of extreme culture clash when a backwoods southern family relocates to Beverly Hills after striking oil. The show's reliance on physical comedy, sight gags, and naïve misunderstandings seem far less politically charged than *M*A*S*H*'s explicit social commentary. However, the central culture clash on *Hillbillies* suggests a deeper set of meanings addressing American social conditions.

The hillbilly Clampett family is often the butt of the show's jokes, which poke fun at Jethro's fifth-grade education, Granny's folk remedies, and the family's confusion over simple modern technology such as doorbells and swimming pools (which they call the "cement pond"). Thus *Hillbillies* reinforces an ideology that celebrates modern consumer culture, city life, and wealth over a rural lifestyle laughably rooted in the past. However, the show treats Beverly Hills with an equally if not more critical eye. The wealthy elitist Drysdales, neighbors to the Clampetts, are characterized as greedy, judgmental, spiteful, and unworthy of their success. While satirized as naïve rubes, the Clampetts are also validated by remaining true to their ideals, generous with their wealth, and uncorrupted by modern indulgences. When they are compared with the Drysdales and other urban characters who try to swindle the Clampetts, their rural simplicity is validated and seen as a refreshing antidote to modern city life. Thus critics have read *Hillbillies* as a forum debating urban versus rural values, critiquing consumerism and wealth, and questioning the norms of 1960s modernity.[3] Because such sentiments would be hard to express explicitly in an advertising-supported program, social commentaries must be embedded within the show's lowbrow humor, allowing the program to debate issues beneath the surface.

According to the model of the cultural forum, television programs usually contain ideological messages, but they are rarely presented without critique or conflict. Frequently, such dissenting voices are contradicted by an episode's conclusion, as ideology reasserts itself through narrative closure, but critics disagree whether such resolutions ensure dominant interpretations. For ideological critics, the dominant ideals asserted by the end of programs frequently invalidate any contrary voices; for cultural forum adherents, the debate is more important than the resolution, allowing viewers to find their own positions within the limits of the debate. How these two understandings of the interpretive process operate for actual viewers cannot be uncovered by analyzing the meanings of the text alone. Chapter 9 explores how viewers make sense of such programming, considering whether they passively absorb ideological meanings or actively negotiate with the content of programs. By looking at the range of meanings offered within any program, you can come to your own conclusions as to how much ideological voices dominate or whether contrary positions are allowed a legitimate place within the debate.

The cultural forum model was developed to explain prime time programming in the classic network era. Since viewers had few choices between shows, networks tried to air programs that would appeal to as many different audiences as possible by including a diverse range of voices and opinions in any individual show. In the multi-channel and convergence eras, mass audience programs are quite rare, as most shows aim for a niche appeal for a specific type of audience. Does this invalidate the cultural forum theory? Some programs and channels clearly strive for uniformity in appeal rather than diversity of opinion, ranging from the ethnic narrowcasting of BET or Univision to the singular political outlook of CBN or CurrentTV. But many shows still present diverse viewpoints in debate, as seen in the satirical commentary on *South Park*, the philosophical debates on *Lost*, or the range of contestants and strategies on reality shows *Survivor* and *The Amazing Race*. Perhaps network television has lost its central role as the "electronic public square" for shared rituals working through cultural anxieties, but television programming continues to offer both ideological and resistant meanings to be debated and dissected by critics and viewers alike.

PUSHING THE LIMITS OF REPRESENTATION THROUGH SATIRE

For some readers, the previous discussions about representations of national character might seem far-fetched. It's only television, right? Most programs are just designed to entertain and distract an audience, and analyzing their meanings as shaping American culture and forging national ideology might appear to overstate television's importance. While it is true that many programs are escapist entertainment and are not trying to send messages or alter the perspectives of viewers, they still help shape the way we see the world. Television exposes viewers to facets of the world exceeding their real-life experiences. When we see something new or different from our own perspectives, television can mold our perceptions of the world.

This type of cultural shaping occurs even with mundane aspects of television's universe. For instance, many young viewers had their first exposure to bars through the hit 1980s sitcom *Cheers*. The producers were not trying to warp attitudes or instill an ideological perspective on drinking, but the program offers a particular vision of a community of drinkers at a neighborhood tavern to people with no other perspective on the subject. Many programs represent aspects of the world unfamiliar to typical viewers, with such images helping to shape how we perceive these facets of American culture. Fans of *ER* feel as if they know how emergency room medicine works, *Six Feet Under* helps mold our understanding of funeral homes, and *Law & Order* shapes our expectations for how the criminal justice system should function. Some research has even proposed a "*CSI* effect," where juries expect more conclusive revelations from forensic evidence than are possible based on their assumptions fostered by the hit crime franchise. All of these programs aim to balance a sense of realism with a desire for dramatically heightened storytelling, but each also helps to shape our perspective of the world in both accurate and distorted ways.

All television contributes to our sense of the world being represented. Even highly fantastic programs such as *Star Trek* and *The X-Files* offer visions of the world that help shape our attitudes toward real-world parallels to alien encounters and government conspiracies. Just because the producers of a program are not trying explicitly to send messages about American culture does not mean that the meanings shows convey are irrelevant or should be ignored as "just entertainment." While considering the intention of producers is a useful question, it should not be the final factor in exploring the importance of representations.

Although many programs may not be motivated by anything more than entertainment, a good number of television shows are created with an agenda beyond just capturing attention. Most creators have a perspective on the world they wish to share in addition to amusing and engaging viewers. Such intentions can vary widely: *Touched by an Angel* was created to celebrate particular religious and moral perspectives, while *Will & Grace* aimed to push the boundaries of gay acceptability in different directions. From *The Cosby Show* to *Roseanne*, *The Waltons* to *Buffy the Vampire Slayer*, many of the most successful programs in television history have come from producers trying to impact viewers with a particular vision of the world and perspective on American culture. Of course such perspectives are not simply imposed on viewers, as producers must offer ideals that resonate with viewers' expectations and that usually come along with the expected pleasures of laughter, suspense, or drama. Studying television's specific strategies of representation can strengthen our appreciation of such television landmarks, and better our understanding of the medium's social impact.

WILL & GRACE

Will & Grace (NBC, 1998–2006): A hit sitcom and part of NBC's "Must See TV" lineup, the show is notable for featuring two gay lead characters and including many references to gay culture not previously seen on network television. While some critics noted that the show's contrast between straight-laced Will and flamboyant Jack reinforced stereotypes, the mere fact of a gay-themed program becoming a ratings hit ensured the series' groundbreaking status.

Satire and Parody as Social Commentary

One of the chief ways television programs engage directly with social issues is through the use of satire and parody. Satirical and parodic programs have often been popular, frequently are controversial, and pose particular problems for critics trying to analyze how they fit within their cultural contexts. The difference between satire and parody is slippery, with some critics using the terms interchangeably, but each term suggests different facets of a similar phenomenon. **Satire** is a broader term, indicating a critical commentary on a topic using pointed and often ironic humor. **Parody** refers to satirical works that directly mimic the form of another text, often changing or exaggerating the content to make fun of the original genre, style, or story. Thus *The Simpsons* offers a satirical commentary on the debates surrounding media violence when Marge campaigns to clean up the airwaves, but it uses parody to mock actual cartoons using the show-within-a-show *Itchy & Scratchy*. Parodies do not have to offer social commentary through their mockery, but at the very least they inspire viewers to take the original forms less seriously—for instance, *Police Squad!* parodies cop shows with little undercurrent of critical satire, but made it difficult for viewers to watch *Dragnet* with a straight face.

Satire and parody have been prevalent since television's earliest years, with 1950s variety/comedy shows *Your Show of Shows* and *The Jack Benny Program* offering gentle parodies of the contemporary culture of their era. Cartoons offered both social commentary, as in *The Rocky and Bullwinkle Show*'s satire of cold war politics, and parody, as with *The Flintstones*' mockery of family sitcoms, but as animated programs they were seen by most as harmless kids' fare, an assumption that would not be changed until the 1990s. The 1960s spy programs *Get Smart* and *The Man from U.N.C.L.E.* both undercut the serious tales of cold war espionage popular on other programs and in James Bond films through parody, but usually stopped short of outright criticism of American foreign policy or its underlying anti-communist ideology. Instead of direct satirical

POLICE SQUAD!

Police Squad! (ABC, 1982): This short-lived parody of cop shows lasted only six episodes, but gained a cult following and led to the successful series of *Naked Gun* movies. Undermining the deadpan style of police dramas with wacky visual jokes, puns, and reflexive humor about television conventions, the show influenced later programs including *The Simpsons* and *Family Guy* with its style of fast-paced throwaway gags.

THE ROCKY AND BULLWINKLE SHOW

The Rocky and Bullwinkle Show (ABC, 1959–61; NBC, 1961–64): A cartoon series with a satirical take on cold war culture, *Rocky and Bullwinkle* combined subtle puns, serialized far-fetched storylines, and parodies with boldly drawn animation. Although never a huge hit, the series developed a cult following and influenced later generations of animated series through its dual appeals to kids and adults.

GET SMART

Get Smart (NBC, 1965–69; CBS, 1969–70): A parody of the spy genre, *Get Smart* focused on an incompetent secret agent and his adoring partner, who accidentally manage to defeat enemy spies each episode, mocking the genre's conventional gadgetry through devices such as the shoe phone and the cone of silence.

commentaries, which typically failed with sponsors in the 1950s and early 1960s, most comedies addressed social issues through fantasy allegories, as on *The Addams Family* and *Bewitched*, or escapist farce with indirect social messages, as on *The Beverly Hillbillies*.

By the late 1960s, television attempted to be more direct in its use of social satire, especially on comedic variety programs. *Laugh-In*, a hit show known for its rapid pace of jokes, music, and go-go dancing, included political comedy among its nonstop barrage of one-liners—for instance, a political joke from a 1968 episode was "We went into Vietnam as advisors. Last week we dropped 400,000 tons of advice"—but sandwiched it among its more apolitical humor, dance numbers, and gaudy graphics. *Laugh-In* typically stopped short of full-fledged social commentary. A more overt form of satire emerged on *The Smothers Brothers Comedy Hour*. Much of the program was wholesome music and traditional comedy from the clean-cut Tom and Dick Smothers, with countercultural appeals coming more from musical guests such as activists Pete Seeger and Joan Baez. CBS actively censored songs and skits it deemed too politically explosive, but the show smuggled in satire by writing in generational code—for instance, ongoing character Goldie O'Keefe hosted a hippie housewife advice program, with nearly every line containing veiled drug references that were missed by the older censors. Even though *Smothers Brothers* was controversially cancelled after a popular but bumpy three-year run, it helped set the stage for the growing politicization of television comedy in the 1970s.[4]

Entertainment television's turn toward political commentary in the 1970s was achieved primarily in the realm of comedy and satire. As discussed in chapter 2, CBS tapped into the youth audience through socially relevant sitcoms that used satirical strategies to comment on current events: *M*A*S*H* used the parallel of the Korean War to critique American policies in Vietnam, while *All in the Family* satirized many forms of discrimination and conservative American ideals through the bigoted buffoon Archie Bunker. *Soap* was an outright parody of soap operas, mocking the genre's twisty plots and convoluted relationships through extreme scenarios such as alien abduction and demonic possession, while using its comedic framework to provide social commentary on homosexuality, race relations, and gender politics.

Hippie character Goldie O'Keefe smuggled drug and anti-war humor under the censors' radar on *The Smothers Brothers Comedy Hour*, until sponsors began to protest the subversive content.

THE SMOTHERS BROTHERS COMEDY HOUR

The Smothers Brothers Comedy Hour (CBS, 1967–69): Although the clean-cut singing comedy brothers Tom and Dick Smothers seemed an unlikely source of political controversy, their variety show included politically volatile musicians and countercultural drug and antiwar humor, and engaged in behind-the-scenes battles with network censors. A clear indication of television lagging behind cultural shifts, CBS cancelled the series to avoid conflicts with sponsors and conservative affiliates, but the series has become legendary as an example of the conflict inherent in television seeking both to engage social issues and serve commercial interests.

ALL IN THE FAMILY

All in the Family (CBS, 1971–79): One of the landmark series in American television, *All in the Family* adapted a British series to focus on the American generation gap, pitting conservative and bigoted Archie Bunker against his liberal, antiwar son-in-law, Mike Stivic. The series tackled issues of racism, homophobia, rape, feminism, the Vietnam War, and other contemporary social issues that television of the 1960s had been scared to touch, surprisingly striking a chord with a broad range of viewers to become a top hit for CBS.

One of the most important programs to popularize satire and parody is *Saturday Night Live,* which incorporates direct parodies of other media, public personalities, and cultural forms in every episode. While many of *SNL*'s parodies gently poke fun at their objects of mockery, the show can also present a more direct critical edge. Throughout its three-decade run, it has offered parodies of advertising, criticizing the basic commercial imperative of American broadcasting in a manner that has been adopted by other comedy programs such as *Mad TV* and *The Simpsons*. *SNL* also features a weekly parody of television news, "Weekend Update," in which both current events and techniques of media coverage are satirized, a clear predecessor for future fake news hit *The Daily Show*. While much of *SNL*'s success has come via apolitical comedic styles, the show has waged crucial battles with NBC's censors to push the boundaries of how television could address current events and it certainly had a clear influence on subsequence socially relevant satires. Along with British import *Monty Python's Flying Circus* and Canadian show *SCTV, Saturday Night Live* helped satirical

Original *Saturday Night Live* cast member Jane Curtin offers an advertising parody for "Fluckers Jam" from the mid-1970s, undercutting television's commercial basis while teetering on the edge of profanity.

sketch comedy emerge as a dominant force and cultural touchstone for young
audiences in the 1970s.

Television programming is certainly cyclical. The 1980s saw a more direct
engagement in social issues in dramatic programs such as *St. Elsewhere, Hill
Street Blues*, and *Cagney and Lacey*, with a decline in satire in exchange for
more character-driven comedies *Cheers* and *The Cosby Show*. Satire and parody
returned in force at the end of the 1980s with the rise of the multi-channel era.
The emergence of the Fox Network was driven partly by successful satires and
parodies, with early successes including sketch comedies *The Tracey Ullman
Show* and *In Living Color*—the latter explicitly engaging racial humor with its
predominantly black cast, pushing the limits of network standards in nearly
every sketch. Most notoriously, Fox offered the dysfunctional family sitcom
Married...with Children, a parody of sitcoms whose working title was *Not the
Cosbys. Married* pushed boundaries of sexual humor while mocking the notion
of the nuclear family as a bastion of American culture, an attitude that resulted
in a viewer-led sponsor boycott and protests to Fox. In a rare decision in which
the network sided with creators over advertisers, Fox continued to air *Married*
with little change in content, a tactic that resulted in a ratings boom from viewers curious about the controversy. Fox used these satirical programs, as well as its
longest-running hit *The Simpsons*, to craft a brand identity of a network unafraid

MARRIED...WITH CHILDREN

Married...with Children (Fox, 1987–97): Fox's first prime time series was one of its most controversial, as this satire of domestic sitcoms was critiqued for being overly lewd and anti-family. The series uses broad parody to mock gender roles and sitcom conventions, making it a less subtle companion to other dysfunctional family sitcoms of the era, *The Simpsons* and *Roseanne*.

to challenge conventions through satire and social commentary, an identity that proved to be most popular among the young and urban audiences its advertisers most desired.

Cable channels also used edgy satire to attract young audiences. MTV embraced satirical British imports such as *Monty Python* and *The Young Ones* in the 1980s, before creating their own hit *Beavis and Butthead*, which satirized both music videos and their dumbest adolescent male fans. Comedy Central embraced satire in the 1990s as well, with imports including the British *Absolutely Fabulous* and Canadian *Kids in the Hall*, and originals *Mystery*

Married...with Children offered a cartoony lampoon of family sitcoms and gender roles.

BEAVIS AND BUTTHEAD

Beavis and Butthead (MTV, 1993–97): An animated series focusing on two moronic teenage boys who crudely mock their peers, comment on music videos, and imagine that they are far cooler than they are. The series was often condemned as possessing no more intelligence than the protagonists by critics who overlooked its satirical tone, and it was notoriously blamed for inspiring a young boy to set his house on fire by emulating the characters' pyromania, despite the lack of evidence that they boy had ever seen the show.

Science Theater 3000, Politically Incorrect, and *South Park* defining the channel as the hotbed of television satire. One of Comedy Central's most striking successes is news parody *The Daily Show.* Under original host Craig Kilborn, *The Daily Show* mocked the news format but rarely engaged with political issues beyond as the object of a quick joke; when Jon Stewart took over in 1999, the "fake news" program became more explicitly engaged in political commentary and pointed criticism of how the legitimate news media fails to inform and educate viewers. As discussed in chapter 4, *The Daily Show* has demonstrated how television satire can be both entertaining and influential, as young viewers use the show as both a source of current events and a guide to decoding real news media and political rhetoric.

While satire can be a successful way to offer social commentary in an entertaining format, it risks being misunderstood. Since most satire uses irony to present an exaggerated form of what it aims to critique, viewers might not recognize such representations as satirical. This was the case with *All in the Family*, as many viewers perceived Archie Bunker's satirical racism as authentic and identified with his position, despite the producers' goal of condemning the character's views. Some misinterpretations of television satire are themselves amusing fodder for parody. For instance, in summer 2006 the legal defense team for indicted congressman Tom DeLay urged supporters to watch an interview on *The Colbert Report* with filmmaker Robert Greenwald as evidence that Greenwald was trying to smear DeLay. DeLay's team clearly missed the point that the Comedy Central program is a satirical parody of right-wing pundits, with Stephen Colbert's character asking intentionally idiotic and baiting questions of Greenwald, such as "Who hates America more, you or Michael Moore?" Obviously such an interview would be less than useful for defending DeLay when recognized as satirizing DeLay's own right-wing positions.

Other satirical programming embraces ambiguity more by design. Comedy Central's *The Man Show* can be understood in wildly different ways. On the

THE COLBERT REPORT

The Colbert Report (Comedy Central, 2005–present): A spin-off from *The Daily Show*, Stephen Colbert's parody of a pundit mocks the excesses of right-wing hosts from Fox News by offering over-the-top hyper-patriotism, an emphasis on "guts over brains," and a mock cult of personality surrounding Colbert. The show's popularity has extended into a robust online fanbase and encouraged viewer participation in various contests and pseudo-activist activities, mocking the "dittohead" audience of real pundits like Rush Limbaugh.

THE MAN SHOW

The Man Show (Comedy Central, 1999–2004): A sketch comedy with an explicitly masculine tone, *The Man Show*, with hosts Jimmy Kimmel and Adam Carolla, simultaneously embraced and mocked the lowest-common-denominator assumptions about male taste, focusing on women in skimpy outfits and toilet humor to appeal to a young, male demographic.

one hand, it appears to be the most unabashedly sexist program ever made—celebrating pornography, mocking women's shopping habits and intelligence, and ending with slow-motion shots of models jumping on trampolines. Yet it also satirizes the persona of the male buffoon who enjoys such entertainment, explicitly mocking the attitudes of the hosts, and by extension the targeted audience of young men, by highlighting their stupidity and presenting clichés of beer drinking and bathroom humor in excess. So is the program a satirical commentary on sexist men or a celebration of male fantasies of beautiful and submissive women? Probably both. The creators clearly recognize they are playing with clichés and satirizing stereotypes, but they also offer those same stereotypes as part of the show's entertainment. Satire, more than most forms of programming, offers widely divergent interpretations and viewer perspectives, a facet of television explored more fully in chapter 9.

Although satire has proven to be a popular technique for attracting young audiences, as with recent hits *Family Guy*, *Da Ali G Show*, and *Chappelle's Show*, programs can be too critical of established norms to secure a spot within the industrial system of commercial television. In the mid-1990s, documentary filmmaker Michael Moore, who had yet to become a household name following his hit films *Bowling for Columbine* and *Fahrenheit 9/11*, brought his political

TV NATION

TV Nation (NBC, 1994; Fox, 1995): Running for two summers on two different networks, Michael Moore's satirical newsmagazine took an explicit position against corporate exploitation, government corruption, and right-wing hypocrisy, making it a difficult fit for advertising-supported networks, despite solid ratings. Much of the program's approach would return to television with the field segments for *The Daily Show*, which found a better fit on cable.

humor to television on the satirical newsmagazine *TV Nation*. Stories plumbed current events with a sense of humor, as with a segment trying to raise awareness about corrupt business practice with comedic mascot Crackers the Corporate Crimefighting Chicken. However, the show's antiestablishment sensibility made it difficult to sell to sponsors—despite decent ratings, it failed to last beyond a few episodes. In general, satirical programming thrives today primarily in the form of animated cartoons, and on cable channels, where lower ratings expectations and more concentrated demographics appeal to advertisers; an influential show combining these two traits is *South Park*.

Animated Satire and the Case of *South Park*

Television animation has traditionally been a marginal genre, restricted to Saturday morning programs and cable channels aimed at kids. But in the 1990s, animation entered the mainstream in the wake of the surprise success of *The Simpsons*. Animation then became more legitimate as a form of entertainment aimed at adults, as well as a vibrant form of social commentary. From the emergence of prime time cartoons *King of the Hill* and *Family Guy* to the growth of Cartoon Network's Adult Swim block of edgy programs featuring *The Boondocks* and *Robot Chicken*, animation has emerged as one of the most creatively adventurous and politically engaged forms of television programming. Animation as a form taps into the long tradition of political cartooning and caricature, allowing satirical representations to push boundaries and challenge conventions in ways that would feel uncomfortable—or be outright impossible—in live-action programming.

South Park is a key part of the rise of animated television satire. Trey Parker and Matt Stone's aggressively vulgar and satirical cartoon helped establish Comedy Central's credibility and push forward the adult animation cycle of the 1990s. *South Park* took the critical tone of *The Simpsons* and *Beavis and Butthead* and made the satire more extreme, tackling issues ranging from hate

Comedy Central's long-running hit cartoon *South Park* is willing to put politically extreme opinions into the hands of young children, pushing boundaries through extreme satire.

speech to euthanasia, as well as plumbing the depths of bad taste from anal probes to pornography, all in a cartoon about eight-year-olds in a "quiet little" Colorado town.

Few television programs moved from the margins of the television industry into mainstream acceptance as quickly and forcefully. Parker and Stone met as students at the University of Colorado at Boulder, creating short films with a crude comedic sensibility. One of their shorts, *Jesus vs. Frosty*, used rudimentary construction-paper cut-out animation techniques to introduce a quartet of eight-year-olds who profanely narrated a battle between the holiday icons. Their films caught the eye of a Fox executive who hired the pair to create a video Christmas card with a similar sensibility. "The Spirit of Xmas," which featured a boorish battle for holiday supremacy between Jesus and Santa, eventually resolved by figure skater Brian Boitano, became a Hollywood sensation in 1995, circulating widely among producers and stars, and eventually becoming one of the first "viral videos" to gain wide distribution on the Internet. Comedy Central capitalized on the video's underground popularity, contracting Stone and Parker to create an animated series based on the kids featured in both short films.

South Park debuted on Comedy Central in the summer of 1997 to much notoriety, cultural disdain, and instant popularity among the channel's young male audience. While following the basic structure of a child-centered sitcom, complete with episode-ending moral messages about what is learned each

SOUTH PARK

South Park (Comedy Central, 1997–present): Comedy Central's most successful series took animated parody to new extremes by tackling both social issues and offering excessively vulgar content. The show has been decried as lowering the standards of American media, and celebrated for being the smartest and most insightful series on the air, highlighting how satire can be viewed in a broad range of ways.

week, the show offers topical explorations into current events and social issues. Parker and Stone use computer techniques to imitate their construction-paper aesthetic, embracing the flexibility of the technology to alter their animated sequences hours before airing programs, referring to their process as "virtually live animation." Viewers quickly made *South Park* Comedy Central's flagship program and the top-rated cable program of the late 1990s, recognizing that between the lowbrow references to "talking poo" and Chef's "salty chocolate balls" resided some of the most clever and sophisticated satire of the era.

Certainly *South Park* could never have come to air without the dual predecessors of *The Simpsons* and *Beavis and Butthead*, programs that used the innocent image of animation to offer a combination of lowbrow humor and highbrow social commentary. Like its two forebears, *South Park* provoked fears concerning its potential influence on children upon its debut. Even though Comedy Central runs the show only after 10:00 P.M. and prefaces every episode with a disclaimer stating "The Following Program Contains Coarse Language and Due To Its Content It Should Not Be Viewed by Anyone," the assumption that all animation must be for kids led to condemnation from a host of critics. Additionally, the profane dialogue and cynicism coming out of the mouths of elementary school kids struck many as the nadir of televisual bad taste. This critique was intensified by the successful merchandising of the characters, with T-shirts and toys that many felt were catering to children. Comedy Central realized that the negative publicity was drawing audiences to its taboo-busting program, especially among its core niche of young men, and thus supported and even highlighted the show's profane content and satire to attract audiences.

Parker and Stone responded to anti-*South Park* critiques within the program itself, creating their own taboo media sensation, *The Terrance and Phillip Show*. The boys' favorite television program is a never-ending succession of poorly animated "fart jokes," mimicking how some critics perceive *South Park* itself. Adults within *South Park* condemn *Terrance and Phillip*, protesting the show's negative effects and profane sensibility to the fictitious Cartoon Channel.

In 1999, Parker and Stone extended this plot in the feature film hit, *South Park: Bigger, Longer, and Uncut*; the highly profane film focuses on the corrupting influence of *Terrance and Phillip*'s feature film, which inspires extreme vulgarity in the impressionable minds of South Park's youth, resulting in a backlash that leads to the United States going to war with Canada and triggering Armageddon. While certainly outrageous in every taboo-busting possibility, the film was also hailed by many critics as one of the finest musicals and social satires in years.

South Park has continued to receive strong ratings and generate controversy throughout its run. Notably in "Trapped in the Closet," an episode from 2005, the show satirizes the Church of Scientology as based on a bad science fiction story, and portrays its celebrity endorsers Tom Cruise and John Travolta as brainwashed dupes, a storyline that dared the notoriously litigious religion to sue the show's producers. While as of yet no lawsuits have been filed, the episode led to the resignation of Scientologist Issac Hayes from his role as the voice of Chef, as well as Comedy Central pulling reruns of the episode due to alleged pressure from Cruise toward parent company Viacom. The show got its revenge on both, running an episode in the following season in which Chef gets brutally killed after being brainwashed by a cult, and another mocking Comedy Central for refusing to air controversial content.

Few shows in television history have as consistently satirized and mocked taboos and touchy subjects, including its own supporters in the media industry, as has *South Park*. The show's role as the contemporary standard-bearer for social satire on television was reinforced in 2003 when television pioneer Norman Lear joined the program as a creative consultant, endorsing Parker and Stone's brand of humor as the direct descendant of his own groundbreaking 1970s comedies such as *All in the Family*, *Maude*, and *Good Times*. In recognition of *South Park*'s commitment to free speech and ability to combine strident commentary with humor, in 2005 the show won a coveted Peabody Award, which recognizes excellence in television programming.

How might we characterize the politics of a show like *South Park*? For some, it might seem left-leaning as it pushes boundaries of free speech, criticizes racism and homophobia, and mocks ideological traditions of family, religion, and group conformity. However, it equally condemns ideals and practices tied to the left, like hate-crime legislation, anti-corporate rhetoric, and the opinions of liberal celebrities such as Barbra Streisand and Rob Reiner. In many ways the show endorses a libertarian perspective, critical of any interventions into personal freedoms and skeptical of authority and institutions of any political persuasion. More than any one issue, *South Park* aims its satire at hypocrisy and threats to the free expression of ideas, and is willing to skewer both liberals and conservatives for such offenses. Some commentators dubbed the term "*South Park* Republican" to stand in for the show's political persuasions and represent its typical fans, although there is little evidence that its fans or creators identify

> **FAMILY GUY**
>
> *Family Guy* (Fox, 1999–present): A brash animated sitcom known for its random vignettes and often crude sensibility, the series was cancelled in 2002 due to low ratings. However, popular reruns on Cartoon Network and a successful DVD release led Fox to reconsider, bringing the show back to the network in 2005, where it has gotten more consistent ratings.

with the Republican Party over any other party or organization. The show's core audience is young men, but their political affinities are far more diverse, attracting fans from across the political spectrum.

Through its defense of free speech and willingness to break taboos, *South Park*—and other shows following in its wake, such as *Family Guy* and *Drawn Together*—is often hailed as battling against **political correctness**, or PC. In many ways, PC is itself an invention of the politicized culture wars of the 1990s. While many media outlets had been challenged by marginalized groups to offer more positive and visible representations, conservative commentators proclaimed that this was a coordinated effort to restrict expression and force a singular orthodoxy of "correct" opinion. While it remains debatable whether PC was ever actually a significant force to restrict speech, or just a dismissive term to belittle attempts to foster more respectful language and inclusive representations, many people do feel that restrictions on potentially offensive expressions have led to a restricted climate.

In the wake of such debates in the 1990s, a "politically incorrect" mode of expression emerged as typified by *South Park*—taboo-busting content that tries to shock viewers and mock attempts to stifle speech. However, much of the boundary-pushing content on such programs has little to do with issues of PC. The mode of "correct" speech labeled as PC is concerned with eliminating stereotypes of identity groups expressing sexism and racism, not policing against the profanity and lewdness that typifies so-called politically incorrect programs *South Park* and *Family Guy*. Right-leaning politicians and pundits who rail against PC restraints in the name of free speech are ironically often in favor of restricting the amount of sexual and obscene content on the airwaves through content regulations, as with those that emerged in the wake of the Janet Jackson Super Bowl performance.

Ironically, it would seem that the reaction against the (perhaps nonexistent) threat of being constrained by PC doctrines actually made more of an impact than any efforts to restrict programming to a singular set of "correct" representations by PC campaigners. While certainly some representations from the early days of television, such as the minstrelsy of *Amos 'n' Andy* discussed in chapter

CHAPPELLE'S SHOW

Chappelle's Show (Comedy Central, 2003–06): A sketch comedy show known for edgy racial humor, the series was among Comedy Central's most popular when host Dave Chappelle abruptly quit during production of the third season. The program's legacy lives on in reruns and DVD popularity, with sketches such as the blind African-American white supremacist and the black George Bush entering everyday pop culture vocabulary.

8, would not be acceptable on today's airwaves, this stems from large-scale shifts in cultural norms and racial equality, not a coordinated campaign of PC activists. Politically incorrect programs revel in offering representations that many claim to be "unacceptable" yet regularly make it to the airwaves—for instance, *Chappelle's Show* offers a blind black man who is a white supremacist spewing racist remarks, while *The Man Show* flaunts sexist language and images unlike anything ever represented prior to the so-called PC era. Many of these programs offer such extreme representations for satirical purposes, following *All in the Family's* legacy. Thus *South Park's* one African-American child character is named "Token Black" and excels at playing bass guitar "naturally" because of his race, a self-aware mockery of racial stereotypes.

To call such representations "politically incorrect" seems to miss the point allegedly motivating PC in the first place: to call attention to how representations and images can be discriminatory and to encourage more self-aware forms of expression. Presenting satirical extremes of racism and discrimination accomplishes such goals, and would likely only be protested by viewers unable to appreciate the show's irony. To understand the full dynamics of how the PC debates relate to representations, we need to focus on the specific ways television represents people's identity, the topic of the next chapter.

FURTHER READING

Many critical accounts of television explore the medium's politics of representation, with theories of ideology, hegemony, and cultural forums explored in nearly all cultural analyses of television. For an overview and application of such theories, see John Fiske, *Television Culture* (New York: Routledge, 1987). Todd Gitlin, "Prime Time Ideology: The Hegemonic Process in Television Entertainment," in *Television: The Critical View*, ed. Horace Newcomb, 5th ed. (New York: Oxford University Press, 1994), 516–36, offers an ideological approach, in contrast with Horace Newcomb and Paul M Hirsch, "Television as Cultural Forum," in *Television: The Critical View*, ed. Horace Newcomb, 5th ed. (New York: Oxford University Press, 1994), 503–15.

A number of specific analyses of television's cultural politics explore the issues outlined in this chapter in specific historical eras. Michael Kackman, *Citizen Spy: Television, Espionage, and Cold War Culture* (Minneapolis: University of Minnesota Press, 2005), considers how American identity is articulated within the spy genre, while Aniko Bodroghkozy, *Groove Tube: Sixties Television and the Youth Rebellion* (Durham, N.C.: Duke University Press, 2000), looks at youth representations in the 1960s as a site of hegemony. The work of Douglas Kellner fits in to this paradigm focusing on contemporary media issues, especially *Media Culture: Cultural Studies, Identity, and Politics Between the Modern and the Postmodern* (London: Routledge, 1995), and *Media Spectacle and the Crisis of Democracy: Terrorism, War, and Election Battles* (Boulder, Colo.: Paradigm, 2005).

Satire has been on the rise as an object of critical analysis. See Jonathan Gray, Jeffrey P. Jones, and Ethan Thompson, eds., *Satire TV: Politics and Comedy in the Post-Network Era* (New York: New York University Press, 2009), for a range of perspectives on the topic, and Carol A. Stabile and Mark Harrison, eds., *Prime Time Animation: Television Animation and American Culture* (New York: Routledge, 2003), provides a range of analyses on animated satires, including *South Park*, while Jonathan Gray, *Watching with* The Simpsons: *Television, Parody, and Intertextuality* (New York: Routledge, 2005), offers an account of television parody focused on the most successful animated program.

NOTES

[1] Barry A. Kosmin and Egon Mayer, "American Religious Identification Survey 2001," The Graduate Center of the City University of New York, available online at http://www.gc.cuny.edu/faculty/research_briefs/aris/aris_index.htm.

[2] See Horace Newcomb and Paul M. Hirsch, "Television as Cultural Forum," in *Television: The Critical View*, ed. Horace Newcomb, 5th ed. (New York: Oxford University Press, 1994), 503–15.

[3] David Marc, *Demographic Vistas: Television in American Culture*, rev. ed. (Philadelphia: University of Pennsylvania Press, 1996).

[4] See Aniko Bodroghkozy, *Groove Tube: Sixties Television and the Youth Rebellion* (Durham, N.C.: Duke University Press, 2000).

CHAPTER 8

REPRESENTING IDENTITY

Some critics following either the ideological or forum approaches outlined in chapter 7 examine how television represents the American nation, focusing on its political and economic systems. Representational analysis in this vein is inherently political, invested in how television helps shape national norms tied to the power of one group of people to rule over the majority. However, for most cultural scholars, politics extend beyond institutional systems of government and economics; the insights of feminism and critical race theory have insisted that the personal is political. Thus television not only defines America's cultural norms concerning democracy and class differences, but also asserts what it means to be female, Latino, or gay, all of which are part of a broader sense of **cultural politics**. Following this approach, many television scholars examine how television represents particular social groups and establishes cultural norms and expectations for a particular category of **identity**.

Many studies of representation and identity focus on how television portrays minorities, considering how groups such as African-Americans or lesbians are represented or even included within programming. However, the "minority" label is complicated concerning gender representation, as women are actually a slight majority of the American population—yet still are often represented as lacking the social power and legitimacy of men, especially in terms of political, economic, and intellectual achievements. Likewise it is hard to view groups such as children or the elderly as "minorities," as each individual passes through

305

different ages throughout his lifecycle. Thus scholars often frame their analysis as focusing on the representation of **subordinate groups**, examining how media present identity categories differing from the socially dominant position of a white, male, heterosexual adult. Additionally, we can examine the representation of this **dominant identity**, looking at how television offers particular meanings surrounding whiteness, masculinity, and heterosexuality. In essence, the study of identity is the study of difference, contrasting the varying norms and assumptions tied to both dominant and subordinate identity categories.

Representations of identity help define what a culture thinks is normal for a particular group, how behaviors and traits fit into a society's shared common sense. Such representations also directly impact how we think about ourselves: when television constructs norms for a group we belong to, we might compare our own behavior to that representation; when it represents a group different from ourselves, television can shape how we view other people. Chapter 9 will explore how actual viewers consume representations and to what degree television shapes our beliefs, but this chapter explores some of the central ways scholars have studied three particular types of identity categories: race and ethnicity, gender, and sexual orientation.

APPROACHES TO STUDYING IDENTITY

How do we study television's representation of identity? It can be quite a daunting process, as there are so many differing groups of people who may be represented, with an almost infinite number of programs across the television schedule to consider. Thus we can never assert that television as a whole represents a particular group with only one set of meanings and norms; there are always exceptions and contradictions surrounding any common representation. But patterns do emerge, within particular historical moments, for specific genres, and surrounding certain identity categories. Thus representational analysis can explore how particular groups are represented in dominant ways within certain parameters, which is the goal of most studies of identity on television.

A study of how television represents particular groups can follow a number of different methods and approaches, all of which can be useful for answering particular questions. No one approach to studying identity can yield all the answers, as each question demands a different approach and method. We can outline some of the major approaches to studying identity representations, considering what each might explain about the ways television creates an image of different types of people.

One facet of representation concerns what we might call **creator identity**: How does the identity of people who produce programming help shape

CAGNEY & LACEY

Cagney & Lacey (CBS, 1982–88): A groundbreaking cop show focused on the life of two female police officers, the show combined crime stories with issues confronting women in the workplace, including family troubles, breast cancer, sexual harassment, and discrimination. The series had a small but dedicated fanbase that successfully lobbied to bring the show back after it was cancelled following its low-rated first season, and eventually became a solid hit, winning numerous awards.

representation? Within literary studies, we often assume that the gender or race of an author helps shape his or her fictional representations; likewise, a female or African-American filmmaker might be studied for offering a particular voice or outlook tied to her own identity. However, television is such a collaborative and industrialized form that it is difficult to regard any producer simply as an "author." All programs are shaped by both the creative decisions of a large number of producers, and the goals and practices of the television industry. Thus there are relatively few studies of television authors and how their identities shape the texts they produce.

We can still consider the role of creator identity in shaping meanings and representations, especially in particular instances. The 1980s police drama *Cagney and Lacey* was created by two female writers, Barbara Avedon and Barbara Corday, who used the show to explore how professional women were treated in predominantly male workplaces, an issue framed by their own experiences and influenced by their involvement in feminist activism of the 1970s. Bill Cosby, who has both starred in and produced such programs as *Fat Albert*, *The Cosby Show*, and *Cosby*, has explicitly worked to present what he sees as "positive images" of African-Americans on television. When Ellen DeGeneres publicly came out as a lesbian, so did her sitcom character on *Ellen*, a show she produced and starred in. In these instances, the identity and perspective of the producers helped shape the way their television programs represented various subordinate groups and framed the perspective each offered on identity.

However, none of these producers was acting as sole creator, as the representations offered by their programs were shaped by a large number of additional producers and network executives, which approved only those representations regarded as appropriate to achieve their respective creative and commercial goals. We can better understand the ways television presents meanings and constructs identities by examining the negotiations between various creative practices and institutional pressures, considering how representations emerge

ELLEN

Ellen (ABC, 1994–98): *Ellen* would have been barely remembered as a mar-
ginally successful sitcom vehicle for comedienne Ellen DeGeneres except
for a bold shift in 1997, when both the actress and her character came
out publicly as lesbians to great public controversy. The resulting notoriety boosted the show's ratings briefly, but the show's shift in tone and
focus eventually wore out its welcome a season later, but not before
opening the door for subsequent gay-centered programs such as *Will &
Grace* to air without generating significant controversy.

through the interaction of these often-competing forces. But while the identity
of creators can help shape representations, they can never be seen as simply the
defining factor in determining the meanings of a television text.

The majority of studies looking at representation analyze television texts
themselves, more than looking at their creators. One early approach to studying representation, which still persists among some critics and everyday viewers, has been referred to as **image analysis**. An image analysis assumes that the
representations of identity offered on television screens can be assessed and
judged around two basic questions: are images accurate, and are images positive?
Thus the images of female bodies commonly presented on television might
be viewed as inaccurate by their overemphasis on thinness and unrealistic (or
even unhealthy) beauty norms. African-American representation could be condemned for overrepresenting blacks as criminals and thus creating an unrealistic and potentially damaging portrait of the world. Image analysis looks at the
surface presentation of characters and meanings, categorizing them based on
accuracy and social value.

Such studies often follow a quantitative research method called **content
analysis**, in which researchers define specific parameters to measure within a
selected group of programs and count the appearance of different image categories. Content analysis is best for answering questions in which the coding
of images is most clear-cut and objective, as with appearance and visibility of
certain identity categories. For instance, one study measured the level of racial
diversity among prime time network entertainment programs as compared to
the U.S. population in 1999. Based on this content analysis, white people were
found to be slightly more common on television than in the actual population
(74 percent of television characters, 71 percent of the population), but television
actually overrepresents African-Americans (18 percent on television, 12 percent
of the population) while significantly underrepresenting Hispanics (3 percent
on television, 12 percent of the population) and Asian-Americans (1 percent on

television, 4 percent of the population). This study further considers whether such characters are presented in positive or negative lights, the significance of their roles, and the genre and network they are found on—thus the overrepresentation of African-Americans might be rethought when considering that almost half of all these characters appeared on WB or UPN sitcoms with predominantly black casts appealing nearly exclusively to black audiences, such as *Malcolm & Eddie* and *The Steve Harvey Show*.[1] While such quantitative statistics might assess television's presentation of racial groups, they do not tell the full story of representation. Each individual character and narrative might offer a range of different meanings and perspectives that cannot simply be counted. Furthermore, attempts to code and quantify representations as "positive" or "negative" are clearly much more difficult and subjective than is measurement of a character's race, gender, profession, or appearance, suggesting some of the limits to content analysis as a research method.

Image analyses and quantitative content analyses tend to draw upon the notion of **stereotypes**: narrow, oversimplified, and inaccurate definitions of cultural identity. While select elements of a stereotype might be true about some members of a cultural group, the stereotype reduces all aspects of the group to a small set of characteristics and erases any diversity within the group itself. The stereotypical behavior of effeminate gay men may apply to some people, but by no means typifies the entire range of behaviors and personalities within the larger population of homosexuals. Media images help reinforce stereotypes in viewers' minds, furthering negative assumptions about subordinate groups for outsiders and belittling people's identities. Critics can examine programs looking to identify stereotypes and label images as harmful, such as sexist portrayals of women or racist representations of minorities. This type of assessment is also quite common among everyday viewers. We have all seen images on television programs that strike us as demeaning toward a particular group or misrepresenting the diversity of our own experiences. Identifying and criticizing stereotypes is an important aspect of studying media representations.

Yet examining stereotypes also poses some problems. Approaches to stereotypes and image analysis assume that images can be viewed as essentially positive or negative, representing a group effectively or inflicting harm. But in practice, such clear-cut assessments are usually somewhat blurred. For instance, *The Sopranos* has been critiqued and boycotted by some groups for perpetuating Italian stereotypes, portraying Italian Americans as violent, uneducated mobsters obsessed with food and hypocritical in their Catholicism. While certainly the show offers many characters who fit that type, *Sopranos* also features Italian American doctors, FBI agents, priests, and students at elite colleges—and even one character who heads an organization protesting media stereotypes of Italian Americans! Additionally, the show is by design about a Mafia family, and thus must feature criminals engaging in immoral behavior; any crime program

Sopranos characters Tony Soprano and Silvio Dante might represent Italian-American stereotypes, but the wide range of behaviors offered by the characters over many years complicates simplistic negative readings.

will necessarily represent loathsome characters regardless of their race or ethnicity. While lead Mafioso Tony Soprano is certainly not presented as an admirable role model, the show does suggest that behind his exterior brutality lies a swamp of moral conflicts and an intelligent and at times even humane person seeking redemption from his actions and lifestyle. Thus while some people focus on the show's stereotypes, other viewers consider its counter-stereotypes and the complications of ethnic identities portrayed in the program. Such a program, therefore, cannot be simply praised or dismissed using the language of positive or negative images.

Image analyses tend to consider the surface representations of a group across a range of programs or episodes. One of the criticisms of such an approach is that it removes representations from their contexts, narrowly evaluating images without considering their role within narratives, genres, industrial strategies, and historical moment. The brief image of someone on the news might be tabulated with the same criteria used to judge characters in a sitcom. Another approach to representation draws attention to such contexts: **textual analysis** takes an in-depth interpretive approach to a program to understand what it might be saying about identity and how representations fit within broader cultural assumptions and contexts. A textual analysis examines how a program creates meanings using formal attributes, production techniques, and narrative strategies detailed in chapters 5 and 6, considering how such elements convey meanings and representations. Thus rather than quantifying identity categories across a range of programming, a textual analysis looks at an individual program or specific

THE SOPRANOS

The Sopranos (HBO, 1999–2007): A landmark series focusing on the family and professional life of a Mafia leader, the show was hailed by many as an artistic peak for television and established HBO as the leader for innovative television drama. The series incorporates many techniques from art cinema and gangster films, raising the aesthetic possibilities of television and featuring some of the most acclaimed performances ever seen on television.

episode as providing a window into broader cultural practices concerning identity, often highlighting how meanings within one given program fit into larger patterns of ideology or debates within a cultural forum.

Textual analyses can still address some of the issues common to image analyses, such as evaluating positive or negative images, or identifying stereotypes. But a close analysis of an individual program usually complicates the simple "yes or no" evaluation typical of image analyses, as most television shows contain more contradictions and conflicting messages than can be coded as positive or negative. Often a character's identity will transform over the course of a narrative: a racist character might learn the error of his ways throughout the episode, or a relationship will develop that challenges our initial impressions of a character. Thus instead of trying to simplify representations as positive or negative, a textual analysis looks more to the processes by which television can convey and change identity categories. For instance, camera angles, costuming, and performance styles might convey different meanings between female characters who are presented as sexually appealing and those who are not portrayed as beautiful; these techniques help reinforce gender assumptions about sexuality and identity, which might link to how the characters behave within the narrative. By looking at more than just the surface image, a textual analysis can highlight the specific ways identity is represented throughout American culture.

Many scholars who analyze identity via textual analysis consider that media not only reflect existing identity norms, but also help shape those norms within the culture. One important theory argues that categories such as race and gender are **social constructions**, not naturally inherent features. Obviously our identities are grounded in physical realities, with biological traits identifying people's gender, and appearance as one factor signalling race. However, to say that race and gender are socially constructed is to highlight how the specific meanings of categories such as "male" or "Latina" are culturally variable and molded by social practices in specific historical moments. While there may be physical traits that indicate someone's identity, it is only through cultural practice that these markers mean anything. For instance, why does skin color define racial identity, while eye color or height does not? These connections between specific physical traits, cultural categories of identity, and the assumed meanings of those identities are generated through social practices with their own distinct histories. Media representation is one of the chief realms where such identity categories are constructed.

For instance, *Gilmore Girls* features Lane Kim, one of the few Asian American characters on a network prime time series, as the best friend of teenager Rory Gilmore. Lane is Korean American, with an immigrant mother who tries to keep her within strict traditions both of her Korean ancestry and evangelical Christian faith. However, Lane is rebelliously focused on her eclectic musical tastes, drumming in a rock band, and dating white boys her mother disapproves of. Throughout the show, Lane and Mrs. Kim represent generational conflicts heightened by the culture clash common to immigrant families. The show clearly offers these conflicts as a cultural forum, debating assimilation into American culture versus retaining ethnic roots and values, and generally siding with Lane's attempts to distance herself from the often-laughable attitudes of her mother. However, the representation of the Kims is complicated when viewed in the context of the entire show: Lane and her mother are nearly always featured as marginal figures within the story, offering a counterpoint to the dramatic action of the white Gilmore family via secondary plots, or by Lane offering

Lane and Rory on *Gilmore Girls* are interracial best friends that seems to offer a "positive image" of Asian-Americans, but Lane always plays a subordinate role within the show's narrative, marking her as different from the Gilmores.

JACKASS

Jackass (MTV, 2000–02): A popular show among young men that has led to a successful film series, *Jackass* features a crew of daredevils subjecting themselves to dangerous and humiliating stunts accompanied by wisecracking commentary among the group. Not surprisingly, the show generated controversy and fears of copycat accidents and the general complaints about lowering standards of entertainment,typical of gripes aimed at media popular with youth.

comfort and support to Rory. Additionally, the actresses playing Lane and Mrs. Kim are actually of Japanese American descent, a crucial difference in ethnic identity that Asian American viewers recognize, but that is typically erased in American media. Thus the program's representations of Asian Americans cannot simply be viewed as stereotypical or positive, but as an ongoing construction of assumed meanings and identities played out within the context of the narrative and performances.

Entire channels can help construct identity categories, too. Since its debut in the early 1980s, MTV has been a primary arena for young people to view visions of American culture and to constitute their identity. Critics have analyzed how the channel's presentation of music videos from hard rock to hip-hop furthers particular norms of gender identity, particularly in representing women as highly sexualized objects of desire for an ideal young male viewer. MTV's non-music programming also works as a site of gender construction. In the early 2000s, most programs, ranging from *Jackass* to *The Real World* to MTV's *Spring Break*, offered two distinct gender norms for teen viewers. Male viewers were offered the figure of "the mook," a crude and obnoxious prankster who mocks social norms using bathroom humor typified by Tom Green and *Jackass* performers. Female viewers were given "the midriff," a hypersexual girl who aggressively flaunts her body and sexuality, following the success of Britney Spears and Christina Aguilera. While certainly these personality types exist in some real-world teens, they are framed as the ideal on MTV, which further reinforces these types in real viewers and legitimizes their representations in an ongoing cycle.[2] Such representations both reflect and construct reality, shaping norms through repetition and validation, and expressly tied to the marketing strategies of the commercial television industry through advertising and branding.

Likewise, genres can be explicitly linked to identity categories, helping to represent particular meanings and to address specific audiences. As discussed in chapter 6, some genres have had a long-established connection to gender identities. The assumed audience of soap operas has always been female, and thus the meanings offered by soaps have been regarded as tied to feminine values and ideals. Likewise, sports and news have traditionally been gendered as masculine in their address, meanings, and assumed cultural importance. The identity categories linked to most genres are typically understood on a continuum in comparison to other genres. While most people would not necessarily think of medical shows as particularly gendered, they are seen as less feminine than soap operas and less masculine than cop shows. Sitcoms are not necessarily linked to a racial identity, but far more shows focused on African-American characters are comedies than dramas. When genres are mixed, their assumed identity categories can often resonate in interesting and creative ways. For instance, *Hill Street Blues* combined the masculine address of the gritty urban police drama with the feminine appeals of melodramatic relationship dramas pulled from soap operas, leading to a show that both confounded traditional genre norms and appealed to a varied audience. Likewise, *Buffy the Vampire Slayer* played with the masculine gender norms of horror fiction by making the supernaturally powerful hero a petite cheerleader, integrating the feminine appeals of teen dramas to create an explicit statement of female empowerment. Genres have no inherent relationship with identity categories and thus can shift assumed identities in different historical contexts, but linking genre and identity representation is a powerful way ideological meanings can be both maintained and debated.

All analyses of representation recognize that television's portrayal of identity categories shapes American culture, molding the commonsense norms defining groups and shaping what we assume about ourselves and others. Whether you use content analysis to count images or textual analysis to analyze identity constructions, it is crucial to realize how the people we see on television programs stand for more than just their individual characters. They often represent an entire racial or sexual identity in the minds of viewers, and thus must be analyzed in their cultural contexts. Such representations do not cause viewers to misperceive the world, but rather they offer the vocabulary for viewers to see themselves and others. For people whose cultural encounters might be limited by age, region, class, or race, televised representations are a chief way of imagining others outside of their context, and thus they bear tremendous power in shaping people's cultural perspectives. Scholars have focused in detail on the specific categories of race, gender, and sexual orientation, examining the historical transformations of representing identity within each of these three areas, with each area offering particular aspects of representation worth considering in depth.

REPRESENTING RACE AND ETHNICITY

Racial differences lie at the core of American society, with its history of violence and divisiveness along racial lines, as well as the centrality of immigration throughout the country's evolution. Racial and ethnic representations have also played a central role in the history of television, charting changing social attitudes and shaping public opinion in powerful ways. Race and ethnicity are both difficult terms to define, as they are dependent on historical contexts and shifting social norms. For instance, in the early nineteenth century, Irish Americans were considered a racial group distinct from whites, while today they would be seen as an assimilated ethnic identity among white people. Generally, **race** is categorized by physical features, most typically skin color, while **ethnicity** is tied to national origins and cultural practices including religion. Both race and ethnicity are cultural systems of identity that group people by their ancestry and presumed behaviors and traits. Recognizing how race and ethnicity categories have shifted over time makes it clear how most of these assumed norms and behaviors of groups are culturally constructed, rather than rooted in physicality or heritage.

Throughout television history, the majority of programs have presented characters and performers unmarked in their racial and ethnic identity. In America, this "default" identity is white: a light-skinned person without explicit ties to any specific heritage, encompassing a range of European ethnic backgrounds, usually without clear identification. Whiteness has persisted as a norm throughout television history, with a presence so ubiquitous that most viewers do not even perceive most white characters as having any racial designation. Typically critics would not choose a program with predominantly white characters, such as *Everybody Loves Raymond* or *Sex and the City*, to analyze race and ethnicity, preferring to focus on representations of non-white characters. However, there is much to be learned by examining the representations of whiteness within a specific program or historical era.

For instance, the late 1950s saw the rise of two genre cycles presenting distinct meanings of whiteness: suburban family sitcoms such as *Father Knows Best*, *The Donna Reed Show*, and *Leave It to Beaver*, and Westerns including *Gunsmoke*, *The Rifleman*, and *Rawhide*. While these programs are quite different in their settings, tone, and meanings, both genres portray white Americans as the norm for their era, at the center of their respective communities and defining national and familial morals. Both genres erase the historical racial differences that defined their eras—between white settlers, Native Americans, Chinese and Mexican laborers, and migrating blacks in the nineteenth-century West, and the emerging civil rights movement in the segregated 1950s—focusing nearly exclusively on white characters as representing the nation's past and present. In both of these instances, it is important to recognize the focus on white characters as an active choice that furthers certain meanings, solidifying the ideology of white identity at the center of the American nation and placing non-white groups on the margins.

While whiteness is certainly the norm for the bulk of American television, racial analyses tend to look at examples of non-white groups from a variety of

KUNG-FU

Kung Fu (ABC, 1972–75): A mixture of the Western and martial arts drama, *Kung Fu* focuses on Shaolin master Caine wandering the American Old West in search of his half-brother, with frequent flashbacks to his Kung Fu training in China. The show was part of the growing popularity of martial arts in 1970s America, and Caine's nickname, "Grasshopper," was a frequent pop culture reference.

perspectives: identifying stereotypes, recovering the work of marginalized minority producers, and considering how television constructs racial categories. When studying racial and ethnic groups, one key issue concerns **visibility**: Are characters presented who are noticeably non-white? For some races, including black and Asian, visibility is literal, as a performer's physical appearance usually indicates racial identity, or at least marks someone as non-white. For ethnic groups, such as Latino and Irish, characters and performers often must be identified explicitly via ethnic names, accents, or direct reference to heritage. At times actors will portray characters across racial and ethnic lines, as with Latina actress Alexis Bledel playing the white Anglo-Saxon character of Rory Gilmore on *Gilmore Girls*, or white actor David Carradine playing part-Chinese character Kwai Chang Caine on 1970s hit *Kung Fu*. Such instances provoke questions about visibility and representation: Is an effective performance more important than playing within an actor's racial identity? And where might we draw the line? Would it be appropriate for an actor to wear makeup to appear to be another race? Can actors play characters only within their own ethnic identity? Does it matter if an actor playing a stereotypical role is actually a member of the represented group? There are no simple answers when confronting such charged issues of racial identity.

Ethnic and racial visibility varies across different historical moments. While the 1950s is remembered as an era of white dominance on television, the early 1950s actually featured a broad range of racial and ethnic representations. Many early programs, often imported from radio, focused on families of distinct ethnic identities, such as the Jewish family of *The Goldbergs*, Norwegian immigrants on *Mama*, and Italian Americans on *Life with Luigi*. African-Americans were represented, although not necessarily with much respect, on *Amos 'n' Andy*, *Beulah*, and *The Jack Benny Program*, and the co-star and producer of the era's most popular show, Desi Arnaz, on *I Love Lucy*, is clearly identified as a Latino American in a mixed marriage, both in real life and on the show. While many of these representations played upon stereotypes and might be regarded as negative images, the range of ethnic and racial identities seen on fictional television

THE GOLDBERGS

The Goldbergs (CBS, 1949–51; NBC, 1953–54; DuMont, 1954; syndication, 1955–56): Based on a long-running NBC radio show, *The Goldbergs* focuses on a Jewish immigrant family living in the Bronx and later suburban Connecticut, and includes ethnic humor and tales of American assimilation across generations. The show, which switched networks frequently during its multi-year run, was created, written, and produced by star Gertrude Berg, making it one of the first and most notable television programs run by a female producer.

in the early 1950s was far more broadly inclusive than it would be for another twenty years, and certainly featured non-white performers far more than non-fiction news and talk shows of the times. This moment of heightened diversity was in part due to the legacy of radio, where ethnic diversity was embraced for the variety of vocal accents and dialects it provided. But critics have also pointed to how these programs served as a nostalgic anchor to tie the emerging communities of postwar homogenous suburbs to the prewar urban ethnic neighborhoods that were dwindling in the 1950s. Television's early ethnic representations reminded viewers of their roots, a function that became less needed as the suburbs became more familiar by the end of the decade. Non-ethnic whiteness then became entrenched as the standard mode of representation across television genres for subsequent decades.[3]

Tracing the history of representations of African-Americans provides the clearest indication of the range of ways a group might be portrayed on television, and the power of such representations to culturally define a group. The portrayals of black characters and performers have shifted throughout television history, alongside developing industrial strategies and social upheavals that have influenced the images that appear on-screen. Early 1950s programs featured blacks in subservient roles, playing to stereotypical notions of African-Americans that had lingered for decades: the overweight black mammy serving as a maid to a white family, as on *Beulah* and *Make Room for Daddy*, or the subservient Uncle Tom characters on *Trouble with Father* and *My Little Margie*. For most fictional programs of the 1950s, black characters functioned to support white characters, offer comic relief at their own expense, and passively justify a segregated American society. Such meanings clearly link to dominant ideologies of the era, as segregation and discrimination were part of the broader American "common sense" that the civil rights movement was working to combat and overturn.

The complicated exception is *Amos 'n' Andy*, which presents an all-black community in Harlem and features what would be the largest number of

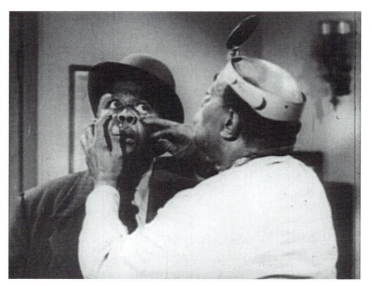

The black characters on *Amos 'n' Andy* were buffoons inspired by minstrel performances, but provided African-American performers an opportunity to star on television that would disappear for years after the show's cancellation.

African-American actors in an ongoing television series until the 1970s. *Amos 'n' Andy* was adapted from one of radio's most popular programs, which portrays highly stereotyped black characters as lazy buffoons and cowardly crooks—all voiced by white actors using minstrel dialects and appearing in blackface makeup for public appearances. For television, the white producers hired an all-black cast to play the minstrel-inspired roles well known to radio audiences. Not surprisingly, many African-American viewers took great offense, fearing that such a sitcom might be viewed as representing an entire race with demeaning images, which led to an NAACP protest and lawsuit against CBS in 1951. For other African-American viewers, however, the show was more ambiguous: it provided opportunities for visibility and employment for black actors, humanizing the stereotypical characters and featuring humor beyond just stereotypes. These supporters of *Amos 'n' Andy* feared that if the program were cancelled under protest, African-Americans would disappear from the screen entirely—a fear that turned out to be true once the show left the air in 1953, as almost no regularly appearing black characters were featured on network television for more than ten years.

Despite the heightened visibility of African-Americans within the civil rights movement and significant legal and political gains in racial equality, the period between 1954 and 1965 featured a virtual absence of blacks in entertainment television. Black actors appeared as guests in single episodes of series, variety

AMOS 'N' ANDY

Amos 'n' Andy (CBS, 1951–53): One of radio's most successful programs transitioned to television with a new cast of African-American actors replacing the white "blackface" performers from the original, but maintaining the humor based on stereotypes of lazy, crooked, and dim-witted blacks. The series was met with resistance from both African-American groups critical of the stereotypes and advertisers unsure of an all-black cast, which led to the show's cancellation and its eventually being pulled from syndication after rerunning into the 1960s.

THE NAT "KING" COLE SHOW

The Nat "King" Cole Show (NBC, 1956–57): The first network variety show to be hosted by an African-American performer, Cole's program was met with overt hostility and racism from many advertisers and affiliates, making it impossible for NBC to sustain the show despite decent ratings. Cole remained successful as a musical guest on other variety shows, but the conservative attitude of the television industry would not gamble on another African-American-led show for another decade.

and music programs featured occasional black musicians and stars, and sports broadcasts showed African-American athletes competing in integrated leagues, but central roles for black performers were quite limited. This invisibility was in part due to attitudes of southern affiliates, many of whom were vocal in their desire to keep broadcasting segregated, and advertisers who feared offending whites by associating products with black stars. Both of these factors doomed NBC's *Nat King Cole Show* in the late 1950s, despite a popular black host with previous success crossing over to white audiences in his musical career.

In this period, the dominant televised images of African-Americans were on news and documentary programming, highlighting passionate civil rights speeches, integration battles, and black protesters being hosed down in the streets by white police—a stark contrast to the upbeat images of all-white suburbs and rural Americana portrayed on popular fictional programming. When issues such as integration and civil rights did emerge, they were cloaked in allegories—fantasy sitcoms *The Munsters* and *The Addams Family* portray the horrified reactions of white suburbanites when a family of friendly "monsters" move

JULIA

Julia (NBC, 1968–71): The first African-American–led sitcom since the early 1950s, *Julia* focuses on an assimilated nurse and single mother living in a mostly white world. However, the narrative stems less from racial conflicts and situations, and more from standard sitcom storylines that avoid the political issues implicit in the show's premise.

in next door, a commentary on contemporary politics without representing non-whites who might offend advertisers, affiliates, or viewers.

African-Americans became more prominent on television in the mid-1960s, as a number of programs cast blacks as regular characters, both in leading and supporting roles. Most notable was 1965's *I Spy*, featuring Bill Cosby as one of two globe-trotting spies. Although the show was not a huge hit, Cosby won the Emmy Award for Best Dramatic Actor for all three years the program ran, marking a breakthrough for black performers and launching Cosby's successful television career. Black actors found work as supporting cast members on numerous series, including *Mission: Impossible*, *Star Trek*, and *Hogan's Heroes*, usually featured as the one non-white character within an ensemble. *Julia*, debuting in 1968, saw the first African-American lead actress in Diahann Carroll's role as the title character, a nurse in an integrated office raising a son after her husband died in the Vietnam War—despite this potentially socially relevant situation, the show was mostly apolitical and escapist in tone throughout its three-year run.

Programs like these can be considered as **assimilationist** texts, offering a vision of an integrated community or workplace in which the non-white characters are treated equally to their white counterparts, although rarely placed in leadership roles. While these shows certainly offer such images as positive statements about a divisive issue, many critics argue that by erasing representations of racism, segregation, and civil rights, such programs paint an idealistic vision of a country that required no further reforms or activism. If black television characters could be equal to their white co-workers, why were real-life blacks demanding more rights and access? At their worst, these representations can be viewed as erasing racial identity beyond the actor's skin color, suggesting a level of color-blindness in which all people are equal but adhere to norms and behaviors associated with white people, a characterization some critics called "white Negroes." Such characterizations are consistent with the era's hegemony of civil rights reform on the surface without challenging deeper-seated cultural norms of racial difference.

In reaction to such assimilationist representations, a wave of fictional programs in the early 1970s highlighted racial struggles, discrimination, and civil

The controversial hit *All in the Family* portrayed generational conflicts frequently focused on issues of race and integration, with the racist Archie Bunker explicitly expressing many combustible opinions that had previously been unstated on television.

rights issues, especially within comedies, where racial tensions could be defused with laughter. The most prominent and successful of these shows is *All in the Family,* presenting the prejudices of racist white patriarch Archie Bunker in conflict with his liberal daughter, Gloria, and son-in-law, Mike. While Bunker's ignorant discrimination is directed at all who are different from him—women, Italians, homosexuals, youth, liberals—the show's most intense conflicts focus on his racist views, primarily those triggered by his new neighbors, the African-American Jefferson family. As discussed in chapter 2, CBS used *All in the Family* to reach younger viewers who might share Mike and Gloria's condemnation of Archie's racism, but by voicing hateful epithets and stereotypes that had never previously been portrayed on television, many critics thought audiences might embrace Archie's views. Research at the time suggested that the show reinforced beliefs for both bigoted viewers who agreed with Archie and progressives who empathized with Mike and Gloria. Producers Norman Lear and Bud Yorkin aimed to highlight generational struggles, especially around racial conflicts, allowing Americans to confront rather than escape from their prejudices, but producers cannot control how viewers make sense of the messages they consume. Critics were divided on whether turning a spotlight on racist views worked to validate and humanize such beliefs, or to highlight their absurdity through argument and discussion; in the end, *All in the Family* probably did both.

The success of *All in the Family* led to a cycle of socially relevant programs directly engaging racial issues and dramatically increased the number of African-Americans on television. Within ensemble programs, the presence of singular black characters continued, but on shows such as *Barney Miller* and *Soap*, black characters were not fully assimilated, as their racial differences were acknowledged and factored into the narrative. Exploring terrain uncharted since *Amos 'n' Andy*, a number of black-centered programs became hits in the 1970s, including *Sanford and Son*, *The Jeffersons*, *What's Happening!!*, and *Good Times*.

Debuting in 1974, *Good Times* embodies many of the contradictions tied to racial representation. At times, the show seems to reinforce negative stereotypes of African-Americans—the impoverished Evans family lives in a Chicago public housing project and struggles to maintain jobs and pay the bills, while the character J.J. is a comedic buffoon in the tradition of the racist minstrel "coon" character of the nineteenth century, scheming to make money and entertaining audiences through broad, clownish humor. Many viewers perceived these as negative images that furthered stereotypes of poor, uneducated, and unemployed blacks on welfare. However, the show was created as an alternative to earlier assimilationist representations of middle-class African-Americans, to highlight the racism, poverty, and social struggles prevalent in many black communities. Additionally, the show features an intact black nuclear family with intelligent characters debating moral and social dilemmas, a first in television history. While *Good Times* certainly uses stereotypes in its representation of an

The all-Black cast of *Good Times* both drew upon and countered television's stereotypes, creating controversy among viewers and critics.

BARNEY MILLER

Barney Miller (ABC, 1975–82): An award-winning sitcom focused on the dynamics of a New York City police precinct, the show mined comedy from its outlandish criminals and burnt-out cops. The cast was racially and ethnically diverse, using the identities of the characters as a source of humor rather than striving for an assimilated color-blind workplace.

SANFORD AND SON

Sanford and Son (NBC, 1972–77): A popular African-American–centered sitcom focused on the life of a father and son running a junkyard business in a Los Angeles ghetto, the show highlights the persona of comedian Redd Foxx and his insult-driven humor. Although designed to acknowledge black culture and the conditions of ghetto life, many critics saw it as playing to stereotypes of African-American poverty and laziness.

THE JEFFERSONS

The Jeffersons (CBS, 1975–85): A spin-off from *All in the Family*, the show focuses on an African-American family that had achieved economic success and moved into a luxury Manhattan apartment, and on the resulting culture clash between the brash George Jefferson and his upper-class neighbors. The show is less explicitly political than *All in the Family*, although it notably featured an interracial couple at a time when such representations were still considered taboo for television.

African-American community, it also offers a look at a facet of American culture that had been previously ignored by television.

Good Times and other 1970s shows present an alternative model to assimilationist programming: a **segregated** presentation of an all-black world. On such programs, racial difference and racist discrimination are often acknowledged, but they are presented through a community that is mostly isolated from a larger white world. These programs often aim to present positive visions of black families, but they also justify what would grow into a segregated system of representation: shows featuring black families and communities in the 1990s and 2000s

GOOD TIMES

Good Times (CBS, 1974–79): Another branch in the *All in the Family* tree, *Good Times* focuses on an impoverished African-American family living in a Chicago public housing project. Designed to highlight life in poor ghettos and comedically discuss racial issues, the program generated controversy as it began to focus more on the minstrel-style antics of the character J.J. and less on the social issues facing the Evans family.

THE GAME

The Game (The CW, 2006–present): A spin-off of *Girlfriends*, this African-American–centered sitcom focuses on a medical student and her boyfriend, a professional football player. The series typifies contemporary African-American sitcoms that play to an almost exclusively black audience, performing poorly in overall ratings but strong among its core demographic.

are mainly targeted to black audiences. This phenomenon has been supported by Fox, The WB, UPN, and The CW, all of which featured a single night of black sitcoms at various times, garnering high ratings among African-American viewers but with virtually no white viewership. For instance, The CW's *The Game* was consistently in the Nielsen top ten among African-American audiences in 2006–07, but was the second lowest rated show among total audiences. The effect of this segregated scheduling is to isolate the majority of black representations away from non-black viewers. However, before this segregated trend took hold, two important representations of black families from the 1970s and 1980s did prove to be major hits among all audiences, both serving as landmark crossover television programs: *Roots* and *The Cosby Show*.

One popular innovation of 1970s television was the rise of the miniseries—and no miniseries was as groundbreaking or as culturally relevant as 1977's *Roots*. The show traces the history of one black family back centuries to its roots in Africa, portraying the dehumanization of slavery in the starkest terms ever seen on television. The miniseries was one of the most-watched shows in television history, gaining a massive audience among all races throughout its weeklong presentation. *Roots* highlights the history of African-American abuse and degradation at the hands of white Americans, but frames the story as a tale of the triumph of human dignity in the face of adversity—the ancestors of author Arthur Haley overcame their hardships to lead to eventual family success in the

ROOTS

Roots (ABC, 1977): A tremendously popular miniseries about author Alex Haley's ancestry, *Roots* traces their enslavement from Africa to life in post–Civil War America. Approximately 85 percent of American television households watched at least part of the eight-night series in 1977. *Roots* featured many high-profile actors, with white stars playing unsympathetic roles as slave traders and racist KKK members and black actors serving as the dramatic center in a manner unprecedented for television.

twentieth century, a tale that some view as denying the lingering effects of racism and slavery. While there is no doubt that *Roots* had tremendous impact by highlighting and confronting the historical racism foundational to the United States, some critics suggest that it downplayed the racism that persists beyond the civil rights era. Additionally, as a miniseries, it had little impact on other programming, as virtually no other television dramas focusing on African-American families or racial issues succeeded in its wake, leaving black families solely as the subject of comedies.

A landmark African-American comedy emerged in the decade following *Roots. The Cosby Show* debuted in 1984 and soon became the most popular series in America. A family sitcom portraying a loving African-American family headed

Surprisingly popular, *Roots* portrayed the brutality of the African slave trade and dehumanized life on a Southern plantation.

The Huxtable family on *The Cosby Show* offered a new model of representation: a successful and functional upper-class African-American family that was embraced by viewers in surprising numbers.

by a respected doctor and a successful lawyer, the show was embraced across racial lines and to many signaled a shift in representational possibilities. Certainly star and producer Bill Cosby designed the program to offer an explicitly "positive" alternative to the ghetto sitcoms of the 1970s. However, research suggests that white and black viewers took differing meanings away from the show. Blacks typically appreciated the vision of success presented on-screen, but doubted how realistic an image it was, while many whites viewed *Cosby* as evidence that racial equality had arrived in real-life workplaces and schools. Other sitcoms presenting African-American affluence followed in *Cosby*'s wake, including *The Fresh Prince of Bel-Air* and *Family Matters*, defining one typical black representation for years to come.

While it was a step forward to have top-rated shows focus on successful African-Americans, *Cosby* unintentionally fueled a backlash to civil rights policies that grew under the Reagan administration of the 1980s.[4] This backlash was heightened by the contrast between *Cosby*'s representation of successful African-Americans in a racially equal world, and the dominant images of blacks on news programming during the 1980s—stories of crack cocaine addicts, so-called "welfare queens," and gang violence. These two representational modes taken together suggested that blacks could succeed if they applied themselves, and that real-world instances of poverty and crime were simply signs of individual failure, not indicators of structural racism or economic inequality. According to many critics, *Cosby* may have promoted tolerance of individuals regardless of race, but it unintentionally undercut many of the arguments for sustaining civil rights policies and continuing to work toward a truly non-racist society.

Cosby was the last major representational shift of the classic network era. In the multi-channel era, black representations became more segmented and targeted to predominantly African-American audiences via channels like BET. More centrally, Fox Network emerged in the late 1980s and early 1990s by appealing to urban audiences through black representations on shows such as *In Living Color, Martin, Roc,* and *Living Single,* drawing upon an outrageous comedic style some critics termed the "new minstrelsy." Once Fox was well established, it turned away from African-American audiences and toward young, white audiences; newer networks The WB and UPN picked up Fox's strategy with black sitcoms *Moesha, The Parkers, Girlfriends,* and *The Steve Harvey Show,* a strategy continuing today with The CW. African-American characters are still a staple on cop shows, medical dramas, and other genres representing an integrated workplace, but such representations typically follow the assimilationist model by downplaying racial identity. Thus while today there are proportionally more black images and a broader range of representations on television than in any other era, they still often follow conventional patterns of identity and are limited by their narrow appeal to limited audiences.

What can we take away from this brief history of black representation? One key lesson is that there is no ideal way of representing a racial group; no single character or program can represent an entire race. One problem throughout the classic network era was that at any given moment, there were too few representations on the air to provide a diversity of images: the 1950s featured mostly minstrel stereotypes, while the 1960s offered mainly assimilated ideals. When a group is less visible on television, each representation must carry more cultural weight, standing in for an entire group. This is especially true for a minority group in the eyes of the majority: for many white youth, televised images of blacks or Latinos may be the powerful first impressions of an entire race. For most critics, the ideal representation would be broad range of diverse images across the television schedule: poor inner-city blacks alongside African-American lawyers, a middle-class black family drama and an African-American sketch comedy. While arguably such breadth of images does exist across the dozens of channels available today, the segmented nature of narrowcasting means that individual viewers still see just a slice of representational spectrum: young MTV viewers see brash hip-hop stars while older CBS fans watch assimilated cops and lawyers.

For many critics, the opportunity to see a diversity of racial identities within one program, exploring the conflicts and differences active within any racial group, has rarely been offered on television. One such series is *The Wire,* which features a majority black cast playing roles ranging from drug dealers to politicians, reporters to cops, with a wide range of personalities and moral codes,

ALL AMERICAN GIRL

All-American Girl (ABC, 1994–95): A failed sitcom starring Margaret Cho about a Korean American family, the series struggled to find a clear tone and frequently retooled its premise before being cancelled after one season. It remains notable as a still-rare attempt to center a network program on an Asian American family.

GEORGE LOPEZ

George Lopez (ABC, 2002–07): A family sitcom about Lopez, his family, and work life follows typical genre conventions, but the focus on a Hispanic American family makes it a rarity for network television. The series was cancelled to protests from Lopez, as ratings were stronger than those for renewed programs, but since the show was not produced in-house by ABC, it generated lower revenue than ABC-owned programs.

SCRUBS

Scrubs (NBC, 2001–08; ABC, 2008–present): A long-running quirky sitcom about young doctors, *Scrubs* plays with formal qualities, using reflexive fantasy sequences and voiceover narration, and employs serialized plotlines involving relationships and career moves. The series has a wide-ranging tone, shifting from wacky physical comedy to more sentimental character studies, frequently within the same episode, with a small but faithful fanbase sufficient enough to sustain it for years across networks.

coupled with an explicit recognition of how racial politics matter in contemporary America. Yet *The Wire* is seen as more an atypical exception on the margins of television rather than the start of a new trend in representation.

The challenge of representing an entire race is more pronounced for other groups beyond blacks, as representations of Latinos, Asians, and other races have been much rarer than those of African-Americans. Only one network show, the short-lived 1990s sitcom *All-American Girl*, centered on an Asian American family, and occasional programs about Latinos, such as *The George Lopez Show* and

Ugly Betty, have fared only slightly better. Television representations that cross over outside a particular racial audience are predominantly seen on programs presenting integrated workplaces, where one Asian character on *Grey's Anatomy* or one Latino on *NYPD Blue* adds diversity to a mostly white program, but offers few opportunities to engage with the issues of racial identity that continue to divide American society. Integrated programs that call attention to the impact of racial differences among their ensembles are rare, as on *Homicide: Life on the Street, Veronica Mars,* and *Scrubs.*

One key difference between African-American representations and other races is the presence of targeted non-English programming on cable and local markets: national channels Telemundo and Univision offer Spanish-language programming quite popular among Hispanic communities, while cities with significant Asian or Latino communities often feature broadcast stations dedicated to programming in native languages and select national satellite channels offering non-English programming. These language-based channels, however, tend to erase intra-ethnic differences among a group: Univision constructs its Spanish-speaking audience with little regard for differences among Mexican, Cuban, or Venezualan heritage, as well as alienating younger generations who do not speak Spanish fluently. Another effect of this system is to continue to segregate representations, with ethnic communities consuming images of their own group, and little access offered to outsiders.

Television's representations of racial and ethnic minorities are often motivated by noble intentions to break down barriers and fight stereotypes. But according to many critics, the system still reinforces the ultimate gap between a dominant position of whiteness and other subordinate groups. Almost all television programs represent a dominant ideology of white identity and norms— non-white characters are seen as either assimilating within those norms, and thus giving up their own unique identity, or segregating themselves from whites, and often reinforcing stereotypes in the process. According to this perspective, there is no such thing as a "positive image," as all representations work in some way to sustain an unequal society divided along racial lines. The only way out of this trap is to directly engage with racial issues in an open and direct manner through a diversity of representations that refuse to ignore how racial identity matters in the lives of all Americans, a tactic that few television programs have embraced. As we can see concerning gender representations, television has been a bit more direct in confronting how gender identity matters throughout television history.

REPRESENTING GENDER

Racial identity has typically been studied by charting the limited set of images represented within a mostly white televised world. For the analysis of gender on television, issues of visibility are far less central: both women and men have obviously been represented throughout television history in nearly every genre. There are a few realms where gender imbalances have been central. Network newscasters have overwhelmingly been men, and children's television tends to feature male characters in far greater numbers than females. But in the majority of studies on television's gender representations, the focus has been less on visibility than on analyzing what roles are played by male and female characters, and how the relationship between genders is portrayed.

To understand gender representations, it is important to distinguish between *sex* and *gender*. **Sex** is the biological identity distinguishing male and female bodies. **Gender** refers to the social and cultural meanings tied to people's biological sexual differences, typically expressed as **masculinity** and **femininity**. While the divide between these categories is not completely clear, as some gender behaviors have biological roots, the vast majority of masculine and feminine traits are not determined by sex, but are learned through cultural practice. Media are one important site of gender learning, as cultural norms of masculinity and femininity are repeated and validated, which encourages viewers to adopt them as part of their own behavior and further reinforces dominant gender norms. While no single representation directly causes our behavior, the repetitive consumption of particular meanings helps shape how we think about gender identity, and shifts our identities accordingly.

Throughout American culture, gender norms are shaped by an underlying ideology of **patriarchy** that privileges male and masculine identity over female and feminine norms. As with all ideologies, patriarchy is historically dependent: certainly many aspects of American patriarchy have been transformed and weakened significantly over time. However, in many key aspects of American culture, male identity is still perceived as the default: within the realms of politics, sports, economics, academia, and the professional workplace, men are much more likely to be in leadership positions and a successful woman is still viewed as exceptional rather than the norm. Likewise, a patriarchal ideology still defines women's primary role as a family caregiver, even as access to professional achievement has been increased. Patriarchy today is not totalizing or determining, as many examples of both men and women actively contradict this ideology, but as a general social norm, patriarchal definitions of masculinity and femininity persist and structure the typical way we view gender.

How does television factor into this system? Within the male-dominated television industry, many women have played important roles as creators, producers, and, to a lesser degree, executives throughout the medium's history. Tracing the success of women in the industry suggests that progress has been made toward gender equality, but that more work is required, especially within executive ranks. While some women have used their positions to challenge patriarchy by offering new gender representations, as with *Cagney & Lacey* or

Oprah Winfrey's talk show and co-ownership of Oxygen Channel, studying gender is not limited to looking at who creates television's images. Given the collaborative and commercial nature of television, exploring on-screen representations regardless of the identity or intentions of producers is more central to studying gender. The study of television's gender representations requires us to look at how the medium constructs norms of both femininity and masculinity, as well as how it presents the relationship between genders.

One way to explore how television portrays gender would be to chart the history of representations throughout the medium, following the previous discussion of African-American representations. But the history of gender representations is more multifaceted than that of race, given that nearly every program might have some perspective on gender roles. Unlike racial representations, there are rarely singular modes of presenting gender at a given time that define the era. While historical developments can emerge that shift cultural norms, typically television offers such a wide range of gender representations at one time that their historical evolution is more subtle to chart. Such historical examinations are important, tying developments in representations to broader social changes such as the rise of the feminist movement in the 1960s and 1970s, or the subsequent anti-feminist backlash of the 1980s and 1990s.[5]

Another way to study gender representations is to examine some of the main traits of masculinity and femininity found on television, considering how they are presented and charting their cultural impact across historical eras. Thus we can identify a number of **tropes** of gender, commonly repeated meanings that help construct gender identities through television representations and in other realms of American culture. Gender is culturally understood as a binary system: even though actual identities typically fall somewhere along a spectrum between masculine and feminine norms, the ideological system of gender depends on a clear distinction between male and female identities. Following this binary mode, most of these tropes of gender can be understood in pairs, highlighting how masculine and feminine are understood only in relation to one another, not as independent terms. Each of these tropes is much more complex in actual representation than simple dichotomies, as there are always exceptions to these tendencies in portraying gender identity. But it is useful to explore the larger binary patterns that persist despite many exceptions and complications, as such tropes function as common norms in television and throughout American culture.

One of the key ways television constructs gender is locating men and women within particular social roles and functions. This is primarily represented by linking masculinity with a **professional** role, and femininity with **domesticity**. The demeaning saying "A woman's place is in the home" is based on the cultural assumption that women belong in the domestic realm of home and family. Throughout television history, women have been represented in the role of homemaker. From 1950s icons the Cleavers on *Leave*

LEAVE IT TO BEAVER

Leave It to Beaver (CBS, 1957–58; ABC, 1958–63): Often remembered as the quintessential vision of 1950s suburban family life, the show was not particularly successful in its initial run. The program reran in syndication for decades, and its portrayal of the low-stress problems encountered by the Cleaver family took hold in the popular imagination as typical of the era, with the show still serving as a nostalgic glimpse of an America that never truly existed.

JUDGING AMY

Judging Amy (CBS, 1999–2005): A drama mixing family with workplace situations, *Judging Amy* follows the mother and daughter main characters as they encounter social issues focused on children through their respective jobs as a social worker and family court judge. The show is notable for its portrayal of cross-generational professional women and its serious treatment of issues rarely addressed on television in the context of a compelling, female-centered drama.

It to Beaver to the quarrelsome Romano clan on *Everybody Loves Raymond*, the vast number of television families depict women as solely responsible for maintaining their homes, doing household chores, raising children, and taking care of their husbands. Even when women are portrayed as working, as on *Roseanne* or *Malcolm in the Middle*, they are still in charge of domestic duties such as cooking and cleaning. Often their need to juggle domestic and professional roles becomes the source of dramatic conflicts, as on *Judging Amy*, as professional ambitions are blamed for interfering with women's domestic and family responsibilities. When television represents male characters in domestic roles, the situation usually becomes a topic of humor, emerges in response to a crisis, as in the death of the wife and mother on *Full House*, or serves as a dramatic problem to be overcome by men reentering the workplace, as on *thirtysomething*—all of which reinforce the seemingly "natural" ideology of female domesticity.

In contrast, men are typically identified with their professional career roles. This trope is common both in family programs, where the father serves as "breadwinner" and provider, and workplace shows, where the majority of characters tend to be male. Shows where men lose their jobs, as with Dan on

Most episodes of *I Love Lucy* show both conventional gender roles, with Lucy serving her husband Ricky in domestic duties, and acts of rebellion, as Lucy strives to find ways to work outside the home.

Roseanne or Graham on *My So-Called Life*, often dramatize the loss of work as a crisis of identity, suggesting that masculinity is defined by professional success outside the home. Shows about working women highlight the inherent conflicts concerning female professionals: *Murphy Brown* showed a successful woman who was viewed as overly masculine by co-workers and friends, while Lynnette on *Desperate Housewives* battles the stresses of reentering the workforce after an extended hiatus to have children. When a male workplace is integrated to include women, as in the newsroom on *The Mary Tyler Moore Show* or the firehouse on *Rescue Me*, the professional woman is typically subjected to doubts about her abilities and even to harassment. Male professionalism is further reinforced by nonfiction programs where the positions of authority tend to be filled by men, such as news anchors, game show hosts, sportscasters, and voice-over announcers. Advertising similarly draws upon the domestic/professional norms to market particular products to imagined audiences of female homemakers and male workers. The vast majority of television representations reiterate this assumed binary, making these gendered associations seem natural and the default function for American culture.

Even though the norms of masculine professional versus feminine domestic are clearly engrained in American culture, television programs can still place these ideals in conflict and generate discussion, creating a cultural forum. A good example of this is one of television's first hits, *I Love Lucy*. The show's central couple, Ricky and Lucy Ricardo, follow typical gender norms, with Ricky as a professional singer and Lucy as homemaker. However, Lucy is demonstrably unsatisfied with her role, envying Ricky's career; she and her friend Ethel Mertz spend most episodes scheming to get out of the home and into some professional opportunity. Each of these schemes fails with comedic flair, typically ending with Ricky chastising Lucy and demanding that she stop her mischief. On one hand, the show reinforces the typical gender divide of the era by dramatizing Lucy's failures and by giving Ricky the last word. However, viewers tune in for the opportunity to revel in Lucy's somewhat misguided attempts at personal fulfillment, potentially empathizing with her sense of domestic confinement. While the show certainly does not offer a serious debate about gender or women's roles, it portrays a woman unsatisfied with the norms of her day, and rebelling against patriarchal authority. In this way, it opened opportunities for viewers of the 1950s to envision other options for their own lives, questioning the assumed "natural" division of labor between men and women. The show does not encourage female viewers to rebel against ideological patriarchy, which would have been off-limits in 1950s culture, but it certainly makes small acts of rebellion entertaining to watch.

Another pair of gendered tropes corresponds to the professional/domestic divide: masculinity is typically shown as being **rational**, while femininity is **emotional**. These traits are not inherently valued as positive or negative, as their worth changes depending on the context. Representations of emotionally engaged and sensitive women validate their domestic roles as mothers and wives, or show women applying their abilities within select professions requiring empathy, such as nurses and teachers. Men are typically seen as thriving professionally in fields such as medicine, law, science, business, and government because of their rational abilities, and professionals must often learn to be less emotionally involved with work to succeed, a common theme of medical and crime programs. In news and public affairs programs, distinctions between types of stories often follow these gendered lines: reports of politics, economics, and foreign policy require the rational analysis more typical of male journalists, while so-called "soft" news features on celebrities, families, and human interest tend to be framed by emotionally engaged female reporters and talk show hosts. Entire genres can break down along these gendered lines: the hyperemotional world of soap operas and daytime talk shows are coded as feminine, while the rational realms of news and public affairs programming are understood as the domain of men.

Individual characters can present these two traits in tension. The title character of *Ally McBeal* is a successful young lawyer who clearly has a sharp, rational mind. She often participates in lengthy debates about contemporary social issues and controversies. But Ally is also driven by intense emotional desires, including romantic intrigue with co-workers and a desire to have a child. The show portrays Ally as neurotic and prone to visual fantasies,

Ally McBeal's main character is both a highly successful lawyer, and a neurotic self-obsessed woman focused on fashion and how she appears to men, highlighting contradictions of 1990s culture.

doubting her own abilities and second-guessing her goals; it ultimately suggests an incompatibility between Ally's role as rational attorney and her feminine emotions.

A more sympathetic example of such a mixture is Allison DuBois on *Medium*. Although she abandoned law school, Allison charts a career as a crime-solving consultant for the district attorney by emphasizing her more emotional and irrational abilities as a psychic whose visions help solve crimes. She is clearly less rational than the male lawyers and police officers with whom she works, but she merges her intuition and psychic powers with logical crime-solving investigation techniques to balance the two sides of her personality, a balance that is emphasized through her own struggle to balance her career and the demands of motherhood. Representations such as Ally and Allison portray the struggles between rationality and emotion typical of female professionals, with varying attitudes as to how best to achieve this balance and success.

The example of *Medium* points to a common way television represents femininity as irrational: linking women to supernatural powers. This mode of representation was popularized in the early 1960s, as *Bewitched* and *I Dream of Jeannie* presented female witches and genies whose powers surpassed the more rational and mundane male world. Just as *The Addams Family* and *The Munsters* tackled racial integration through supernatural allegory, these programs addressed the rhetoric of the emerging women's movement, which

I DREAM OF JEANNIE

I Dream of Jeannie (NBC, 1965–70): A fantasy sitcom playing with gender roles that cloned the more successful *Bewitched*, *Jeannie* portrays an astronaut who finds a magical genie for whom he becomes a reluctant master and eventual husband. The wacky comedy plays with sexual innuendo between the sexy but naïve Jeannie and the pair of astronauts who keep her in her bottle.

argued for gender equality and female power, by creating supernaturally powerful female characters such as *Bewitched*'s Samantha and the title character Jeannie. Still, these powerful women generally dedicated their power to helping the men in their lives: Samantha Stevens agrees to give up her powers upon marrying her husband, Darrin, although this pledge is broken every episode, while Jeannie literally serves her "master" Tony Nelson. As on *I Love Lucy*, these shows comedically present the struggle between genders, but the 1960s fantasy sitcoms raise the stakes by heightening female power and mocking the bumbling "rational" minds of male characters. While again television does not offer a clear, outright message promoting the overthrow of patriarchy, *Bewitched* and *Jeannie* value women's abilities and offer a female-centered power that would later be celebrated in programs more explicit in their engagement with feminism, including *Wonder Woman*, *Buffy the Vampire Slayer*, and *Xena: Warrior Princess*.

While *Jeannie* celebrated female powers countering male rationality, it also drew upon a common stereotype: the dumb blonde. Numerous television representations offer attractive women lacking brains, dating back to comedy legend Gracie Allen, whose ability to win an argument based on "illogical logic" made her a brilliant comedienne on the 1950s program *The Geroge Burns and Gracie Allen Show*. However, most representations along this type forsake Allen's clever twisted logic, simply making a stupid woman the object of laughter. On *Jeannie*, the title character's lack of intelligence regularly leads to magical mischief, while on *Three's Company*, Suzanne Somers became a 1970s icon by playing a dumb blonde whose constant confusion causes comedic misunderstandings. Since the rise of reality television, the dumb blonde figure has returned as part of "celebreality" programming—Paris Hilton, Jessica Simpson, and Anna Nicole Smith all headlined reality programs highlighting their ignorance and lack of common sense, making them famous primarily for being stupid. This lingering stereotype furthers the patriarchal ideology of locating intelligence and rationality within the realm of masculinity by offering an extreme and ridiculous form of irrationality in the representations of women.

THREE'S COMPANY

Three's Company (ABC, 1977–84): A sexy farce that was part of the mid-1970s "jiggle TV" craze, the show focuses on three single roommates, with the man pretending to be gay to be allowed to live with two women. The over-the-top innuendos, risqué misunderstandings, and parade of skimpily dressed women propelled the show to high ratings, but the program looks like a dated 1970s relic today.

Not all representations follow these tropes of rational men and emotional women. One common male characterization runs counter to this dichotomy and serves as the counterpoint to the dumb blonde: the masculine buffoon. Dating back to the 1950s with Ralph Kramden on *The Honeymooners*, the buffoon is represented as full of masculine pride and assertiveness, but overestimating his own intelligence; buffoons typically carry out ill-conceived schemes and poor decision-making that require frequent rescuing, typically from their more rational and levelheaded wives. Buffoons can be a blustery exaggeration, as with *All in the Family*'s Archie Bunker or Homer on *The Simpsons*, or more understated, as with Darrin on *Bewitched* or *Everybody Loves Raymond*'s title character—but they all serve as the object of mocking humor by the more rational members of their families. Male buffoons are also a staple of advertising, popularized by beer commercials highlighting the stupidity of the men featured using the product.

How does this representation fit into the patriarchal scheme of gender? Buffoons do mock the conventions of male rationality, but they reinforce male power within the family at the same time: while a buffoon's wife will mock her husband's idiocy, she never overtakes his masculine power within the family. The buffoon representation knowingly acknowledges that the patriarchal family structure is based on an illusion of male superiority, but still reinforces the system by repeatedly allowing the buffoon to assert his power in each episode, placing the more rational wife in a subservient role that she accepts.

The dynamic between such buffoon characters and their wives highlights another key trope in television's representation of gender: masculinity is defined as **active**, while femininity is seen as **passive**. This trope differs by genre. On crime programs, men are more likely to be investigators with women are represented as victims; on medical dramas, men are typically doctors in command of female nurses. On family programs, the phrase *Father Knows Best* is frequently followed, with men serving as heads of household with support from their wives, even when the all-knowing father is a buffoon. On action and adventure programs, women are typically placed in jeopardy to be saved by male heroes. In

FATHER KNOWS BEST

Father Knows Best (CBS, 1954–55, 1958–63; NBC, 1955–58): One of a number of idyllic late 1950s suburban domestic sitcoms, *Father Knows Best* was an adapted radio show portraying life in a midwestern suburban family. Although the title suggests a patriarchal norm, episodes frequently saw mother Margaret Anderson trumping father Jim in terms of family wisdom and parenting know-how.

journalism, male reporters are more commonly sent out into dangerous conditions of wars and disasters, with female reporters more focused on interviewing victims and offering compassion. Televised sports are overwhelmingly male, portraying active athletes as masculine ideals. There are obviously many exceptions to this tendency, as active women and passive men can be found across the television schedule, but as a broadly circulating norm, more representations reinforce these traditional notions of female dependence on take-charge male figures.

A good example of the active/passive dichotomy is the spy program *24*. The first season of the show represents heroic agent Jack Bauer fighting to save his wife, Teri, and daughter, Kim, from unknown terrorists with a personal vendetta. Throughout the season, which tells the story of one eventful day, Jack is constantly using investigative techniques and physical violence to rescue the two women in his family, while Teri and Kim primarily function as passive objects to be kidnapped, abused, and saved. Most of Jack's fellow agents are male, aiding his efforts to bring down the terrorists, who are similarly male and capable of action, albeit of a malevolent nature. The other victim of the terrorists' plot is presidential candidate David Palmer, who is far more active and take-charge than Teri or Kim, able to assert his power through launching investigations and confronting enemies. Two women are characterized as active but malicious figures: Palmer's wife, Sherry, continually undercuts his family and political authority in order to gain power through his success. More starkly, Jack's colleague (and former mistress) Nina Myers is revealed to be a double agent working for the terrorists, eventually killing Teri before being captured by Jack. While these villainous women are far from passive, the only female power in the world of *24* is corrupting and malicious, needing to be subordinated to a male authority; even the main male terrorists are seen as nobler and more worthy of respect than the duplicitous and treacherous figures of Sherry and Nina. The show thus establishes a representation of the world in which male power and action is legitimate and necessary to save women from both villainous men and dangerous women who overstep their place.

On action programs like 24, female characters like Teri and Kim Bauer frequently function as passive objects under threat and needing rescue by heroic men, and often framed via the camera as the object of the male gaze.

Many programs, especially in recent years, have tried to reverse these cultural norms by focusing on active and heroic female characters. Whether through the fantasy superpowers of *Buffy the Vampire Slayer* and *Xena* or the semi-realistic espionage of *Alias* and *La Femme Nikita*, the action heroine is a rising mode of representation that aims to counter the long tradition of passive women through both creative genre mixing and innovative characterization. On *Buffy*, this reversal is heightened by the character of Xander, who functions as a male version of the "damsel in distress," the passive and typically female victim needing to be rescued. Often such heroic women are less powerful than typical male heroes, as they lack the exaggerated range of skills found in men. Buffy is super strong, but her physical abilities are undercut by her lack of intelligence, often making her resemble the dumb blonde character. The female incarnation of intelligence is found in her friend Willow, who offers research and computer skills to augment her physical timidity—but in later seasons, Willow's growing powers as a witch overwhelm her, making the combination of intelligence and power unstable within one female character.

Alias's Sydney Bristow might be the closest network television has come to presenting a fully powerful and capable female heroine comparable to male action heroes. Sydney possesses outstanding intelligence and technical skills, speaks nearly every language, displays inhuman bravery and resistance to torture, and can defeat any enemy in hand-to-hand combat. In contrast to Sydney's unrealistic perfection, nearly every other female character on *Alias* is a conniving villain or a passive victim, while most of the other male characters are more

XENA: WARRIOR PRINCESS

Xena: Warrior Princess (syndication, 1995–2001): A cult fantasy show spun off from *Hercules* and filmed in New Zealand, *Xena* focuses on an ancient Greek princess and her sidekick, Gabrielle, battling monsters and saving innocents. The show generated a significant fanbase, particularly around the lesbian subtext between Xena and Gabrielle, a facet of the series that producers regularly hinted at to acknowledge knowing fans.

well rounded and complex. Thus even with programs attempting to counter stereotypes, it is difficult to escape well-established cultural norms.

One particular subset of the active/passive binary is so central as to count as its own trope: in representing sexuality, masculinity is typically portrayed as the **sexual subject** and femininity is seen as the **sexual object**. The difference between subject and object corresponds to the passive/active divide: a subject is someone who carries out an action, or expresses desire toward an object. Concerning sexuality, this means that men are represented as expressing and exerting sexual desire toward passive and receptive women, and that men are the initiators of sexual and romantic relationships. As with all of these tropes, television did not invent this dichotomy, but it typically represents the cultural norms of ideologically "proper" sexual roles at any given cultural moment. In television narratives, men typically initiate romances and advance relationships to new levels of intimacy.

Additionally, the very act of visual representation has been analyzed by many critics as configuring women as sexual objects of a **male gaze**. Typically the producers of images are male, and the camera frequently photographs women as objects of sexual desire. Sometimes such objectification is made explicit, with women as sexualized decoration in music videos featuring scantily clad dancers, or as goals to be attained in advertising presenting a product as a tool to "obtain" a beautiful woman. Slightly more subtly, game shows such as *Wheel of Fortune* or *The Price Is Right* use beautiful women as mute spokesmodels to highlight products and facilitate games for the benefit of the more powerful male host. In such programming, the default mode of watching these images is figured as a male gaze upon desirable female bodies, which are frequently linked to products to be consumed and purchased.

This division is further reinforced by the differing beauty norms for men and women on television. While most performers are typically attractive, there is more tolerance for conventionally unattractive men on television than for unattractive women. For instance, it is not rare for an overweight or balding man to be dating or married to an attractive woman, as on *Seinfeld* or *The King of*

Seinfeld's short, portly, and bald George Costanza is presented as an unattractive and unpleasant man, who still manages to date a series of attractive women.

Queens, but there are virtually no examples of women not fitting typical beauty norms attached to conventionally attractive men. Television makes a spectacle of beautiful women's bodies as part of nearly every genre, from sports cheerleaders to makeover show contestants, soap opera vixens to fictional lawyers in miniskirts. Even the news follows this double standard, demanding a level of physical attractiveness of female newscasters not demanded of men. The rare case of female television personalities not adhering to such norms becomes a story itself, such as Oprah Winfrey's regular weight fluctuations or Camryn Manheim of *The Practice* embracing her self-proclaimed "fat" body. The range of acceptable body types for men is much broader, as demonstrated by sexually active characters portrayed by Dennis Franz on *NYPD Blue* or Jason Alexander on *Seinfeld*.

Since cultural norms about sexuality have changed significantly throughout television's history, the modes of representing the sexual facet of gender have transformed as well. In the 1950s, representations of sexual practices were virtually absent from television screens out of concern for offending sponsors or more traditional family audiences. Fictional couples slept in separate beds, and any references to sex were couched in veiled innuendo. *The Ed Sullivan Show* even famously refused to show the lower half of Elvis Presley's dancing body in 1956 for fear of offending viewers. The 1960s saw more explicit sexuality for its day, but still with strict lines not to be crossed: Barbara Eden on *I Dream of Jeannie* dressed in skimpy outfits with a bare midriff, but was forbidden to expose her

THE PRACTICE

The Practice (ABC, 1997–2004): A legal drama from producer David E. Kelley, the series focuses on idealistic Boston lawyers and the compromises they must make to sustain a business. Following declining ratings in the show's seventh season, more than half the cast was fired and the drama was retooled; the resulting series was reframed again into the more lighthearted spin-off *Boston Legal*, which proved to be successful in reaching an affluent audience.

NYPD BLUE

NYPD Blue (ABC, 1993–2005): This long-running crime drama was initially controversial, prompting boycots for its inclusion of profanity and partial nudity, but it soon was hailed by most critics as one of television's most effective and popular cop shows. The series combines gritty views of New York City crime with the personal lives of the police, especially the tortured male cops at the center of the program.

THE ED SULLIVAN SHOW

The Ed Sullivan Show (CBS, 1948–71): Originally known as *Toast of the Town*, Sullivan's quintessential television variety show featured a broad array of performers, including musicians, magicians, comedians, animal tricks, and dancers. The show played to a mass audience and offered something for all tastes, ranging from the Metropolitan Opera to legendary television appearances by Elvis Presley and The Beatles, making Sullivan one of the most influential figures in entertainment for decades.

navel. Groundbreaking prime time soap opera *Peyton Place* was most explicit in discussing (though not showing) adultery, premarital teen sex, and illegitimate children, and new female action heroes in British import *The Avengers* and *Honey West* gave women role models who both solved crimes and took charge of their bodies in ways previously unseen on television, but still within strict limits of decency and explicitness.

THE AVENGERS

The Avengers (ABC, 1966–69): A rare example of a direct import airing in American network prime time, the British spy show *The Avengers* was a global sensation in the mid-1960s. Focusing on gentlemanly spy John Steed and a series of spandex-clad female fighters, the show imported a combination of sophistication and sexuality that seemed distinctive on American airwaves.

ALL MY CHILDREN

All My Children (ABC, 1970–present): A long-running and popular soap opera that was conceived as a way to make the genre more topically engaged with social issues, the series is best known for Susan Lucci's portrayal of Erica Kane, one of the most famous and notable characters in television history.

The 1970s transformed the role of sexuality on television and throughout American culture in the wake of the sexual revolution and the feminist movement, which questioned social norms concerning sexuality and gender relations. Daytime soap operas had been pushing sexual boundaries throughout the 1960s by offering narratives of various sexual behaviors, but the genre became more explicit in the 1970s: soap operas portrayed infidelity, increasingly steamy scenes, and even an abortion, on *All My Children*. Most notably, daytime soap operas offered a flurry of rape narratives in the late 1970s, representing male sexuality as an act of violence. Some of these televised rapes adhered to an older notion of rape as unbridled passion often triggered by women "teasing" their rapists, but most sympathized with a feminist definition of rape as an act of brutal violence, not sexually justifiable or caused by its victim. The most famous televised rape was its most ambiguous: when Luke raped Laura on *General Hospital* in 1979, it initiated their romance, which would evolve into daytime's first "supercouple." The show offered Luke as a rapist who would be rehabilitated by Laura's love, acknowledging her victimization but reframing the violent act as the trigger of a mutual passion. Within a year, the couple became national heartthrobs, and their 1981 wedding still stands as the most-watched soap opera episode in television history. While rape narratives are comparably rare on television, they do draw upon the typical dynamic of sexual power assumed to be normal in many programs: men have the power to initiate sex with objectified women.

CHARLIE'S ANGELS

Charlie's Angels (ABC, 1976–81): A popular detective show featuring three beautiful women investigating crimes that frequently forced them to undress and employ their sex appeal, the program simultaneously gave women powerful active roles and objectified them as the "possessions" of the faceless detective agency owner Charlie.

Prime time tackled sexual issues in the 1970s as well, especially in made-for-television movies and through satirical comedies such as *All in the Family*, *Maude*, and *Soap*. Though some of these shows questioned the sexual politics of passive women following the lead of active men, the bulk of the more explicit programs of this era highlighted women as objects of male desire—most notably, *Charlie's Angels* became a smash hit by creating television's first sex symbols in Farrah Fawcett-Majors, Jaclyn Smith, and Cheryl Ladd. *Angels* and similar shows *The Bionic Woman* and *Wonder Woman* launched what was termed the "jiggle era" of late 1970s television, which featured attractive women in action sequences wearing skimpy outfits. While these programs did offer active women with skills beyond their looks often rescuing other women and defeating male villains, the women typically acted in service of a man, as with the *Angels'* off-screen voice Charlie, and strategically used sex appeal to achieve their crime-fighting goals. Thus while women were granted more agency and power, they were also represented as titillating sexual objects for male viewers. Throughout 1970s television, female sexuality was represented as a site of contradictions and ambiguity, with women's bodies offered as both objects to be looked at by male viewers and a source of feminine power and identity.[6]

By the multi-channel era, sexual representation became more fractured: the most explicit images and storylines moved to cable television and out of the regulatory reach of the FCC, while prime time television continued to push the boundaries of what could be shown and heard. By the 1990s, network shows *Friends*, *Seinfeld*, and *Roseanne* regularly offered women as sexual subjects, with women initiating relationships on their own frank terms, while cable programs such as *Sex and the City* offered sexually active women in more explicit representations. However, the male subject/female object divide continues to persist across the majority of programs, in the standards of beauty and imagery, and in the regulatory policies of the industry. Like all of the gender norms explored here, sexual representations are far more diverse than encompassed by a single pair of terms, but these binaries still exert power to shape cultural norms as a broad tendency across a range of programs, genres, and channels.

REPRESENTING SEXUAL ORIENTATION

Throughout the discussion of how television's representations of sexual relations shape gender identity, all of the examples presume heterosexuality as the only way of representing sexual relationships. This is typical for the vast majority of television, where homosexuality has been absent from the spectrum of representations offered on-screen. However, in recent years, television has become more open and forthright about presenting a broader range of sexual orientations. Since the 1990s, representations of gay and lesbian characters and people have become more acceptable and commonplace on television. How did this transformation occur? And what norms of representing homosexuality have emerged in the wake of this increased visibility?

As with the history of racial representation, the issue of visibility is central to representing homosexuality. However, visibility is more complicated for gays and lesbians; since sexual orientation is typically identified by openly presenting sexual practices or relationships, the visibility of homosexuality is tied to the representation of sexuality in general. As previously discussed, all sexual practices were restricted from television screens for much of the medium's history, a tendency even more pronounced for homosexuality. Until the 1980s, even the most modest expressions of sexual practice, such as kissing, hugging, or dancing, were off-limits for gay and lesbian couples. Thus while blacks can be integrated into programs subtly, without explicit identification of a character's or performer's race, the same is not true of gay or lesbian character or performers. Given the taboo of even representing heterosexual practices in the first decades of television, homosexuality has been even more absent and invisible for most of television's history. Homosexuality did emerge occasionally in news and talk shows, typically framed as a "social problem" to be addressed or debated, but rarely seen as an identity category within fictional programming.

Even though explicit representations of homosexuals were mostly absent for television's early years, veiled innuendos and unacknowledged representations did find their way on to television. From the popularity of pianist Liberace in the 1950s, to 1970s game show staples Paul Lynde on *The Hollywood Squares* and Charles Nelson Reilly on *Match Game*, the presentation of gay performers allowed a double address to audiences: mainstream viewers saw such figures as flamboyant, while gay-savvy viewers recognized the performers' often-closeted homosexuality as part of their personas. Given that the creative communities of Hollywood and New York were much more open to acknowledging and accepting homosexuality than was most of the country, producers often slipped gay-friendly subtext and humor into programs such as *Get Smart*, *Bewitched*, and *The Monkees*, offering inside jokes that would go unnoticed by the majority of unaware viewers.

As with representations of race and gender, the 1970s was a transformative decade in presenting sexual orientation, as gay rights social movements began

Jodie Dallas, *Soap*'s cross-dressing gay character played by Billy Crystal, started as an extreme stereotype but became one of the show's most popular and humane characters, launching Crystal's career.

to make homosexuality more acceptable and visible throughout American society. As television became more explicit in presenting heterosexual practices and issues, gays and lesbians also became more acknowledged and presented in explicitly visible roles. Often these roles were as guest stars in a program, playing with stereotypes on a sitcom or portraying dangerous homosexual characters as sexual predators on police and medical dramas. Episodes of *All in the Family* challenged Archie Bunker's prejudices with lesbians and transvestites, while dramatic series *Family* offered a sympathetic portrayal of a lesbian teacher. Probably the most notable gay representation of the era was on the farcical comedy *Soap*, where a young Billy Crystal played Jodie Dallas, an openly gay character. While Jodie was never allowed happiness in a homosexual relationship—he actually dated more women than men over the show's four years—he evolved into one of the show's most likeable and morally admirable characters, raising a daughter as a single parent. The high-rated show was greeted with protests and attacks concerning its explicit sexual frankness concerning adultery, promiscuity, and homosexuality, and it always struggled to sell ad time due to sponsor fears of boycotts and bad publicity. However, *Soap* helped break taboos by showing that a well-rounded gay character could be embraced by viewers.

In the 1980s, gay characters appeared with more frequency and acceptance. Additionally, gays and lesbians were featured more positively in news coverage, gaining legitimacy in the public realm. The emergence of AIDS helped fuel this coverage, as the disease ravaged the gay male population with a great deal

FAMILY

Family (ABC, 1976–80): An earnest family drama incorporating social issues of the day into the lives of a suburban family, the show was among the first in prime time to seriously address breast cancer, homosexuality, infidelity, teen sex, alcoholism, and adoption in the context of an ongoing set of characters rather than as external problems to be solved on a medical or cop show.

ST. ELSEWHERE

St. Elsewhere (NBC, 1982–88): A critically acclaimed medical drama that similarly transformed the genre as *Hill Street Blues* reinvented the cop show, *St. Elsewhere* combines medical cases, serialized stories of interpersonal relationships, a subtle dark comedic tone, and an exceptional cast. The show was one of the first to tackle AIDS as an issue, foregrounded many crises within the medical industry, and ended with a renowned final scene that reframed the entire series in a thought-provoking way.

of publicity. Television was less active in covering the AIDS crisis than other media, but activists lobbied network news agencies to treat the subject seriously and without prejudice. The decade's most noteworthy representation was the award-winning made-for-television movie *An Early Frost*, aired in 1985. The film dramatized a gay man's AIDS diagnosis, his family's reaction, and the relationship between him and his partner. While criticized by some for being too idealistic and timid in its representations, *Frost*'s success opened the door for AIDS becoming an issue to be addressed on dramatic television, with both single-episode cases and ongoing characters dealing with the disease on medical drama *St. Elsewhere* and sitcom *Designing Women*. Yet openly gay ongoing characters were still a rarity, more commonly represented in "code," as on the sitcom *Love, Sidney*, which featured Tony Randall's title character as a single, neat, and fussy fan of musical theater, to be read as "gay" for viewers in the know.

The 1990s saw a marked boom in the frequency of open gay and lesbian representations, and a shift in their tone. An important breakthrough came on the innovative reality show *The Real World*, as nearly every season includes at least one openly gay or lesbian cast member. Most notably, the 1994 cast featured Pedro Zamora, an openly gay Hispanic man with AIDS, who used the platform of the popular show to educate viewers about the stigmatized disease

MELROSE PLACE

Melrose Place (Fox, 1992–99): A spin-off from teen drama *Beverly Hills, 90210*, *Melrose Place* is a prime time soap about young professionals living in a Los Angeles apartment complex. The show became known for its outlandish plotlines and sexy attitude typifying Fox programming.

shortly before his death. Dramas *thirtysomething* and *Melrose Place* offered ongoing gay characters as part of their ensembles, while sitcoms *Friends*, *Frasier*, *Mad About You*, and *Roseanne* presented gay-friendly leads accepting of homosexual minor characters. Additionally, such sitcoms brought their gay subtext into the foreground. On *Friends*, Chandler and Joey were teasingly offered as a closeted gay couple, while *Seinfeld* famously coined the phrase "not that there's anything wrong with that" as a caveat to Jerry and George's denials of being gay. By the late 1990s, Ellen DeGeneres came out of the closet as a lesbian in real life, bringing her fictional character on *Ellen* with her. Homosexual representations had gone mainstream.

One of the landmark representations of homosexuality was *Will & Grace*, television's first hit comedy starring two gay characters. While there is little doubt that the success of this surprise hit broke ground in mainstream acceptance of gay characters, its representational strategies have been criticized for both embracing stereotypes and failing to present gay relationships. The lead character of Will Truman is a successful gay lawyer who defies stereotypes of effeminate behavior. This idealized representation is reinforced by making his most stable relationship that with his once-girlfriend and sometime roommate Grace. While Will is always clearly identified as gay, his sexual identity is consistently downplayed and thwarted by his coupling with Grace; he is denied a long-term romantic partner until the show's final season and is rarely shown physically involved with men at all. Will stands in direct contrast to his friend Jack McFarland, a stereotypical "queen" obsessed with fashion, musicals, witty repartee, and sex. Jack's over-the-top flamboyance is allowable because it is contrasted with straight-laced Will, and thus the show offers a spectrum of gay representations that denies either extreme as being typical. As a comedy with a broad and campy sensibility, *Will & Grace* rarely delves into the politics of homosexual rights or equality except as the setup for a gag, but as America's most popular images of gay men, Will and Jack need to be taken seriously: over its eight seasons, the show helped define the cultural norms of homosexual identity to millions of viewers who may have had little other exposure to "out" gays and lesbians.

Even though such representations suggested that there was nothing wrong with being gay in the 1990s, this was far from a consensus opinion throughout

The characters of Will and Jack on *Will & Grace* offer a contrasting pair of gay representations: the straight-laced, straight-acting professional versus the flaming queen.

America. While homosexuality was emerging as fashionable within popular culture, gay rights were a wedge issue among voters, and controversies raged concerning issues such as gays in the military and equal rights legislation. Commercial television rarely offers representations contrary to consensus ideologies, for fear of offending sponsors, typically following social change rather than leading it. So why did fictional television seem to offer an accepting vision of homosexuality in the 1990s counter to ideological norms? As discussed in chapter 2, industrial motives often will fuel shifts in representation. In this case, acceptance of gay and lesbian characters was seen as a way to appeal to a desirable audience segment for networks: socially liberal, urban-minded professionals, or what one critic terms *slumpies*. While certainly many of the gay and lesbian producers and executives in the television industry wanted to offer a more positive and accepting vision of homosexuality, if such meanings could not be sold to advertisers as a way to attract desirable audiences, such representations would never have aired. Similar to the shift toward provocative content on early 1970s hits *M*A*S*H* and *All in the Family* being motivated by the desire to reach young urban viewers, gay and lesbian representations in the 1990s thrived because profits trumped politics.[7]

Just as the history of racial representations suggests that visibility does not ensure successfully positive images, the growth of gay and lesbian representations has not simply been a tale of progress. Open representation of homosexuality has been virtually absent among nonfiction performers, such as

The Fab Five of gay fashionistas on *Queer Eye* embrace a straight guy to make him over into a metrosexual, both highlighting and playing with stereotypes.

sportscasters, broadcast journalists, and game show hosts—MSNBC's Rachel Maddow became the first openly homosexual national news host in 2008, although her sexuality is rarely referenced on her program. Some reality programs have featured openly gay contestants and performers—most notably, *Queer Eye for the Straight Guy* was a surprise hit in 2003, offering a Fab Five of gay savants to make over a straight guy in the "metrosexual" vein. While *Queer Eye* certainly promotes straight acceptance of gay culture and identity, it does so using typical stereotypes of gay flamboyance, consumerism, and wit, while ignoring the sexual dimension of gay identity entirely; on this show, homosexuality is simply an accessory used to help improve straight men. When gays and lesbians are featured on network television, whether on reality programs *The Amazing Race* and *Big Brother* or fictional programs *Will & Grace* and *ER*, the standards for representing intimacy and physical contact are quite limiting, and more restrictive than for heterosexual behavior. Premium cable channels HBO and Showtime, on the other hand, have been more explicit in representing gay and lesbian relationships, sexuality, and communities on programs such as *Six Feet Under*, *Queer as Folk*, and *The L Word*. Thus even though gays and lesbians are visible across television, there are distinct limits on how they can be represented and what roles they can serve within commercial television.

This discussion of television's representation of identity categories has focused on three main types of identity: race and ethnicity, gender, and sexual orientation. Other identity categories could be explored along similar veins—for

QUEER EYE

Queer Eye for the Straight Guy (Bravo, 2003–07): A merger of the reality trend and gay chic, *Queer Eye* became a surprise hit in featuring a quintet of fashionable gay advisors to make over straight slobs. The show simultaneously embraces and pokes fun at gay stereotypes, which led to an ambivalent reception from the gay community.

THE L WORD

The L Word (Showtime, 2004–09): A drama about a community of lesbians in Los Angeles, this show, along with *Queer as Folk,* helped brand Showtime as a gay-friendly channel and differentiate it from HBO's more male-centered programming.

instance, representations of class differences can be understood as pertaining to cultural identity. Scholars have studied how television represents rural versus urban identities, and considered how age groups such as teenagers or the elderly are presented. No matter what specific identity category is considered as part of television's representational role, we must consider how the issue of representation is not simply contained by what is presented on-screen within programming. Television's industry, regulatory framework, technological shifts, and viewing practices all impact how meanings are conveyed, constructed, and consumed. Textual representations are part of a larger puzzle of the cultural impact of television explored throughout this book.

Even though representations and meanings coded within texts are powerful, we must remember that their cultural importance becomes relevant only when seen by viewers. There are no controls as to how viewers will interpret such representations, and thus intended meanings can be missed or altered in the process of watching and discussing television programming. Beyond the institutions forming American television and the meanings created by programs themselves, we must consider how viewers engage with television as part of their everyday lives, making sense of the medium and gauging the impact television has on people. This facet of viewer practice is the focus of the next chapter.

FURTHER READING

Representations of identity are one of the most studied areas of television scholarship. Gail Dines and Jean Humez, eds., *Gender, Race, and Class in Media: A*

Text-Reader, 2d ed. (Thousand Oaks, Calif.: Sage Publications, 2003), provides a wide assortment of relevant scholarship, while nearly any collection of television scholarship will have some work focused on representational issues.

The representation of African-Americans has been widely studied in scholarship including: Herman Gray, *Watching Race: Television and the Struggle for "Blackness"* (Minneapolis: University of Minnesota Press, 1995); Sasha Torres, *Black, White, and in Color: Television and Black Civil Rights* (Princeton, N.J.: Princeton University Press, 2003); and Darnell M. Hunt, *Channeling Blackness: Studies on Television and Race in America* (New York: Oxford University Press, 2005); as well as an excellent documentary, Marlon Riggs, dir., *Color Adjustment* (PBS, 1991). Sut Jhally and Justin Lewis, *Enlightened Racism:* The Cosby Show, *Audiences, and the Myth of the American Dream* (Boulder, Colo.: Westview Press, 1992), offer an important study of the reception of one key program, while Robin R. Means Coleman, *African-American Viewers and the Black Situation Comedy: Situating Racial Humor* (New York: Garland Publishing, 2000), focuses on the important genre of black sitcoms.

The study of other racial groups has been less developed. Arlene M. Dávila, *Latinos, Inc.: The Marketing and Making of a People* (Berkeley: University of California Press, 2001), explores the construction of the Latino market segment, including television, while Yeidy M. Rivero, *Tuning Out Blackness: Race and Nation in the History of Puerto Rican Television* (Durham, N.C.: Duke University Press, 2005), explores the specific realm of television's representation in Puerto Rico. Darrell Y. Hamamoto, *Monitored Peril: Asian Americans and the Politics of TV Representation* (Minneapolis: University of Minnesota Press, 1994), explores Asian American representation in the classic network era. George Lipsitz, *Time Passages: Collective Memory and American Popular Culture* (Minneapolis: University of Minnesota Press, 1990), offers an important history of 1950s ethnic television, and Sasha Torres, ed., *Living Color: Race and Television in the United States* (Durham, N.C.: Duke University Press, 1998), includes articles on an array of racial representations.

Gender has been explored by a wide range of scholars, with relevant work collected in Lynn Spigel and Denise Mann, eds., *Private Screenings: Television and the Female Consumer* (Minneapolis: University of Minnesota Press, 1992), and Charlotte Brunsdon and Lynn Spigel, eds., *Feminist Television Criticism: A Reader,* 2d ed. (Maidenhead, UK: Open University Press, 2008). Susan J. Douglas, *Where the Girls Are: Growing Up Female with the Mass Media* (New York: Times Books, 1994), and Bonnie J. Dow, *Prime Time Feminism: Television, Media Culture, and the Women's Movement Since 1970* (Philadelphia: University of Pennsylvania Press, 1996), both offer engaging histories of female representation, while Amanda D. Lotz, *Redesigning Women: Television After the Network Era* (Urbana: University of Illinois Press, 2006), focuses on more contemporary programs.

Representations of sexuality have been increasingly prevalent as a topic of scholarship in recent years. Elana Levine, *Wallowing in Sex: The New Sexual Culture of 1970s American Television* (Durham, N.C.: Duke University Press, 2007), provides an examination of both heterosexual and homosexual representations in the 1970s. Stephen Tropiano, *The Prime Time Closet: A History of Gays and Lesbians on TV* (New York: Applause Books, 2002), surveys the shifting representations of homosexuality, while Ron Becker, *Gay TV and Straight America* (New Brunswick, N.J.: Rutgers University Press, 2006), provides a compelling analysis of the rise of gay representations in the 1990s.

NOTES

[1] Joan L. Conners, "Color TV? Diversity in Prime Time TV," in *Race/Gender/Media:Considering Diversity Across Audiences, Content, and Producers*, ed. Rebecca Ann Lind (Boston: Pearson Education, 2004), 206–12.

[2] See Barak Goodman, dir., *Frontline: Merchants of Cool*, PBS, 2001.

[3] See George Lipsitz, *Time Passages: Collective Memory and American Popular Culture* (Minneapolis: University of Minnesota Press, 1990).

[4] See Sut Jhally and Justin Lewis, *Enlightened Racism: The Cosby Show, Audiences, and the Myth of the American Dream* (Boulder, Colo.: Westview Press, 1992).

[5] See Susan J. Douglas, *Where the Girls Are: Growing Up Female with the Mass Media* (New York: Times Books, 1994), for such a historical account.

[6] See Elana Levine, *Wallowing in Sex:The New Sexual Culture of 1970s American Television* (Durham, N.C.: Duke University Press, 2007), for a detailed history of 1970s sexual representation.

[7] See Ron Becker, *Gay TV and Straight America* (New Brunswick, N.J.: Rutgers University Press, 2006).

SECTION 3

Television Practices

This book explores the intersection of television and American culture, with the first section focusing on the private and public institutions responsible for creating, distributing, and regulating television, and the second section considering the cultural dimension of meaning more fully. In examining the form and content of television programming, section 2 follows one definition of the term **culture**—the meanings that circulate within a society, especially in the realms of art, media, and communication. This section will add to that discussion with another facet of the term culture, considering *practices of everyday life* as the location of American culture. Thus we can define culture in this regard as a general term for "how people live," encompassing a broad array of behaviors and beliefs. This definition of culture derives from traditional anthropology, where Western scholars examined little-known societies that often differed drastically from their own. However, more recently anthropologists and other scholars have used similar methods to explore their own societies and cultures. To understand the common everyday practices typically left unexamined in the United States, we can turn an anthropological eye toward the mirror, examining the seemingly mundane everyday life of Americans.

Understanding culture as everyday practice spans a range of issues. Chapter 9 focuses on the specific practices involved in viewing television, including issues concerning media violence and fandom. Chapter 10 considers the particular segment of children viewers, as many of the concerns and debates around television's impact focus on youth. Finally, chapter 11 turns to the technology of television, considering how technological change impacts and shapes viewer practices. Together, this section serves as an important reminder that television's power is not lodged solely in institutions and texts, but also in the ways we engage with the medium.

CHAPTER 9

VIEWING TELEVISION

What role does television play in American everyday life? Certainly watching television is a key pastime for many, and the meanings gleaned from the screen have significant social impact. But the act of watching television itself is more than just receiving meanings: people interact with media through a wide range of practices, and thus we need critically to question the assumed position of the television viewer as "couch potato." Likewise, television's impact goes beyond the moments in front of the screen, as television is talked about, debated, and studied in a range of ways. Thus to understand the variety of roles television plays in the everyday practices of Americans, we need to study viewers and critics, fans and activists, educators and children—all of whom help shape the important ways television matters in our lives and culture.

TELEVISION VIEWERS:
PASSIVE OR ACTIVE, EFFECTS OR INFLUENCES?

One of the questions surrounding television that has been most studied concerns the medium's impact on viewers: How does television affect us? An entire subfield of academic study of television has developed around this issue of media effects, researching the medium's impact on the people who consume it. Other researchers, who embrace a model of active viewers, have questioned the underlying assumption of the media effects paradigm that television viewing can even be understood within a framework of causes and effects. This debate rages among media scholars and causes such sharp division that some adherents to each side regard the research produced by the other side as simply illegitimate. While this book makes no claims to reconcile this division, this section lays out the core arguments and criticisms of both media effects and active viewer research, suggesting how the insights from both models might inform our understanding of television's role in everyday life.

The Media Effects Paradigm and Passive Viewers

For a large number of scholars, the dominant research agenda for understanding American television is to measure how the medium affects its viewers, an approach generally known as the **media effects paradigm**. This approach is common among researchers, and used quite frequently by policymakers, critics, and the television industry to justify regulatory policies, condemnations of programming, and marketing campaigns, respectively. It is most commonly found in research within the discipline of **mass communications**, which emerged in the mid-twentieth century in the United States and still thrives as an academic field. Underlying early mass communications research was a three-stage model of the communication process: a sender creates a message and transmits it to a receiver. This **sender–message–receiver** model follows basic common sense regardless of the medium—someone speaks to other people in the hope that he will understand the intended message, just as I write this book trying to convey ideas to its readers. If we analyze either a conversation or book, we might consider communication successful only if the receiver understands the message as intended by the sender. In this model, senders have the power to communicate effectively, and success is judged by whether receivers accept the messages they receive—in other words, receivers primarily function as passive recipients of messages that they can accept or reject.

Early mass communication research was particularly interested in analyzing **propaganda**, as the field emerged in the wake of World War II and during the rise of the cold war. Propaganda messages are designed to have a direct **persuasive** effect on their receivers, shaping opinions and motivating actions. Not surprisingly, the research on persuasion and propaganda has been most directly applied to television advertising, where senders are highly motivated to generate specific effects upon viewers, as discussed in chapter 2. For some researchers, the fact that propaganda and advertising can have direct and measurable effects on viewers is evidence that all media operate similarly, with clear effects upon viewers. However, we must be careful to distinguish between media designed expressly to persuade, such as advertising and propaganda, and programs created with less persuasive goals, such as to entertain, to inform, to amuse, or to provoke emotions of fear, sadness, or excitement. Do such programs, which comprise the bulk of television besides advertising, have similarly measurable direct effects?

This is a question that divides the field of media studies. For media effects researchers, the answer is a firm "yes": all kinds of media can potentially affect viewers in significant, direct, and measurable ways. Such researchers have developed a number of different methodologies and theoretical models to account for the effects of media on viewers. The most commonly employed approach follows the paradigm of **behavioral effects theory**, in which the actions and behaviors of viewers are directly affected by an outside stimulus such as television. In its most extreme form, such research adheres to a **hypodermic needle** model of media effects: television is a foreign substance injected into a passively viewing victim, which directly causes a change in behavior. While almost no researchers subscribe to such a crude approach today, the metaphor is still powerful in the common sense of many media critics, policymakers, and parents looking to "save" children from perceived deadly and addictive effects of drug-like media.

More subtle approaches to media effects still believe that the stimulus of television can cause direct effects, but reactions are much more variable and linked to a variety of factors and contexts than the metaphor of a direct injection. Researchers looking to prove behavioral effects commonly rely upon **experimental research** that measures changes in attitudes, actions, or physiology after exposure to particular media content. Many such experiments have demonstrated behavioral effects of media upon some viewers—for instance, experimental research has suggested that viewing violent programming increases the immediate likelihood of some viewers exhibiting aggressive behavior. Such experimental research must be understood with some important caveats, as it typically demonstrates only immediate short-term effects, not the long-term social impacts of television that many media critics ultimately believe shape viewers' attitudes and behaviors. Experimental research is also always removed from the way actual viewers experience media, as the laboratory setting itself can influence behaviors. Additionally, even when direct effects are observed, it is always in only a statistically relevant portion of the research subjects, not as a universal reaction to the experiment. Thus the bulk of media effects research suggests a model of **limited effects**—*some* media have *some* effects on *some* viewers in *some* circumstances—far from the overwhelming claims of television's harmful impacts that are often repeated in the press and by politicians.

Another way of measuring media effects relies on real-world behaviors rather than laboratory experiments. Via **survey methods**, viewer attitudes and behaviors are collected and coded, and researchers attempt to find connections between variables, such as links between the amount of television viewed and beliefs about violent crime. One of the most well developed approaches to analyzing media effects via survey research is called **cultivation theory**. This approach uses long-term surveys to chart the correlation between television viewing and social attitudes, based on the hypothesis that people who view a large amount of television are likely to share opinions and values that are reinforced by programming. Cultivation analysis typically does not consider specific programs or genres, but rather looks at how consuming television as a medium impacts people's perspectives of the world. Cultivation researchers view the medium of television as an entire ecological system or environment, as discussed more in chapter 11, rather than conveying particular meanings within specific texts. Researchers chart the broad cumulative patterns of meaning offered by television, and then pose questions via surveys to chart how varying degrees of television viewing might cultivate opinions that mesh with television's meanings. In many ways, cultivation theory follows an ideological approach to textual analysis as discussed in chapter 7, but uses quantitative methods to measure the correlation between television viewing and beliefs in areas such as consumerism and racial identity. The most well known hypothesis offered by cultivation theory is called the **mean world syndrome**, which argues that heavy viewers of television are likely to view society as more dangerous and violent than it actually is, a belief that fosters emotions of fear, distrust, and anxiety.

While survey research and cultivation theory offer provocative claims about how media consumption might shape our world views and cultural norms, such methodologies can only demonstrate a **correlation** between factors, showing that it is statistically more probable than by chance that particular variables coincide. This mode of research cannot prove **causation**, or that one variable causes another. Thus a survey might show that children who watch more

News stories designed to provoke fear and anxiety pervade the airwaves, arguably shaping viewer perception about a "mean world" that is unsafe and threatening.

televised violence are more likely to behave aggressively, but this does not prove that television caused the aggressive behavior. Viewers with aggressive personalities might be more likely to enjoy violent programming, or both behaviors might be tied to a third variable, such as educational aptitude or family situations. Such correlational research generally finds that the statistical linkages between media and behaviors are less significant than other structural and contextual variables, so again these studies point to a limited effects model for some viewers in some contexts, positioning media consumption as a potential "risk factor" for particular behaviors, rather than as a direct catalyst. Surveys can also fall prey to a number of research flaws: questions can bias respondents toward particular answers; or there may be inaccuracies inherent in reporting people's behaviors and attitudes. Well-constructed surveys showing correlations between media and behaviors can be quite useful, especially as long-term studies measuring changes within the same group over time, but it is crucial not to mistakenly equate evidence of correlation with proof of causation, as press and policy summaries of such research often do.

The bulk of media effects research focuses on the impact of violence upon viewers. Researchers typically use techniques of content analysis, as discussed in chapter 8, to quantify and label the amount of violence in varying programs. These quantitative accounts of violence are then used as evidence to support the cultural impact of more limited experimental or survey findings. It is crucial to note that no reputable researcher claims that simply identifying the content of a program proves its impact. While the most adamant voices against media violence believe that experimental and survey research have conclusively proven definitive harmful effects of television violence, the content of the texts themselves does not provide evidence regarding its impact on viewers. For adherents to the media effects research paradigm, the evidence from experimental and survey research appears to suggest conclusively that media violence produces the effects of fear, aggression, desensitization to violence, and lowered inhibitions toward actual violent behavior. They acknowledge that such effects are only strong in a small percentage of viewers with predispositions toward violence or other contextual factors, but they contend that television causes small negative effects upon the majority of the population. However, a large number of scholars question the core foundations of media effects as a paradigm.

Part of the criticism of media effects research stems from a broader divide between **quantitative** social scientific research, which nearly all media effects researchers embrace, and adherents to **qualitative** methods more common in the humanities and certain social sciences such as anthropology and sociology. For qualitative researchers, the meanings of television programs and the ways viewers respond to those meanings are far too varied and complex to be easily quantified into simple categories, "violent" and "nonviolent"—such criticisms point out that in some quantitative studies, an image of Bugs Bunny hitting Elmer Fudd might be coded identically to news footage of a war zone or a bloody shootout in a fictional police drama. Likewise a broad range of viewer attitudes and opinions is typically reduced to one or two variables for statistical purposes, oversimplifying the breadth and complexity of human behavior for analytical convenience. For qualitative researchers, the phenomenon of media viewing must be understood through more interpretive means: in-depth analyses of programs and representations, as explored in chapters 7 and 8, and via interviews and observations of actual viewer behaviors, considered more below. The disagreement between quantitative and qualitative researchers is perhaps an irreconcilable divide, as each side can argue that their method is the only way truly to understand the phenomena they study. A reasonable middle ground is to acknowledge that insights can emerge from each approach, and that the specific research questions being posed might effectively be explored from a variety of relevant methodologies.

Media effects research has also been criticized for its core assumptions and attitudes toward television. Media effects researchers typically hold a negative opinion about television, seeing it as a destructive social influence. Their research looks to prove the specific ways they believe television causes problems. Yet this perspective arguably clouds their analysis in key ways: by searching for problems caused by television, they typically ignore both the potential social benefits of the medium and the additional factors that might be more powerful causes of the social ills linked to television. For instance, if the social problem being researched is youth violence in America, many factors correlate much more strongly with violent behaviors than television viewing, including poverty, drug use, peer influence, parenting styles, educational achievement, and psychological conditions. Likewise some studies of television viewing suggest that just as violence can provoke negative effects in some viewers, the same content might reduce or redirect aggressive behaviors in other viewers, an aspect that media effects researchers rarely explore seriously. According to the strongest critics of media effects research, the inherent anti-television biases of researchers undermine the entire field, as studies are designed and interpreted only through the lens of proving researchers' already-held beliefs about the medium's lack of value.

The final major critique of media effects research concerns how the field conceives of television viewers as passive recipients of messages and social effects. The basic model of media effects conceives of senders and messages as much more powerful than receivers in a communication system. At its extreme, the hypodermic needle assumption treats viewers as entirely passive recipients of drug-like media injections, but even more nuanced and complex accounts of viewing through the models of cultivation theory and limited effects assume that the primary place of viewers in the media system is to receive messages and feel their associated effects. Even the use of the term *effects* implies that what happens to viewers is caused by external factors, similar to the effects of ingested substances such as drugs or medicine. Another school of media research avoids the language of *effects* by focusing more on "media influences," considering how the media function within a larger cultural context of people's lives.

The Media Influence Paradigm and Active Viewers

No media researcher would argue that the content of television has no impact on viewers. Obviously television provides information, persuasive messages, and emotional experiences that significantly influence both individual viewers and society as a whole. The divide within the field concerns both the relative power of such messages versus the actions and choices of viewers, and the most appropriate methods to understand the influence of television. While media effects researchers attempt to measure direct effects of television upon viewers using quantitative methods, a competing approach could be understood as the **media influence** paradigm. Under this approach, researchers believe that the impact of television is best understood by studying actual lived experiences, rather than abstracted surveys or laboratory experiments, using qualitative methods of interviews and interpretation. Scholars studying media influences look at television as one of many factors that help shape behaviors and attitudes, avoiding claims of simple causality or direct effects. Rather, media are considered as part of a broader cultural context to be studied from the perspective of a viewer's everyday life.

Media effects researchers tend to regard programs or entire media systems as stimuli with measurable effects, gauging average effects on a large number of viewers. The media influence approach looks at the power of messages in relation to the power and practices of the viewers themselves. This shift in emphasis requires a different understanding of the basic act of communication, a rethinking of the core process of sender–message–receiver. An influential revised model of communication, developed for understanding television news, but applicable to all media, focuses on the **encoding/decoding** of messages.[1] According to this approach, the creation of media texts involves multiple meanings and competing ideas included in the production process. As discussed in chapter 5, formal choices conveying meanings in a television program might signify a broad range of ideas and represent the input of dozens of production personnel. Thus texts are seen as encoded with multiple meanings through their production, rather than a singular "sent" message. Most scholars looking at texts through this framework consider how a program encodes ideological and hegemonic representations; as discussed in chapter 7, many messages are not explicitly intended by creators, but reflect an unquestioned set of "common sense" norms and assumptions. By looking at a range of multiple encoded meanings, scholars explore how programs allow for a cultural forum of ideas, rather than for a singular uniform message.

The process of consuming or decoding a text allows for a similar range of interpretations and understandings, rather than a simple "reception" of an intended meaning. For scholars of media influence, understanding the varying ways to decode a program is crucial to assessing its cultural impact. This decoding process is not an open free-for-all to interpret any meaning into a program, but is framed by cultural and social limitations. Obviously many encoded messages frequently convey their intended meanings, as news programs communicate facts about current events or a soap opera projects its emotional tone. However, it would be a mistake to think that all encoded meanings are conveyed equally, or that the only meanings people take away from programs result from intended messages. Viewers bring their own frameworks and expectations to the decoding process, including their particular social situations, such as age or economic class, as well as their personal tastes and experiences. Thus the process of decoding is an intersection between a text that contains a multitude of encoded messages, and a viewer with a range of influences that shape his or her perception. Out of this junction emerges a limited number of different possible interpretations.

Scholars have charted a spectrum of decoding as it specifically relates to the ideological messages within a text. At one extreme is a **dominant decoding**, which fully accepts ideological messages as common sense, similar to the "hailed" viewer discussed in chapter 7. Thus for a shampoo commercial, a viewer with a dominant decoding might see her own hair as worse than the woman in the ad and believe that happiness could be achieved by better hair, as obtainable through this shampoo. At the other extreme is an **oppositional decoding**, which recognizes the ideological messages of the text and rejects them as flawed or irrelevant to the viewer's own social position and experiences. A viewer with an oppositional decoding looks at the shampoo advertisement as misleading and manipulative, trying to convince her to be unhappy for failing to live up to unrealistic beauty norms.

Most viewers fall somewhere between these two poles, engaging with texts via **negotiated decodings** that accept some dominant meanings while rejecting others, based on how they relate to viewers' own experiences and social positions. There could be many different negotiated decodings of this hypothetical ad, such as a viewer who identifies with the problem of split ends but doubts that this shampoo could solve it, or a viewer who uses the advertised shampoo but does not see split ends as a real problem—or even a bald viewer who finds the messages and product ironically amusing. Such readings are always subject to the limits of the text, as viewers have the ability to negotiate with textual meanings but not to invent completely new interpretations: a viewer who saw the shampoo ad as advocating for universal health care would be dismissed as misinterpreting the text. Thus this approach to studying television consumption examines both the degree to which media messages influence viewers, and how viewers' backgrounds and beliefs influence how they might embrace, reject, or negotiate with those messages.

Advertisements are typically straightforward messages to examine for media influence: they are encoded with explicit messages designed to influence viewers, and resulting consumer behavior is a fairly direct measure of that influence. Most programming is much more complicated, both in terms of the complexity of encoded messages and the various ways viewers might decode them. For instance, the political thriller *24* is encoded with a broad array of meanings, ranging from reinforcing traditional gender roles with helpless female characters rescued by powerful men, to offering commentary on government corruption and bureaucracy. For a media effects researcher, the show's central meaning might concern its portrayal of violence, conveying the message that extreme violence and even torture can be a heroic solution to problems. Researchers might use experiments or surveys to gauge how viewer behaviors and attitudes toward violence and politics might be affected by consuming the program. A media influences scholar would look at a broader range of meanings and ways of decoding the show, trying to account for how a viewer's background and beliefs influence the way he makes sense of *24*. A viewer with a law enforcement background who believes that terrorists and criminals must be stopped using every available technique might find that *24* reinforces his dominant beliefs, while other oppositional viewers might find the graphic violence and ideological messages so distasteful that they watch the show only to be outraged. Other viewers might enjoy the show despite the violence, embracing its narrative suspense and complex storytelling but rejecting the morally questionable behaviors of characters, thus negotiating with the program to focus on the particular meanings and pleasures most relevant to them. Such negotiations might be motivated by other aspects of the text: the show's representation of an African-American president, the quirky personality of Chloe, or the visual style of split screens and hand-held cameras. Media influence researchers reject a simple model of direct effects, arguing instead that meanings are made at the intersection between a broad assortment of elements within a show such as *24* and the range of viewer experiences and social positions.

How do researchers proceed in making sense of the various elements and possibilities that factor into media influences under this model? Most scholars under this paradigm follow an approach known as **cultural studies**, a set of related methodologies and theories that explores culture as a site of negotiation and struggle, rather than simply the cause of social problems. To understand how people are influenced by television, cultural studies scholars use two primary methods. The first is textual analysis, as discussed in chapter 7, where researchers analyze the range of meanings encoded in texts and consider how particular meanings might uphold or challenge dominant ideologies. Textual analysis can outline a spectrum of potential meanings, forming the limits of multiple interpretations that might be activated by viewers' decoding, and highlighting how a text might privilege particular meanings through narrative structure or other formal elements. But to understand the decoding process, cultural studies scholars use qualitative **reception research** to investigate how actual viewers make sense of texts. Such research can use open-ended surveys, interviews, focus groups, observations, analyses of published reviews or comments (in a magazine or online forum), or other related methods, sometimes in tandem with quantitative methods to correlate the decoding process with people's social identities via categories such as race, age, or economic class. The goal of cultural studies reception research is to capture the ways people actually consume and decode media in their everyday lives, charting both how media influence viewers and how various viewers influence the interpretive process.

This reception research has pointed to some broad trends concerning how people make sense of media. Foremost, the research has highlighted the inability of media messages uniformly to determine their own influences, as actual viewer responses and practices are much more wide ranging and variable than either media effects researchers or traditional ideological critics claim. These diverse interpretations are typically limited by what is encoded in the text, but also are directly shaped by a viewer's **context**: preexisting beliefs, social situations, identities, attitudes, and modes of viewing are central factors in shaping how people decode and make sense of media texts. While certainly messages can have powerful influences on viewers, and people's social contexts can guide their interpretations, cultural studies research argues that television viewers are ultimately much more active than the passive model portrayed by media effects research, and engage with a television program in a broader variety of ways than simply absorbing singular messages.

Critics have questioned both the methodologies and findings of cultural studies research, highlighting some of the limits of the paradigm. The qualitative methods of interviewing and interpretation are certainly not designed to be the controlled scientific measures that media effects research often claims to be. Qualitative studies typically focus on a small number of non-random viewers, not statistically representative pools of viewers. Such studies claim that their usefulness is not in predicting behaviors or measuring cause and effect, but in examining the range of practices comprising everyday life that viewers might follow. Just because one viewer offers a particular interpretation does not mean that others will see the program in the same way, but that interpretation points to a distinct possibility among a range of options. Such research is inherently interpretive rather than framed by controlled experiments or statistical surveys, and thus must rely on the power of persuasive argument to convey the broader relevance of such real-world viewing practices. Cultural studies research is dependent on viewers relating their own practices and perspectives, and thus can be critiqued both for relying on questionably subjective self-reported information and for offering only inconclusive interpretations of what people say about themselves. At its worst, cultural studies research simply reports the opinions of viewers without sufficient analysis of those opinions' significance and contexts, but well-done research can point to how broader social factors help shape our viewing experiences and attitudes in a more complex and varied fashion than media effects models of direct causality.

How can two groups of well-respected scholars studying television viewers paint such divergent pictures of how messages impact people? In part, the difference between media effects and influences paradigms stems from the core attitudes and starting points of the researchers. Many media effects researchers start with a core belief that television is a negative social influence, and thus they conduct studies to prove this influence; while cultural studies scholars tend to be more focused on understanding the social practices of everyday life, and thus they start by regarding viewers more sympathetically to see how television fits into their lives. One of the key differences between the media effects and media influence approaches is the willingness to consider the activity and agency of viewers in making cultural judgments, interpretations, and decisions through the act of watching television. Thus researchers might view the same data on viewing behaviors quite differently: a media effects scholar would foreground the evidence that some viewer behaviors shifted negatively in reaction to programming, while a media influence scholar would emphasize the broad range of responses viewers can take away from programming, complicating simple negative/positive characterizations.

The biggest danger in trying to understand the effects or influences of television is the tendency to oversimplify what is a tremendously complex and multifaceted social practice into a simple slogan or generalization. Almost no studies claim to have definitively proven that television causes real-world violent behaviors, or that television viewers are free to make whatever meanings they care to. However, these claims are often made by people referring to such studies, used to justify industrial and policy decisions, and offered as justification for condemning or celebrating television as a medium. The impact of television programming on viewers is much studied, but still up for debate. Understanding the methodological strategies and findings of such research, and looking at competing models to compare competing viewpoints, is the key to discerning the important question of how viewers are impacted by what they see on television.

NOT JUST WATCHING:
THE CULTURAL PRACTICES OF TELEVISION

By focusing on the questions of media effects and influences, we run the danger of reducing the complex practice of television viewing solely to its social impacts.

While there is no doubt that the influence of television on its viewers is a crucial area to explore, such impacts are not the only way the television matters in the everyday lives of Americans. Television is such a pervasive medium that its presence is felt in nearly every facet of our lives. Taking a broader account of how television matters in American culture forces us to consider questions about why we watch television, how we relate to television within our everyday conversations and practices, and what role television plays in our lives even when we are away from the screen.

One uncontroversial claim about television is that watching it occupies a great deal of time in the lives of most Americans. According to a 2007 survey, Americans watch an average of 2.6 hours of television each day; only sleeping and working occupy more of people's time.[2] Watching television is by far the most popular leisure activity among Americans of nearly every imaginable demographic grouping, and people also spend time talking and thinking about television in their time away from the screen. Television's importance in people's everyday lives cannot be reduced to the effects or influences the medium might have upon viewers. Instead, we must consider how people think about and engage with television in a broad variety of ways.

Talking about Television

Research on television viewers tends to focus solely on the act of watching programming. For the television industry, the ratings research discussed in chapter 2 reduces all viewer practices into approximate measures of who is watching what. Media effects and influences researchers alike focus on the meanings and impacts viewers take away from the act of watching a television program. But if you think about the various roles television plays in your own life, you will probably realize that time in front of the screen is only one part of television's everyday importance. Television often serves as a key topic and source of social interactions and engagement. People discuss programs with friends, share television memories as a common cultural bond, go online to find information about their favorite programs, and even read books or take courses about television. How we understand television extends to these practices outside the act of viewing.

One key concept for understanding television is how the medium is framed by **discourses**, or the way people talk about a topic. Television itself has many meanings and possible functions, as illustrated throughout this book. However, certain discourses help define particular ways of thinking about television. For instance, a commonly used metaphor is to conceive of television as a drug. Terms such as "the plug-in drug," referring to viewers as "TV junkies" or "addicts," and describing the act of watching as "narcotizing" or "getting a TV fix" all help reinforce the connection between consuming television and drug use. Academic research into media effects might consider the "hypodermic needle" model for television's impact on viewers, while policymakers condemn television's effects of "dumbing down" youth in terms matching a substance abuse epidemic. These phrases are rarely based on actual evidence of how television might function similarly to drugs, but rather they follow a metaphorical discourse for defining the medium in drug-like terms. Examining the discourses that frame how television is understood and discussed helps us more carefully understand how the medium is actually used versus what is just overblown rhetoric about television.

One common tendency among discourses concerning television is to present the medium as part of a **moral panic**, a concept describing exaggerated fears of popular culture trends throughout history, from nineteenth-century vaudeville theater to contemporary video games, and typically justified in the name of protecting children. Television violence, representations of sex, and alleged negative physiological effects from watching television have all been framed as moral panics, and have generated outrage and calls for increased regulation. These discourses all function to frame television as a negative social influence, furthering a seemingly commonsense assumption that the medium is a destructive factor in American life. Such discourses have even spurred activists to call for eliminating television from cultural life, through organizations such as TV Turnoff Network and scheduled TV Turn-Off weeks. While such attempts are certainly legitimate ways of calling attention to television's potential negative impacts on American society, it is important to examine critically the assumptions behind discourses that universally condemn the medium, as such claims are often exaggerated and subject to debate.

For many people, watching television is a cultural contradiction: it is a pleasurable activity we spend a great deal of time doing, but we feel guilty about it and ultimately doubt the medium's cultural value and worth. Television occupies a low level of cultural prestige compared with other media: dedicated film fans are "cinephiles" or "film buffs," and music fans are "aficionados" or even "snobs," but anyone who admits their devotion to television is a "couch potato," "vidiot," or "TV junkie." This distinction is in part due to the commercialized system of American television, where the industry often embraces formula and avoids creative risks in search of mass audiences, as discussed in chapter 1. However, even the most innovative and sophisticated television lacks cultural prestige, as the discourses used to define the medium for decades have framed television as uniformly lowbrow and devalued. Programs that do garner critical praise and prestige typically rise above the average value of television via metaphors to other media, hailing shows like *The Sopranos* or *The Wire* as "cinematic" or "televised novels." Scholars and students taking a closer look at television need to look beyond its assumed lack of value and consider how the medium might be reframed as a legitimate and worthwhile cultural form on its own terms, and to reframe its viewers as doing more than "wasting time."

Even though television is devalued in comparison with other media, it is still the central form of communication, information, and storytelling in American culture. Viewers do experience legitimate and authentic pleasure in watching television, embracing a wide range of programming and ways of engaging with the medium. One important pleasure for many is television's role as a **cultural ritual**, a regular part of people's daily lives that can reassure, relax, and provide consistent enjoyment for viewers. Certain programs and nightly lineups can be embraced as **appointment television**, valuable parts of people's daily or weekly routines that viewers schedule as they would lunch with a friend. In the 1990s, NBC notably capitalized on this phenomenon with its lineup of "Must See TV," building a group of programs into a mandatory part of viewers' weekly schedule. Many viewers embrace the ability to start each day with the familiar face of a favorite news anchor, immerse themselves in the interwoven stories featured on a long-running soap opera, or relax with the vicarious participation of a game show, all of which provide legitimate pleasures that comfort and reassure them as a stable and consistent part of their lives.

For some people, television can become an activist cause; they invest their time, energy, and money to help shape the programs featured on television. The group Viewers for Quality Television was formed to lobby networks and advertisers to renew programs with poor ratings but high acclaim, including *Hill Street Blues, Cagney and Lacey,* and *Homicide: Life on the Street.* Other groups engage with the television industry around the politics of representation; the Gay & Lesbian Alliance Against Defamation (GLAAD) lobbies against stereotyped characters and offers awards for more inclusive programming, as well as creating newsletters and websites highlighting and critiquing representations. On the other end of the political spectrum, the Parents Television Council lobbies and critiques programming it believes offers so-called "anti-family" messages of profanity, violence, and homosexuality. These organizations and their supporters engage with the content of the medium and the industry in order to make television fit with their drastically differing visions of what American culture should stand for—but they are united in the belief that television should be taken seriously and that it serves a central cultural role in everyday life.

Many of television's pleasures are social, fostering connections and common ground among people. In the medium's early decades, watching television often served as a family ritual, as families gathered together in the same room to share common entertainment and information. In the earliest years of television, this communal function extended to neighborhoods, as groups would congregate in the street's one house or apartment with a television to watch "Uncle Miltie," or in a local tavern to watch a boxing match. In the multi-channel and digital convergence eras, family members typically have their own dedicated programs, channels, and even separate screens, leading some critics to decry the loss of the

HEROES

Heroes (NBC, 2006–present): A surprise hit for NBC, *Heroes* takes a comic book premise of people developing into superheroes and ties it to other genres of soap opera and conspiracy mystery. The series is notable for its use of multimedia, running an online comic book and alternate reality game to supplement its core television narrative.

SPONGEBOB SQUAREPANTS

SpongeBob SquarePants (Nickelodeon, 1999–present): One of television's most successful children's programs, *SpongeBob* portrays the wacky adventures of a group of sea creatures with an absurd sense of humor. The show has been highly successful in creating tie-in merchandise, a feature film, and soundtracks incorporating numerous well-known musicians who add to the show's appeal to teenagers and adults.

"electronic hearth" in the wake of narrowcasting and fragmentation. However, social bonds still are forged around television outside the home: co-workers discuss the previous night's episode of *Heroes*, college students gather in a dorm lounge to watch *Grey's Anatomy*, teenagers instant-message one another while watching *American Idol*, and children act out episodes of *SpongeBob SquarePants* on the playground. Additionally, key moments in American history are still experienced via television. From the Kennedy assassination and moon landing of the 1960s to more recent events of the September 11 attacks and Hurricane Katrina, television coverage unites viewers across demographics and forges shared cultural bonds. Even though narrowcasting has reduced the number of shows that reach a mass audience across demographic categories, television viewing still binds Americans together as they share cultural experiences both within communities and across groups.

For many skeptical critics, television viewing is conceived as a passive and hypnotic activity, with an endless flow of programming washing over a mesmerized viewer parked on the couch. Certainly this is how some people watch some television, but most viewers watch in a variety of ways that contradict the discourse of the passive couch potato. Television is often part of a larger practice of **multitasking**, mixed in with other activities of household chores and social interaction. In many homes, the television set is on regardless of whether people are watching, fading into the background as people carry out their daily routines. Multitasking is especially common among youth, as a 2005 study found that while watching television, more than half of teenagers frequently use other media and three quarters engage in other practices such as homework and phone conversations, a mode of viewing that goes against the stereotype of the passive couch potato.[3] For multitasking viewers, television offers a consistent presence and ongoing stream of information and entertainment, enabling people to selectively engage with the material or direct their attention elsewhere.

The distracted glance of the multitasking viewer occupies one pole of a spectrum of how people watch television; on the other extreme are viewers who are intently focused and engaged with what is on the screen. However, the engaged viewer is not necessarily passive: such viewers are often focused on television programming in an active process of comprehension and emotional stimulation reminiscent of watching films in a darkened theater. Viewer engagement has been further enabled by recent technological developments, as home video recording, prerecorded television on DVD, and online downloads allow viewers to schedule and control their own viewing beyond the constraints of network schedules. For viewers watching a DVD of their favorite program on their high-end entertainment system, pleasure stems from active engagement with a show's narrative and textual style, not a passive acceptance of whatever might be on. The emergence of highly complex narrative structures discussed in chapter 6 furthers this mode of engaged viewing, as it would be hard to imagine how a distracted, disengaged viewer might make sense of *Lost* or *The Wire*. Viewers also take their engagement beyond the confines on the screen, participating in online discussion forums and interpersonal conversations to dissect the latest developments in a range of programs, including the serialized twists of *Heroes*, the relationship tangles of *Days of Our Lives*, and the strategic machinations of *Survivor*.

Even when we are away from our television screens, the medium plays a key role in constituting our perspective on the world. Terms from television are used to describe a wide range of cultural phenomena: We often look at the unfolding narratives of public figures using the lens of soap operas, charting scandals such as President Clinton's infidelity or the ups and downs of a political race as serial dramas complete with betrayals, cliffhangers, and relationship turmoil. Spectators at a live sporting event typically compare their experiences to how the sport appears on television, even casting their eyes toward giant screens to watch the live event mediated through the familiar set of camera angles and replays. Tourists to particular regions view the real world through the lens of their television representations, noticing New Jersey sights as captured by the credit sequence opening *The Sopranos*, or imagining *Northern Exposure*'s fictional town of Cicely while visiting rural Alaska. Such pilgrimages have inspired a growing industry of "teletourism," where viewers visit and tour the shooting locales of favorite programs. Television's influence on our everyday lives is so

NORTHERN EXPOSURE

Northern Exposure (CBS, 1990–95): A critically acclaimed dramedy that grew into a ratings success, the show chronicles the experiences of a New York Jewish doctor forced to live in a small Alaskan community. The series was known for its experimental storytelling, inclusion of mysticism and spirituality, and representation of Native Americans.

pervasive as to frame our fields of vision almost regardless of how much we watch the screen. Television matters in ways that we hardly notice in shaping our experiences and expectations for the everyday.

There are clearly many different ways people watch and engage with television, encompassing a wide range of pleasures, practices, beliefs, and attitudes. It is important to work against the discourse of the passive couch potato as the typical television viewer. Such dismissive attitudes toward the most popular and prevalent leisure activity in America are a dead end, unable to explain the range of reasons why people watch and how television matters within their broader lives. We need to be aware of the many reasons people might watch television—to gather information, to relax within a routine, to reinforce social bonds, to be immersed in and engaged by a fictional world, to provide a backdrop for other practices, to fit within their social community, and to experience a broad range of emotional reactions. Television programming and its viewers get little respect when compared to other cultural forms, but we need to be careful when condemning a practice that we might not fully understand. Detailed research of viewer practices and of the role of television in everyday life suggests that blanket dismissals of the medium are often based on faulty assumptions.

Fan Cultures

As one detailed example of how viewers engage with television programming, we can consider the practice of television **fandom**. Every medium and cultural form has its own type of fandom, whether it is the highbrow world of food epicures and opera enthusiasts or the more lowbrow heavy metal headbangers and hardcore video gamers. Television fans might flock to any genre. Obviously sports broadcasting has passionate fanbases dedicated to particular teams or sports, while fan communities have evolved surrounding home improvement shows, newscasters, and even The Weather Channel. For fans of nonfiction programs and genres, typically the investment stems from an attachment to the subject of the program, as with political junkies or sports diehards, and such interests are typically viewed as culturally legitimate and valid pastimes apart from the television medium. Other television fandoms are more maligned, especially when directed to fictional or lowbrow genres commonly seen as a waste of time for viewers. However, by looking at how fans of genres such as game shows, soap operas, and science fiction define their own practices, we can see a more complicated perspective on how television matters in viewers' lives.

For dedicated fans, watching a program is only the beginning of their involvement with the show. Often fans have a routine for how best to watch their favorite shows, ranging from solitary immersions into the text to social celebrations experienced as part of a broader community. In early decades, television fans were technologically limited to watching programs only as they were scheduled by broadcasters, making most programs ephemeral experiences—although fans in these eras did use available technology, such as audio taping and photography, to partially capture programs as they aired. The spread of VCRs in the 1980s allowed fans to begin archiving their favorite programs, reliving pleasurable moments and engaging in a broader community of videotape collectors and traders. In the 2000s, DVD sales and direct downloads of television programs brought fan collecting into the mainstream, complete with detailed extras of behind-the-scenes information and bonus materials that have typically been highly valued rarities within fan communities. Today owning the complete run of a popular television series is commonplace, while such behaviors in earlier decades typically viewed as obsessive and wasteful.

Television fandom is simultaneously both personal and social. Many fans have their own private relationships with programs, forging intimate connections with a show and investing a great deal of time and emotion into their relationship with a fictional world. For some fans, their connection to programs is tied directly to their social identities. For instance, a number of gay fans of *Star Trek* have noted how its utopian science fiction world made them feel included when they felt like outcasts in real life, even though the show itself contains no overt representations of homosexuality. Fans incorporate elements of favored texts into all spheres of their everyday lives: using television quotations in casual conversation, wearing clothing and accessories tied to programs, decorating homes and office spaces with images from shows, and incorporating traits from favorite characters into everyday behavior. For many dedicated fans, self-identifying as a fan is a central aspect of personal identity, with fandom worn as a badge of pride.

Fandom is also a social practice for most fans, fostering interpersonal bonds and communities that often become central to people's lives. Fan groups emerge within larger communities of a city or college campus, with viewing clubs developing to share tapes, swap stories, and collaboratively enjoy mutual objects of media consumption. **Fan conventions** bring together fans of a particular program or genre more broadly via large-scale events to celebrate their communities, complete with guest appearances by actors and producers,

STAR TREK

Star Trek (NBC, 1966–69): The original *Star Trek* was a struggling utopian science fiction series with a small but dedicated audience that led NBC to renew it for a third season after cancellation. It lived on in syndication, generating a cult following that eventually spawned numerous spin-offs, merchandise, and a series of successful feature films, establishing the paradigm for cult media fandom.

elaborate costume play, trivia contests, and pervasive merchandise to create a special realm outside of the everyday life of television viewing. With the spread of the Internet in the 1990s, online fan communities enabled social interactions beyond the boundaries of physical locale: discussion forums, email lists, bulletin boards, group wikis, online video sites, and chat rooms have all flourished as virtual spaces for fans around the globe to discuss programs and share fan activities. Even as every fan has a personal connection to favorite programs, most share their individual passions within larger groups of both friends and strangers, turning the solitary act of television viewing into a broader social community engagement.

Although fandom typically centers on television texts, fans also are invested in **paratexts**, the additional layers of textual material surrounding a program. Some paratexts are direct results of the promotional process discussed in chapter 1. Program promos, official websites, and billboards are designed to attract viewers to the actual show, but fans often collect and celebrate such promotional materials as extensions of their favorite programs. When a program becomes successful, paratexts expand to include **licensed merchandise** to be sold via the industry's logic of cross-media synergy. Officially sanctioned merchandise can include soundtracks, games, books, calendars, toys and action figures, clothing, food products, watches, household items, and holiday decorations, all of which might be embraced by fans as a way to extend the experience of their fandom—or condemned as selling out or misrepresenting the "true" nature of the program. While fans often are hyper-consumers of television merchandise, they can also be quite discriminating when judging licensed goods, skeptical of products that they see as untrue to their perceived vision of the program.

Fans often transcend the typical role of consumer by becoming producers of paratexts, too, creating new texts that build upon their knowledge and passions for a program. Before the rise of the web, photocopied fanzines were a common form of fan creativity, sharing images and ideas about a program through subscriptions and convention distribution. As the technology has emerged, online **fansites** have become the most common and accessible way for fans to create and share their tribute to a favored program, including both

A fan playing with *Star Trek* toys, as featured in the film *Trekkies*, is a way to extend fandom beyond the act of viewing, and to allow fans to actively construct their own meanings and intepretations.

original and recycled images, details about the show, interpretations and evaluations of episodes, and links to other fansites and online resources. A show with a complex mythology will often generate highly elaborate fansites dedicated to solving the show's mysteries and chronicling its plot. For instance, fans collaborate on Lostpedia.com to develop a wiki-based comprehensive encyclopedia with thousands of entries for all aspects of ABC's *Lost*. Fans also create visual art that inflects the world of a show with their own personal vision, developing a range of images capturing the spirit of a program and its fans. While such fan resources are often freely shared online, an underground market of fan-created merchandise, zines, and art circulates through websites and conventions, allowing some fans to make a living selling and trading objects connected to their passionate engagement.

Many programs inspire the creation of **fan fiction**, stories that extend a show's storyworld with new adventures, revised relationships, and even imaginative shifts across genre and crossovers with other programs, as in an unlikely meeting between the science fiction series *Highlander* and the sitcom *Friends*. Fan fiction often explores elements of a program that go beyond the boundaries of the primary text, offering interpretations of themes or aspects of characters that stimulate fan pleasures but will never be explored within the framework of mainstream television, such as dark secrets in a character's past or erotic relationships following a broad range of sexual orientations and practices. Fans use other media for paratexts, including fan "vids," songs, and video games, spending

FIREFLY

Firefly (Fox, 2002–03): This quirky short-lived science fiction/Western mixture created by *Buffy the Vampire Slayer*'s Joss Whedon was never given adequate time to develop and generate significant ratings by Fox, but its hardcore fanbase made its DVD sales such a success that eventually led to a feature film adaptation.

hours creating material that can never be sold (due to copyright restrictions), but will be shared and enjoyed throughout fan communities. Fan fiction and "vidding" are practices circulating in overwhelmingly female fan communities, often built upon an ethic of collaborative support, mentoring, and sharing that runs counter to the merchandising exclusivity of most media industries. Fan-created narratives thrive within a comparatively small subculture of fans, but often serve as a creative outlet that inspires writers and producers to publish their own work and enter into the mainstream media industries, or happily remain as a subcultural community that finds pleasure in sharing its own creative revisions of shared mass media narratives.

What programs inspire such dedicated and passionate fan communities? One type of show that often generates active fanbases can be called **cult television**, named for its ability to inspire a devoted following. Cult television typically falls outside of mainstream popularity, often coming from genres such as science fiction, fantasy, and animation rather than typical television staples of sitcoms and workplace dramas. While some cult shows are on major networks, such as *The X-Files* on Fox or ABC's *Twin Peaks*, they often air on smaller cable channels like Sci Fi Channel or Cartoon Network, or even in first-run syndication, as with *Xena: Warrior Princess*. Cult shows can be quite short-lived, as with Fox's *Firefly*, which lasted less than a season but spawned a passionate fan community called "browncoats," named after the failed resistance fighters depicted in the show's science fiction future. These fans generated sufficient enthusiasm and revenue via DVD sales to justify a spin-off feature film, *Serenity*. For many fans, a show's cult status as a beloved but marginal program can be part of its appeal, as fans enjoy being in a minority subculture they view as sufficiently discerning to discover and appreciate a hidden gem in the television schedule. However, one of the core activities of fandoms for cult programs often involves lobbying a show's network or channels to prevent a show's cancellation due to marginal ratings.

The paradigm for cult television fandom is certainly the *Star Trek* franchise. The original *Star Trek* ran on NBC in the late 1960s, garnering low ratings but inspiring an avid fanbase attracted to the show's utopian vision of the future.

Star Trek fans dress as various characters and alien races, as with this group of Klingons crossing the street, to celebrate and participate in the show's fictional world.

Fans launched a successful letter-writing campaign asking NBC to bring the show back for a third season, which proved to be its last. Despite the show's cancellation, fans sustained interest in it throughout the 1970s and 1980s, inspiring Paramount Pictures to create multiple feature films and to license additional products such as action figures and novels. Fans entered into the production process, spawning a passionate fan community that shared music videos, fan fiction, fanzines, and other paratexts decades before online distribution made fan media broadly accessible. Paramount capitalized on the fanbase by reviving the franchise for television in the late 1980s, with first-run syndicated series *Star Trek: The Next Generation* and *Star Trek: Deep Space Nine* in the late 1980s and 1990s, and UPN series *Star Trek: Voyager* and *Star Trek: Enterprise* in the late 1990s and 2000s. The fans of *Star Trek* are the model for how people think of a dedicated and passionate fan community, both as a positive attribute and an easily mocked stereotype of obsessive behavior. However, it is important to remember that fan engagement with television programs is more complex and multifaceted than parodies of sci-fi "geeks" typically offer.

While cult fandoms often seem the most typical mode of fan engagement with television, many more mainstream genres and programs generate thriving fan cultures. Soap operas cultivate a dedicated fanbase, with specialist magazines such as *Soap Opera Digest*, hundreds of fansites, online forums, tape-trading communities, newsletters, and live events drawing a robust fan community

TRL

TRL (MTV, 1998–2008): As MTV shifted away from music videos and toward reality and scripted programs in the 1990s, *Total Request Live* became the primary place for the channel to air music videos each afternoon, playing the top-requested videos from its website, along with live performances and commentary from fans in studio and online celebrating their favorites.

that can span decades and across generations. Game shows can also inspire fandoms, especially long-running programs such as *The Price Is Right*, as fans make pilgrimages to attend a studio taping and even recreate elaborate games in their own homes. Televised wrestling has a huge fanbase, typically propelling programs to the top of cable ratings charts, turning memoirs of wrestlers into bestsellers, and generating tremendous revenue and cultural influence from a phenomenon mostly overlooked by most of the media. News and talk shows can also generate fanbases, as with the crowd that gathers outside *Today's* studio each morning, or the devoted followers of figures such as Oprah Winfrey or Bill O'Reilly, who follow on-camera suggestions for consumer and political behavior. Satirical show *The Colbert Report* even generates a mock fanbase, who follows the host's ironic self-promoting edicts to deface Wikipedia, remix videos, or vote in online polls to name sports mascots. Nearly any program or genre can find a small but passionate fan community that dedicates its time and energy to creating tribute websites or other paratexts celebrating the object of their devotion, from the obscure to the mundane.

How might we view the political overtones of fan cultures? Are they individualists daring to express their passions and interests in programs that most people regard as banal or worthless? Or are they conformists following a trend by investing emotions into a manufactured piece of mass culture instead of something more worthy of their time? As with most aspects of television, fan practices cannot be seen simply as supporting or resisting dominant social forces. Certainly some fans embrace programming with a subversive attitude, rewriting the series via fan fiction and videos that bring subtexts to the forefront, as with a large genre of "slash fiction" stories asserting a homosexual relationship between Kirk and Spock on *Star Trek*. But other fans seem to embrace fandom as a mode of conforming to social norms. Watch the behaviors captured on MTV's *TRL*, with young music fans sending emails or appearing on-camera to offer a steady stream of nearly identical comments celebrating mainstream bands.

Like most social practices, fandom is a complex phenomenon, simultaneous embracing mainstream culture and offering a community defined in opposition to certain social norms. We must be careful with any proclamations of television fandom as a waste of time, as many examples of today's elite culture, such as Shakespeare's plays or Dickens's novels, were regarded by many in their day as popular forms appealing to undiscerning masses lacking sophistication. Perhaps in another century, television programs such as *Buffy the Vampire Slayer* and *The Simpsons* will be viewed as comparable masterpieces, legitimizing their fandoms in hindsight. Any claims arguing that all fans are either inherently dupes of mass culture or resistant fighters against a dominant ideology should be viewed skeptically. Only by close examination of actual fan practices can we get a sense of how a particular fan community operates and negotiates within greater social forces.

Fans are certainly not typical of all television viewers, but most people exhibit aspects of fan behavior around some cultural form, from sports to music, food to politics—all of which frequently appear on television screens. As technological developments have made fan communities more publicly accessible beyond the subcultural tape-trading groups and fan conventions, fan practices have become more mainstream. Many viewers who would not consider themselves "fans" in the traditional sense collect DVD sets of programs, watch behind-the-scenes documentaries, participate in online forums, search the Web for episode guides or recaps, and purchase merchandise tied to their favorite programs. While we should not assume that a highly active fan making remix videos or wearing costumes from a program is typical, television viewers fall along a spectrum that embraces a wide range of practices countering the stereotype of the passive couch potato. Understanding and accepting the practices of television fans strengthens our understanding of how all viewers can choose to engage actively with programming, just as much as they can choose to take in passively whatever might be on the air.

Active fans can also help us understand the appeal of television programming and the investment many viewers make in it, even if they are not moved to create their own paratexts or engage in role-playing. Fans are nearly always emotionally engaged in the programs of their affection, finding pleasure in moments that exceed rational explanation—the glances between characters, subtle references to previous episodes, the visual composition of a shot. It is tempting to want to provide concrete reasons why viewers enjoy what they watch, but beyond clear ties to identifiable characters or realistic situations, pleasure is often wrapped up in the inexplicable emotional investments people make in programs and in these unique details. To an outsider, such emotions may seem almost pathological, especially when aimed at lowbrow forms such as soap operas or cartoons, but they are legitimate and authentic to the dedicated viewer. Fans make their emotional investments public, testifying to their engagement via their self-identification, creativity, and pronounced adoration for their fannish devotions. For non-fans, viewing television can still stimulate such moments of private pleasure and engagement, providing a cultural experience that matters despite its lack of explicit rationale or purpose. Thus by looking at fans not as irrational outsiders but rather as extroverted and heightened examples of typical viewers, we can better understand the various ways television matters in people's everyday lives.

FURTHER READING

Debates over theories of media effects versus influences are prevalent among television scholars. For the media effects side, see Elizabeth M. Perse, *Media Effects and Society* (Mahwah, N.J.: Lawrence Erlbaum Associates, 2000), and W. James Potter, *The 11 Myths of Media Violence* (Thousand Oaks, Calif.: Sage Publications, 2003). For the media influences position, see David Gauntlett, *Moving Experiences: Media Effects and Beyond*, 2d ed. (Eastleigh, UK: John Libbey, 2005), and Martin Barker and Julian Petley, eds., *Ill Effects: The Media/Violence Debate*, 2d ed. (London: Routledge, 2001). James Shanahan and Michael Morgan, *Television and Its Viewers: Cultivation Theory and Research* (Cambridge, UK: Cambridge University Press, 1999), provides a good overview of cultivation theory.

Reception studies of television viewers have been quite influential in the field. See David Morley, *Television, Audiences and Cultural Studies* (New York: Routledge, 1992); Ien Ang, *Desperately Seeking the Audience* (New York: Routledge, 1990); Justin Lewis, *The Ideological Octopus: An Exploration of Television and Its Audience* (New York: Routledge, 1991); and Ellen Seiter, *Television and New Media Audiences* (New York: Oxford University Press, 1999), for important works in the field. Although focused on British viewers, David Gauntlett and Annette Hill, *TV Living: Television, Culture, and Everyday Life* (London: Routledge, 1999), offers the most detailed account of the ways television matters in people's everyday life.

The scholarship of television fandom tends to focus on specific fanbases and genres. Henry Jenkins, *Textual Poachers: Television Fans and Participatory Culture* (New York: Routledge, 1992), is an influential account focused on *Star Trek* fans; while Jonathan Gray, Cornel Sandvoss, and C. Lee Harrington, eds., *Fandom: Identities and Communities in a Mediated World* (New York: New York University Press, 2007), provides case studies of a wide range of fandoms. C. Lee Harrington and Denise D Bielby, *Soap Fans: Pursuing Pleasure and Making Meaning in Everyday Life* (Philadelphia: Temple University Press, 1995), focuses on the realm of soap opera fans; while Matt Hills, *Fan Cultures* (London: Routledge, 2002), offers an important theoretical exploration of fandom.

NOTES

[1] See Stuart Hall, "Encoding/Decoding," in *Culture, Media, Language*, ed. Stuart Hall et al. (London: Hutchinson, 1980), 128–40, for the development of this influential theoretical model.

[2] American Time Use Survey, United States Department of Labor, 2007 ed., available at http://www.bls.gov/tus/. Statistics offered by Nielsen suggest that average Americans watch more than four hours of television a day, although this is based on Nielsen's sample, who tend to be more active television viewers by virtue of their accepting the offer to serve in the ratings sample.

[3] Donald F. Roberts, Ulla G. Foehr, and Victoria Rideout, *Generation M: Media in the Lives of 8–18 Year-Olds*, Kaiser Family Foundation, March 2005; available from http://www.kff.org/entmedia/7251.cfm.

CHAPTER 10

TELEVISION FOR CHILDREN

Many of the debates surrounding media effects and influences discussed in chapter 9 acknowledge that for most adults, television is at worst a distraction from activities seen as more important, or a force perpetuating negative values of consumerism, discrimination, and shallow participation in civic affairs—but that adults have the ability to choose their own practices concerning media. However, the stakes rise when critics discuss the imagined audience of children, framed as vulnerable victims of the worst negative impacts television might inspire. Much of the rhetoric and policies surrounding television viewing pose the fearful question of "what about the children?", focusing on the possible harmful effects of television on the social body of American youth. Yet we need to think carefully about this issue, asking what about children makes them seem vulnerable, and questioning our assumptions about their passivity and engagement beyond the simple role of victim.

THE IMAGINED CHILD AUDIENCE

Chapter 2 outlines the difference between audience categories constituted by the industry and actual viewers. Audience categories comprise more than just marketing strategies and ratings reports, however, as broader cultural discourses about viewers can help shape the assumptions and meanings linked to an audience group. This is especially true of the child audience, as academic researchers, politicians, pundits, educators, and parents all spend a great deal of time defining and classifying the child audience, generating a range of meanings that get attached to the category in our everyday understanding of children watching television. But actual child viewers are often left out of these discourses, and are rarely consulted in policymaking or asked to help define their own viewing practices. To understand how the child audience functions in American television, we have to consider both the discourses working to shape the category and the actual practices of child viewers, highlighting the frequent contradictions in and gaps between these definitions and assumptions.

For the television industry, the child audience is a highly lucrative and desirable segment, with a high frequency of television viewing, a trendy, consumerist mind-set, and an impressionable mentality, presenting the potential for the creation of lifetime brand dedication at an early age. This was not always the norm, as direct advertising to children was a rarity in the early years of television. It was not until the mid-1950s with the dual success of ABC's *Disneyland* and *The Mickey Mouse Club* that sponsors such as Mattel toys and Kellogg's cereal discovered that direct advertising to children could inspire parental purchases in record numbers. Additionally, Disney found that the tie-in products, new film releases, and theme park promoted on these shows all saw large bumps in business, ushering in the creation of the child audience as a target for both programmers and sponsors. By the early 1960s, kids were clustered around the scheduling block of Saturday morning cartoons, inundated with cereal and toy ads that drove parents away from the screen. Throughout the classic network era, children were seen by most as a undiscerning audience, willing to watch whatever cartoons might be on the air and passively taking in the persuasive messages of advertising and conveying their desires to their parents.[1]

Just as the multi-channel era led to greater segmentation of the entire television audience, children were subdivided into smaller segments with the rise of cable. PBS grew in popularity throughout the 1970s by offering educational, noncommercial programs for children that appealed to adults looking for something more valid than crass cartoons for their kids to watch. Nickelodeon emerged in the 1980s by branding itself as a mix of network Saturday morning shows and PBS fare—the channel offered an empowering "kid-first" mentality focused on child heroes and poking gentle fun at adults, while assuring parents of its "pro-social" programming with less violence and commercialism than network cartoons. Disney Channel emerged in the 1980s as a premium channel comparable to HBO for kids, commercial-free (although heavily promoting the Disney brand) and wrapped in Disney's long-standing rhetoric of wholesome all-American values; shifting to basic cable in the late 1990s, Disney still avoids advertising, aside from promotions for Disney programs and enterprises. Cartoon Network embraced the spirit of Saturday morning while highlighting its library

DISNEYLAND

Disneyland (ABC, 1954–61): A groundbreaking example of a Hollywood studio embracing television in its first decade, *Disneyland* was a popular anthology series hosted by Walt Disney that presented a range of segments, including ongoing series such as "Davy Crockett," reused short cartoons, and clips promoting the forthcoming Disneyland theme park in California. The show was retitled *The Wonderful World of Disney* and has aired and been revived on all three original networks regularly for decades.

of classic Warner Bros. and MGM cartoons, offering more cultural legitimacy and appeal for adult audiences than many of the toy-based cartoons filling network schedules in the 1990s. Later channels, such as Noggin, were skewed more toward PBS's educational brand, and Toon Disney focused on Disney's library of animation for both kids and adults. Each of these channels seeks to define a slice of the children's audience by highlighting particular genres, values, attitudes, and marketing strategies.

The child audience is defined by more than just industrial strategy, as nearly every type of adult has participated in constructing the category: parents, educators, politicians, activists, and researchers. One reason why so many adults assert forceful opinions about children's media consumption is because we were all children once ourselves: it seems natural to think back to previous generations of youth in contrast to today's norms of childhood. But while such nostalgic glances are typically tinted with idealized memories of "pure childhood" free from mass media, images of violence, and commercialism, historical research suggests that there never was such an era. In America, children have nearly always been linked to commerce, whether as a source of cheap labor or as a target market. Likewise, the realm of children's play and cultural tastes has never been an ideal one, free of violence and fear, as fairy tales, war toys, and various media have captivated young imaginations via often brutal and stark imagery for centuries. Scholars have analyzed historical constructions of childhood to debunk the myth of childhood innocence, highlighting more complex histories of children across generations.[2] Thus adults repeatedly make decisions about media and children relying upon questionable nostalgia for an ideal of childhood that never really existed.

Likewise, memories of youth can never capture the actual logic and mindset of being a child. Many adults with the power to produce and regulate children's television imagine the childish mind as a blank slate, with media images imprinting values and behaviors directly upon it. Such conceptions of the child audience draw directly on the media effects tradition of the passive viewer absorbing meanings and messages, a perspective that resonates with many adult assumptions about children. Many imagine watching television to be a passive activity by default, and that people learn how to be more active and discerning only with maturity. Based on these assumptions, children are regarded as the most passive of all viewers, simply accepting whatever they see on the screen as persuasive and real. These concerns become more pronounced with the presence of questionable content, such as violence, sexuality, and hyper-commercialism, as many adults react defensively to protect children they imagine as helpless victims of an overzealous television industry. However, some research on children as viewers argues that young viewers practice more direct engagement, active negotiation, and cognitive discernment than typically assumed by many media effects researchers, policymakers, programmers, and educators.

Children certainly engage with television differently from adults, but that does not necessarily mean that they are passively absorbing programming. Some researchers have found that children are more likely to watch and enjoy programs that request direct participation, including talking back to characters or performing physical tasks, a set of guidelines that helped develop highly interactive programs for young children such as *Blue's Clues* and *Dora the Explorer*.[3] Additionally, children embrace repetition and familiarity, not because they are undiscerning viewers who will watch anything, but because they are actively learning how to comprehend visual and audio media codes, narratives, and other content. The narratives structuring many children's television programs focus on simple problem-solving tasks, as characters try to overcome situations that to adults may seem trite or overly formulaic—but for young children, repeating and engaging with narrative problems and solutions encourages mastery and command of scenarios rather than boredom or confusion. Repetition, problem-solving, and direct participation are techniques frequently used in formal education; clever producers of children's television incorporate these same techniques into programming to engage youth and make them feel stimulated by the programs, whether they are explicitly educational or not.

Of course not all child viewers engage in television viewing in such active ways, and certainly much (if not most) children's programming does not seek to inspire such participatory viewing practices. But even shows that may appear to adults as mindless, lowbrow distractions might stimulate a more subtle form of engagement than assumed by many. One key example is the Japanese import *Pokémon*, probably the most popular children's media phenomenon of the 1990s, with highly successful television, video game, collectable toys, card games, and book and film incarnations. Many adults condemned the show and its associated products as brainless and shameless commercial manipulation, which implored kids to "catch them all" by purchasing products and staging violent

BLUE'S CLUES

Blue's Clues (Nickelodeon, 1996–2006): One of the most successful programs for preschoolers, *Blue's Clues* used child development research to create an interactive puzzle-solving show about a man and his animated pet dog solving a mystery. The show uses repetition and direct address toward young children to engage them, and its success established the Nick Jr. block as an alternative to PBS for preschool television.

DORA THE EXPLORER

Dora the Explorer (Nickelodeon, 2000–present): Another successful part of the Nick Jr. block, *Dora* presents the adventures of a Latina girl and her pet monkey, Boots, as they locate new places with the help of her friends and a map. The show is notable for incorporating Spanish language and encouraging active participation among preschoolers in helping Dora accomplish her goals.

Pokémon's narrative focuses on collecting and mastery of creatures, which encourages children both to learn and acquire knowledge, and to purchase merchandise.

POKEMON

Pokémon (syndicated and The WB, 1998–2006; Cartoon Network, 2007–present): One of the most popular imports to American television, this Japanese anime show created a huge trend among children, who obsessively watched the series, collected the trading cards, played the video games, and bought licensed merchandise. The series is based around the adventures of a boy striving to become a "Pokémaster" by collecting creatures and learning fighting strategies.

contests between fantasy creatures. While certainly this commercial strategy was quite profitable, the appeal looked different from a kid's-eye view: young *Pokémon* fans exhibited encyclopedic mastery of the various traits and abilities of more than 150 creatures, and developed elaborate strategies to incorporate *Pokémon* knowledge in a wide range of social and personal activities. A dedicated fan of *Pokémon* is anything but passive, as he must actively learn and study the narrative universe and apply those skills to his social interactions. Although the knowledge mastered and practiced by such "Pokémasters" is ultimately not practical beyond the world of fans and games, scholars have argued that such active engagement with media texts teaches children how to learn, research, and apply their knowledge, regardless of its practicality.

As the *Pokémon* example suggests, the practices of active, engaged viewing can be quite compatible with the commercial marketing goals of the television industry. One of the chief ways children engage with television is through imaginative play, acting out scenarios and portraying characters from the screen. For producers, such participatory viewing leads to merchandising opportunities, as they offer tie-in products to saturate the everyday life of child viewers, from licensed breakfast cereals and clothing in the morning to branded toothbrushes and bedsheets at night, and hundreds of other ancillary products in between. It is easy to see the aisles of licensed merchandise in a toy store as a sign of the commercial takeover of children's imaginations, but we must remember that children being sold particular meanings or products is no guarantee that they will embrace those products or use them in predictable ways to reinforce meanings encouraged by marketers. Research on children's toys and play demonstrates how children make active choices and negotiations in how they use such merchandise, often employing toys to act out scenarios and characters quite contrary to the toys' assumed commercial messages. From Davy Crockett coonskin hats in the 1950s to today's action figures and dolls, children's toys are frequently used to "play against the grain," and children embrace products that serve their own developmental and social goals, rather than simply adhering to what marketers sell them.[4]

Concerns about hyper-commercialism and the pervasive reach of media in children's lives have led to another mode of active engagement with television: activist groups lobbying for regulations and industrial codes to limit the potential excesses of television. As discussed in chapter 3, the FCC has taken a hands-off approach to regulating the content of television, mostly employing free market solutions, except in extreme cases. Children's programming has been the most regulated aspect of American television, with numerous policies emerging in response to activist consumer and citizen groups lobbying to make television viewing a "safer" and more rewarding experience for youth. One important organization, founded by mainstream "suburban mothers and housewives" in the late 1960s, was Action for Children's Television, which successfully advocated for reduced commercialism and more quality educational programming throughout the 1970s and 1980s. Due in part to their efforts, the FCC instituted policies requiring "bumpers" separating children's programming and advertising with messages like "And Now a Word from Our Sponsors," restricting the amount of advertising per hour aimed at kids, and banning a show from airing commercials for its own tie-in merchandise, all restrictions motivated to make children more aware of the differences between programming and advertising. ACT was disbanded shortly after the successful passage of the Children's Television Act of 1990, which required broadcasters to air a quota of educational programming each week and instituted clearer legal guidelines for advertising restrictions.[5]

Throughout these regulatory, industrial, and activist debates around children's television, the voices of actual children are rarely heard. This differs from other debates over television content discussed in chapter 8, where critiques and advocacy around racial, gender, and sexual representations typically emerge from the people whose identities are most at stake. Practices and debates concerning children's television typically take place without the participation of children themselves, as youth are rarely granted the privilege of publicly speaking about their own identities or behaviors. In the United States, children are disenfranchised as citizens to participate in their own regulation or governance, even as they are highly valued as consumers and market segments by commercial industries using the public resources of the airwaves. While broader legal participation of children in governance and regulation of the media might be beyond the scope of possibility, one avenue that engages children as citizens and active participants has been on the rise in the United States: the media literacy movement.

MEDIA LITERACY EDUCATION

For many educators, the idea that television should be taught in schools seems somewhat ludicrous. Traditionally schools have regarded mass media as a force to be resisted, as it is believed to pull students away from more valued cultural activities such as reading, writing, art, and music. Television's role in schools has most often been as a teaching tool, used to screen a documentary to supplement a history lesson, a newscast for current events, or maybe a fictional film as a pleasing substitute for recess on a rainy day. But for a number of educators, television has become part of the curriculum, a topic to be studied, analyzed, and produced. Such educators are part of a growing international movement called **media literacy**.

What is media literacy? There is no single definition of the term or subject area, but a number of common principles unite most approaches to media education. At its core, media literacy is tied to critical thinking, encouraging students to be active consumers of media and to analyze the aspects of their communication environment that are typically taken for granted: the lessons about television explored in this book might be included as part of a media literacy curriculum. Many media literacy practitioners believe in teaching how to consume media critically, as well as the skills and vision necessary to create media, emphasizing the term *literacy* as including both reading and writing. This hands-on facet of media education has emerged in part through the rise of video production and computer equipment in schools, as well as through connections with community-based media organizations and public access cable, as discussed in chapter 3. Although media literacy is not embraced by all media educators, a fairly broad consensus statement created in 1992 defines it as "the ability to access, analyze, evaluate and produce communication in a variety of forms."[6] Such a statement applies to any medium, including traditional studies of print and literature, but media literacy education has been particularly focused on studying the mass media of television, advertising, and popular culture.

Media literacy has grown slowly in the United States, especially when compared to the more aggressive incorporation of media education into primary and secondary curricula in Europe and Canada. The 1970s was a decade of expansion for American media literacy education, as political energies from the 1960s connected with revisionist pedagogical models aimed at empowering students and inspiring critical thinking. Media literacy in the seventies was often focused on helping transform young people into informed and engaged citizens, providing the critical tools necessary for them to filter out and resist the power of advertising, stereotypical representations, and other perceived dangers of the commercial mass media. Throughout the 1970s, media literacy was supported by a range of sources, including local schools, nonprofit organizations and foundations, academic researchers, churches, and federal agencies; through such innovations, educators helped build a number of national organizations and associations committed to expanding media education in public schools. Since this boom decade, media literacy has been less funded and supported, especially as public education has shifted toward "back-to-basics" models centered on standardized testing of a core curriculum. Nonetheless, media literacy continues to seep into the teaching practices of many educators looking to engage students, employ new technologies, and connect traditional lessons to today's media of everyday life.

A number of different approaches comprise American media literacy education. One model might be termed a **vocational approach** to media education, teaching students the skills needed to create mass media such as broadcast television, journalism, radio, Web design, and video making. Vocational media education has flourished in schools and alternative programs that focus on teaching practical job skills, often involving internships and connections with local media professionals and organizations. Although a vocational approach can introduce a critical mind-set to studying the media, typically, such media education is less focused on critical thinking found in other media literacy models. The vocational approach is often viewed by traditional educators as not particularly serious or intellectually engaged, and is stigmatized by the assumption that students are simply being taught how to make television. Two other approaches to media literacy have more critical and intellectual focus, and thus have been more integrated into traditional subject areas and curricula.

The activist pedagogy of the 1970s helped shape one of the dominant approaches to media literacy. The **protectionist approach** to media education is based on the assumption that media are a negative external force that students must be insulated from to avoid their influence. The protectionist approach shares many common beliefs with media effects research, assuming a one-way flow of harmful media impacts that must be resisted, as well as a distrust of corporate control of media institutions tied to the political economy model discussed in chapter 2. Pedagogically, protectionist approaches try to break through students' complacency and acceptance of mass media by teaching them critical skills to analyze and subvert the messages offered by television and other forms, unearthing persuasive and manipulative techniques lurking beneath glossy media surfaces. Supporters of this approach argue that such activist and confrontational pedagogy is necessary to combat what they see as powerful, antidemocratic, and even inhumane messages offered by mass media. But just as some critics have questioned the models of media effects, another approach to media education has critiqued protectionism and its underlying assumptions.

A **culturalist approach** to media literacy education views mass media as an integral part of the cultural lives of youth, not an outside force to be resisted or overcome. Culturalist educators see the protectionist approach as breeding cynicism and disinterest toward media, not critical engagement and discovery, as the protectionist educator's hostility toward mass media works to persuade students of a totalizing model of corrupt and socially damaging media. Yet most students approach media with a sense of pleasure, engagement, and identification that protectionist approaches often critique and try to dispel. Culturalist educators aim to build upon students' own pleasures and practices with mass media, infusing these everyday experiences with critical reflection and awareness of the institutions and systems underlying the media, and developing abilities to create their own engaging media forms. Building on cultural studies theories of active consumers, media educators try to encourage students to explore their own viewing activities and nurture critical engagement with media, not a rejection or dismissal of popular culture. One of the chief goals of culturalist media education is to promote active engagement and participatory citizenship among youth, building upon their already strong attachments to mass media to foster other social and cultural activities beyond media consumption.

The differences between these approaches concern some of the key questions surrounding media education. One debate focuses on how best to situate media literacy within school curricula. Some educators, especially vocational practitioners, frame media education as a distinct area of study needing dedicated courses in media creation and criticism. Others, including some protectionist and culturalist educators, argue for media literacy across the curriculum, bringing the study and use of media into classrooms in all disciplines, from science to social studies, art to literature. As media literacy has slowly developed in the United States, it has typically been seen either as a vocational area or as an add-on to the curriculum, placed as a unit within established courses in English, history, or health. Media literacy advocates continue to work to convince administrators, school boards, and families that teaching both *with* and *about* the mass media is a crucial and invaluable facet of education in the twenty-first century, and media literacy must be integrated throughout a student's educational experiences.

One of the chief hurdles for the expansion of media literacy education in schools is the comparative cost of teaching media. Educators need access to expensive televisions, computers, and video production equipment to institute broad-based media literacy curricula, technology that many school districts struggle to afford. Some schools have turned to corporate sponsors to help fund media education, with computer and media companies donating equipment and educational materials. The issue of corporate sponsorship has created a deep divide within the media education community: Protectionist educators feel that corporate money inherently corrupts the critical pedagogy driving media literacy, and many have created independently financed nonprofit organizations and curricula to fight what they see as the corporate takeover of media education. For others, corporations are seen less as an enemy and more as a potential partner; vocational educators often work with media companies to place students for employment and training, while culturalist educators try to engage with media corporations to improve their policies, representations, and programming, using educational sponsorships as a bridge to foster collaboration rather than hostility.

Probably the most controversial participant in American media education is Channel One News. A highly successful for-profit company, Channel

One provides free satellite receivers, television sets, and video recorders for any school that signs up for the service. In exchange, the school is required to have all students watch a daily twelve-minute newscast containing two minutes of commercials. The system has been widely adopted, with nearly eleven thousand schools subscribing to Channel One, reaching around one third of American teens. Protectionist educators regard the forced consumption of advertising to a captive audience as an affront to media literacy, and argue that much of the news contained on the program is uninformative and often supports the mission of the sponsors more than informing about actual current events as taught in the classroom. Advocates, including some culturalist educators, suggest that the free equipment is essential to improving educational access for many schools with limited resources, and some teachers even use the content on Channel One as the object of media literacy analysis, examining how the programming addresses students as consumers and citizens. Few educators see Channel One as the solution to media education, and the controversy continues over whether the potential gains of access to equipment outweigh the concerns about commercialism and questionable educational quality of their news coverage.

As mass media have transformed in the digital convergence era, media literacy philosophies have also adapted to a digital environment. An approach termed **new media literacies** implies both an attention to *new media*, such as video games, social networking, and online video, and an acknowledgment that the digital era requires *new literacies* to move beyond the models of reading, writing, and critical viewing traditionally explored in media literacy. The shift to embrace new media literacies, funded in large part by the MacArthur Foundation, emphasizes that many young people are no longer exclusively media consumers, but are also producers of media via easily accessible technologies such as phone-based digital cameras, online video sharing, networked gaming, blogs, and wikis. Framing today's media environments as a **participatory culture**, new media literacy advocates seek to build upon the creative practices already embraced by young people and ensure that all students have access to the skills and technologies of media creativity. Although such an approach to media education clearly shifts its sights beyond television as the central screen that engages young people, the technological shifts discussed more in chapter 11 force critics and educators to see the variety of screens used by media industries, creators, and viewers as inherently linked together, making television an integral part of digital participatory culture.[7]

Although media literacy education is typically centered within schools, arguably it is also needed as a facet of lifelong learning, especially for parents to better understand how to incorporate media effectively into their children's lives. Researchers, educators, policymakers, and activists often try to influence how families use television, seeing it as a powerful shaper of children's opinions and behaviors. The division between protectionists and culturalists also applies to adult and family education. Protectionists often lobby for eliminating or greatly reducing television's role within households, working with organizations like TV Turnoff Network to push television out of its central role in everyday life. Often citing media effects research as conclusive evidence that television is a clear cause of social, physical, and psychological harm, protectionists frame the television medium as a problem potentially triggering a range of ills from obesity to autism, rising violence to declining political participation. Protectionists often advocate using television only as a monitor for prerecorded videos that can be chosen carefully by parents, and avoiding commercialism of all forms—if allowing children to view television at all. Many major medical organizations, including the American Academy of Pediatrics, have endorsed this line of argument that television should have the most minimal role in a family as possible, although some argue that these recommendations are based less on medical expertise than on a narrow reading of the relevant research and a general distaste for mass media among pediatricians.

Culturalist researchers and educators believe that television can serve a productive role in family life, providing young viewers exposure to a range of ideas and perspectives and offering an opportunity to foster healthy habits of engaging with the medium. According to culturalists, parents should be active in helping children learn to watch television critically, and should teach the differences between programming and advertising, discuss the representations seen on the screen, and encourage children to incorporate television stories and characters into their play to foster interactivity with television. Some specific guidelines offered by media educators include setting consistent family policies for moderation in the amount of television viewed as appropriate to the child's age, parents and children actively participating in choosing appropriate programming, not using television as a behavioral reward or punishment or an "electronic babysitter," and ensuring that adults model appropriate television viewing habits for children in the home. According to many culturalists, eliminating television from family life altogether both establishes it as a taboo for kids to seek outside the home, and ignores responsibility for teaching healthy ways to become critical and literate viewers. One type of programming particularly embraced by culturalist media educators is television designed to educate children, as many media literacy practitioners have put their philosophies in action to help create effective and engaging educational television.

EDUCATIONAL TELEVISION AND THE CASE OF *SESAME STREET*

It would be difficult to think of a program more influential or central to American culture than *Sesame Street*. Since its debut in the late 1960s, *Sesame*

SESAME STREET

Sesame Street (PBS, 1969–present): Arguably the most influential and successful television series in American history, *Sesame Street* transformed children's television, helped establish PBS as a major source of educational programming, and generated vast amounts of research on the influence of television on young viewers. It has also had a global impact, with localized versions produced in more than 120 countries, making it the most widely disseminated American television program in the world.

Street has had a direct impact on generations of children, helped sustain the American model of public television, and inspired an entire genre of educational television. For people who grew up with the show, it is such a staple of television that it seems so conventional as to escape notice. But when it was created, it was a radical departure from the industrial and cultural norms of children's television, and no account of television and American culture can be considered complete without an exploration of how *Sesame Street* matters, both in the everyday lives of viewers and as tied to the other facets of television outlined in this book. Even today, when *Sesame Street* is less popular and important to kids than numerous other preschooler programs, all educational television owes a tremendous debt of influence and existence to the show.

For a program that has been on the air for almost forty years, *Sesame Street* is definitely a product of its original moment, born of a risky experiment in education and social activism amid the transformative politics of late 1960s America. This era saw a great deal of public policy attention to the links between racial discrimination, poverty, and early childhood education, with a belief in extending opportunities to minority and poor children through subsidized preschool programs and the new Head Start initiative. Believing that early intervention providing educational opportunities for marginalized children was a highly efficient long-term strategy for combating social and economic inequality, teams of educators, legislators, researchers, and philanthropists worked together to devise innovative solutions to help children at risk. Television offered one key means of reaching poor children: for many impoverished families, television was a comparatively inexpensive source of entertainment and information, but prior to *Sesame Street* many activists and educators assumed the protectionist position, assuming television was part of the problem, not a potential solution.

Children's television in the 1960s was regarded by many, as FCC chair Newton Minow memorably termed it, as a "vast wasteland." The majority of children's television programs in this era were cartoons airing on Saturday mornings and afternoon syndication, with low budgets, no prestige, and few ambitions beyond generating ratings and merchandising revenue. The few educational programs at the time tried to appear as distinct as possible from such cartoons, using slow pacing, minimal visual variety, and earnestly direct educational lessons: not surprisingly, in retrospect, these programs were neither particularly popular nor educationally effective. In the minds of many critics and educators, the television that children typically watched, including cartoons, Westerns, cop shows, sitcoms, and advertising, all made them less ready for school, encouraged low attention spans, promoted violence and poor nutrition, and generated the expectation of being entertained rather than taught.

In 1966, television producer Joan Ganz Cooney and Carnegie Foundation executive Lloyd Morrisett met and began brainstorming about an experimental educational television program that might reach disadvantaged preschoolers and teach them using production techniques more common to commercial television. With Carnegie's financial backing, Cooney developed a program that would appeal to kids using the formal strategies of advertising and cartoons; in her proposal, she suggested that the show be "highly visual, slickly and expensively produced . . . [with] frequent repetition, clever visual presentation, brevity and clarity."[8] Such a description ran counter to many of the assumed tenets of both education and educational television, which often viewed the formal qualities of the television medium as impediments to education, not potential ways to engage kids with educational content. Cooney enlisted a broad range of psychologists, educators, and media creators to consult and work on the show, and formed an organization called Children's Television Workshop, with funding from the federal government and private foundations to develop the show. In November of 1969, after more than three years of research and development, CTW finally debuted *Sesame Street* on public television stations across the country.

The program was constructed in a highly segmented format, with individual sequences rarely lasting more than four minutes and virtually no continuity between segments, beyond some consistent characters. This decision was motivated in part by the assumption that children's attention span would be best served by frequent shifts of scenario rather than continued narratives, as well as to compete with the quick pacing of commercial television and advertising itself, a strategy acknowledged within the show with each episode "brought to you by" a letter and number. Each segment presented a specific learning objective, using a range of production techniques, including animation, live-action film, puppets, and studio-produced street scenes. The "street" itself was designed to resemble an inner-city block, complete with front stoops and a multicultural mix of adults and children speaking both English and Spanish. While these strategies were used to appeal to the inner-city youth targeted by the creators of the show, they were designed to be as inclusive as possible in appealing to all kids, regardless of race or socioeconomic background.

Mixing puppets and humans of a wide array of races, *Sesame Street*'s integrated inner-city locale reached out to poor, urban children but appealed to kids from a range of backgrounds around the world.

Among the many creative talents that CTW collaborated with to produce *Sesame Street*, probably nobody had as much of a direct on-screen impact as Jim Henson. A puppeteer who had achieved modest success via television commercials and appearances on *The Ed Sullivan Show*, Henson found his breakthrough in *Sesame Street*, with his Muppet characters Ernie and Bert, Kermit the Frog, Big Bird, and Grover becoming the iconic symbols of the show. In initial test episodes, the Muppets appeared only in sequences separated from the live-action street scenes, as psychologists had suggested that children needed clear distinctions between fantasy and reality. However, research with focus groups of kids suggested that the street scenes without the Muppets did not engage young viewers. CTW retested segments including Muppets on the street, and found kids more involved and responsive to the content, with little problem distinguishing between puppets and humans. In the revised episodes, Big Bird and Oscar took up residence on the street, and the Muppets soon became the central and most appealing characters on the show; they factored even more as the show progressed over the years, especially with the rising popularity of Elmo in the 1990s. The Muppets brought a distinct image to the show, but also incorporated adult references and satirical humor. These adult appeals, which included famous guest stars and parodies of cultural references like "Monsterpiece Theatre" and The Beetles singing "Letter B," were designed to encourage parents to watch with their kids and facilitate active conversation about the show and its educational content. This cross-generational appeal extended in the mid-1970s, when Henson created the spin-off *Muppet Show* for older children and adults, launching a multimedia Muppet franchise still going strong years after his untimely death in 1990.

One of *Sesame Street's* most distinctive aspects was CTW's insistence on testing and conducting viewer research on every segment, scrutinizing how well children were paying attention, retaining lessons, and emotionally responding to the show, both before and after airing. Such detailed research was not uncommon with advertisers looking to maximize sales effectiveness or with networks choosing among television pilots, but with its home on PBS, *Sesame Street* was insulated from sales and ratings pressures; instead, the research was used as evidence to foundations and other funding sources that the show's pedagogical model was sound and effective. Additionally, producers believed that the only way the show was going to succeed was to capture kids' attention and successfully create opportunities for learning, and thus developed research protocols measuring viewer attention, eye movement, and learning retention to develop a set of strategies for how best to both entertain and educate preschoolers.

Sesame Street is certainly the most researched show in the history of television, and perhaps the most documented case of any media text's consumption. The bulk of this research supports the media influence approach more than the media effects paradigm. Even the youngest viewers are quite active and selective

Jim Henson spun Kermit the Frog off from *Sesame Street* in the mid-1970s to be the host of the more mature variety program, *The Muppet Show*, which turned into one of the most successful first-run syndicated programs in history and spawned a broad range of popular characters and films.

THE MUPPET SHOW

The Muppet Show (syndicated, 1976–81): A comedic variety show featuring *Sesame Street*'s Kermit the Frog as host to a group of new Muppets, including Miss Piggy, Fozzie Bear, and Gonzo the Great, *The Muppet Show* appealed to older children and adults through wacky physical humor, puns, and savvy cultural references. The series was a hit in first-run syndication, leading to a successful series of movies and further spin-offs including *Muppet Babies*.

in their viewing, negating the stereotype of the mesmerized couch potato with evidence that kids negotiate what they see in the context of their personal and social experiences. Some protectionists still condemn the show for diluting educational lessons into commercial-style entertainment, claiming that television is inherently an ineffective way to teach; the research done both by CTW and outside academics counters these critiques, showing that *Sesame Street* viewers typically perform better in school than non-viewers, and learn positive social values of tolerance and diversity in both the short and long term. Television certainly has the power to influence, which *Sesame Street* producers harness for educational ends, but it is not a one-way power that can override the contexts, agency, and actions of viewers.

The success of *Sesame Street* is obvious: running continuously for decades, spawning international adaptations into more than 120 countries, winning more Emmy Awards than any other television program, and boasting more than 74 million "graduates" who received part of their preschool education from the show. As its popularity rose in the 1970s, *Sesame Street* embraced merchandising and cross-media tie-ins both as a strategy to fund itself outside of government and foundation grants, and as a way to extend its educational strategies into books, toys, audio recordings, software, and live events. The show's educational evidence and popularity led directly to an upswing in educational children's television. CTW, since renamed Sesame Workshop, has produced numerous other programs for public television, including *The Electric Company*, *Dragon Tales*, and *3-2-1 Contact*, all offering different learning goals for various audience segments. Other successful PBS programs followed in the wake of *Sesame Street*'s success, such as *Barney and Friends*, *Arthur*, and *Teletubbies*. In the mid-1990s, Nickelodeon saw an opportunity to create educational television for preschoolers as a for-profit model under the Nick Jr. label, with programs such as *Blue's Clues* and *Dora the Explorer* airing with minimal advertising by relying on merchandising opportunities. Other cable channels, including Disney Channel, Noggin, and TLC, have since started showing educational programming, despite the lack of any regulatory mandates requiring them to. Thus the growth of educational television in recent decades primarily relies on alternative industrial models to the commercial advertising sales market, suggesting that the industry can respond to viewer and societal demands outside the commercial ratings system.

The success of *Sesame Street* was certainly fueled by viewers embracing the show in surprisingly high numbers, but how do the show's viewers engage with and participate in the program? Both preschoolers and adults watching the show have proven to be highly participatory viewers, not passive consumers accepting whatever is on. The success of merchandise and other media incarnations of *Sesame Street* suggests that fans are actively seeking out ways to make the show part of their daily lives beyond the scheduled viewing. We probably would not consider *Sesame Street* viewers as part of a fandom in the same ways we look at the fans of *Star Trek* or other cult media, but children do engage in similar participatory practices: dressing in Muppet costumes, adorning their rooms with tie-in merchandise, role-playing scenarios as a version of live fan fiction, and even making their own videos with *Sesame Street* toys. Anecdotes of many viewers who grew up with the show attest to this engagement, as *Sesame Street* remains one of the most vivid memories of childhood for many Americans. For a few young people it has proven even more formative, as many of the future Muppeteers and other educational television creators have mentioned the direct influence of *Sesame Street* on inspiring their future careers.

Even if it is no longer the most popular and influential educational television program, *Sesame Street* still plays a central role in defining childhood media in today's digital media age. A robust online fan community has emerged around the show and the Muppets, offering material for both kids and adults. As with many media properties, a sign of the show's influence can be seen through its incorporation into parodies: online video sites have featured popular fan parodies that infuse the urban *Sesame Street* and its characters with the distinctly adult violent and vulgar sensibility of movies such as *Mean Streets* and *Do the Right Thing*. The most successful parody was the hit Broadway show *Avenue Q*, which featured Muppet-style puppets on an inner-city street singing about drinking, homosexuality, and pornography. Although these parodies and tributes are clearly intended for adults, they are a tribute to how iconic *Sesame Street* has become in representing the idealized model of children's television for generations of viewers and creators, far from the vast wasteland of children's television imagined by many.

The issue of children and television has been a vexing and controversial topic for decades, and remains one of the hot-button issues driving governmental regulation, consumer activism, and industrial innovation. The rise of quality educational programs and media literacy education has certainly helped producers and parents envision ways that television can be used as a productive and beneficial facet of children's media consumption. Another facet of television has also helped shape the way all viewers, children and adults alike, interact and engage with television as part of their everyday lives: the technology of television itself. We now turn to this final facet of television to understand how all of the other elements of the medium are shaped by, and help shape, the technologies we use to create, consume, and engage with television.

FURTHER READING

To understand children's television, we must first explore how childhood functions in American culture. See Henry Jenkins, *The Children's Culture Reader* (New York: New York University Press, 1998); Marjorie Heins, *Not in Front of the Children: "Indecency," Censorship, and the Innocence of Youth* (New Brunswick, N.J.: Rutgers University Press, 2007); and Gary S. Cross, *The Cute and the Cool: Wondrous Innocence and Modern American Children's Culture* (Oxford: Oxford University Press, 2004), for overviews of children's culture and relevant social debates.

Norma Odom Pecora, John P. Murray, and Ellen Wartella, eds., *Children and Television: Fifty Years of Research* (Mahwah, N.J.: Lawrence Erlbaum, 2007), summarizes many of the research traditions surrounding this broad topic. For a good account of the children's television industry, see Cy Schneider, *Children's Television: The Art, the Business, and How It Works* (Chicago: NTC Business Books, 1987), and Norma Odom Pecora, *The Business of Children's Entertainment* (New York: Guilford Press, 1998). Ellen Seiter, *Sold Separately: Children and Parents in Consumer Culture* (New Brunswick, N.J.: Rutgers University Press, 1993), provides an important account of children's television advertising and reception, while Heather Hendershot, *Saturday Morning Censors: Television Regulation Before the V-Chip* (Durham, N.C.: Duke University Press, 1998), offers a history of viewer activism and content regulation. Joseph Jay Tobin, ed., *Pikachu's Global Adventure: The Rise and Fall of* Pokémon (Durham, N.C.: Duke University Press, 2004), explores the important Japanese import, and Heather Hendershot, ed., *Nickelodeon Nation: The History, Politics, and Economics of America's Only TV Channel for Kids* (New York: New York University Press, 2004), details the impact of Nickelodeon.

Many of the discussions surrounding media literacy focus on the broader role of media in children's lives—see David Buckingham, *After the Death of Childhood: Growing Up in the Age of Electronic Media* (Malden, Mass.: Polity Press, 2000), and David Buckingham, *Media Education: Literacy, Learning, and Contemporary Culture* (Cambridge, UK: Polity Press, 2003), for the perspective of a major figure in the culturalist approach. Victor C. Strasburger and Barbara J. Wilson, *Children, Adolescents, and the Media* (Thousand Oaks, CA: Sage Publications, 2002), summarizes the research from a more protectionist approach. Kathleen R. Tyner, *Literacy in a Digital World: Teaching and Learning in the Age of Information* (Mahwah, N.J.: Erlbaum, 1998), explores more theoretical issues involved in media literacy education.

For research on *Sesame Street*, see Robert W. Morrow, Sesame Street *and the Reform of Children's Television* (Baltimore, Md.: Johns Hopkins University Press, 2006), and Gerald S. Lesser, *Children and Television: Lessons from* Sesame Street (New York: Vintage Books, 1975).

NOTES

[1]See Jason Mittell, *Genre and Television* (New York: Routledge, 2004), chapter 3.

[2]See Henry Jenkins, *The Children's Culture Reader* (New York: New York University Press, 1998).

[3]Daniel Anderson, "Watching Children Watch Television and the Creation of *Blue's Clues*," in *Nickelodeon Nation: The History, Politics, and Economics of America's Only TV Channel for Kids*, ed. Heather Hendershot (New York: New York University Press, 2004), 241–68.

[4]Jenkins, *Children's Culture Reader*; Marsha Kinder, ed., *Kid's Media Culture*, ed. Marsha Kinder (Durham, N.C.: Duke University Press, 1999).

[5]Heather Hendershot, *Saturday Morning Censors: Television Regulation Before the V-Chip* (Durham, N.C.: Duke University Press, 1998).

[6]Quoted in Kathleen R. Tyner, *Literacy in a Digital World: Teaching and Learning in the Age of Information* (Mahwah, N.J.: Erlbaum, 1998), 119.

[7]See http://www.digitallearning.macfound.org and http://projectnml.org for more on new media literacies.

[8]Quoted in Robert W. Morrow, Sesame Street *and the Reform of Children's Television* (Baltimore, Md.: Johns Hopkins University Press, 2006), 50.

CHAPTER 11

TELEVISION'S TRANSFORMING TECHNOLOGIES

This book started with an apparently simple question: What is television? Thus far we have explored the public and private institutions that shape American television, examined the content and form of television programming, and discussed how people interact with television on a daily basis. But so far we have avoided much discussion of the television set itself, the black boxes and glowing screens found in millions of American households. This chapter turns to the material form of television, considering television's role as a technology, and how technological transformations have impacted—and will continue to reshape—all facets of the medium covered so far in this book.

More than any other chapter, this one is almost guaranteed to be out-of-date while you're reading it, as the technological models of television are undergoing rapid shifts in the digital convergence era. New distribution systems, transmission protocols, software innovations, and hardware components will certainly emerge in unpredictable ways that will supplant many of the terms, devices, and examples discussed in this chapter. However, it is important to look toward the future of television's technology with a knowledge of its technological origins and history. How we perceive and use television may shift, but the history of television technology will definitely still matter in helping us understand how technologies change and what impacts such transformations have upon American culture.

THE CULTURE OF TELEVISION TECHNOLOGY

To truly understand the various technologies involved in making your television work would require advanced study in physics, electrical engineering, computer science, and other scientific specialties far outside the expertise of this book. However, we can approach technology not from the perspective of an engineer trying to build a device, but as cultural critics seeking to understand how technologies matter to their users, both the producers and consumers of television. While it is important to have a general sense of what various technologies do, it is more central to the cultural study of television to explore how technological developments change social relationships, creative possibilities, or economic practices, rather than a detailed understanding of how they work scientifically.

The Message of the Medium

One challenge in trying to understand television technology is isolating what makes the technology distinct from its uses; after all, every form and use of television covered thus far in this book is tied to and enabled by the technology of television. One influential approach to studying technology offers three different metaphors that we might consider in analyzing the television medium.[1] The first metaphor approaches a medium as a **conduit** for content, conveying meanings and representations like those discussed in chapters 7 and 8. A second metaphor considers a medium as a **language** with its own form or grammar, as with the norms of communication employed by producers, as detailed in chapters 5 and 6. Both content and grammar are impacted by technology: for instance, the rise of portable camcorders and remote satellite transmitters enabled the model of electronic news gathering that typifies television journalism today, as discussed in chapter 4.

The third metaphor is the broadest and most abstract, conceiving any medium as a distinct **environment** independent of any specific content or form it might convey. Every medium has its own possibilities and limitations of communication that shape the production and consumption of texts. For instance, reading a book is generally an individual experience that can be done almost anywhere within the control of the reader, who can choose at any time to stop reading, reread a section, or even skip to the end; you are free to reread this sentence as frequently as you want, or skip to the next section. Compare reading a book with going to see a film in the theater, which is a shared group event in a specific and constrained space that controls the viewer's time and ability to experience the narrative. Books and films can share content, as in the case of adaptations or tie-ins, but no matter how faithful an adaptation might be in terms of content or even storytelling form, the two media environments are quite distinct and lead to different experiences of consumption.

The study of media environments has been termed **media ecology**, analyzing how a medium creates possibilities of communication and social impacts apart from the specific content it might convey. Media ecologists take a macro-level perspective on communication technologies, charting broad historical transformations between eras of communication, such as the shift from oral to written culture. In this view of history, communication technologies are seen as a central defining attribute of a society, shaping social relations, economic systems, and political structures. The ways people interact with one another are transformed with the adoption of a new technology; for example, the spread of writing changed our ability to communicate across time and space, with wide-reaching social implications. Additionally, media ecologists argue that a medium has direct impacts on individual psychologies. For example, the rise of writing fostered a mode of logical analysis that some claim was not possible in an oral culture; writing enables modes of thinking including historical and scientific reasoning, which arguably could not thrive in an oral culture. For media ecologists, these large-scale changes in a culture's dominant forms of communication are more important and influential than the specific messages that media convey.

The most influential and controversial media ecologist was Marshall McLuhan, a Canadian literary critic who became internationally famous in the 1960s for his proclamations about electronic media. McLuhan was not only the first well-known scholar of television, but he himself was also a visible television personality, appearing on talk shows throughout the 1960s to offer his insights into the medium and its social significance. McLuhan's ideas are difficult to summarize, as he was less interested in detailed arguments and evidence than in making sweeping pronouncements in the form of provocative phrases and axioms—among the most famous of McLuhan's phrases are "the medium is the message," "we drive into the future using only our rearview mirror," and "electronic media recreate the world in the image of a global village." McLuhan purposely wrote using such "exploratory probes" to evoke creative and provocative thinking. His elliptical style makes it easy to misread or dismiss some of his more exaggerated proclamations. However, we can look back at McLuhan's ideas to see how they shape a particular way of looking at media that has remained influential decades later, and even might be more relevant in the digital era than they were in the 1960s.

The core idea in McLuhan's work is that "the medium is the message." This central tenet of media ecology argues that content and messages obscure the great impact of an entire medium at the macro level. McLuhan saw media as creating pervasive environments that shape human consciousness as fully and invisibly as water shapes the experiences of a fish: we cannot perceive the power of a media environment while we are swimming in it. Our awareness of media is rooted in the past; we think that the technologies of a previous era still matter even as we communicate using the tools of today. Consider the term *email*, which maps an old postal technology onto a new electronic medium. For McLuhan, the ways a medium shapes our communication and social experiences is lodged in the technology itself, not in the specific messages conveyed by the technology. While McLuhan may have been too quick to dismiss the study of content, we can strike a middle-ground approach that considers media environment as a key filter that shapes television's content and form. There is no doubt that particular aspects of the television medium shape social relationships and modes of communication in ways that McLuhan's probes encourage us to think about.

McLuhan generally embraced the changes in media during the 1960s, seeing the development of technology as moving the world toward a better place, or at least enabling a return to a "new orality" through electronic media. He conceived of media as "sensory extensions," connected to our bodies by providing technological appendages that allow us to see, hear, and feel beyond ourselves. He saw television as the most balanced sensory medium since orality, and imagined that it would enable society to return to a tribal culture of shared values and experiences. But unlike local preliterate tribes, McLuhan envisioned a "global village" joined by television's universal address and shared culture. Probably more than any other of his futuristic predictions, many of which seem off-base today, a modified model of the global village seems to have taken shape in the digital era, with the World Wide Web, a medium with a McLuhanesque name, enabling an interconnected population. Given the narrowcasting tendencies of both global television and Internet circulation, however, it might be more appropriate to point toward a number of overlapping global villages rather than one shared universal culture.

Many critics both in the 1960s and since then regard McLuhan as less of a prophet than an eccentric footnote in the study of mass media, a distraction from the more detailed and grounded study of media content, form, institutions, and cultural practices that comprise the bulk of this book. But the subfield of media ecology does continue to explore the environmental dimensions of various media through a wide range of methods and critical approaches. Other media ecologists tend to be more pessimistic than McLuhan, claiming that the shift from print to television as the dominant mass medium has led to many social problems, including illiteracy, civic disengagement, increased violence, media addiction, and environmental collapse. The title of a famous McLuhan-inspired treatise against television dismissively sums up this perspective as "Amusing Ourselves to Death."[2] If the danger of overlooking the impacts of a medium environment is that we risk ignoring how technologies shape our experiences like fish in water, it can be equally risky to focus on media ecology with a nostalgic vision, comparing the negative elements of today to the positive features of yesterday.

At its best, however, media ecology can focus our attention on macro-level elements of medium and technology that other facets of television studies might miss. One of the best-regarded studies of media ecology combines McLuhan's sweeping historical claims with more detailed accounts of shifting social relationships in the television era. Instead of imagining that television alters sensory balance or consciousness, we might consider how television changes the way we relate to one another, providing access to social relationships and behaviors in a manner distinct from other media. As discussed in chapter 4, television news and advertising allow politicians to appeal to viewers at an emotional register much more intensely than print typically can, altering the style of politics encouraged by the medium. Another example involves how children experience television: unlike with reading, there are few barriers of comprehension for young children to view programming aimed at older audiences. Thus even in programs designed for families, children watching television can see adults interacting in ways that they rarely would witness in real life, whether it is romance behind closed doors or parents talking about how to discipline children, thus making boundaries between children and adults more fluid. Television, because of its medium-level attributes of accessibility and emotional resonance, helps break down and shift social boundaries beyond the content it conveys.[3]

Social Constructions of Technology

The central critique of media ecology is that often offers too limited a sense of how technology fits into social history and practices. A number of critics have labeled McLuhan and his followers as **technological determinists** because they generally situate technology itself as the key factor causing historical changes and transformations. Although nearly no scholar would actually adhere to a pure form of technological determinism, this tendency to overvalue the power of technology to shape its own uses and impacts runs through both academic thought and common sense. Technology can certainly be a central influence in social change, but we need to remember that technology itself emerges from social forces: any claim that television transforms culture needs to understand how television itself is shaped by the culture that created it. Technologies do not simply pop out of nowhere, but are shaped by the same societies they help define, requiring a more nuanced approach to the complex relationship between a technology and its culture.

An alternative perspective on studying media technology fits more closely with this book's approach. Instead of viewing technologies as deterministic environments, we can study them as **socially constructed**, influenced by a broad range of factors and embedded in their specific historical contexts. Following this approach, technologies are not external factors that generate historical changes, but they need to be understood as representative of their historical eras and as shaped by more than technical specifications. We cannot predict either the use of technologies or their social impacts from the technologies themselves, but need to examine how technologies are used, promoted, understood, and debated within their cultural contexts. The insights of media ecology might still apply, but they are less determined by technological innovations themselves and more shaped by the cultural history of any medium's production and consumption.

To study the social construction of a medium, we can look at three different facets that help shape technology's cultural role and impact. The first is a medium's **technological capabilities**. Every medium has its own potential ways it can be used, as well as limitations that restrict other possibilities. The technology of television combines audio and visual communication using live, simultaneous broadcasting, a combination of capabilities unique in the twentieth century. These technological elements helped mold how television was adopted into homes, driving the dominance of live broadcasting discussed in chapter 5, and helping to distinguish what television could do differently from its competing forms of film, radio, and theater. Clearly these technical dimensions powerfully shape television's use and cultural impact, but they do not determine them on their own.

Institutional practices are a second layer of technological shaping, as the influence of private industries and public regulatory bodies helps drive technological change and guide key historical decisions. Television's technological capabilities initially privileged local broadcasting over high-power national stations or complex interconnections between local stations, but the immediate dominance of national networks ran counter to the technology's easiest path to development; it was because of the institutional practices of networks, station owners, and compliant regulators that the network model became the medium's norm. Similarly, historical decisions about television's screen resolution, delayed shift to color, and slow spread of cable all developed less from technological capabilities than from institutions making choices and lobbying for policies that would increase profits and help them maintain control of national networks. Institutions also shape technology by investing in particular inventions over others, as demonstrated by the reluctance shown by networks and advertisers to embrace alternative technologies to measure ratings, as discussed in chapter 2.

A third factor driving the social construction of technology is the **cultural circulation** of any medium. Although institutions and technologies offer their own capabilities and preferences for how a medium will be used, viewers have the ability to exert preferences in what they purchase and how they use media. Just because a technology exists and a company pushes it to market does not guarantee its long-term success, as failed television innovations such as Sony's Watchman or WebTV suggest. Additionally, we cannot simply reduce technologies to their core technical or institutional functions; we invest a tremendous degree of meaning and significance in our media, with particular technologies serving as status symbols, signs of identity, or markers of subcultural affiliation.

Some of these meanings are offered by institutions, as with advertising and design elements that frame any new technology's potential uses and cultural values, but many emerge unpredictably from how people connect with or reject a technology. Ask nearly any TiVo owner about the device to hear a sincere outpouring of celebratory cultural values that could not be determined by technological or institutional forces alone.

Analyzing the social construction of technology allows us to look more closely at how media both shape and are shaped by a society, seeing a complex relationship between new technologies and American culture. We can still follow the analytic impulses of media ecology to explore how a new medium can potentially alter social relationships, psychological models, and economic and political systems, but we need to be careful not to grant technologies a deterministic power apart from their social contexts. For a study of the television medium, we can trace out some key moments in the medium's technological development, institutional practices, and cultural circulation. Through this examination of the medium's history, we can see how what we know as television is neither natural nor inevitable, but rather the product of particular social practices with significant cultural consequences.

A BRIEF CULTURAL HISTORY OF TELEVISION TECHNOLOGY

Entire books have been written about the origins and emergence of television technology, charting the various devices, patents, and inventors that came together to create such a powerful medium. For the purposes of this book, it is less important to know who invented what than to explore how our understanding of the television medium emerged through these innovations and their associated technological, institutional, and cultural developments. The television medium can be understood not just as a blank screen to pursue commercial aims, or a collection of tubes and transistors enabling the uncanny achievement of viewing the world from our living rooms, but as a collection of meanings and metaphors that shape our relationship to the medium's institutions, programs, and everyday practices.

Television's Origins and Original Meanings

It is tempting to start the history of American television at one defining instant when television was born: for instance, the 1939 New York World's Fair is often hailed as a key moment of the public unveiling of television, with RCA's high-profile exhibition and its broadcasting subsidiary NBC debut of television by broadcasting the opening events. However, a long history of inventions, institutional battles, and cultural debates about the new medium preceded this moment of television's grand debut—and more negotiations would follow throughout the next decade before television truly became a mass medium. The varying ways that television was understood and imagined leading up to its publicized debut help us understand how television became the device it is today.

Although television is often seen as the technological synthesis of the early twentieth century's two dominant media, motion pictures and radio, experimentations in television actually preceded the emergence of both film and radio. A number of parallel inventions and discoveries of the nineteenth century were instrumental in the development of television, with key technologies emerging in the United States, Europe, and Russia. Although the term *television* was not used until 1900, its etymology suggests the goals of many earlier inventors. The term means "seeing from a distance," evoking the idea of extending human vision outside of its immediate spatial context. While some inventors were less invested in the specific applications of their discoveries, a shared goal of most was the desire to transmit visual images across space through a range of technologies.

Many of the key devices that would come together to form modern television were invented prior to the 1920s. Much of the early experimentation in the medium's prehistory in the 1800s was in developing **mechanical television**, a system for capturing and transmitting images using spinning discs. Some of the core principles of mechanical television became influential in the medium's electronic form: images were scanned and broken down into smaller bits of light, which would then trigger reproduction on a screen using a photochemical process. These inventions were aimed at creating not a wireless broadcast mass medium, but rather a visual parallel to the telephone, striving toward a wired two-way device, or a form of remote "telephotography," or "telescopy," similar to what later became the fax machine. Had these systems of mechanical television proved to be technically and economically feasible, the cultural functions of television might have turned out quite differently.

The **electronic television** was developed in the 1910s and 1920s by a number of inventors, who used vacuum tubes to scan and project images via an electron beam. The most notable invention was the **iconoscope**, created in the mid-1920s by Russian émigré Vladimir Zworykin while he was working for American electronics firm Westinghouse. The iconoscope used a **cathode ray tube** (CRT) to scan images and crudely reproduce them on a screen. The system was refined in the 1930s as Zworykin shifted to RCA, refining the invention to build on the company's core business of wireless radio broadcasting and manufacturing. A competing inventor, a young self-educated engineer named Philo Farnsworth, developed his own television camera in the late 1920s, one that more effectively dissected an image into small "picture elements," or what would later be called **pixels**. Farnsworth battled RCA throughout the 1930s over patents before agreeing to merge the two systems into the basic model of television that would last for decades. Under RCA's primary control, television developed as a form of visual wireless—not because it was determined by the technology itself, but due to institutional practices pushing to extend the business model of commercial radio to the new medium.[4]

American television broadcasting was far slower to emerge than in Germany and Britain, which both launched national television systems in the mid-1930s. While the British and German systems met with limited popularity, curtailed in part by World War II, Europe's public service models encouraged launching of the technology to serve viewers as soon as the technology was feasible. In the United States, RCA and other manufacturers were unable to settle on uniform standards in the 1930s, and the FCC refused to step in to force a technology upon the industry. The late 1930s saw some experimental television broadcasting and marketing of a few retail television sets by manufacturers trying to gain a foothold in the new industry of television, with RCA aggressively pushing its own system over the objections of many competitors. In 1940, the FCC finally forced a compromise, which led to the creation of the **National Television System Committee** (NTSC) to determine a set of industry standards. In 1941, the NTSC recommendations, which were largely modeled after RCA's system, were adopted by the FCC, setting in place the basic system of television still used into the twenty-first century.

What did the NTSC standards specify? While there were many technical elements dictating issues of signal encoding and tube specifications, the most noticeable standards involved the television screen resolution: NTSC defined a resolution of 525 horizontal lines and a frame rate of 30 screens per second, deemed adequate resolution to match the image quality of 16-millimeter film.

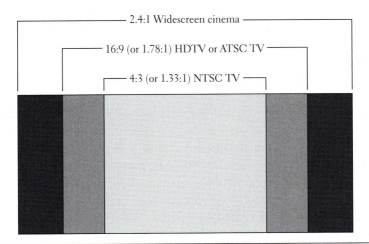

Figure 11-1 The NTSC standard of 4:3 aspect ratio has given way to the DTV standard of 16:9, which is still less broad than widescreen cinema.

Additionally, NTSC dictated a screen shape of a 4:3 aspect ratio and the use of the VHF band for signals. Just as important was what the NTSC did not include: CBS had innovated a color television system that it was advocating to become part of the emerging standards. The NTSC and FCC followed RCA's influence to endorse a black-and-white system that was incompatible with CBS's color model, effectively limiting the technological influence of CBS on the development of television. Additionally, the NTSC standard froze screen quality for decades, leading to higher resolution in other standards adopted later around the world, such as the European systems of PAL and Secam.

Although television standards were set in 1941, the medium did not truly become a viable form until the late 1940s. This delay and expansion was mostly due to U.S. involvement in World War II. After the United States entered the war in 1941, American electronic firms shifted the majority of their efforts to producing military devices, which led to a significant expansion of the electronics industry. After the war, many firms adapted their manufacturing base to produce the emerging technology of television, which created widespread availability and growing competition among brands. Early television was still a luxury, with a small-screen television measuring seven inches costing upward of $400 in the late 1940s, more than $3,000 in today's dollars. But by the early 1950s, competition had driven down prices by almost 50 percent, allowing more than a third of American households to own televisions by 1952.[5] By the early 1950s, with the growing sales of television sets, the rising numbers of broadcast stations, and the emergence of programs such as *Texaco Star Theater* and *I Love Lucy* as shared landmarks of American culture, television had truly arrived as a dominant mass medium.

While the technological and industrial innovations and practices account for much of television's early emergence, new media do not take hold without broad cultural circulation. Today it is hard for most of us to imagine life without television, but in the 1940s, it was not clear what life *with* television might look like. Early television sets were not only large investments, they were also large pieces of furniture, typically with heavy wooden cabinets to house the bulky electronic components. How would American households place these devices in their homes and allow families to gather around the screen? Technological capabilities helped shape these decisions, especially in determining screen and cabinet sizes, and institutional practices such as design and marketing definitely influenced how consumers perceived this new medium, but we need to explore the meanings and practices circulating around television in its earliest years to understand how it emerged as America's dominant medium.

One of the chief concerns surrounding early television focused on its impact on family dynamics. Television emerged in the postwar era of suburbanization, the baby boom, and a return to more traditional gender roles of female domesticity, all of which centered much of American life on the individual

Televisions in the 1950s were thought of as furniture to be integrated into homes, creating potential conflicts amongst family members and shaping the everyday lives of Americans.

family home more than the communal neighborhood of urban life. Magazines aimed at homemakers directly addressed how to reconcile television in the home, offering suggestions for arranging a living room to avoid focusing on the "eyesore" of a television, and expressing anxieties that television screens might serve as a competition for male attention. Early on, the medium was framed as appealing to fathers and children, while being a domestic disruption for women trying to maintain an ideal suburban home. One common discourse framed the medium as an "electronic hearth," where the family could gather to share in the nightly ritual of watching variety shows and sitcoms, with the television as the glue that bonded families together.

Television was also framed in a positive light as an essential component of the American household, especially through advertisements for television sets and representations of the technology in programming itself. One prominent way of understanding the new medium was as a "window to the world," allowing viewers to travel to exotic locales from the privacy of their homes. Additionally, early television programs highlighted their theatricality and sense of presence, claiming to transport viewers to new places through the "home theater" of live broadcasting, with every television viewer described as part of a community of millions of others simultaneously watching the same program. Liveness was an essential component of the early television experience, as the simultaneous nature of broadcasting made the medium feel less isolating and individualistic, and helped ensure its ties to the radio industry over Hollywood film production, as discussed in chapter 5. These meanings of television, harking back to the literal definition of the word, "seeing from a distance," worked to combat the potential isolation of suburban living by framing television as an electronic connection to build community: television created an imagined community of individual viewers experiencing shared culture from a distance.[6]

While we primarily think of television as a domestic medium, in its earliest years many viewers first experienced it in public spaces. For urban men in the 1940s, television was commonly watched in taverns as a form of public amusement, not private isolation. Although such venues typically featured sports broadcasting, serving as the ancestor of the modern sports bar, tavern television sets showed a broad array of programming, from prime time variety shows to afternoon cartoons. Another public venue for early television was the storefront: many retailers placed televisions prominently in their windows to draw consumers and promote sales of sets, but these displays also functioned as gathering sites to watch programming outside of the home. Television has certainly been more defined by its domestic incarnation, but we should not forget the proliferation of screens where television still can be watched outside the home: sports in bars, news in airports, health information in medical lobbies, advertising on enormous screens in urban centers such as Times Square, and promotional videos in large retail stores.

In trying to define the aspects of the television medium that operate at the broader level, beyond specific content or form, it is clear that early television foregrounded the centrality of liveness, shared access among a community of viewers, and the ability to overcome spatial boundaries through broadcasting. Another important aspect of the medium that has been influential in the study of television is **flow**. As discussed in chapter 1, flow refers to the continuous connection between segments and programs that typify the television schedule. Flow is less technologically defined than institutionally created, as the television industry devised modes of scheduling and production that work to build continuity between a set of programs and commercials, rather than treating each segment as a distinct and separate object to be analyzed or understood on its own. For many critics, flow creates a mode of engagement with television that passively absorbs a viewer into a steady stream, blurring boundaries between segments of programming, commercials, distinct genres, and juxtapositions of different types of content—all of television can be seen as one constant flow of content. As we will see with the technological shifts in the convergence era, flow and liveness are arguably becoming far less central as a defining experience for television.

A Transforming Box

While the basic NTSC system and most of the meanings associated with the television medium endured throughout the twentieth century, a number of key transformations in television technology triggered changes in how we think about the medium. Even though CBS's color system was dismissed in the 1940s, another protocol for color broadcasting was approved by the FCC at the end of 1953, following industry leader RCA's technology. But color television would not become standard in the industry for more than a decade, with the networks converting to full color broadcasting by the mid-1960s. This delayed adoption was less technological than economic: by the time color standards were approved, there were more than three hundred television stations operating across the country, with more than two thirds of them having been on the air for less than two years. Upgrading the cameras and transmission equipment that these stations had just purchased at great expense was an additional cost with no additional revenue. NBC and its affiliates were most aggressive in the shift to color, trying to drive sales of the color television sets of NBC's parent company, RCA, but color sales were slow for a decade. By 1965, only 5 percent of television households had color receivers. Even after network programming had converted to full color, viewers made the shift slowly, taking until 1975 to reach the 75 percent saturation point for color, which highlights how technology itself rarely determines its own cultural impact and dissemination.

Few technological innovations have had more impact on the entire world of communications than the proliferation of **satellites** since the 1960s, with television feeling their impact at all levels, from production to consumption practices. Communications satellites orbit in constant sync with the Earth, allowing dishes on the ground to communicate signals with the multiple transponders mounted on each satellite, with each transponder reaching a specific "footprint" of a large geographical area able to receive its signal. The television industry uses satellites in all phases of its system, receiving content from remote locations for live news or sports coverage, distributing programs across a network or to cable systems, and transmitting signals directly to DBS subscribers. In the 1970s, the first form of home satellite reception was through enormous dishes commonly found in rural areas with no other television service. Today DBS service requires only a small dish suitable for urban apartments as well as rural locales. Satellite technology helps reduce the geographical boundaries that have traditionally made international communication challenging, allowing television and other communication systems to traverse the globe almost instantaneously. Satellite technology has been a chief agent in creating a global village, enabling a shrinkage of time and space through the practice of live or simultaneous broadcasting.

Many of the transformations in television technology occurred at the levels of production and distribution: telefilm, videotape, satellite links, captioning, and special effects discussed in previous chapters all made significant impacts on television programming and institutions. For the technology of everyday life, transformations of actual television sets have been quite dramatic, but so commonplace as to potentially escape notice. Television sets in the classic network era were typically bulky consoles with small black-and-white screens, while the way viewers selected programs was vastly different from today. Televisions had dials that required fine tuning to get a quality signal, along with adjusting antennas either mounted on the console as "rabbit ears" or on rooftops, sometimes with electric motors to rotate the antennas for better reception. The effect of this tuning system was that it often took up to a minute to change the channel; the practice of "channel surfing" was nearly impossible. This system encouraged flow due to the technical difficulty of changing channels. Even though newer technologies have made such practices obsolete, the phrases "don't touch that dial" and "tune in" still resonate in American culture.

Early in the medium's history, television manufacturers began offering alternate ways of tuning in television: instead of rotary dials, some televisions in the 1950s featured push-button interfaces that allowed viewers to set the tuning for individual channels and access them at a single click. Another lasting innovation from the 1950s was the **remote control device** (RCD). Early RCDs were connected to televisions by wires, but by the mid-1950s, ultrasonic wireless devices were available as an option on expensive televisions. In the classic network era most viewers could receive only a few channels, making RCDs a less essential part of watching television. With the rise of cable in the 1980s, RCDs became more critical for navigating dozens of channels. More sophisticated infrared remotes became a standard component of many televisions in the 1980s, with more than three quarters of television homes using RCDs by 1990. While the RCD technology did not directly cause a shift in viewing practices, it certainly enabled a mode of channel grazing that disrupted flow, simultaneously making viewers more active in choosing programming and allowing the passivity of staying on the couch.

Along with cable and RCDs, the 1980s saw the rise of two more technologies that would help extend the use of television: home video and video game consoles. Following the spread of videotape in the studio production process in the 1960s and the portable recorders of the 1970s, the home **video cassette recorder** (VCR) emerged in the late 1970s with two competing technical standards: Sony's Betamax system and JVC's standard called VHS. While JVC licensed its technology to other manufacturers to make VHS recorders, Sony retained proprietary control as the only manufacturer of Betamax. In the so-called format wars, Betamax lost control of the market, despite having better picture quality, as consumers preferred the lower-priced VHS machines and the emerging video rental industry tended toward VHS to reach the more widespread customer base. VCRs were initially marketed primarily as devices to **time-shift** programming, disrupting flow and allowing viewers to watch television on their own schedules. However, a minority of VCR owners used time-shifting capabilities; instead, pre-recorded videotape rentals became much more popular, allowing viewers to watch films on television, while a small portion of collector fans used VCRs to record and archive programs. These varied uses helped lead to the saturation of VCRs, found in two thirds of television households by 1990.

Other home video technologies were marketed to compete with VCRs, including a number of different **videodisc** systems. Throughout the 1970s and 1980s, the range of videodisc options included SelectaVision and LaserDisc, which used different technologies to create a read-only large disc the size of a phonograph record. Videodiscs offered higher image and sound quality than VHS, with a direct appeal to collectors and the rental market. While some fans embraced the technology, most viewers preferred the flexibility of VCRs, making videodiscs a failed addition to television's technological expansion; although the basic idea of videodiscs would return with great success in smaller form with DVDs.

Home video components allowed viewers to watch television with more control of timing and choice of content, but the core content and form of programming remained consistent, featuring the shows and movies already available via broadcast and cable. **Video game consoles** more directly transformed both the mode of engagement and the type of content featured on television, although most discussions of television do not even consider video games as part of the medium. Yet today video games are a crucial component of home entertainment systems and a key part of digital convergence. The roots of this development trace back to the earlier consoles of the 1970s, such as the single-game Pong and programmable console Atari 2600, which appealed to players despite crude graphics and fairly simple game play. The video game market boomed in the late 1980s and into the 1990s, with Nintendo, Sega, and Sony consoles driving demand for this expanded use of the television as a site of play and interactivity, with more than a third of television households owning video game consoles by the mid-2000s.

By the end of the twentieth century, television was a transformed technology. While the core function of using television to watch programs received through broadcast signals still matters, the television set has expanded and multiplied into the hub of broader home entertainment systems, with numerous boxes surrounding it. Home video devices such as VCRs and videodiscs enable viewers to disrupt the television schedule and choose what they wish to watch on their own time, with many consumers integrating the television into their stereo systems to create a virtual theater with surround sound. Video game consoles make televisions a site for interactive play rather than just watching programmed content. Penetration of cable systems and DBS add additional boxes to the mix, with more than three quarters of households receiving cable and 15 percent subscribing to DBS. With all of these expanded components come additional remote controls, making the television set the centerpiece of the home electronics universe—and the majority of households have multiple sets of various sizes and functions scattered throughout their home, a far cry from the early days of the electronic hearth.

It would be easy to see this transformation as a case of technology driving social change, presuming that multiple sets, narrowcasting channels, and niche components such as video games push families apart and foster social isolation. But we must remember that technologies do not determine their uses, as the ways consumers engage with technologies help shape those technologies' social functions, influencing the institutions that manufacture and program technology in how they address such cultural practices. One important aspect of the everyday practices of technology is how different technologies are understood as gendered, coded as masculine or feminine in their daily uses. Research has suggested that although most entertainment technology is assumed to be a masculine domain, varying perceptions are linked to different components: video game consoles, remote controls, and recording via VCRs are typically tied to male users, while basic television viewing and playing videotapes is more gender neutral and can even skew toward assumed female users. The gendering of technology is understood both at a broad cultural level as a general trend and as part of specific family practices, where tendencies might follow or contradict such general patterns. These assumed gender practices matter for technology manufacturers and the television industry, who either reinforce the assumptions by catering to the targeted gender, or work to counter the trends to reach consumers outside the core demographic—for instance, Nintendo's Wii console successfully targeted players outside the core young male gaming demographic with its easy-to-use motion controls and appealingly sleek white design, along with a marketing campaign specifically aimed at women, young kids, and seniors. Such an example highlights that in trying to understand how technologies matter, we need to focus on the interactions between industries and users, not just on the devices themselves.

TELEVISION IN TRANSITION: CONVERGING ON THE DIGITAL

It is hard to imagine a more transformative period in television's history than the 2000s. More significant technological shifts have emerged in this decade than since the invention of the medium, with all facets of the television industry forced to adjust to a transforming medium and an uncertain future. Any attempt to survey the shape of the television medium in the digital era is nearly impossible, as a significant change might become irrelevant or overtaken by something new at any moment. Yet with the caveat that any of these developments, names, and technologies might appear passé by the time you read this, we can chart some of the key ways television is making the transition to a digital media environment, and consider how the convergence era is altering many of the core attributes tied to the medium.

The Resolution Revolution

The NTSC standard persisted as the only way to receive over-the-air broadcasts into the 1990s not because it was the most technologically advanced system—it was surpassed in the 1960s by higher-resolution European standards PAL and SECAM—but because changing broadcast standards is a costly and complicated task. The television industry made slight upgrades to NTSC over the years, incorporating color and stereo sound, but these changes were made without requiring an entire overhaul of stations' transmission equipment or consumers' television sets. Yet in the 1990s, the federal government started the process to convert American television broadcasting into a digital television standard, a transition still underway as this is being written in late 2008.

The story of digital television is quite complicated, influenced by the competing interests of broadcasters, television technology manufacturers, the computer industry, congressional budget priorities, and countless other parties. Possibly the most confusing element for everyday consumers is the issue of terminology: the phrase "digital television" can refer to a wide range of different technologies, including DVDs, video games, HDTV, digital cable, DBS, downloadable programming, and online video. For the purposes of clarity, this book will use **digital television** and its abbreviation DTV to refer to the system of digital broadcasting and its associated set of standards, also known as Advanced Television Systems Committee (ATSC), designed to replace analog signals and NTSC screen specifications.

The technical specifications for DTV broadcasting require that the signals transmitted by stations use digital standards, encoding the visual and sonic information of television into binary data rather than the analog information traditionally used by television. The effect of this shift is to increase both the fidelity and amount of information that can be broadcast on a television signal, reducing the interference and variable reception that typify many over-the-air broadcasts. To accomplish this transition to a more reliable and efficient broadcast signal, the Telecommunication Act of 1996 directed the FCC to allocate a new portion of the spectrum for DTV, issuing licenses for all analog TV stations to create parallel DTV channels. As discussed in chapter 3, this decision to duplicate existing television broadcasting licenses at no cost was seen by many as a corporate giveaway and a missed opportunity to strengthen both competition and public service obligations among broadcasters. The television industry countered that this process of duplication was needed to allow stations to fund the high cost of transitioning to DTV equipment, a change requiring new broadcast towers, cameras, and transmission infrastructure.

The DTV transition was launched with a series of deadlines for analog conversion, starting with major markets in 1999 and with a final requirement that all analog stations mirror their broadcasts in DTV by 2003, with a planned elimination of the analog spectrum and full switch to digital in 2006. These deadlines were routinely missed, leading the FCC to roll back the proposed timetable for eliminating analog broadcasting to February 2009, at which point all stations will be exclusively available in DTV. The FCC will then convert the analog television spectrum to serve wireless communications services, which will have to pay for their licenses at auction, in stark contrast to the free licenses receive by commercial television broadcasters. When analog broadcasting ceases operation, all traditional television sets will need to be outfitted with a converter box to receive over-the-air DTV signals or be hooked into a cable or DBS system that provides analog conversion. These analog conversions will not be able to take advantage of the higher resolution pictures afforded by DTV. All television sets sold since 2007 are mandated to have built-in DTV tuners, although there is a good deal of confusion among consumers as to how to interpret phrases such as "Digital Ready" or "HDTV Monitor" on television sets, as these terms do not necessarily indicate the presence of a DTV tuner.

DTV and the ATSC standards do more than just change the way transmissions are coded; they significantly upgrade the resolution of images available through television. For most consumers, DTV is most recognizable as **High-Definition Television** (HDTV), the highest-quality image resolution available via DTV transmissions. Unlike NTSC's single-image specification, DTV allows for more than a dozen different variations on the image resolution, shape, scanning technique, and frame rate. DTV can feature either **progressive scan** images, where every line of resolution is rendered in each frame, or **interlaced scan** images, which render every other line per frame in an alternating pattern. This difference was crucial to satisfying the competing interests of companies involved in creating ATSC standards, as televisions have traditionally used interlaced scanning, while computer monitors use progressive scan; the compromise allowing for dual systems appeased both industries, ensuring them that their existing technology would be compatible with DTV monitors. The three highest-quality ATSC resolutions, measured by the lines of resolution and either interlaced or progressive scanning, qualify as HDTV: 1080p is considered "true HD," while 1080i and 720p systems both offer slightly lower HD quality. HDTV features a 16:9 aspect ratio, allowing for a wider rectangular screen than NTSC. This widescreen rectangle has become the standard shape for nearly all DTV sets.

While HDTV's image resolution has become the main selling point for early adopters of digital television sets, not all DTV broadcasts are in HD. Many local stations have found the upgrade of production technology to HD too costly, and it is questionable whether people really wish to see local news in such high definition. Likewise, much of the television schedule consists of older rerun material, most of which is impossible to upgrade to HD resolution. DTV allows for broadcasting in other standards with lower resolution than HD, including **Enhanced-Definition Television** (EDTV) images in 480p or 576p. These images are still higher than **Standard-Definition Television** (SDTV) of NTSC, in 480i resolution, although DTV can still display SDTV programming with improved image quality due to its better signal reception.

For broadcasters, the biggest advantage of EDTV and SDTV is not lower production costs, but the potential of **multicasting**: the efficient DTV signals allow for multiple simultaneous SD or ED broadcasts to be transmitted on one station license, creating up to five **subchannels** of SD programming. Potential uses for multicasting, which broadcasters see as an opportunity to compete with the niche programming typical of cable, include public television offering a broad array of educational programming at any given time, sportscasts providing access to multiple games simultaneously, or local stations offering continual weather and traffic broadcasts on a subchannel. While these practices are still emerging, networks have shifted much of their prime time entertainment and sports programming to HD, but have been slower in upgrading daytime and news programming. Additionally, each DTV channel has sufficient bandwidth to include a **datacasting** signal in addition to television programming or subchannels, allowing any device that can receive a DTV signal to access a stream of data. Datacasting allows for high-speed broadcast of digital software data for a range of purposes, including advertiser information, educational content, video-on-demand, or computer upgrades, although these usages are still being explored and have yet to become widespread as of this writing in 2009.

DTV has most direct implications for broadcast stations, which must transfer all of their operations from analog to digital, but the transition has also impacted cable and satellite providers and channels. Many subscribers receive "digital cable," and all DBS service is digitally encoded, but these systems do not necessarily feature DTV signals. Typically DTV service, including HDTV programming, is an extra feature of cable or DBS systems, requiring a special set-top box to receive HD reception, at an extra fee. In 2007, a provision of the Telecommunications Act of 1996 finally went into effect after years of legal battles that mandated cable systems to offer consumers the ability to use a CableCARD inserted into a digital television set or DVR, eliminating the necessity of a separate set-top cable box to access HD programming. The cable systems industry has been resistant to shifting to DTV in full, as it requires carrying numerous local subchannels and upgrading infrastructure to be able to transmit dozens of HD signals effectively via cable. However, for some cable channels, including ESPN and the upstart HDNet, it has been an effective way of building an audience among early adopters of DTV technology.

The broader cultural impacts of DTV have yet to be fully felt, as the technology has not penetrated most American television households: less than

23 percent of Americans had DTV sets in 2008, although this number is certain to grow rapidly in the face of the 2009 analog cutoff. DTV is potentially fostering class distinctions, as the current cost of HDTV-equipped sets is prohibitive for most working-class families. Television has long been one of the most economically diverse media, with consumers of all incomes owning sets, and DTV threatens to create unequal access to America's central medium except through low-fidelity converter boxes. Currently around 15 percent of American households receive television only through over-the-air signals, presumably with many of those opting for the free broadcasting service for economic reasons. These households were most impacted by the switch to DTV, forced to purchase converter boxes, subscribe to cable or satellite, or invest in an expensive DTV set. Another social impact of the switch to digital is the environmental impact of millions of analog sets being discarded after digital upgrades, as cathode ray tubes contain a large amount of lead, requiring recycling and processing to avoid serious pollution of toxic waste.

For early adopters willing to invest thousands of dollars in their television setups, HDTV has been a chief appeal in building home entertainment systems to screen films and sports in a home theater experience to rival cinema. Some viewers complain that certain programs look worse in HDTV because the high-resolution images highlight visual imperfections, often undermining makeup and other techniques designed to make performers appear attractive, a complaint that has spanned genres from newscasts to game shows to pornography. It will be interesting to see if particular genres or modes of programming become more or less popular under the DTV paradigm and high-resolution of HDTV. For one potential sign of cultural shift, Discovery Channel's 2007 HD presentation of the British nature documentary *Planet Earth* set records for cable ratings driven in part by the spectacular visuals featured on the program. Perhaps the higher fidelity of visual resolution afforded by DTV and HD will increase the fortunes of naturalistic styles, such as documentary, sports, and gritty dramas, over more presentational modes, such as multi-camera sitcoms, studio newscasts, or game shows. However, it is far too soon to tell how the DTV change will impact American culture and the formal norms of television.

From Flow to Files

The shift to DTV clearly changes the technological basis of American television, but it remains to be seen how it will alter how viewers engage with the medium or its underlying industrial system. Another shift under way over the past decade may have been less technologically transformative, but has had more of an impact on both the production and consumption of television. As discussed earlier, for many critics the essence of the television medium is tied to liveness, simultaneity, and flow: watching television means viewing whatever is

PLANET EARTH

Planet Earth (Discovery Channel, 2007): This BBC nature documentary re-aired in the United States to set record ratings for the genre, driven by the program's spectacular photography showcasing the newly emerging HD format.

airing at the moment along with millions of others around the country, following the schedule determined by broadcasters. This flow paradigm began to be challenged by the VCR, which offered an alternative to this dominant mode by introducing time-shifting and the ability to watch prerecorded tapes, but a series of newer digital technologies have more directly threatened live simultaneous viewing.

The rise of the VCR in the 1980s spurred the home video industry, which has proven to be a crucial market for Hollywood studios. Initially prerecorded tapes were priced at high rates to be purchased exclusively by video rental stores and dedicated collectors, with prices ranging between $70 and $100 per copy. Feature films were the most popular slice of the home video market, with rentals transforming the film industry by creating another lucrative market for a film after its release. While made-for-television movies fared well in the home video rental market, ongoing series were generally not released on videotape. Even as retail prices for home video dropped throughout the 1980s and 1990s, to "sell-through" prices of under twenty-five dollars, making film collections more commonplace, material originally broadcast for television was a marginal part of the home video market.

The minor role for prerecorded television programming in the 1980s and 1990s can be attributed to a number of factors. Certainly a television series was a large investment to collect on videotape: Each tape could hold approximately two hours, so the cost to purchase multiple tapes of any series was significant to both consumers and rental stores. Perhaps even more challenging was the size of the tapes, as a season of a series might take up an entire shelf in a retailer or home collection. Additionally, the thought of purchasing a program that was generally available to viewers via syndication at no cost, save for advertising, seemed daunting for all but the most serious fan. Notably the few series that did have major home video releases were cult shows such as *Star Trek* and *The Twilight Zone*. The industry was wary to invest in bringing television series to the home video market, as they saw it as a risky move that also threatened to undercut syndication sales and advertising revenue. Thus before the emergence of DVD, the bulk of series television videotapes were repackaged "Best of" collections or selected special episodes of series that were rarely syndicated.

DVDs, which were commercially launched in 1997, changed many of these practices. Even though DVD players became popular quite quickly, the first few years saw the bulk of releases mirroring the videotape market by focusing on Hollywood films. The technological capabilities of DVDs enabled a new opportunity for home video release of television series: because of digital compression and fidelity, an entire season of a series can fit into a box set that takes the shelf space of one videotape, with a higher resolution and better resistance to wear and tear. Television institutions did not take immediate advantage of this possibility, as the industry still doubted that a market for retail sales of television programming would be significant beyond a cult audience. However, the successful release of Season 1 of *The X-Files* in 2000 set an industry standard, and established precedents for successfully marketing home video releases: use high-quality and well-designed packaging, include significant "extras" such as commentaries and behind-the-scene documentaries, and highlight the high fidelity of DVDs. This model of releasing television on DVDs transforms the flow model of broadcasting into a publishing strategy more common to the book and music industries, turning television programming into an object to be bought, collected, and viewed multiple times.[7]

In the 2000s, the majority of new scripted television series have been given DVD releases, even short-lived programs that had trouble lasting on network schedules. Notably, *Family Guy*'s DVDs sold so well that Fox reversed its cancellation by returning the series to its lineup, while sets of cancelled single-season series such as *Freaks and Geeks*, *Wonderfalls*, and *Firefly* sold far better than their low broadcast ratings would have predicted. DVD sales offer another measure of viewer interest and consumption beyond ratings, although clearly the advertising industry sees the commercial-free release of television as more of a threat than an opportunity: the rise of product integration has been partly in response to the home video shift, as promotions integrated into an episode's content pay longer-term dividends as part of an archived collection of media rather than commercials featured in a one-time-only broadcast.

DVD box sets are changing both the cultural use of television programming and the creative choices made by producers. Many viewers have been so taken with the freedom, flexibility, and lack of advertising enabled by DVDs that they wait for video releases to follow favored series. This mode of consumption is particularly tied to the rental market, with the rental-by-mail model of Netflix as a popular way of working through a television series. Television writers have latched on to the possibilities of DVD viewing to redefine the way they tell stories—because DVD viewers are more likely to watch series with smaller gaps between episodes and frequently will rewatch favorite series, shows such as *Lost*, *Arrested Development*, and *Heroes* feature more complex storytelling strategies that demand regular viewing with close attention, supplemental commentaries and extras, and the ability to rewind for details. Viewers have embraced "binging" marathons for the series *24* on DVD, and have even attempted to mimic the show's real-time narration within a twenty-four hour viewing block. The transformation of television programming from a fleeting broadcast flow into a collectable and archived object on DVD has helped raise the cultural legitimacy of the medium, with acclaimed shows such as *The Wire* and *The Sopranos* embraced as the cultural equal of literature and cinema on the shelves of some collectors and connoisseurs.

In many ways, the DVD set makes the ephemeral flow of programming into something more tangible and material, an object to be owned and purchased; however, DVDs also transform television in a less tangible and more abstract way by shifting programming into the digital realm. Once a show is on DVD, each episode enters the familiar realm of computer interfaces, organized by menus rather than schedules. Although copy protection protocols make it difficult for most viewers to make copies of DVDs, even for personal backups or other fair uses discussed in chapter 3, downloadable software exists that allows consumers to "rip" DVDs and transfer the content to personal computers. This digitization redefines programs into **computer files**, with an associated set of uses and possibilities common to the digital realm. Online file sharing, video remixing and reediting, and proliferation across multiple screens are all enabled by the DVD's native digital format.

DVDs are far from the only way television programs function as computer files. In part to try to offset the illegal file sharing that confounded the music industry in the early 2000s, the television industry has embraced a variety of online distribution platforms to bring programming to technologically advanced viewers. In 2005, production studios and networks began to offer episodes of current and classic programs for **pay-per-download** for $1.99 on iTunes, Apple Computer's online media store. While broadcast hits *Lost* and *Desperate Housewives* were among the top programs, lower rated shows *The Office* and *Battlestar Galactica* also fared surprisingly well on iTunes, helping to keep them on the air despite marginal ratings. Other official downloading options have followed from the success of iTunes, including Amazon.com's Unbox, alongside numerous illicit methods of downloading through software protocols like BitTorrent, making downloaded television into a popular option, especially among younger viewers.

The television industry has been eager to embrace online **streaming video**, using network or channel websites as platforms to deliver advertiser-supported programs from their current schedules and archives. In many ways, streaming video is more consistent with the traditional distribution and transmission roles of the television industry, with programming delivered at no cost in exchange for delivering viewer's attention to advertisers. Networks and channels retain their role in promoting programming, directing viewer choices, and branding their own online identities. Just as downloading comes in both sanctioned and

iTunes offers direct downloading of dozens of programs, such as these ABC offerings, enabling consumers to pay directly for owning television shows more like music or movies.

illicit forms, streaming video can be found both legally, on network websites, and on non-licensed illicit sites that collect a wide range of online video, including YouTube and more explicitly illegal sites that emerge and disappear frequently. The television industry has been aggressive in trying to shut down illicit online video options with copyright lawsuits, while offering its own alternatives through licensed platforms including Joost and Hulu.

The industry-controlled transformation of programming from scheduled flow to digital files has been driven partly by the rise of DVDs and downloadable video, but new consumer technologies have also added significantly to this shift. VCRs enabled time-shifting, but were used far less frequently for this purpose than for playing back rented or purchased prerecorded tapes. In 1999, a new time-shifting device was introduced: the **digital video recorder**, or DVR, which was first marketed by TiVo and the now-defunct Replay TV. While TiVo remains the most common brand-name DVR, with diehard advocates among its user base, most DVRs are offered by cable and satellite companies as part of a subscription package. While DVRs received a tremendous amount of hype in the early 2000s, their adoption has been gradual, with a saturation rate of only around 25 percent of households in 2008. However, for people in the media industries, who were among the earliest adopters of DVRs, the technology clearly pointed to a radical shift in viewer behavior, with many industrial strategies of the twenty-first century designed to react to an anticipated sea change.

DVRs capture the flow of the television schedule, converting all programming into digital files stored on a hard drive and accessible via a menu interface.

With a DVR, viewers are always in the time-shifting mode, as the DVR's interface is actively standing by, ready to time-shift, pause live television, rewind up to thirty minutes of material, or record an entire program even midway through it. DVRs can be programmed to record all episodes of a favorite program, and even can recommend programs based on similar program tastes. If time-shifting is an exceptional practice for a VCR, it is the norm with a DVR. Our default mode with a DVR is always ready to disengage from the schedule-driven flow that traditionally structures the experience of watching television. The majority of DVR users embrace time-shifting for most genres, with news and sports still most commonly viewed in real time and series programs often recorded. A DVR transforms the schedule grid into a menu of options for present and future viewing. DVR users rely less on network scheduling strategies, thus undoing many of the promotional techniques detailed in chapter 1: a program on a DVR is detached from its original network or channel, moved into a list of choices accessible with a computer-driven menu.

One common fear provoked by DVRs concerns the technology's impact on advertising, as most DVR users fast-forward through commercials. Nielsen has adapted its measurements to include DVR users as a category of ratings, but many advertisers have questioned the usefulness of measuring viewers who are probably fast-forwarding through their ads. However, some research has suggested that DVR users can recall brand names from ads as well as traditional viewers: a viewer fast-forwarding through an ad break is actually paying close attention to the screen to detect the show's return, while traditional viewers often leave the room or allow their attention to wander during muted commercials. Some advertisers have tried DVR-friendly ads, with clear text on the screen to deliver the message. In an extreme example, fast-food chain KFC embedded a code word in a single frame that viewers needed to access to get a coupon for free food in one highly publicized 2006 ad, requiring DVR users to scan the ad slowly for the hidden information. More widespread impacts of DVRs on the advertising industry include the rise of product integration in the 2000s to create promotional opportunities immune to the fast-forward button, ads on sports and news programming becoming more desirable, and higher value being placed on the placement of ads near the beginning and end of commercial breaks.

While many in the television industry see DVRs as a threat to the advertising model, the technology also offers significant opportunities for market research and audience measurement. TiVo's software logs every time a viewer pauses or fast-forwards, changes the channel, or records a program, enabling a detailed account of how viewers engage programming with far more precision than traditional ratings systems. TiVo compiles this data and sells its reports to networks and advertisers, enabling the industry to get a different sense of viewer behavior. While it is true that TiVo users are a small minority of the television audience, they are typically a more economically desirable segment, appealing to advertisers as technologically savvy consumers whose tastes and habits are trackable through the technology. TiVo also allows advertisers to deliver targeted commercials directly to its users, with lengthy promotions available for interested TiVo viewers to watch on demand. Thus the DVR cannot be seen simply as a threat to advertisers, but also as offering a shift in how sponsors can reach out to and engage viewers—as well as raising privacy concerns for viewers uninterested in having their viewing patterns monitored.

The most significant impact of DVRs might not be felt for a generation, as many of today's young viewers will grow up never knowing television as a medium defined by liveness, synchronous viewership, or industry-controlled scheduling. For today's DVR children, "what's on television?" refers to what is on the DVR menu. As viewers grow up in an on-demand programming environment, the strategies used to harness their attention in the twentieth century will appear out of place with their definitions of what television is, just as many older viewers today have a hard time imagining why viewers might want hundreds of channels or to pay for premium television. DVR and DVD technologies do not determine their own cultural uses and meanings, but we can see a broad and significant transformation under way as the flow model of television yields to the convergent logic of computer menus, archived discs, and portable files, leading to still unforeseen shifts in the medium's institutional practices and cultural circulation.

Multiplying Screens, Multiplying Content

Typically when we speak of "television," we refer to both the hardware itself and the programming it offers. Just as the ways in which we time-shift and organize programs are transforming in the era of digital convergence, the screens we are watching are also changing. DTV is redefining the resolution and scope of our television screens, with the native digital format making the television a more suitable monitor for other components and applications. Tech-savvy viewers can patch their computers into large-screen DTVs, allowing a high-resolution option for computer gaming, viewing downloaded or streaming media, or accessing an array of digital photos and music. The Apple TV device allows computers to connect to televisions via wireless Internet, while game consoles such as Xbox 360 or Wii can deliver downloadable video or websites to a television. Such components all enable convergence by intermixing computer and television, in terms of both content and interfaces. Even if you are sitting in front of a television, are you really "watching TV" when playing online games on an Xbox or surfing the Web via a Wii?

Just as we're using television screens for more than watching television, programming forms that have traditionally been considered unique to broadcasting are also migrating away from the television screen. Downloadable and streaming programming is one key way, with younger viewers commonly using laptops and desktop computers as video viewing stations. Much of this online video has migrated from traditional television sources, with network and channel sites allowing viewers to watch full episodes of programs at their convenience, or share clips from popular shows on Comedy Central or MTV. With the shift to DTV moving slowly, many viewers find that their computer screens offer higher resolution than NTSC televisions, allowing some consumers to opt out of conventional television sets while still accessing television programming via the Internet.

Watching downloadable or DVD video on computers enables **portability**, the potential to watch television in a wide range of locations. Television has traditionally been defined as a domestic medium. Even though televisions have always had a presence in public spaces, today people are more commonly watching television programs on the move: on subways via video iPods, in the backseats of cars via on-board video monitors, or on airplanes via portable players and personal seat-back screens. Video screens are becoming more pervasive and portable, enabling the experience of television to become more public, but also transforming public spaces into private television-viewing environments. While HDTV and home theater setups are increasing the size and resolution of some television screens, portable screens are offering small images for ease of transportation and flexibility, a change that suggests that television visuals are being pulled in two opposing directions.

Portable video typically uses recorded programming, whether downloaded or on disc, to view on demand. **Mobile television** similarly allows television to be consumed away from home, but via the more time-based feeds of broadcasting or streaming. Wireless phones are emerging as a central mobile video platform, with "mobisodes" offered both to genres demanding immediacy, such as news and sports, and as extra features for scripted programs such as 24 and *Lost*. Slingbox technology allows users to "place-shift" to conventional broadcasts from their homes onto a portable laptop, enabling viewers to watch their home local broadcasts while traveling, a convenience that has proven popular with business travelers eager to keep up with their home sports and news broadcasts, or even access their DVRs from the road. The dual emergence of portability and mobility break television away from its assumed domestic role, making the medium more centrally part of people's lives regardless of their place or schedule, while challenging the basic definition of the medium's core qualities.[8]

Potentially even more transformative than the ability of digital media to shift television's time and place constraints is how online video has upended the industry's control of television production and distribution. Throughout the network and multi-channel eras, the television industry's oligopoly was based on scarce access to the distribution platforms of over-the-air transmission and spots on the cable lineup. Unlike with the film, music, and publishing industries, television has lacked an independent alternative to the mainstream industry, with the marginal and generally underused exception of public access cable. Throughout the twentieth century, if you wanted to distribute a television program in America, you typically needed to gain access through the gatekeepers of commercial broadcasters and cable channels, or the noncommercial but still restricted realm of public broadcasting.

Online video provides easy and low-cost access to distribution in the twenty-first century, fueled by the growth of broadband Internet and the user-friendly interface of YouTube and other Web platforms. With the simultaneous proliferation of affordable video cameras, including stand-alone camcorders, cameras embedded in phones, and webcams attached to computers, and easy-to-use video editing programs such as iMovie and Windows Movie Maker, the technology of the mid-2000s allows anybody who can afford basic home computer technology to have the chance to make videos and get them seen. While most people may not see YouTube as a direct extension of television, the very name refers to the now-obsolete technology of tubes that used to be synonymous with television: YouTube features no "tubes" per se, but could be seen as functioning like the shared cultural meeting ground that television served in previous decades. Of course the rate of technological change in the digital era raises red flags about the longevity of any of these platforms, as YouTube might soon be eclipsed by other ways of presenting and sharing video unimagined as of this writing in 2009.

While the technology of online video certainly enables its widespread use and importance, we need to look at the institutional and cultural practices that have responded to and shaped the medium of online video, considering how the medium both converges and diverges from the traditions of television. It is tempting to see YouTube and other online video sites as wholly separate from media industries, with the majority of material created as **user-generated content**. Certainly the way YouTube users upload video is quite different from the centralized network system of controlled television distribution: online videos of all different types and production values can coexist, from professional music videos to bedroom lip-sync performances, sophisticated remixed film trailers to low-tech webcam commentaries. Many critics see such a platform as inherently democratic and participatory, with **viral videos** gaining notice through the votes of viewers and links from blogs and emails.

YouTube's popularity rankings via user rating and counting views suggest a far different sense of what viewers want to see than Nielsen ratings. The site's list of the all-time most viewed videos as of 2008 include such eclectic entries as a two-minute video of a baby laughing, a finger puppet show featuring the characters from *Harry Potter,* and a young Korean guitarist's performance of Pachelbel's Canon. However, the list also includes many professionally produced music videos by major label artists Avril Lavigne and Timbaland that also get

heavy rotation on televised music video outlets MTV and BET. YouTube's popular videos differ from most television primarily due to their short length, with
content appropriate for quick consumption and viral appreciation. Such format
constraints seem to privilege musical content, comedic shorts, or brief clips with
one sensational or notable feature, whether a dangerous stunt, a quick display of
an impressive talent, or an amusing gag that encourages a user to forward a link
to friends. The first few years of popular online video resemble the early years
of motion pictures in the 1890s, which critics have called the "cinema of attractions": storytelling is less important than spectacle, impressive performances, or
a quickly understood and amusing premise.

YouTube and similar video-sharing sites are not the exclusive means of distributing independent online video. Many creators use their own websites to
create popular series, especially via animation. *Homestar Runner* and *Happy
Tree Friends* are two examples of cult online animations, each with an eclectic sense of humor and aesthetics that would be hard to imagine thriving on
mainstream television. *Red vs. Blue* uses videogame footage from *Halo* to create
an ongoing **machinima** series, merging gaming and television technologies to
create a new mode of entertainment. Some professional creators and performers
have used online video as an outlet for new material, presenting comedic clips
on sites such as Super Deluxe and Funny or Die as a means of bypassing the
mainstream industry. During the writers' strike of 2007–08, *Buffy* creator Joss
Whedon produced an independent musical comedy mini-series, *Dr. Horrible's
Sing-Along Blog*, that successfully generated an audience and revenue through
paid downloads, ad-supported streaming, and DVD release; the show's success
pointed to an alternate distribution platform for selling programming outside of
television, especially when linked to well-established talent and creators. And
musicians regularly use their own websites or MySpace pages to host videos,
among other content, promoting bands through a direct connection to fans.
Even outside of YouTube, the genres of comedy and music dominate the short
format of online video.

Will online video replace traditional television? It is impossible to know
the future of technology, but the history of previous media suggests that new
forms rarely replace older technologies. Instead, old media shift their uses and
cultural roles in the face of newer formats. Neither cinema nor radio disappeared in the wake of television, as some predicted would happen in the 1940s
and 1950s, but film became more focused on big-budget spectacles unavailable on small-screen television, and radio embraced music and talk show formats that did not require a visual dimension. What seems almost certain is that
television will not successfully imitate the user-generated "video of attractions"
style of YouTube, but rather will focus on long-form, high-budget storytelling
and factual programming genres that are difficult to achieve via user-generated
content.

While some critics see user-generated content as a democratic or even utopian alternative to mainstream corporate media, we must view the phenomenon with a bit more skepticism. Many of the most popular YouTube videos are professional productions and advertisements, suggesting that it is not solely non-commercial or grass-roots phenomenon. Additionally, many popular online videos turn into "calling cards" for their producers, who go on to sign development deals with Hollywood, translating their online fame into traditional fortune within the film and television industry. Video sites are following similar commercial patterns of television, with advertising-driven revenues and corporate consolidation, as with Google's purchase of YouTube for $1.65 billion in 2006. And while user-generated content does allow free expression and access to an audience more than traditional television, it is important to remember that the users are often generating revenues and wealth for these host sites without compensation. In response to critiques of this free labor situation, some online video sites have developed some revenue-sharing models for contributing users, but the imbalance persists where the creators receive far less for their work than the owners of the distribution platforms—a scenario quite similar to the model of television and other media industries.

No discussion of online video would be complete without a mention of the role of copyright and piracy issues. File-sharing networks of users sharing high-quality copies of copyrighted programs are one target of the industry's legal attack, but the most notable action in recent copyright battles was Viacom's $1 billion lawsuit against YouTube, filed in 2007. Viacom and other television corporations claim that online clips of their programs posted by users are clear breaches of copyright law, and Viacom retains the online rights to their programs, and requires viewers to watch their content (and the associated advertising) on their own websites. YouTube claims that it responds to copyright violations upon complaint, as the law does not hold a website responsible for content uploaded by its viewers if they remove clips upon request. The issue is still undecided in court, but it is important to remember that even if user-posted clips do violate copyright, they can still generate revenue for producers by generating new fans, who might then watch shows on television or purchase downloads or DVDs. For instance, NBC's *Saturday Night Live* experienced a significant ratings boost after an illicit copy of its music video "Lazy Sunday" became a viral hit on YouTube. *SNL* has been aggressive in courting online fans via NBC.com and Hulu.com ever since, a strategy that paid off especially well in Fall 2008, as Tina Fey's imitations of Vice Presidential candidate Sarah Palin resulted in both online sharing and record ratings for NBC's long-running show.

The assumption that all copyrighted content posted without permissions constitutes a copyright violation ignores the crucial area of fair use, as discussed in chapter 3. Many clips posted on YouTube and other sites are presented in the framework of criticism and commentary, which are typically granted fair use.

The *Saturday Night Live* digital short "Lazy Sunday," featuring actors rapping about cupcakes and going to see the film *Chronicles of Narnia*, became a viral video sensation that drove viewers both to YouTube and *SNL* in 2005.

Even more commonly, bits of copyrighted works are incorporated into new creative work in the form of fan-created music videos, parody clips, and remixes. Such transformative works vary in their fair use claims, as criticism or parody are specifically allowable under fair use law, but remixes to show a fan's devotion and reinterpretation of a work are not. However, it is clear that such remixes are not piracy but rather examples of fan creativity. Different copyright holders take various attitudes toward such work, but there is a danger in potential computer protocols or legal policies that treat all work that includes materials copied without permission as piracy by default.

While many of the corporations in the television industry have battled against unlicensed use of their programming online, they have also proactively built popular extensions of content via network websites and other multimedia platforms. Some of the Internet's most popular websites are extensions of television channels, including CNN.com and ESPN.com, featuring embedded video that both reuses footage from cable programming and extends the content beyond what is available on television. Many of these sites feature extensive original content: in the case of ESPN, its online columns, podcasts, and associated *ESPN Magazine* and ESPN Radio extend the channel's brand name into a large multimedia presence that many readers might not even associate with the original cable channel. Such channels combine the logics of multimedia synergy and the niche creation of narrowcasting to ensure that the channel's brand name carries across media and comes to define the subject, whether it's ESPN's sports brand or Food Network's extension into various culinary realms.

For channels and networks tied to the more typical model of broadcasting a wider range of genres and reaching various audiences, websites function more as a portal to specific areas for each program. In addition to offering programs for online viewing, a number of shows use the Web's multimedia capabilities to extend how viewers can interact with their programs. Nearly every television program offers a companion website with promotional materials, behind-the-scenes information, and opportunities for online discussion among viewers. Reality and game show websites, with interactive voting, extended information about contestants, and opportunities for audience participation, are particularly popular at drawing in online users, with sites for *American Idol*, *Deal or No Deal*, and *Dancing with the Stars* as the three most popular program sites in the spring of 2007. While we rarely think of such programs as synergistic franchises, the long tradition of "home game" versions of game shows now extends beyond board games to multimedia properties such as websites, video games, and various tie-in products. Other shows have experimented with providing licensed footage to encourage fan remixing: for example, *The Colbert Report*'s "green screen challenge" asked fans to overlay footage of Stephen Colbert into their own videos. Such online extensions encourage fans to participate directly in a program's brand and offer opportunities for communities to develop through a show's online portal.

For narrative programs, online content often embraces a model of **transmedia storytelling**: websites not only reproduce and summarize content from the program, but also extend a show's narrative universe. Such paratextual material, such as in-character blogs or online diaries, often deepens the life of specific characters, especially when written from the perspective of a marginal or fan-favorite character. Blogs and other online supplements focus on characters who are particularly popular in soap operas and other dramas whose audience appeal is typically driven by investment in characters and relationships. Such extensions have also proven popular with comedies, as with *The Office*'s Dwight Schrute writing a blog that extends his character's unique worldview.

Some programs have extended transmedia storytelling even further. One of the most innovative examples is *Lost*, which has featured a number of online games and websites that contain information about the show's mysterious universe. In the summer of 2006, the show launched "The Lost Experience," an **alternate reality game** that put viewers in the position of investigating the show's suspicious Hanso Foundation. The game includes numerous websites, podcasts, in-person events, talk show appearances by fictional characters, and other avenues for fans to collaborate to solve puzzles, exploring a deeper narrative level than presented on the television series—as well as participating in explicit marketing opportunities for companies Sprite, Jeep, and Verizon. NBC's *Heroes* has similarly extended its storytelling possibilities with online comic books, games, and videos that both provide character backstories and fill in narrative gaps.

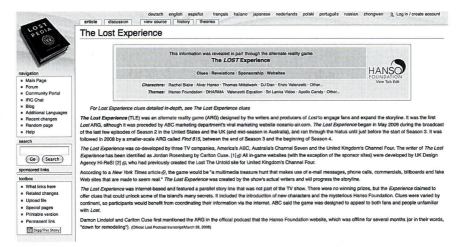

Lost fansite Lostpedia uses wiki technology to collectively decode both the television show and its transmedia extensions, like The Lost Experience.

One impact of transmedia storytelling and other online extensions of television programming is that they make the culture of fandom more mainstream and accessible. Years ago, such extended narrative universes, transmedia tie-ins, and opportunities for viewer participation would have been seen as appealing only to the most marginal group of cultish fans. While most viewers today still do not participate in online television culture, a significant portion of the audience does extend its viewing into multimedia forms and participatory culture. As such, creators pitch their programs to multiple levels of engagement, with some stories and characters aimed at the mainstream viewers watching only the televised series, and a more in-depth level of content appealing to hardcore fans willing to invest time and often money to consume transmedia tie-ins and participate in a series across formats.

The rise of transmedia extensions of television has created a good deal of industrial controversy. The Writers Guild of America strike of 2007–08 was triggered by a number of disagreements between the writers and the film and television industry, but at the center was how the industry would compensate creators for online distribution. Networks termed online viewing of programming and online content including webisodes and fictional blogs as "promotional content," and thus would not pay writers residuals for such material. Writers argued that online distribution was another revenue source more like DVDs and syndication, and that extra content online should be compensated as original creative work. The outcome of the strike redefined writing for online material as creative work and subject to compensation, as well as granting residuals on downloaded sales and online advertising, although not in the terms that the writers were seeking. The conflict points to the challenges facing the media industry in the era of digital convergence, as it struggles to define the boundaries of television and revise an industrial model based on a broadcast system facing competition from a range of media sources.

This chapter has explored television's history of technological change, with some glimpses of what might be on the horizon. New transmission protocols, such as Internet Protocol Television (IPTV), might prove to be significant and transformative—or might be one of many failed innovations, as with WebTV of the 1990s. Regardless of how technology continues to develop, we must always view technological shifts as not solely determined by technical means. Instead, the roles of institutional practices to shape how a medium is used, and cultural circulation to shape how people think about the medium, are powerful factors that will continue to matter if we are to understand television's present and future. All of the facets explored in this book connect with technology, and it is hoped that this approach to the medium will be able to account for whatever new developments arise.

FURTHER READING

The field of media ecology is built on McLuhan's writings, with Marshall McLuhan, *Essential McLuhan* (New York: Basic Books, 1995), providing an effective introduction. For examples of media ecologists following from McLuhan, see Neil Postman, *Amusing Ourselves to Death: Public Discourse in the Age of Show Business* (New York: Penguin Books, 1986); Joshua Meyrowitz, *No Sense of Place: The Impact of Electronic Media on Social Behavior* (New York: Oxford University Press, 1985); and Casey Man Kong Lum, *Perspectives on Culture, Technology and Communication: The Media Ecology Tradition* (Cresskill, N.J.: Hampton Press, 2006).

Cultural approaches to technology reference Raymond Williams, *Television: Technology and Cultural Form* (Middletown, Conn.: Wesleyan University Press, 1992), as a key text, especially for introducing the concept of flow. Brian Winston, *Misunderstanding Media* (London: Routledge & Kegan Paul, 1986), and Brian Winston, *Media Technology and Society: A History: From the Telegraph to the Internet* (New York: Routledge, 1998), offer historical accounts of the technological emergence of television. Lynn Spigel, *Make Room for TV: Television and the Family Ideal in Postwar America* (Chicago: University of Chicago Press, 1992), is an essential account of the early cultural dynamics of domestic television technology, while Anna McCarthy, *Ambient Television: Visual Culture and Public Space* (Durham, N.C.: Duke University Press, 2001), explores television outside of the home. Robert V. Bellamy and James Robert Walker, *Television and the*

Remote Control: Grazing on a Vast Wasteland (New York: Guilford Press, 1996), discusses the impact of the remote control.

Analyses of the shift to the digital convergence era are still being written. Amanda D. Lotz, *The Television Will Be Revolutionized* (New York: New York University Press, 2007), provides an account of the institutional shifts involved in the digital era, while Henry Jenkins, *Convergence Culture: Where Old and New Media Collide* (New York: New York University Press, 2006), explores how digital technologies alter viewer practices and storytelling models. Lynn Spigel and Jan Olsson, eds., *Television After TV: Essays on a Medium in Transition* (Durham, N.C.: Duke University Press, 2004), provides a range of perspectives on the shifting medium, and William Boddy, *New Media and Popular Imagination: Launching Radio, Television, and Digital Media in the United States* (Oxford; New York: Oxford University Press, 2004), compares the shifts in television to other media transformations.

NOTES

[1]See Joshua Meyrowitz, "Images of Media: Hidden Ferment—and Harmony—in the Field," *Journal of Communication* 43, no. 3 (1993): 55–67.

[2]Neil Postman, *Amusing Ourselves to Death: Public Discourse in the Age of Show Business* (New York: Penguin Books, 1986).

[3]Joshua Meyrowitz, *No Sense of Place: The Impact of Electronic Media on Social Behavior* (New York: Oxford University Press, 1985).

[4]See Brian Winston, *Misunderstanding Media* (London: Routledge & Kegan Paul, 1986); and Brian Winston, *Media Technology and Society: A History: From the Telegraph to the Internet* (New York: Routledge, 1998), for more details on television's technological origins.

[5]See Christopher H. Sterling and John M. Kittross, *Stay Tuned: A History of American Broadcasting*, 3rd ed. (Mahwah, N.J.: Lawrence Erlbaum, 2002), 315–17, 864.

[6]Lynn Spigel, *Make Room for TV: Television and the Family Ideal in Postwar America* (Chicago: University of Chicago Press, 1992).

[7]See Derek Kompare, "Publishing Flow: DVD Box Sets and the Reconception of Television," *Television and New Media* 7, no. 4 (2006): 335–60.

[8]For more on the distinction between mobile and portable television, see Amanda D. Lotz, *The Television Will Be Revolutionized* (New York: New York University Press, 2007).

CONCLUSION

AMERICAN TELEVISION
IN A GLOBAL CONTEXT

This book explores television as an American phenomenon, limiting its analysis by national boundaries. In many ways, this makes sense, given the distinctly national aspects of television: the FCC's jurisdiction is limited by the borders of the United States, and the transmission systems of local stations and municipal cable franchises place most television institutions under national norms and regulations. American television is different from that of the rest of the world, with its highly commercialized system, limited role for public broadcasting, and distinct perspective on news and political coverage. Even fictional genres have distinctly American identities, as with the American soap opera's differences from *telenovelas* and European serials. There is much to be learned by focusing on how American television stands apart from that of other countries and focusing on the role the medium plays in American lives.

However, if we don't recognize how American television operates in a global context, we will miss an important facet of the medium. Even though the FCC is distinctly national, the corporations that dominate television's oligopoly are not. For instance, News Corporation owns the Fox network, 20th Century Fox studio, numerous cable channels, Direct TV, and many local stations in the United States, but it also owns the Asian satellite service Star, the European satellite system Sky, the Australian cable system FOXTEL, and numerous other production, distribution, and transmission companies around the world. As the television industry has become more conglomerated, it has also become more transnational, with American cable channels and programming distributed around the world. The long history of American television's foreign distribution has had a key impact on the American television industry, and has often affected the type of programs produced for American audiences. Thus this conclusion will briefly consider the interplay between American television and the rest of the world, with the acknowledgment that such a complex topic is truly deserving of its own book.

EXPORTING AMERICAN TELEVISION AND CULTURAL VALUES

It is tempting to see the foreign distribution of American television as part of the broader trend of **globalization**, the 1990s buzzword highlighting international economic trade and cultural exchange. While certainly global television has accelerated in recent years, the international distribution of American television programs actually dates back to the medium's earliest decades. The United States produced more television than most other national systems that developed later in the 1950s and 1960s, and given the commercialized system of American television, its programs often had larger budgets and more impressive production values than most television produced under public service systems. The commercialized American industry followed the precedent of Hollywood film in seeking foreign distribution to supplement its domestic income, and found numerous opportunities to sell American television to foreign television stations and networks in need of content. Early telefilm programs such as the Westerns *Hopalong Cassidy* and *The Lone Ranger*, kids' show *Rin Tin Tin*, and sitcom *I Love Lucy* received significant distribution to fill schedules in emerging television systems in Latin America and Europe, making exports an early component of the programming exchange. The financial incentives for foreign distribution provided yet another motive for producers to switch to telefilm over live production.

The role of foreign distribution of American television grew more important in the 1960s and early 1970s, as more television systems matured across the world and international syndication companies emerged to serve the growing market. Foreign distribution declined somewhat in the mid-1970s, with FCC's Fin-Syn rules shaking up syndication markets, which in turn led distributors to pull back from international markets. However, American television thrived around the world in the multi-channel era, spurred by technologies of satellite distribution that made it more cost effective to deliver programming globally. Cable channels themselves became global distributors, with channels such as MTV, CNN, and ESPN all having numerous international versions spanning the globe. Localized versions of American channels typically offer both American content and regionally or nationally produced programming in differing proportions, as channels need to customize to fit the interests and tastes of local audiences. But no matter how localized a version of MTV or CNN might be, these channels are still generally understood as American imports, not as television indigenous to other regions.

International distribution can shape the programming choices made by American producers, networks, and channels. Foreign distributors often express preferences for the types of programs that will be most popular abroad, with action-oriented dramas tending to appeal more broadly than sitcoms or social dramas with distinctly American content. Such preferences encourage producers and networks to target genres with both American and international appeal. One remarkable example is the 1990s program *Baywatch*, which was cancelled by NBC but reemerged as a first-run syndicated program. The show achieved unprecedented global success, with its action-oriented stories featuring beautiful lifeguards in skimpy swimwear appealing to billions of viewers across the globe, making it arguably the world's most popular television show of all time.

Why has American television become such a powerful export? Because of the differences between the American commercial model and the more widespread public service broadcasting system, it is often more economically efficient for non-American broadcasters to import American programs than to produce their own. American television producers typically deficit-finance their productions per the system described in chapter 1, but revenues from foreign

Baywatch's use of glamorous beauties in tight-fitting swimwear has contributed to its global success, offering sexual appeals that need no subtitles.

BAYWATCH

Baywatch (NBC, 1989–90; syndication 1991–2001): After a first-season cancellation by NBC, this beach drama garnered great success in first-run syndication and via global distribution, reaching an estimated audience of more than one billion viewers each week. The show's simple format, combining action and beautiful actors in swimwear, made it an ideal program to catch on worldwide, with little translation necessary.

distribution are usually seen as "extra" income, not a crucial part of the economic package necessary to produce a program. Thus producers will charge varying rates for a program depending on the economic situation of each foreign distributor: poorer countries pay far less than wealthier ones for the same packages of programming. The effect of this variable pricing is that American producers use their flexibility to make programming affordable across the globe, and provide strong economic rationales for distributors to import rather than produce much of their programming.

There are clearly other motivations in programming strategies beyond the economic, however. Under public service broadcasting systems, television stations and networks explicitly serve the public interest of their countries: for many nations, that interest is explicitly linked to developing their own television productions and representing their own cultures, not importing American media. Many countries resist imports via **quotas**, which mandate a percentage of programming that must be domestically produced, a strategy practiced by Canada, France, Australia, and elsewhere at various times. But as television schedules expand and additional channels and networks emerge in addition to national public service broadcasting, American imports typically fill schedule gaps in greater proportions than local productions; thus the emergence of multi-channel systems is often tied to a process of Americanization, as well as broader global flows within regions, as in Latin America and Asia.

What is wrong with featuring American television across the globe? One clear issue is that other nation's media production companies cannot compete with American programming on a level economic playing field, which creates concerns that importing media can lead to the underdevelopment of domestic creativity. Television importation differs between genres, with news, sports, and public affairs programming having a stronger domestic basis, while drama, comedy, and other entertainment forms tending more toward imports. American television has been shaped by tight access to its own domestic distribution, which has led to limited avenues for creative expression and innovation in the United States; when other countries find their airwaves dominated by American imports, their own creators face limited opportunities to try out new forms and often must emulate American models and genres.

Another main concern about importing television stems from media's role in conveying norms and ideals, as discussed in chapter 7. Many critics regard international distribution of American media as a form of **cultural imperialism**, forcing American values and ideologies upon viewers around the world. There are powerful arguments to be made about the dangers of such cultural imperialism, as other cultures often embrace American norms including consumerism, restrictive beauty ideals, and patriotic identity as conveyed through television and other popular media. There is little doubt that the widespread dissemination of American media has helped spread capitalist values throughout the world, and the global rise of commercially driven television systems that augment or replace public service broadcasting has been fueled by the successful distribution of American programming as a vehicle for both commerce and ideology.

While fears of cultural imperialism cannot be overlooked, we must also remember that television's meanings are not as simple as a hypodermic needle: the fact that global audiences are viewing a program does not guarantee that they will all interpret the show uniformly. Research on international viewers tends to sustain the cultural studies approach to wide-ranging decoding discussed in chapters 7 and 9. For instance, research on the popular 1980s serialized drama *Dallas* showed that while the series was highly popular across the world, it rarely served as a direct conduit of American values celebrating big business and capitalist expansion. Instead, many viewers watched the show as a commentary on American excess, seeing the characters' extreme wealth and greed as objects of satire, not celebration.[1] Regardless of the program, we must remember that viewers around the world, as well as in the United States, actively negotiate with American television rather than passively consuming it, and frequently watch such shows as commentaries on America, not simple vehicles for embracing American values. While we might cringe at the idea that millions of viewers around the world might see *Baywatch* as a representation of American culture, we should remember that they might view the show with cynicism and camp pleasure as much as seeing it as a simplistic celebration of beautiful people on a beach.

IMPORTING GLOBAL TELEVISION

American television's global function is primarily as a programming supplier and exporter, but there are significant flows of foreign programming coming into the United States. One common form of global influence is through American **remakes** of foreign programming. Shows from the 1970s such as *All in the Family* and *Three's Company,* and contemporary, favorites *The Office* and *Ugly Betty* are adaptations of scripted series originating in other countries. Unscripted programming typically uses global format adaptations as discussed in chapter 1, with reality hits such as *Survivor, American Idol,* and *Big Brother,* and game shows *Who Wants to Be a Millionaire* and *The Weakest Link* all originating from templates established in Europe and adapted throughout the world. In most of these instances, the American versions and remakes are marketed as American programs, not global adaptations, fitting with the perception that American audiences are not interested in viewing foreign programming.

There have been many direct imports of foreign programming for decades, although most non-American programs emerged in the margins of network dominance. British programs have been the most prevalent throughout American television history, starting with the 1960s wave of espionage imports such as *The Saint* and *The Avengers,* which aired briefly on network schedules. With the rise of PBS in the 1970s, British television found a home, addressing sophisticated viewers interested in adaptations of literature via *The Forsyte Saga* and *Masterpiece Theatre,* high-quality detective shows such as *Prime Suspect,* the quirky sci-fi of *Doctor Who,* the eccentric wit of *Monty Python's Flying Circus* and *Fawlty Towers,* and the continuing importation of "Britcoms" such as *Are You Being Served?* and *The Vicar of Dibley.* A number of cable channels used British imports in the early years to help build an audience, with MTV airing both *Monty Python* and *The Young Ones* and Comedy Central's hit import *Absolutely Fabulous.* Today, BBC America offers an entire channel of British imports spanning across genres, expanding access to alternatives to American programming. Although these imports range in genre and tone, they are typically marketed as explicitly British, suggesting a more literate, culturally daring and serious sophisticated tone than typical American programming.

Canadian television has also gained a foothold in American markets, as with the cult sketch comedy series *SCTV* and *The Kids in the Hall.* Probably the most successful Canadian imports stem from the *Degrassi* franchise, with numerous programs aimed at children and teenagers with a grittier and more socially engaged tone than typical of American teen programming. Canadian broadcasting can be viewed directly along the northern border of the United States, with viewers in Detroit and Seattle receiving Canadian programming on cable and over the air. Often viewers in these markets embrace Canadian news and sports coverage as less commercialized and more in-depth options than those offered by American markets, and alternative sources of programming as highlighting how American television is not the only possible model of television.

Another important source of programming for American viewers is Japan, specifically with the rise of anime, or Japanese animation. Unlike British and Canadian programming, Japanese television rarely airs in the United States in its "native" form, but is localized through dubbing and editing. Animation lends itself to such localization, as poor lip-synching or editing of risqué or culturally specific content is less noticeable. Anime grew in popularity slowly, with heavily edited cartoons such as *Speed Racer* and *Robotech* placed alongside American animation aimed at kids. Anime fandom grew as a subculture throughout the 1980s, mostly accessed through an underground videotape-trading network rather than through broadcast television. By the 1990s, anime saw higher-profile film and video releases, with television embracing hit kids' series including *Pokémon, Sailor Moon, Dragon Ball Z,* and later *Yu-Gi-Oh!, Naruto,* and *Cardcaptors.* Cartoon Network embraced anime in the 2000s, running series aimed at adolescent and adult audiences during its Adult Swim block, including *Cowboy Bebop, InuYasha, Neon Genesis Evangelion,* and *Fullmetal Alchemist.* Contemporary anime programs in the United States do edit and dub to meet broadcast standards, but they often retain a clear identity of their Japanese origins. The anime boom has led to a great demand for Japanese-language education and a strong interest among young Americans in Japanese culture, suggesting that one of the functions of international media is to promote intercultural exchange. A few dubbed and adapted live-action Japanese programs have also taken hold in America, including *Power Rangers* and *Iron Chef.*

As the multi-channel era enabled more narrowcasting to target smaller audience segments, television programming emerged aimed at specific immigrant communities. National broadcast networks Univision and Telemundo provide Spanish-language programming that mixes domestically produced and imported shows across numerous genres. Long-running Univision series *Sábado Gigante* straddled this boundary itself, as it started as an import from Chile before relocating to Miami in the mid-1980s. Many Spanish-language programs airing in the United States are produced in Mexico, with the American market serving as a primary audience for these global media products. The rapid growth of Spanish-speaking audiences in the United States has made Univision a key player in the television industry, with ratings rivaling The CW Network and beating those of most cable channels.

Other niche channels target dozens of different language communities, with premium packages available from satellite and cable providers to access imported programming in foreign languages. In metropolitan areas with concentrated immigrant populations, local stations can broadcast to specific communities, as with Los Angeles's KSCI, which features locally produced and imported programming in numerous Asian languages to target specific ethnic communities. Additionally, immigrant communities have turned to alternative ways of acquiring video beyond broadcast, cable, and satellite, using videotape, disc, and file-sharing networks to trade and access programming from around the world. While the bulk of American television is dominated by domestic English-language programming, many immigrants regularly consume non-American programming as a way of maintaining a connection to their native countries and languages, complicating any simplistic notion of what constitutes "American television."

BLURRING NATIONAL BOUNDARIES
AND THE GLOBAL *SIMPSONS*

The concept of American television is certainly made more complex by both foreign imports and international exports, but the very notion of domestic programming is not as simple as it might seem. Increasingly, some domestic programs are produced at least in part outside the United States: many notable American series including *The X-Files, Smallville,* and *Battlestar Galactica* have been shot in Vancouver, Canada, which has been dubbed "Hollywood North" due to its strong film and television production industry. In such cases, the business, writing, and postproduction offices typically remain in Hollywood, with only the actual filming and some special effects work done in Canada, taking advantage of lower production costs, a beneficial exchange rate, and Canadian tax incentives. This model of **runaway production** has led Vancouver to become second only to Los Angeles in participating in the global share of television production.

While business incentives can make runaway production appealing, the practice raises a key question: Is a show shot outside the United States truly an American program? *The X-Files*, which takes place in the United States, focuses on American F.B.I. agents, and originally aired on American television, appears to be an American program to its fans, as few viewers even realized that it was shot in Canada. However, its production company, 20th Century Fox Productions, and its distributor, Fox Network, are both owned by News Corporation, which was officially an Australian company in the 1990s. Such an example highlights how even programming that seems clearly American can have mixed origins when one traces the various countries that may be involved in production, funding, and ownership of a show. As such, we must be careful when assuming that the programs airing on American channels and networks are simply American products, as various companies and practices involved typically have transnational ties and origins.

As a concluding case study, it would be hard to think of a program more tied to American culture than *The Simpsons*, but still bearing many traces of global television flows. *The Simpsons* is one of the great unlikely success stories in television history: starting as transitional bumpers before ad breaks on Fox's sketch comedy show *The Tracey Ullman Show* in 1987, *The Simpsons* was launched as its own program in 1990 as the first network prime time animation series to air since the heyday of *The Flintstones* in the mid-1960s. In the late 1980s, Fox was still a fringe upstart network with little successful programming, and thus had an incentive to take major programming risks. An animated series satirizing family sitcoms was an unlikely hit, with major potential for failure, given the fairly high production costs and restrictive timeline for producing animation. The show became Fox's first hit program, helping to make the network a legitimate competitor to the Big Three of ABC, CBS, and NBC; as of this writing, the show has been on the air for nineteen years and counting, making it the longest-running prime time comedy in television history, and one of the most successful series ever made. For many viewers, the show is one of the best arguments for the value of television as a socially engaged and valuable creative medium, especially through its pointed satire of American culture and media.

Although the show's content is quintessentially American, its production and consumption are more global, with blurred boundaries. In developing the program, 20th Century Fox needed to reduce production costs to keep the show profitable; the production team decided to follow the trend for many American animated programs by outsourcing animation production to South Korea. Since the 1960s, American animated programming, which was mostly constrained to Saturday morning and late-afternoon scheduling blocks for kids, subcontracted with Asian animation firms to complete much of the labor-intensive animation process. American artists and designers typically draw storyboards of action and illustrate *key frames* of a sequence; they then send these drawings and the recorded voice track to Asia, especially South Korea, Taiwan, and Thailand, to

For the decades, *The Simpsons* has presented an image of the American family where watching television plays a central role, a satirical portrait that has been embraced by viewers throughout the world.

animate the programs via the processes of "in-betweening" and coloring, before returning it to the United States for final postproduction. Such labor practices parallel some of the more notorious sweatshop manufacturing common in clothing and toy manufacturing, although animation jobs in Asia are considered comparatively high-paying skilled labor with above-average working conditions. Additionally, the training and equipment needed to produce American television animation has helped spur the animation industries in Asian countries, making Korea the third largest producer of animation in the world, behind only the United States and Japan.

The process of overseas animation employed by *The Simpsons* and most other cel-animated American television is primarily tied to economic conditions, as the labor costs are greatly reduced by outsourcing, but there are interesting cultural ramifications. Korean animators frequently do not understand the references and actions found in *The Simpsons*, needing cultural translation for actions foreign to their society. For instance, Korean animators allegedly needed guidance from American producers on how to animate a gun being shot, as firearms are outlawed in Korea, and thus they were not familiar with the physics of bullets. There are certainly some interesting ironies in the fact that a show hailed as one of the most insightful commentaries on the United States is produced, at least in large part, in Korea, where many of its satirical jokes and cultural references are not understood.

Once episodes are completed in the United States, *The Simpsons* is branded as an American media production, making its global origins invisible to all except the most dedicated fans reading the closing credits. But the cultural circulation of the show transcends its American identity, as *The Simpsons* is among the more popular television exports around the world. The show is particularly popular in English-speaking countries, including Canada, the United Kingdom, Australia, and South Africa, but dubbed versions have also become significant in Latin America and the Middle East. The show has not found a particularly welcome audience in Korea or most other Asian countries, despite its hybrid production origins, in large part because the cultural references do not resonate with Asian social norms and values. Factoring in the extensive multimedia tie-ins, such as video games, toys, comics, merchandize, and a hit film, *The Simpsons* is a global media franchise worth billions to News Corporation and its corporate partners.

An American media product with such global reach and popularity might raise concerns of cultural imperialism, fearing that *The Simpsons* spreads American values across the globe, and leaving little room for local cultures to resist the media-driven domination. There is no doubt that two key consequences of the show's global popularity are reduced opportunities for locally produced programming to find a place on television schedules, and an economic flow of foreign consumer spending toward American-based media corporations. But is

The Simpsons an effective conduit for American ideology, expressing dominant values of the United States?

Cultural imperialism becomes tricky when applied to satire. Much of what makes *The Simpsons* a popular television program is its ability to mock traditional notions of American dominant values and the television medium itself. The show highlights a dysfunctional family; satirizes the capitalist values embodied by Mr. Burns; undercuts civic institutions of politics, education, and law enforcement; criticizes consumerism and advertising; and even frequently mocks a wide range of television genres, from news to sitcoms. Research into the show's global consumption highlights how, for many viewers, *The Simpsons* is regarded simultaneously as a uniquely American program, but also as actively mocking American values and norms, an attitude that is appealing to many viewers across the globe whose media consumption has been frequently dominated by American products. Homer's representation as a caricature of the "ugly American," chanting "USA!", waving a flag, or condemning immigrants, can hardly be seen as an uncritical vehicle for American values, as much of the show's content functions as a criticism of cultural imperialism and mindless nationalism itself.[2]

The case of *The Simpsons* and global circulation highlights the complexities of how television both can support and undercut American cultural values. Certainly both foreign and domestic viewers can watch the show as a critical commentary that challenges dominant norms and pushes back against the consumerist ideology pervading most television programming. However, we cannot forget the political economy of the show, in which multinational corporations have profited greatly from the series; its successful tie-ins and licensed products certainly promote consumerism quite explicitly, even as the show's jokes mock its own overt merchandising. In the end, it is too simple uniformly to celebrate the show's critical edge or to condemn its consumerist imperialism: like most successful media products, *The Simpsons* contains multiple meanings and a wide range of cultural impacts, not reducible to a simplistic bumper sticker slogan praising or denouncing the show's politics and values.

The Simpsons is an apt place to end this book. It is certainly one of the most important texts in American television history, and it brings together all the facets of television we have explored—from textual form to multimedia technological transformations, corporate power to satirical consumption. By viewing television as a complex, multifaceted entity, we cannot come to easy conclusions about how such a show functions as a positive or negative part of American culture. Rather, we are left with a picture of a medium that offers a wealth of contradictions, competing influences and impacts, and a complex set of interwoven institutions and individuals. I hope that this book has raised your awareness and knowledge about television; but through that heightened understanding, the medium should appear less simple than you might have initially thought. Through this sophisticated understanding and heightened media literacy, television can become not "just TV," but a more enjoyable, significant, and vital aspect of American culture.

FURTHER READING

For an overview of global television, see John Sinclair and Graeme Turner, eds., *Contemporary World Television* (London: BFI, 2004); and Lisa Parks and Shanti Kumar, eds., *Planet TV: A Global Television Reader* (New York: New York University Press, 2003). Kerry Segrave, *American Television Abroad: Hollywood's Attempt to Dominate World Television* (Jefferson, N.C.: McFarland, 1998), focuses on America's global television exports, as does Timothy Havens, *Global Television Marketplace* (London: BFI, 2006). For an account of British imports on American television, see Jeffrey S. Miller, *Something Completely Different: British Television and American Culture* (Minneapolis: University of Minnesota Press, 2000).

For a taste of *Simpsons* scholarship, see Jonathan Gray, *Watching with The Simpsons: Television, Parody, and Intertextuality* (New York: Routledge, 2005); and John Alberti, ed., *Leaving Springfield: The Simpsons and the Possibilities of Oppositional Culture* (Detroit: Wayne State University Press, 2004).

NOTES

[1] See Ien Ang, *Watching Dallas: Soap Opera and the Melodramatic Imagination* (London: Methuen, 1985); Tamar Liebes and Elihu Katz, *The Export of Meaning: Cross-Cultural Readings of Dallas* (New York: Oxford University Press, 1990).

[2] Jonathan Gray, "Imagining America: *The Simpsons* Go Global," *Popular Communication* 5, no. 2 (2007): 129–48.

INDEX